Interpreting Cultures: Literature, Religion, and the Human Sciences

Jonathan Hart

INTERPRETING CULTURES
© Jonathan Hart, 2006.

First published in 2006 by
PALGRAVE MACMILLAN™
175 Fifth Avenue, New York, N.Y. 10010 and
Houndmills, Basingstoke, Hampshire, England RG21 6XS
Companies and representatives throughout the world.

PALGRAVE MACMILLAN is the global academic imprint of the Palgrave Macmillan division of St. Martin's Press, LLC and of Palgrave Macmillan Ltd. Macmillan® is a registered trademark in the United States, United Kingdom and other countries. Palgrave is a registered trademark in the European Union and other countries.

ISBN-13: 978–1–4039–7128–9
ISBN-10: 1–4039–7128–5

Library of Congress Cataloging-in-Publication Data

Hart, Jonathan Locke, 1956–
    Interpreting cultures : literature, religion, and the human sciences / Jonathan Hart.
      p. cm.
    Includes bibliographical references and index.
    ISBN 1–4039–7128–5 (alk. paper)
     1. Literature—Philosophy. 2. Literature—History and criticism.
    3. Literature and history. 4. Civilization. I. Title.

PN49.H343 2006
801—dc22
                                                    2005045624

A catalogue record for this book is available from the British Library.

Design by Newgen Imaging Systems (P) Ltd., Chennai, India.

First edition: May 2006

10 9 8 7 6 5 4 3 2 1

Printed in the United States of America.

CONTENTS

For Julia Jackman Marshall Hart

De Guiche—C'est un fou,—mais c'est un fou savant.
Cyrano—Non, je n'imitai rien de ce qu'on fit avant!

Edmond Rostand, *Cyrano de Bergerac,* Acte III, Scène XI, 1633–34

PREFACE AND
ACKNOWLEDGMENTS

It often takes me a great deal more time to write a book than I would like. This is probably a fairly widespread phenomenon. In this labyrinth, I have tried to wind a thread from introduction to conclusion without the journey being too full of rectilinear hedgerows or too much a garden of forked paths.

Whereas the book seeks some unity through interpretation of culture(s), especially but not exclusively in terms of recognition, and with regard to literature, religion, and the human sciences, it is not something straightforward in the linear movement of a single-minded argument. It is meant to be suggestive and heuristic, a tentative book with a series of linked (but not locked) hypotheses and possibilities. This is the possible realm of the actual world and its fictions, theory as a way of seeing, not as a one-eyed vision of the world. This is not a system to put the lock on my readers. Here is one person seeing and one person interpreting culture(s) for a reader with a different pair of eyes. I hope we will meet in some enabling and helpful space of intersubjectivity. We are moving objects in a paradox of objectivity even as we are the subject of our subject.

Different readers will garner different experiences from this book. As usual, I hope to reach an array of students, colleagues, and members of the general public. This is always a fine line to walk, perhaps a trapeze or high wire as much as a thread, but I think that books are as much of an engagement as a conversation or a seminar, so I am always pleased if each reader takes something from my books. Books teach. Teaching is an interaction, an engagement, perhaps a kind of love letter. So I am trying once more, recognizing the improbable and probable shortcomings along the way, to write something that is as inclusive as possible. All of us are subject to the shadows of Plato's cave or, with Ariadne in the labyrinth, find it difficult to see as well as we would like. Insight is hard to find. This whole book is an "essay" to discuss topics vital to people outside as well as inside the university: those with an interest that allows a break from something else, or those starting intensive study and those who, as expert as they are, might find a few new tatters to turn to threads of their own. For all these readers, my hope is that they spin their own silk. Virgil points to paradise, but cannot proceed there though Dante can, and it may be, in this purgatory of culture and its signs, that all I can do is point to Virgil and Dante. Along the way, I can also show other figures that swim around Beatrice and all of us. Rodin placed the thinker at the top of his gates of hell in a maze of figures. That might have been optimistic for the katascopos, even if the creator does not even have the place of the thinker. What I am attempting to essay is to present perspectives without one that brings everything into one stable focus, like the kaleidoscopes we turned into a pattern as children. The points of view of the reader will bring a new perspective to the interpretation of cultures.

Culture and interpretation are something that seep into us from all directions from an early age. Over the years, I have tried to acknowledge some of those who have helped me along the way, and I still wish to thank those I have in earlier books. Here, I would especially like to remember the course of Northrop Frye and Jay Macpherson I audited all those years ago on the Bible and mythology, showing how slow I can be to bring something to fruition. My thanks to Terence Cave, who was a Distinguished Visitor at Alberta, and shared with me his fine work on recognition and other topics. To Ross Chambers, another Distinguished Visitor to Alberta, many thanks for his suggestive ideas on culture and interpretation and for his inspiring example.

More generally, I would like to thank my schoolteachers who taught me many subjects, including literature, history, and geography, in English and French, and, above all, to John Bickell, who pursued the study of Canadian literature in the classroom when it was not the fashion. My thanks also to Timothy Findley, Robertson Davies, and others who encouraged my own poetry decades ago now. As a student, I was once at a meeting at University of Toronto where Robertson Davies felt obliged to come to defend Canadian literature as part of the curriculum. It was also a pleasure to audit classes given by Marshall McLuhan, who included Canada in his global village, and, with his permission, to read his Ph.D. thesis. My study places Canada in a multilateral context, especially, but not exclusively, in the Atlantic world, but also a temporal space that is related to a biblical and classical milieu and to European culture. My thanks to Doug Cole, Bill Byrick, and others at Sainte-Marie-among-the-Hurons, where I worked during the 1970s in various roles, including staff supervisor (although we also dressed up as French carpenters, blacksmiths, and Jesuits—much to the amusement of actual Jesuits who visited this historic site), for allowing me, even during the summer months, the privilege to pursue this history of encounter between the French and the Ouendat, and to reconsider and reinterpret the battle with European diseases and the final destructive war with the Iroquois in the 1640s.

This book was written over a long period. It often takes others to encourage, respond, and help to shape ideas. At Toronto, I learned much from many, but in particular I wish to thank Michael Sidnell who was exemplary in his teaching of modern drama and to Brian Parker, who with as much wit as wisdom led me into the ways of American drama and encouraged my interest in Shakespearean and other forms of drama. At Harvard, Daniel Aaron, Alfred and Sally Alcorn, G. Blakemore Evans, Marjorie Garber, Stratis Haviaris, Seamus Heaney, Barbara Johnson, Harry Levin, Donald and Cathleen Pfister, and Jan Ziolkowski were especially inspiring and supportive. My thanks to Peter Burke and Anthony Pagden at Cambridge for their encouragement of my historical work on the Atlantic world. At Princeton, my particular thanks to Jeremy Adelman, Sandra Bermann, Anthony Grafton, Michèle Lamont, Dale Miller, Kenneth Mills, Nigel Smith, and Harold Shapiro for their support, along with others, of my interests in history and literature, and especially in Canadian culture in a wider context of the Americas, the Atlantic world, and elsewhere. At Alberta, Ronald Ayling, E.D. Blodgett, Patricia Clements, Patricia Demers, Milan Dimić, James Forrest, Michael Lynn-George, Nicole Mallet, Juliet McMaster, Peter Meekison, Robert Merrett, Edward Mojżeko, Gordon Moyles, John Orrell, Winnie Thom, Robert Wilson, Linda Woodbridge, and others were welcoming and supportive in my first years there. My continued thanks to the University of Alberta for its long-standing and ongoing flexibility and support for my teaching and research. To the librarians at these four universities, where I have spent the most time of any universities, and at the British Library, the Bodleian, the Bibliothèque Nationale, the Archive d'Outre Mer, the John Carter Brown Library, and elsewhere, I reiterate my thanks to you, which I have set out in earlier books. To the curators of the exhibits I have seen in museums and galleries in North America, Asia, Australia, and Europe (too many to list), my gratitude.

To all those who have invited me to give related talks in various places in different parts of the world or have given me invitations to write

essays or articles, my thanks. In particular, my thanks to the organizers
and hosts of the conference on Philosophy and Literature at George
Mason University, where I presented a brief paper on recognition
(I decided not to publish this or the considerably longer work, which
appears here for the first time in any form); to Balachandra Rajan and
Elizabeth Sauer for inviting an earlier version of my essay on Canadian
colonial history in context; to Klaus Martens and his colleagues at
Universität des Saarlandes for inviting me to a splendid conference
on poetry (including poetry readings) and an earlier form of the essay on
Canadian women writers; to Charles Stang for providing an invitation
for a briefer and earlier essay on T.E. Lawrence and the Shaws; to
Dorothy Figuiera and colleagues at the International Comparative
Literature Association for inviting me to wonderful executive meetings—
where I presented a brief paper on the topic, an earlier version of the
essay on poetry in the age of technology, which has been revised here;
to Michael Trussler and his colleagues for publishing my earlier essay on
poetry and mythology (and to Christian Riegel for his interest in this
essay); to David Boyd and Imre Salusinszky, at University of Newcastle
in Australia, for inviting a different version of my essay on Northrop
Frye as a writer and for publishing a version in their collection on Frye;
to Philip McGuire for inviting me to write on television drama and to
speak on it on a couple of occasions at Michigan State University, and,
most germane here, on a production of Miller's *Death of a Salesman*, and
to James M. Welsh and his fellow editors for their interest in and publication of an earlier version; to Nat Hardy and his coeditors for inviting
an essay on Irish poetry and another review of Paul Muldoon; to Jüri
Talvet for issuing an invitation for the keynote of a conference on the
novel at Tartu and for publishing a previous form of this chapter. Any
specific acknowledgments to these works may be found in the notes to
each chapter. This book has involved revision, framing the "argument,"
and an extension and an extensive revision of the notes. In the rewriting, I have been searching with Ariadne for the thread in the labyrinth
of interpretation and culture.

For those who have shown support and have taught me through
example, I thank all of you, especially Anne Barton, Catherine Belsey,
Jean Bessière Mary Baine Campbell, Nicholas Canny, Margaret
Ferguson, Stephen Ferguson, Philip Ford, Thomas Healy, Shelagh
Heffernan, Robert Kroetsch, Thomas McAlindon, Kenneth Mills, Steven
Mobbs, Christopher Norris, Peter Sinclair, Irene Sywenky, Gordon
Teskey, Pauline Thomas, and Michael Worton. I also wish to remem-
ber Thomas M. Greene and Edward Said, who led seminars in which I

participated at the School of Criticism and Theory (SCT). Robert Stepto and Valerie Smith, also at SCT, helped to develop my interest in African culture in the Americas. Many thanks, too, to those who have been so supportive at Palgrave. More specifically, it has been once more a great pleasure to work with my editor, Farideh Koohi-Kamali, and her associates, Julia Cohen, Elizabeth Sabo and Lynne Vande Stouwe. At Newgen, I thank Maran Elancheran and his colleagues for their work on production. For permission to reproduce Roy Kiyooka's splendid painting, "Toronto Boarding House 1950," my thanks to Kiyo Kiyooka and the Kiyooka family, the Alberta Foundation of the Arts Collection (AFA), and Barbara Johnson of the AFA. Further thanks to Alan Brownoff for making me aware of that work. This painting suggests an urban landscape, with all its suddenness and transitoriness, that has come to dominate the industrialized world. It is of a boarding house in Toronto, a city in which I have spent a lot of time, but gestures beyond this locale.

Thanks to my parents, George and Jean, whose interest in art, drama, literature, history, and other subjects has been an example for me. They met playing in Macbeth, and my mother's painting and my father's writing keep inspiring me as they still create in their eighties and nineties. They continue to lead me to leads. To my brothers and sisters, Charles, Gwendolyn, Deborah, Alan, and Jennifer, my thanks and appreciation for continuing in this spirit. All their commitment to arts and creativity have been a delicate but exuberant gift. Finally, thanks to my wife, Mary Marshall, and our twins, James and Julia, who have been with me for so much of this journey and who inspire love and gratitude. For Julia in particular—she who loves language, drama, literature, and culture, this work is dedicated. Cyrano follows his own threads, imaginary and otherwise, as we all might, at best in the service of love.

Introduction

It is not easy to see. Samson with or without eyes is a figure that suggests the distinction between physical sight and vision, between perception and perceptiveness. He learns wisdom as we do through his story. The same could be said for Oedipus, whose blindness with eyes leads to an insight that causes him to blind himself. Samson and Oedipus come to blindness through different routes, but they wrestle with the gap between appearance and reality, delusion and wisdom. Ways of seeing in nature, culture, and science vary in a kind of shifting labyrinth over time. The nature of eyes and brain changes at different rates than that of cultural perception and mind. To recognize something is neither easy nor singular. Recognition is something gained with various faculties, even with an eyeless insight, and across differences in experience and fields of expression or disciplines. Interpreting culture is a reading of the world and of words and images of, in, and about that world. Humans are interpreting animals. We make stories, theories, arguments, and, in turn, interpret those. Culture is a kind of lived interpretation. People and peoples are involved in an interpretation of interpretation. Where fact ends and interpretation begins is difficult to know.

Early on, I sensed that a premise in logic contains conclusions, so that the relation between early and later assumptions is as interesting as it is problematic. Where nature ends and nurture begins is something people have wondered about for such a long time. Culture, recognition, and reading (interpretation) seem to stay the same and change. Body and brain in humans have evolved slowly, whereas the mind has attempted to adapt to the ever-quickening change of technology. Perhaps we have Stone Age bodies and brains thrown into the swirl of technology. We the medium may change with the world as medium in some kind of interplay. This book discusses recognition in the arts and human sciences, a way of seeing in the world of a particular culture or nexus of cultures in the Atlantic world—continental Europe, Britain, Ireland, the Americas—in texts and images made by people of African, Native American and European descent.

The recognition of recognition here is that this way of seeing, although cognate with observation and discovery in science, is not identical to it. Owing to the prestige and power of science in our culture, it is tempting to elide difference. The art of writing, perhaps even of reading and interpretation, in the arts and human sciences is not always a matter of progression. The interpretation in this book leads to a more provisional recognition because Arthur Miller is not necessarily making progress over Shakespeare or he over Aeschylus. Nor do the drama critics who write about them necessarily leave each other behind in a kind of history of a discipline that is a curiosity or the domain of the history of science. Nor do these critics and theorists use what works or has been proven through testing, thereby leaving the rest to historians, who examine dead knowledge. Drama and dramatic criticism and theory, any more than poetry and poetics, are probably not given to the same dynamics as physics. On the other hand, it is possible, but not desirable, to freeze science in its early stages or those understandable to humanists rather than to consider the ever-more intricate ways of seeing or theories in the natural sciences and the very creativity that endows scientists as artists. Science is not simply the domain of positivism. Rather than look into the great variety of recognition and interpretation in the sciences, I would like to note how easy it is to parody or reduce different cultural practices and intellectual methods and how counterproductive that can be. Instead, it would be interesting for scientists to see whether recognition and "reading" in the arts and human sciences have implications for, or affinities with, ways of seeing and interpreting in the natural sciences. To recognize and to interpret are such complex activities that even a book such as this that concentrates on a few aspects and possible underlying affinities mainly through specific examples in the arts and human sciences cannot cover the topic even in those domains let alone in science itself. The interplay of all the realms of science and of arts, however difficult, is a desirable goal.[1] Mutual misunderstanding can lead to a dangerous or daunting gap whose division does not move people forward in new recognitions of problems or in facing the ethics of genetics, computers, medical, and pharmacological technologies separate from the cultural knowledge and wisdom gained from recognitions and interpretations in literature, religion, and fields that study the human beyond the physical. Culture has some play with materialism whether it is in the sciences or arts.

The roots of the terms in my title are suggestive. *Interpreting* derives from *interpreter*, which comes from Latin by way of French, and means to expound, translate, explain, and understand. Its roots suggest spreading between or spreading out. The etymology of *culture* is through the Old French, *couture*, which derives from Latin *cultūra* or cultivation. To interpret culture is to understand the fruits of labor or of communities, it is to explicate sacred and secular texts. *Recognition* is, etymologically from the Latin, a thorough acquaintance with, investigation, getting to know once again. *Reading* derives from the verb to "read," which has many meanings in Teutonic languages. The original senses of the Teutonic verb meant taking care or charge of or having or exercising control over something and taking or giving counsel. These significations also occur in Old English and the sense of "advise" still survives. Considering or explaining something obscure or mysterious is shared by these various languages. However, "the application of this to the interpretation of ordinary writing, and to the expression of this in speech" happens only in English and Old Norse.[2] Reading is an interpretation not simply of literary texts but of everyday works and of ordinary speech. Its ancient cognate roots seem to involve thought and accomplishment. Moments of coming back to knowing, thinking, and seeing what texts, speech, and images grow up over time, what is a cultivation of speech and signs, will be the main focus of *Interpreting Cultures*.

Culture is as contested a term as interpreting/interpretation, recognition, or reading. As Clifford Geertz has said, "The trouble is that no one is quite sure what culture is," and he adds that it is not simply contested with multiple definitions and uses, but is fugitive and an unlikely idea to build a science around—"Almost as bad as matter."[3] Despite the imprecision and protean nature of culture, literature, philosophy, and anthropology all pay it great heed while embodying it. The semantic haze and maze of culture can involve a gap between theory and practice, so that whereas I discuss definitions of various terms in the body of this book, I also examine texts and images in specific contexts and try to garner something from instances of recognition and through readings or interpretation from my own limited perspective culturally but also in terms of my training and practice as poet, literary scholar (critic, theorist), and historian. I have limited the examples to the Atlantic world that I have lived in most, trying the difficult task of reading or recognizing the otherness of other cultures but also of my own culture or adjacent cultures. This is an attempt to discover who I am or think I am and who others are and think they are. This is being a stranger in one's own land as well as in another's. As Bertolt Brecht assumed—and he advocated the estrangement or alienation effect in drama as a counterpoint to Aristotle's mimesis—a pocketful of theories help to explain the world and the world of art. As Geertz observed, we cannot go native (I would say go back and go there), but we can understand other frames of meaning even if we cannot feel their feelings or think their thoughts—"enact their lives."[4] Plato, Aristotle, and Longinus might argue that we can, at least in fictions, feel the feelings and think the thoughts of the characters. Plato thought that a danger. Geertz seems to see things in a similar way to Brecht—frames of understanding, and not private emotions, are the focus. Brecht counters all this empathy and sympathy, the anagnorisis leading to catharsis, with an emphasis on distance and science. His epic theatre is meant to appeal to reason because it is comprehensible and not to empathy because feelings are limited and private.[5] Part of what the spectators in the audience are supposed to do is to consider alternatives and embark on decisions as part of their witnessing or seeing of the play.[6] Brecht's theatre, the theory of which is most fully expressed in *Kleines Organon für das Theater* (1949), attempted to place the present in a historical context, to allow for distance between the actors and their roles (*Verfremdungseffekt*), the emphasis on estrangement as a means of emphasizing change.[7]

Recognition is originally related to *mimesis* (imitation, representation). Whereas Plato's ideas are reflected shadows of the material world that art imitates, Aristotle expands that imitation to creation, a fulfillment or supplement and not simply an embellishment.[8] As Francis Cornford notes (speaking about Plato's *Republic*, 392 C–398 B), mimesis is a form of dramatic representation: "The Greek schoolboy was not allowed to repeat Homer or Aeschylus in a perfunctory gabble, but expected to throw himself into the story and deliver the speeches with the tones and gesture of an actor."[9] This is an imaginative embodiment or identification with the character that affects the actor and the audience permanently. Plato's mimesis includes imitation and the copying of natural sounds in music. Plato, as Cornford notes, extends mimesis to something akin to what we mean by "representation" in English, uses *mimetes* as we would artist, and thinks that the work of art is a likeness or image (*eikon*) of the original, holding up a mirror up to nature. Socrates argues that knowledge cannot be gained by studying the poet's picture in words or representation of life—his portraits of heroic characters—because poets do not work with a conscious intelligence but from inspiration, using a beautiful language without understanding its meaning, so that they cannot instruct us through descriptions of chariots or of war.[10] Long before the skepticism of David Hume, the theories of estrangement of Bertolt Brecht or the deconstruction of Jacques Derrida and Paul de Man, there was a suspicion of mimesis. In fact, key people among the early Church fathers and their Christian successors were antimimetic or showed, in the phrase of Jonas Barish, an antitheatrical prejudice.[11] Here, mimesis is a kind of imitation that leads to an illusion that leads away from reality, so the Platonic inheritance of this strand of Christianity is apparent here. Aristotle is more hopeful than the Platonic Socrates over the possibility of gaining knowledge from art. His discussion of tragedy admits that simple plots (ones he favors less than complex plots) can lack peripeteia or anagnōrisis. Aristotle defines *peripeteia* as "a [sudden] change [over] of what is being done to the opposite" and *anagnōrisis* as "a change from not-knowing to knowing," and gives the example of Oedipus as the finest instance of recognition. Such an example will involve *katharsis* (catharsis), a purging of pity or terror.[12] Emotion in Aristotle, as opposed to in Plato, Brecht, and Geertz, is something important to knowledge even if the audience comes to purge pity and terror (the first an empathy, the second a revulsion or moving away). There are various kinds of recognitions that occur by signs and tokens, made up by the poet through recollection and logical inference: Aristotle favors the recognition that comes from the shock of surprise. Aristotle discusses recognition in the context of tragedy and his observations have come to be applied and extend to other kinds of literature and beyond drama and literature themselves into a wider realm of culture. A number of types of recognition occur in Aristotle's *Poetics* let alone in Western culture, so that if I use recognition as a singular, it is because it is a collective noun and not a singular singularity.

To return to Hume, in his *Treatise of Human Nature*, it is possible to see his interaction with Plato, for the mind only has perceptions present to it and these consist of immediate impressions and ideas that replicate faintly these impressions.[13] Whereas Hume faces perceptions in the present, Jacques Derrida denies the existence of perception.[14] Paul de Man was able to talk about allegories of reading and about blindness and insight, so that reversal and recognition could also have analogues in deconstruction or poststructuralism.[15] Northrop Frye's double vision, Roland Barthes's double sign, and Derrida's double writing might well differ on the notion of the integration and disintegration of texts, but recognition and misrecognition through reading and interpretation concern them all.[16] What is a double bind or double blindness and what is prophetic vision might be a question that goes back to Plato and carries on through philosophy and literary criticism or theory. Barthes's view of Balzac's realism is not unlike Plato's of the poets, at several removes from reality. Barthes's Balzac copies painting, which is already a copy of the world. In Barthes's text, the reader is also meant to see double between Barthes's words and Balzac's.[17] Each estranges and denaturalizes the other in a kind of reverse Aristotelianism that Brecht also practiced. Derrida has also attempted to shake up the way we see the world of texts and the textual world, so that just as Plato uses the allegory of the cave to suggest the tentative, tenuous, reflective, and shadowy world of human perception, understanding, and reality, Derrida and others challenge the readiness or shape of knowledge with their theory and philosophy. Derrida saw two interpretations of interpretations, one that dreams of deciphering an origin or truth and another that affirms play and looks ahead to something beyond humanism and full presence.[18] One philosopher's insight might be another's blindness. Metaphors of light and dark, so widespread in religious, literary, and philosophical texts, are ways of seeing for some and means of blinding for others. Tropes and representations are intricate and refractory.[19] In this book, I attempt to call attention to recognition and readings in their multiplicity across faculties, periods, cultures, and contexts, so that readers, can make of them what they will. Reading can mean many things. For Wolfgang Iser, reading has a dialectical structure, involves the capacity to decipher, and involves "discovery" not simply of the unformulated meaning but of the possibility of formulating the different readers' selves through a discovery that had previously appeared to elude each consciousness.[20] Interpretation and reading are for readers to decide: they would have to assume that they could recognize recognition or that one person's subjectivity can be communicated to another's despite the difficulties of representation and reading or interpreting.

It might be argued that any play, written text, or image is an artifact of the past. History, as an experience, is something that stresses this pastness. The past, as R.G. Collingwood said, is not a given fact that historians can apprehend empirically through experience, which leads him to advocate that "the historian must re-enact the past in his own mind."[21] Even though the idea of perception and of individual communication and understanding are fraught with difficulty, Collingwood suggested dramatic embodiment as something that might bring together the disparate views on writing, recognition, interpretation, and reading. Whether or not Aristotelian empathy or Brechtian estrangement provides the main emphasis in representation/antirepresentation, the dramatic has been part of the Platonic dialogue, Aristotle's analysis of tragedy, Freud's discussion of Oedipus, and other key episodes in recognition. My book concentrates on recognition across boundaries and on readings or interpretations of history, poetry, and drama (film). Aristotle's discussion of "discovery" bears on that of Columbus and his successors and on Arthur Miller's tragedy of the common man. Writer and reader, then and now, here and there, all enter into a dramatic space. Without framing the job of the interpreter of the past explicitly in these terms, Collingwood does use a description that plays on discovery:

> When a man thinks historically, he has before him certain documents or relics of the past. His business is to discover what the past was which has left these relics behind it. For example, the relics are certain written words; and in that case he has to discover what the person who wrote those words meant by them. This means discovering the thought (in the widest sense of that word [)] . . . . To discover what this thought was, the historian must think it again for himself.[22]

Discovery or recognition is a matter of much discussion even if such terms, including "thought," mean many different things to different people in different times. The dramatization, reenactment, and embodiment of thought, in the present of the past, means that an attempt is made to merge the two temporalities in understanding historical difference. The language of Plato and Aristotle and their successors, whether critical or not of these seminal philosophers, uses the language of discovery and representation in fiction and not. The philosopher of history shares this kind of language with the poet, dramatist, and other kinds of writers. Erich Kahler, a philosopher of history, distinguishes between history and the representation of history (historiography) and, as much as he admires Collingwood, says that Collingwood does not make this distinction and thereby causes confusion.[23] Kahler attempts to distinguish between meaning as purpose and as form: design, action, search, or quest bears meaning as end and aim; works of art are meaning as form. Part of what is suggestive about Kahler's view, however much one agrees with it, is how he discusses the relation between finding and making meaning:

> [S]omething has a meaning only *for somebody*, only for the human mind which comprehends it, and by comprehending it actually creates it; he who grasps a meaning for the first time creates *something new*; by his mere act of comprehending he changes the picture of the world and—since that picture involves a reflexive change in

his environment—changes his world itself, the reality of his world.
And this is precisely how history came into being.[24]

Perhaps the main exploration of this book is to range through the representations of discovery or recognition in such texts as well as to widen
the scope to reading or interpretation in general that include anagnorisis
as one of its keys. Kahler is using comprehension in its root sense, as an
encompassing and connection of various data in a mental act, which
reveals a "latent connection" between these data. His view involves an
interpenetration of subject and object in the process of history, an intricate
interdependence of human consciousness and time, whereas Theodor
Lessing sees it in more subjective terms as the meaning of history is what
a person gives himself and historical evolution develops from that self to
self. For Lessing, history originates in volitions, desires, needs, and intentions and "is a realization of the 'dream visions' (*Traumdichtungen*)."[25] Ways
of seeing are contentious in the philosophy of history: disputes occur
over understanding, comprehension, and recognition. What happens in
the world and the means of representing and reading (interpreting) are
not settled. One point of agreement might be that recognition and misrecognition are central to the human experience and the representation
of that experience.

Technology has also affected notions of perception and knowledge.
The relation between science and human sciences might also be about
understanding and comprehending. During the 1960s, Derek J. de Solla
Price spoke in such terms: "Perhaps the greatest revelation to me in my
professional odyssey from physicist to historian of science was the discovery that research in the two subjects felt much the same from inside.
The desire of the physicist to achieve some great new understanding of
the universe matches that of the historian to comprehend the workings
of our society, and the lust for idol-breaking is quite similar."[26]

Marshall McLuhan's famous dictum that the medium is the message
implied many things, including the possibility of a proliferated plurality
of media and the messaging, massaging and massing that it would
involve.[27] Recognition and reading are related even in new technologies. For instance, in *Reading Television* (1978) John Fiske and John
Hartley argue against television being simply rubbish—they say the
Elizabethan drama and theatre was denigrated by some contemporaries—
or being a normative, conservative, commercial, and conventional
medium. Instead, Fiske and Hartley set out a paradox—the very
familiarity of television allows it to be an agent of defamiliarization.[28]
Here is a new context for the familiar friction between empathy

(sympathy) and distance—the drawing near and away—that occurs within Aristotle in pathos and catharsis but comes to be dramatized in dramatic, literary, and cultural theory as mimesis and estrangement between Aristotle and his critics (such as Brecht). In speaking about the particular manner in which plays were constructed in Greek, medieval, and Elizabethan drama, especially in terms of the changes brought about by naturalism, Raymond Williams also uses the language of recognition: "And I think we have to go on to recognize that 'design,' in these senses, is radically different from 'representation,' in its modern senses. There is a critical and revolutionary change from dramatic reproduction of a different and more locally human order of experience."[29] For Williams, there is "experience," whereas for some others, as we have seen, experience is a welter, a kind of inchoate present that makes little or no sense. Thinking implies recognition leading to knowledge: for a skeptic, knowing doubt about knowledge seems to imply some form of recognition. My interest is to show various instances of recognition across time, place, and kinds of writing and also to present historical, literary, and cultural readings. The interpretations of texts must begin somewhere. If there were truly no sense in texts, then there would be no sense in writing about them. Meaning, recognition, and reading are all fraught, but examples should allow for some better understanding of them. Communication is difficult but not impossible. There is a rhetorical contract between speaker and audience, writer and reader even as it involves some shifts. It may be, as Richard Lanham suggested decades ago, that there is a clash between the rhetorical and "serious" view of the self, between the sincere and the playful.[30] I would contend that this tension or friction or clash (depending on what metaphor is stressed) helps through its conflict or opposition to create drama and interest. The literary and the descriptive, the fictional and the nonfictional share elements in representation, including in recognition and interpretation. I cannot pretend to resolve these philosophical or epistemological differences, but the drama and interest of recognition and reading in all their differences are suggestive.

Performance and role playing suggest something about the nature, words, and actions of the humans over time in all their variety. These elements can connect dramatists with anthropologists, as Clifford Geertz suggested in the 1960s: people "may change their roles, their styles of acting, even the dramas in which they play; but—as Shakespeare himself of course remarked—they are always performing."[31] It is not surprising that in the study of tragedy over the past century that anthropology should also, in conjunction with the study of myth and archeology, have affected ways of seeing that form. For instance the work of Jane Harrison, Francis Cornford, and Gilbert Murray were especially influential in the first half of the twentieth century.[32]

Although in his study of mimesis or imitation Erich Auerbach did not focus on *anagnôrisis* or recognition, he did a great deal to concentrate attention on the interpretation of reality through literary representation. Homer and Plato were key figures in this history, and Auerbach was able to point out how in the Middle Ages the representation of the story of Christ and nineteenth-century Romanticism more generally were able to break with the doctrine of the levels of representation. Interpretation involved different emphases and allowed for leeway in what the interpreter individually and over time saw in the texts and images before him or her.[33] Terence Cave revisits Odysseus's scar as Auerbach had. Unlike Auerbach, Cave makes recognition the primary focus of an extensive study of poetics. Moreover, Cave traces the history of recognition from Aristotle through the Renaissance, its decline in French neoclassicism and the eighteenth century to more modern manifestations in theory as well as recognition in practice in playwrights, narratives, and fiction from Shakespeare to Conrad. Even though Cave makes many contributions to the topic, two are especially important for my purposes. First, Cave notes the virtual equivalence of anagnorisis with peripeteia in formalist and structuralist uses of recognition and reversal. Second, Cave argues throughout his study that in literary texts recognitions are problematic moments rather than times that produce satisfaction and completion.[34] My discussions of moments of recognition and of reading and interpretation should provide a supplementary view to the ones that Auerbach and Cave produce (and of Northrop Frye who comes between them). E.H. Gombrich has done much to explore the mimetic and interpretative connections between image and word. In discussing Leonardo da Vinci, Gombrich raises the issue of the social rank of artists and suggests that Leonardo explored nature not to be recognized as a natural philosopher (Gombrich uses the word "scientist") but as a means of increasing his knowledge of the visible world, thereby transforming painting from a craft to one of the gentlemanly liberal arts. This transformation would lift him from the manual and therefore menial world of Shakespeare's rude mechanicals—Snout the tinker, Bottom the weaver, and Snug the joiner, those players in Shakespeare's *A Midsummer Night's Dream*—into the world of Aristotle's liberal education (grammar, rhetoric, dialectic, geometry). Gombrich implies, after bringing Aristotle and Shakespeare to bear on his discussion of Leonardo, that ways of making and seeing art have a social dimension. Moreover, he sees Leonardo as trying to affect how his patrons saw the paintings and the painter more in accordance with how Leonardo saw himself. Gombrich is explicit in saying that Leonardo wanted to raise this visual art to the status of poetry: "It was the ambition of such men as Leonardo to show that painting was a Liberal Art, and that the manual labour involved in it was no more essential than was the labour of writing in poetry."[35] Here, for the purposes of this discussion, I wish to emphasize his exploration of architecture and rhetoric in Guilio Romano's Palazzo del Te. In this examination, Gombrich revisits the subject of his dissertation of the 1930s and reinterprets both the palace and his thesis. What the palace teaches, for the older Gombrich, is that sermons and the popular press, and not garden facades or frescoes, are means of propaganda (efforts to influence public opinion), that rhetoric does not always intend to persuade, that the autonomy of art deserves respect, and "that what mattered is the existence of a world of art, a world of dreams, a universe created for our delight."[36] There is, as Auerbach suggests, a change in each of our interpretations over time. The question is whether our recognitions are personal or objective, subjective or intersubjective. Gombrich has changed his mind: " 'The painter,' said Plato, 'makes a dream for those who are awake,' not his personal dream and even less his private nightmare, as I once believed. What counts is the power of the imagination to leave empirical reality behind."[37] Writing and reading are ways of representing or seeing: they involve interpretation. How we imagine, reason, and recognize is a matter for debate. Thomas Greene has provided a historical view of mimesis or imitatio and relates them to discovery in Renaissance poetry, so that the drawing together of representation, interpretation, and recognition, so central to my study, is not outlandish.[38] The approach I have taken, beyond brief theoretical frameworks, is to use examples from texts to suggest the variety of ways to recognize and read. This book is meant to be suggestive and not definitive or exhaustive. It is one interpreter speaking of recognition and reading to other interpreters—my readers. I hope that this study will be read not by specialists alone or solely by those who teach and study within the university.

Experience and reading, the concrete and the abstract, all bear on how we see and what insights, small and large, we have. More than Auerbach, Frye, and Cave, I have also placed recognition in and the reading of literature side-by-side with those aspects of history and related fields. Historians have their interpretations and recognitions, too. One example of recognition is the language Carlo Ginzburg uses to describe his method: "I suddenly realized that in my long research on the

sabbat I had been pursuing a method that was much more morphologi-
cal than historical. I was collecting myths and beliefs from different cultural
contexts on the basis of formal affinities. Beyond superficial similarities
I recognized (or at least I believed I recognized) profound connections,
being inspired more by Longhi than Morelli."[39] Readers and interpreters, whether literary scholars or historians, can experience a new
recognition or think they are members of the audience in the theatre.
This moment of recognition or discovery can come after a long time or
a lifetime as much as after two hours traffic on the stage.

   History and literature have a long relation that is more intricate than
Aristotle in *Poetics*, placing poetry above history for being more universal
than particular or noting that poetry expresses possibility (what can
happen) rather than actuality (what happens).[40] Political writers, historians, and literary theorists—whether Tocqueville, Burckhardt, Hegel,
Nietzsche, or Frye—discuss tragedy.[41] Whether it is metatheatre or
metahistory the shape of the text matters. Word, world, and the genre of
writing all include notions of tragedy. History as fiction is something
that G.W. Bowerstock discusses from Nero to Julian and in doing so
finds Northrop Frye's idea of the secular scripture useful, especially in
discussing the connection between the scripture as truth and story.[42]
Religion, history, and literature have inescapable relations between
language generally and rhetoric, narrative, and poetics specifically. Frye
himself shows that romance is a type that affects religion and literature
and the connection between myth and truth that also concerns history:
"Romance, the kernel of fable, begins an upward journey toward man's
recovery of what he projects as sacred myth."[43] Recognition, as well as
kinds of writing, brings together different fields and academic disciplines.
Lionel Gossman stresses the close relation between literature and history
and discusses narrative, an element so important to both the literary
and the historical.[44] Content and context, as well as the role of value
judgments, affect notions of meaning and signification over time, so that
re-cognizing might depend on understanding what the text implies
that is necessary over time in the changes that occur in life experience
and history.[45] Recognition is contested. One reason I have, as Auerbach
did, emphasized that I am one reader recognizing and reading is that
whereas there may be communication between people and times, I am
not assuming one universal transhistorical person or interpretative community. There are many differences in people and places.[46] One of these
alterities is feminist difference.[47] Reading as or like a woman is such a
difference that assumes biological or cultural differences depending on
which of the two projects in feminist literary criticism we are discussing.[48]

Questions of otherness can also be racial and cultural. The expansion of Western European powers in various parts of the globe affected these notions and intensified differences from the fifteenth century onward.[49] Limited points of view could be, through a kind of technical and industrial dominion and even domination, thought to be normative and universal. Being representative, for Europeans, could mean their European advantage taken for vantage. Rivalries, cultural mixing, and shifting boundaries could, as I have argued elsewhere, complicate the encounters, exchanges, and clashes experienced by different cultures.[50] The "discovery" of the New World was momentous in the tensions between misrecognition and recognition.

As Prospero says to Miranda in Shakespeare's *The Tempest*, this brave new world was new to her: she is looking at the Italians who have arrived on her Mediterranean island. Although Miranda was born in Milan and left their home early when her father's brother had usurped his throne, she is like a Native looking at Europeans arriving as almost-gods, invaders, and usurpers. The island was *terra nullius*, an empty island that Sycorax, the witch, and her son, Caliban (often described as a monster), inhabited with Ariel, a spirit, before Prospero arrived as liberator, magus, tyrant, depending on the point of view. The inhabitants do not get along well: for instance, Caliban is said to have attempted to rape Miranda, but he claims he simply wanted to people the island with their offspring, and Miranda calls him "Abhorred slave."[51] Caliban understands the importance of learning language from Prospero and considers his teacher to have betrayed him. Language becomes a contested ground—who gets to represent the past, the present, the future. Prospero reinterprets Miranda's recognition and interpretation of Ferdinand. In fact, Prospero's magic controls the play and provides its internal framework, at least as a fiction, because Shakespeare has constructed him and the plot for his audience. Meanings become a matter of contention.

Drama was a craft and also, in the case of blank verse, a liberal art, so Shakespeare's status would be a mix of Homer and Leonardo in terms of art. Shakespeare's theatres were outside the city walls because of religious objections to this art of illusion (the devil's work) as well as the Christian incorporation of some of Plato's charges against Homer and the poets. Social context, history, and law were all part of mimesis and the related aspects of recognition and interpretation (reading, viewing). Representation was and is, then, not literary alone. Choosing representatives in government who stand in for the community or constituency is another mimetic activity in which the part representing the whole of synecdoche vies with the displacement of the whole by the part of metonymy. This is an ancient human practice. In classical antiquity there are a number of examples of political and legal representation: for instance, Roman law was also used to support later parliaments of political and legal representatives in terms of powers given to attorneys and the legal theory of representation. In Western Europe, parliaments and similar representative bodies grew up in the second half of the Middle Ages.[52] Edmund Burke, for example, thought that mimesis or imitation helped to form manners, opinions, and lives and is one of the strongest links in society.[53] Politics, history, and colonialism are part of my study of "recognition" and "reading." This is one of the reasons for the range of texts and images I include in the book that follows. Text and context are varied and change over time, although they have some persistent attributes that allow for an attempted communication and understanding over time. The distinction between texts and contexts, as Hayden White has said, has become problematized.[54] One of the aims of my study is to bring text and context together and to show the blurring of their boundaries.

In discussing actual and possible worlds I have argued that they intermingle, so to divide them through definition is more a matter of necessary convenience than determined accuracy. Such distinctions, as in Doreen Maitre's between a possible non-actual world and a possible actual world, cannot be made in a neat division. She herself argues for a reciprocal interaction between fantasy and actual worlds.[55] To delight and to instruct, as Horace may well have known, are not readily divisible, so that the distinction between possible and actual worlds is problematic, especially in theory. Delight, deflection, and escape, as I noted in the 1980s, are not frivolous activities: legal fictions permeate our society and the history of science is full of discredited or revised theorems and laws that we now regard as fictions. History can turn truth into fiction. Today's reality is tomorrow's historical fiction. Possibility, probability, and necessity become ways of discussing fantasy and verisimilitude. Fiction is not necessarily what Plato and the Church Fathers, who adapted his view, thought, a copy of nature that is more illusory the more it veers from nature. Form and content constitute meaning and are part of recognition and "reading." It is also interesting to question, as Thomas Pavel does, the reliability of texts representing worlds faithfully because the assumption of a reliable text is an act of faith.[56] The light of history is refractory; fiction shares distance and relevance with other activities; and I, like Pavel the novelist and theorist, tell fables, use metaphors, and see in the theory of fiction the importance of logic, game theory, linguistics, and science.[57] Jerome Bruner relates actual and possible worlds, theory, and psychology. Two modes of coming to terms with narrative is one bringing to a text argument and theory and another of working from the text.[58] This distinction can blur into what I have called elsewhere, story-argument, where narrative and thesis intertwine.[59] Whether a story-argument is enough is a question for all of us in an age that has responded to an earlier swing to the power of the argument. Writers are readers and readers are writers. Writerly readers may be fictionalizing fictions as much as realizing them. Narratives make history, science, and fiction, so that these human knowledges share something. Conversely, argument occurs in all three. Returning to Bruner, it is interesting to see his own variations on world making, a process akin to recognition and interpretation. Bruner recognizes the elasticity of the real and describes how discourse enlists the imagination. He speaks of three aspects of the human subjunctive in which discourse, rather than establishing certainties, opens up possibilities, allowing the reader to create his or her own world or virtual text. First, presupposition is the creation of meanings. Second, subjectification is the depiction of reality through the protagonists' consciousness. Third, multiple perspective is beholding the world prismatically. Language, mind, and vision are all connected in Bruner's exploration of possible worlds.[60] It is important, as I argue in this book, that while recognizing the importance of literary texts, we realize the significances of the role of other kinds of texts and images. The actual–possible world is an intricate continuum. Recognitions and readings do not need to be final, solid, and definitive. They might suggest intuition, insight, knowledge, and wisdom that change with texts and images and with readers and audiences coming back to them. Subject and object change over time in a dance.

The structure of the body of *Interpreting Cultures* is divided into three parts. In part 1, "Recognitions," I discuss the general nature of gaining recognition or what constitutes discovery across faculties, examine the background to recognition—including embarrassment, mythology, and ideology, explore biblical, classical, and philosophical instances (epic, tragedy, and comedy in the classics), analyze from history exempla from crossing cultures, talk about examples from psychology but mainly psychoanalysis, and offer some tentative conclusions about recognition.

Part 2 of the study, "Readings—History and Poetics," moves from recognition as its primary focus to reading or interpretation and is divided into five chapters. In chapter two, "History and Empire," I discuss a number of key topics: texts and first contacts; narratives of the New World; English colonial hopes, permanent colonies, British and French America: consolidation and contestation; British America: from triumph to loss and continued tensions, and Canada as and at a cross-roads. This discussion of history from the "discovery" of the New World and the significance of North America should help to provide a textual context for other discourses of the West, Europe, and the Atlantic world that appear in the book. Chapter three, "Recognizing Canadian Women and Women in Canada," examines Native, Black, and European women writers in a key colony then state—Canada—that lay between Britain and the United States as it was part of the British Empire and then Commonwealth; however, much of its early English-speaking population came from the American colonies and even the early republic. The topics under discussion are: seeing double, Elizabeth Bishop, Native poets and poets and Natives, African Canadian writers and the double bind/doubly blind, and more dualities. There is a dou-bleness that runs through this discussion, but oppositions are sometimes blurred. Elizabeth Bishop, for instance, lived in Nova Scotia with her maternal grandparents during key years, but is a celebrated American poet. The crossing of boundaries is an important part of recognition and reading. In chapter four, I examine history and writing in terms of the relation between T.E. Lawrence and Bernard and Charlotte Shaw. Lawrence considered himself a writer and not. I also discuss the Shaws's Lawrence, including the Shavian belief in him, and the posthumous film, *Lawrence of Arabia*. Lawrence lost one of his posts, which I describe as the sack of a hero. There are various types of recognition, and one of these is Charlotte Shaw's of Lawrence. His ambivalence over writing was like a wound, and he worried over his privacy and about publication: Lawrence was a genius of publicity who professed to shun it. Chapter five, "Poiēma, Theoria and Tekhnē," emphasizes the importance of the ancient Greeks for poetry, theory, and technique or technology, kinds of making and seeing. Topics that comprise this part are the poetics of communication, theory, poetry and poets, technology and poetry then and now. The text and contexts of poetry affect interpretation: recognition is a key part of reading. In chapter six, "Poetry and Mythology: Coda," I relate poetics to story and argument, myth and ideology, and explore possibilities for poetry in the context of interpretation and other fields but also in and of itself. In part 3, "Readings: Writers, Images and Poets," I begin chapter seven with a discussion of Northrop Frye and writing. The topics are divided into these aspects finding a context, looking for self-expression, the paradoxical visionary, critic, and writer, and the road not taken. Frye was a theorist who reconsidered Aristotle's poetics and discussed mimesis, including interpretation and recognition. Like T.E. Lawrence, he was a scholar who considered the nature of writing and also wrote literary texts and plans for them. For Frye, although he wrote poetry and fiction, what is now called creative writing was a road not taken because he did not concentrate on it as much as on his critical and theoretical works. His recognition of writing had different facets. Chapter eight discusses the possibility of seeing inside the head of Willy Loman, the protagonist of Arthur Miller's *Death of a Salesman*. In analyzing Dustin Hoffman's portrayal of Willy, I examine the tragedy of the common man on film and what kind of tragedy the play is. One of my strategies is to look at the end of the play in terms of the end of tragedy. The role of the Requiem and the question of whether film can get inside this salesman's head are other concerns. In chapter nine of part 3 of the book, I discuss some Irish lyric poets to round out my examination of the Atlantic world, which involves the triangular relation among Europe, America, and Africa. The poets I concentrate on are W. B. Yeats, Seamus Heaney, Paul Muldoon, and Mary O'Malley. Chapter ten focuses on narratives and fictions, on representation and travel accounts, moving to a discussion of recognition and misrecognition.

I conclude with some suggestions about reading and recognition. It is to recognition first and then to reading that I now turn in this study, ranging over various disciplines and times, from texts to images and back again. To interpret culture involves recognition, its insights, and problems.

PART 1

Recognitions

CHAPTER ONE

Discovering Recognition

1.1   Gaining Recognition or Discovery across Faculties

In *The Name of the Rose* the deafness to laughter and the lack of insight into the comic aspects of the human condition lead to murder, inquisition, and torture and the destruction of the lost book on comedy of Aristotle's *Poetics* in a fire at a monastery.[1] This lack of comedy and laughter has all too often led to a blind solemnity that undervalues the comic and sets up a dreary hierarchy of disciplines. Although a master of the poetic and fictional, Plato wanted to banish the poets who would not sing paeans to the republic. Aristotle restored a place for poetics, but it was beneath philosophy, which was more universal, and above history, which was less so.[2] Philip Sidney put poetry on top because its universal and concrete images were more accessible in moving people to virtue, yet he kept history in the basement.[3] Either through a loss of Aristotle's discussion of comedy or through a sense that men were like Saint Paul and had shed childish things when they came of age, comic recognition or insight (*cognitio*) seldom if ever gained the same status in literary theory and criticism that tragic recognition (*anagnôrisis*) achieved.

Neither history nor comedy has been neglected, but both have been undervalued by those who were not historians or comic writers respectively. History was not to be a pattern that would glorify Providence or progress but was to act in the service of philosophy, art, or science. History has made great gains in literary studies since the advent of Marxism, intellectual history, cultural studies, and cultural materialism. Whereas comedy has received attention since antiquity, it seems to have found some recognition with the rise of modernity. Theories of comedy and laughter appear to have multiplied with the flourishing of comic plays—especially in Italy, France, Spain, and England—during the Renaissance, with the rise of the novel, and with the practice and theoretical celebration of satire and irony from the eighteenth century onward.[4] In the first decades of the twentieth century, with the "anthropological" school of Jane Harrison at Cambridge, more balance occurred between tragedy (Gilbert Murray) and comedy (Francis Cornford).[5] Theorists and critics as diverse as Northrop Frye, Harry Levin, and Anne Barton have written eloquently about comedy.[6] My interest here is not to place comedy above tragedy or to proclaim the particular in order to secure the highest place for history, but it is to observe how literary blindness and recognition, in both tragic and comic senses, relate to ignorance and discovery in philosophy, history, and other disciplines. Although my scheme is my own, it owes two debts, one to Paul de Man's notion of blindness and insight (which itself derives from literature and philosophy) and Terence Cave's ground-breaking study of the types of recognition.[7] This discussion of comedy also grows out of my teaching and writing on the subject for more than twenty years. How blindness is resolved in a laughable recognition or in a clear view amidst tragic suffering or death represents the extremes that the author, characters, and readers experience. Even though my discussion of recognition is general, it should also shed some light on the comic and historical aspects of discovery. How recognition crosses generic and disciplinary boundaries is another primary concern here. What then are the different kinds of blindness and recognition in literature and literary theory and do they occur in philosophy, history, religion, psychology, and other fields? Is there a poetics that applies to the various ways of discussing culture?

Recognition is a moment that involves a movement from ignorance to knowledge or self-knowledge, which can represent a whole range of experience, from the tragic through the absurd to the comic. It can bring relief, clarity, a sense of loss, terror, ridicule, suspicion, shock, and a whole host of other effects.[8] From Aristotle, who has anagnorisis, which refers to a knowledge of a tragic situation, to Brecht, who does not fore-ground the term but who wants the audience to gain knowledge of its situation through historical difference or estrangement, discovery or revelation in the characters and in the audience plays a central role in the drama and its contiguous genres.[9]

Perhaps the first critical recognition is that Greek tragedy and comedy originate in the same religious festival, which may have been an embar-rassment to Aristotle and subsequent theorists, who tried, in the wake of

Plato's attack on Homer and on poetry generally, to redeem poetry as a serious endeavor.[10] Another embarrassment is comedy itself as Aristotle defines it in chapter 2 of *Poetics*, that is because it aims at representing people as worse than in life, whereas tragedy makes them better.[11] In chapter 4 Aristotle credits Homer with laying down the model for comedy (*Margites*) and tragedy (*Iliad*, *Odyssey*), so that although the Aristotelian schema elevates tragedy above comedy, it also dignifies the comic, intentionally or not, with Homeric provenance. The comic mask is ugly but does not give pain: comedy involves the ludicrous but not the full range of villainy. Aristotle says that comedy has no history because, at first, it was not treated seriously.[12] The "at first" implies that Aristotle and others are now taking comedy seriously. He then tries to give comedy a history. The *peripeteia*, or reversal, and recognition scenes are the heart of tragedy.[13] Comedy represents the possible (what might happen), whereas history shows what has happened. Tragedy presents both the possible and the historical. Neither Aristotle's *Poetics* nor the *Coislinian Tractate* associates recognition with comedy. The origins of recognition are tragic. Cicero's *On the Character of the Orator* follows suit: Great vice and misery are not fit subjects for ridicule or laughter.[14] In classical times recognition seems to have been a tragic element, and comedy had its scope strictly limited in theory. In practice, Menander adapts the recognition plot to comedy.[15] Not until the fourth century A.D. does theory catch up with practice. Donatus adapts Aristotle's analysis of tragic structure to that of comedy: "Catastrophe is the change of the situation to a pleasant outcome, a change made clear to all through the knowledge of what has happened."[16] Donatus alludes to Livius Andronicus's view of comedy as a mirror of daily life and Cicero's dictum that it is an imitation of life, a mirror of custom, an image of truth.[17] Despite the disclaimers, comedy is being taken seriously, and part of that seriousness is recognition. The disturbing nature of comedy is recognized through the disturbance of recognition. The author, character, and audience/reader share this public act even when it involves apparently private- or self-knowledge.

1.2   Recognizing the Background: Embarrassment, Mythology, and Ideology

Although my schema might make the subject of blindness and recognition (ignorance and knowledge) look synchronic or transhistorical, this topic does have a historical dimension. Closely related to religious vision and the lifting of the veil of human ignorance of the divine, blindness and recognition also have tragic dimensions. Cave speaks of the "scandal" attached to recognition, which owes something to the etymology of *skandalon*, the way such awareness seduces the reader into its trap, and to scandal as a stumbling block or an obstacle to belief, which derives from the French *scandale*, something that disturbs decorum and that calls attention to the difficulty of talking about literature.[18] The scandal arises from the undervaluing of comedy and romance, which underscore their own fictionality, so that such an undervaluation also means an underestimation of fiction or literature itself, which is one of the greatest fictions. My argument here is that comedy and romance, although not solemn, are serious, that the imagination of literature is at the root of culture. Although certain views, such as Plato's, have tried to banish the mythical impulse or to limit it to sing for the soul of politics, myth—although not entirely separable from political ideology—is not so readily exiled or contained. In my brief account, recognition is enlightening and embarrassing as it brings characters, readers, audiences (theatrical and religious—congregations) from ignorance to knowledge.

Recognition embodies fictions of truth or the truth of fictions. Religious recognition contains its own demonic parody. *Cognitio* haunts *anagnorisis*. What is remarkable about recognition is that it represents or reenacts a whole range of human experience, from the ecstasy of religious vision and the discovery of truth to comic illuminations of love and satiric unmaskings of pretension. Through irony, recognition gives a great overview of a life without blindness or it calls attention to our all-too-human sightlessness. Recognition shows how the doors of perception open and shut, or, perhaps, how they revolve and reverse, sometimes catching us in one of the compartments during stops, starts, and reversals. The scandal of recognition may be that people have long underestimated fictions, especially literature, and within literature the so-called frivolity of comedy and romance.

Aristotle, Sidney, and others have sung the praises of poetry and philosophy at the expense of history, but it has been the ideology of politics, at least from Plato onward, that has made literature and the recognition of the truth of its own fictionality an embarrassment and a breach in the decorum of the world.[19] But even political ideology possesses its own myths. The shadows on the wall of the cave in Plato's allegory are another form of recognition that emphasizes the difficulty of coming to a knowledge of truth and justice, to an enlightenment, in a world of shadows. It may be that disputes and scandals arise over the types of recognition and not over the existence of that subject or the possibility of epiphany or a comic or tragic knowledge of a self or situation. The power of irony or embarrassment might even enhance the ability to know. A smug blindness might be, like a little learning, a dangerous thing.

A complication of the embarrassment or disturbance over literature, particularly as recognition draws attention to its fictional nature, arises in the conflict between, and conflation of, story and argument, myth and ideology. The worldliness of argument, especially in rhetoric but to some extent in dialectic, calls into question the use and truth of *muthos*, the plot Aristotle discusses but also the root of the story of mythology that underlies literature. Rhetorical argument, and perhaps all argument, has a *telos*, an end that is supposed to be a truth or understanding of and in the world. Literary plots also have such ends, but they are, in such a view, at best, mere representations of the world and, at worst, flights of fancy from reality. When arguments, such as those in science, can be tested by experiment, through an appeal to nature, the hope for truth or knowledge may, for a time, live up to its veridical, worldly, and dialectical promise, but how many arguments are clearly so? Analogy is used in argument and in story. Stories contain arguments and arguments stories. Perhaps, as I have suggested elsewhere, most of the time what we find ourselves in is story-argument.[20] The ghostly plot of literature haunts the movement of argument. Both seek to clarify ignorance through recognition: they are teleological. The trouble is literary recognition may question the possibility of achieving actual recognition and thereby achieve the notoriety of scandal, at once as a trap, block, and disturbance. Possibly, each clarification reminds us of more ignorance or mystery or how inadequate human explanation is before divine, natural, and human forces. The latter force relates to aggregate human behavior in and over time. Each recognition in science, philosophy, history, and literature may be, to some degree, a failure owing to the limited scope of human cognition. Truth in fiction may be a scandal for truth in the world.

Two ways of looking at the relation of mythology to ideology should clarify the difficulties of distinguishing the two terms or in conflating them. In keeping with the rhetorical tradition Roland Barthes says that mythology is ideology, whereas Northrop Frye, while admitting they overlap in many cases, sees mythology, especially in its displaced form in literature, as being a critique of ideology and the foundation of poetics. More like Marshall McLuhan, Barthes attempts a semiology that reads visual and verbal signs as mythologies that try to naturalize their ideology through an aesthetic seduction or a proclamation of their worldliness as realism or naturalism. Barthes and Frye make strong cases, and I am loath to do without their insights. Their views alone do not provide a whole enough picture. Barthes's position is harder to maintain in relation to lyric poetry and apparently neutral description in fiction. Does it adequately take into account the displacement of the world into fiction? Goethe's view that art is art because it is not life is barely noticed. Frye, like the structuralists, sees literature as music, so that the form is the content.[21] This view, although powerful (as after all literature does have its own formal properties), neglects the politics of form. Even music has its political origins and uses, and we might not be able to separate the musician from the music any more than we can the dancer from the dance. The aesthetic may be an ideology and a critique of ideology. That is my principal theory. It is my prime recognition about recognition, which lies at the heart of human knowledge. Hayden White's content of the form, like Frye's, raises similar questions about the relation between fact and interpretation, mythology and ideology, in the writing of history and historiography.[22] Literature, history, philosophy, and other fields of human vision are subject to blindness and recognition. They are heterodox disciplines with a heterodoxy of texts. Perhaps in practice readers might accept a difference between story and argument (despite what Milton calls the headnotes he added to *Paradise Lost*) while observing the difficulty of proving any difference in theory.

The movement from religion to theology, if we were to accept this working, but not theoretical, difference, would constitute a move from story to argument. My theoretical view would be one that sees practice and experience as upholding theory and not simply a metatheory, which asserts that practice is wholly already a theory. The line between practice and theory is like the boundary between mythology and ideology. An uncertain circularity can paralyze such debates. Appealing to practice, then, as mutual as it is (between experience and a theory of that experience simultaneously with varying stresses), is the way to begin. We must start somewhere. The biblical stories yield many different interpretations. Theological differences arise from these hermeneutical variants. These theological recognitions are sometimes contrary and, indeed, have led to some of the greatest political battles in European history, at home and in the European empires. The religious wars in France, the Inquisition, and the treatment of the Natives in the "discovery" of America are three examples from a multitude of instances. How do we move from the originary religious impulse of revelation or ecstasy to a reasonable recognition of this irrational visionary knowledge? If a Native were of a different religious view, was he or she othered from "civil" society or from the "city on the hill" or from another earthly city based on the City of God with dire material and political circumstances? Recognition inhabits the borderlands between stories about recognition or with discoveries and interpretations that discover what might be called a recognition of recognition. Behind those recognitions is the insight that no human recognition is complete even if it allows for *katascopos*, or overview. Even the theorist, having seen the recognition behind the tension between recognitions, is not at the end of history but inhabits something that may be analogous to the end of Hegel's history even as time has passed by, has limited the one who has made the claim of standing at the end of history, or has caused him or her to experience something that resembles a recognition of one of Aristophanes's characters. Irony or time may keep recognition from becoming tyrannous, destroying others for different beliefs or insights, often in response to the same stories, but the ironic and the temporal have their own possible tyrannies in potentially destroying any beliefs or discoveries. Negatively, this possible destruction can create an ethical, social, and political paralysis, but positively, it can allow for a dialectical form of knowledge and self-knowledge. The paralysis occurs Hamlet-like. With irony and time enough, with the pattern of history, how much matters that mattered before? But the ironic, as an antithetical, skeptical, or katascopic force, would be essential for dialectical knowledge

1.3 Biblical Instances

My interest here is to concentrate on recognition in the stories in the Bible rather than on the myriad recognizing and recognizable interpretations that make up commentary and dogma in Christian theology. The main reason I use the Bible is that the Koran and other religious texts have not had the same direct effect on Western literature over time. Recognition in the Judeo-Christian tradition is one of revelation even if, as Etienne Gilson suggests, theology tries to reason with the revelatory.[23] One might expect an unambiguous use of recognition in the Bible that would show the wisdom and seriousness of humans. On the contrary, many shades of recognition are cast in the Bible, although, principally, there are two kinds of blindness and recognition in it: structural and situational. Within these two types, knowledge, according to biblical values, exists in true and parodic forms.

The structural myth of a fall into knowledge, sin, and death informs the situations that comprise that myth. The comic structure of the Bible,

from the Fall through Christ's crucifixion to the Last Judgment, shows
various comic subplots of blindness and recognition in addition to this
larger structure of bliss lost. In this superplot, happiness is restored
through a recognition of disobedience in the quest for knowledge and a
regaining of paradise after Christ enters human history and experience
through the crucifixion and then ascends to make possible once again an
atonement between human and divine. The various blindnesses of Eve,
Adam, Cain, Jacob, Job, Judas, and others and the recognition of error
or ignorance at various stages in a series of u-shaped or "comic" narratives contribute to the great movement of the biblical superplot.[24] A friction occurs in these moments of recognition between the tragedy of the
situation and the comic structure of the larger recognition in the Bible.
That comic structure is a movement from an old order through chaos to
a new order, from innocence through experience to a higher innocence,
from one happiness through exile and misery to a new happiness.
Whether a recognition is tragic or comic depends on how short or long
a view of the plot or *muthos* one takes. Most often, and this phenomenon is particularly true in the Bible and works like Dante's *Divine
Comedy*, the tragic, diachronic aspect of recognition works together with
its comic, synchronic element. Recognition of sin or joy, which has
tragic and comic dimensions, is central to the Bible and the many biblical analogues and displacements in Western literature. Knowledge of
truth is hard to see behind the shadows of the pseudo-knowledge of sin.
Pride is the worst sin, and the desire for knowledge to rival God is not
the same thing as the wish to have knowledge of God. Christ embodies
a humanity that allows humans to gain a better understanding of the
divine. The typological structure of the Bible makes Christ a new Adam:
he breathes new life into the clay (the etymology for Adam). The New
Testament supplies a humility in knowledge that redeems the proud act
in Eden that pursued forbidden knowledge.

A few key examples of situations of blindness and recognition should
elaborate this large structural theme (or thematic structure). In Genesis 3,
knowledge is a temptation and a dangerous thing. The serpent contra-
dicts the unnamed woman (whom Adam later calls Eve because she was
the mother of all living things), who quotes God as saying of the fruit of the
tree in the midst of the garden: "Ye shall not eat of it, neither shall ye
touch it, lest ye die."[25] This is a well-known story, so in it I stress
blindness–recognition only. The serpent tells the woman: "Ye shall not
surely die: For God doth know that in the day ye eat thereof, then your
eyes shall be opened, and ye shall be as gods, knowing good and evil."[26]
The woman sees that the tree is good for food, pleasant to sight, and

desirable for knowledge, so she ate and shared the fruit with her husband: "And the eyes of them both were opened, and they knew that they *were* naked; and they sewed fig leaves together, and made themselves aprons."[27] This recognition leads to shame and punishment: the serpent and the woman will have their own offspring that will have enmity toward one another; Adam and his wife will be cursed with sorrow and know death from dust to dust. Their knowledge of good and evil, says God, has made Adam and Eve "become as one of us," so God exiles them both before they can eat of the fruit of the tree of life and become immortal like God and the cherubims, who, along with the flaming sword, guard the eastern gate of Eden and the tree of life itself. The tragic nature of the knowledge of good and evil is sin, pain, exile, and death.[28] The vision of recognition here is something to remind Adam and Eve of their shameful bodies and their fall from grace. For the reader and for the Christian who knows the story, this Fall precipitates a series of other falls and redemption from blindness to insight until the ultimate recognition of the Last Judgment. Human reliance on divine grace and revelation might serve as an embarrassment for readers in this secular age, but that unease depends on how far they take irony.

The story of Jacob shows how recursive, ambivalent, and multilayered recognition can be. It also illustrates how a reader might take a more tragic view on first reading—or if thinking of each episode individually—than an experienced reader who keeps in mind the larger structure of Jacob's story or of the Bible. A brief account of Jacob should illustrate the strong mythological dimension of the story. The conventions and devices of storytelling are foregrounded. God prophesies to the pregnant Rebekah that her elder twin shall serve her younger twin as will the two nations that they will found.[29] Jacob and she trick Isaac into disinheriting Jacob's elder twin, Esau. She overhears Isaac, who is nearly blind, instruct Esau to make him savory meat, which Isaac will eat before blessing Esau. Rebekah tells Jacob to substitute himself for Esau and she puts Esau's raiment on Jacob and makes him hairy, like his elder brother, by putting kidskins on his hands and neck. Jacob, impersonating Esau, then lies to Isaac, "I *am* Esau thy firstborn."[30] Isaac questions, feels, kisses, smells, and blesses him even though he hears the voice of Jacob. Soon after Jacob leaves, Esau arrives: now, too late, Isaac recognizes his mistake and trembles at the trick. Esau cries in his bitterness and wants his father's blessing, but although his father blesses him, he cannot undo the favored status he has given to Jacob. Esau swears his revenge on Jacob, and Rebekah, overhearing once more, sends her favorite son away until her eldest forgets the cause of his anger.[31] Jacob feels shame but

God reassures him in the dreams of the ladder. Jacob goes to his mother's brother, Laban, who has a daughter Rachel: Jacob falls in love with her and pledges to work seven years to marry her, an offer Laban accepts. But after the marriage feast, Laban tricks the trickster. At nightfall, Laban brings Jacob his bride, but in the morning he sees that it is Leah.[32] Jacob works another seven years in order to have Rachel as his second wife. God punishes Jacob by making Leah fertile and Rachel not. A few sons later, by the maids of Rachel and Leah, Jacob, once God has forgiven him for loving Rachel most, has a child with Rachel: Joseph. The interpretation of this series of tricks and their recognition depends on how long a view the reader takes. In the short term, Jacob knows a little of how Esau felt, but in the long term, he makes his peace and covenant with Laban as God desires it.[33] He also wrestles with a stranger who blesses him as Israel, as a prince, and whom Jacob comes to recognize as God.[34] Esau receives, kisses, and forgives Jacob.[35] The story of Joseph becomes the next main concern. Reversals and tragic aspects of Jacob's stories are part of a series of such falls, reversals (chaos), and triumphs, all occurring within the comic structure that extends within the Bible. Recognition is diachronic and synchronic, fragmentary and whole. The dramatic irony the reader experiences comes from the situation and the structure and from the difference between the human view (that of Adam, Eve, and Jacob) and the divine perspective. At a human level, even a trickster, such as Jacob, can be tricked, a kind of irony that teaches the reader epistemic skepticism or religious humility or both. Paradoxically, it is a framework of belief, or ideology, that gives the mythological structure a comic shape, although it might be the pattern that determines the hope.

Recognition surrounds Jesus. He foretells Peter's three denials, which Peter recognizes when the cock crows.[36] Judas kisses Jesus, a betrayal through a sign of love, so the soldiers will recognize and take him, thereby fulfilling Christ's words: "behold, he is at hand that doth betray me."[37] This recognition of the disciples' betrayal is also repeated in Mark 14, Luke 22, and John 13–18. Repetition emphasizes the supreme importance of these recognitions in the Bible and gives to them, despite their similarity, different contexts. Situational repetition stretches the structure in a kind of fluid triptych. In John 14, the disciples show anxiety in their questions to Jesus about how they will know him. Judas, not Judas Iscariot, asks "how is it that thou wilt manifest thyself unto us, and not unto the world?"[38] All these recognitions of betrayal happen, ironically, when Jesus is bringing them together in the communion of the last supper. Christ's glosses on peace, the Holy Ghost, and other matters, as well as his parables, mix explication and story. Whereas Jesus's parables and images baffle and are irreducible, this glossing in John seems to welcome interpretation and ideology as a kind of prolepsis to a new theology. What is being recognized here is revolutionary, and the means are both story and precept, as if mythology and ideology cannot do without each other and sometimes lose distinction. The allegory seems more apparent here than in some of Christ's other parables: the prophetic and the poetic clash and combine.

The recognitions surrounding Jesus's betrayal look forward to secret signs, mysteries, allegories, and other difficulties while being part of a post-crucifixion typology that is a telescoping of the technique of Christian typology between the Old and the New Testaments. Christ will give signs by which the disciples will know his resurrected body. But some of the prophecy-actualization pattern occurs before Jesus stands trial. Always conscious of earlier prophecies, which help to form the Christian typology, Christ says at the last feast: "The Son of man goeth as it is written of him: but woe unto that man by whom the Son of man is betrayed! it had been good for that man if he had not been born"[39] Judas Iscariot kisses him in a moment of recognition/betrayal/love.[40] Recognizing his error and Jesus's innocence, Judas repents and gives back the thirty pieces of silver to the chief priests and elders only to find them indifferent to Judas and ready to persist in their plans against Christ. In despair, Judas hangs himself.[41] Jesus's curse has taken hold. When Christ is dying on the cross, he calls out, "Eli, Eli, lama sabachthani?" or "My God, my God, why hast thou forsaken me?"[42] Some, Matthew reports, thought Jesus called for Elias to save him. The dead are raised in an earthquake as a celestial sign, but Jesus's human doubt is displaced and elided here with the story of Elias (a confusion of sounds) and the landscape mourning and proclaiming the death of God. Variations on this calling out at the crucifixion occur at Mark 15, who gives less quaking earth while still providing the centurion who proclaims in supreme recognition: "Truly this man was the Son of God."[43] Luke's account represents a prelude to a description of the superscription, "THE KING OF THE JEWS," with "Father, forgive them; for they know not what they do."[44] After telling the believing thief that today he shall be with Jesus in paradise (after this thief had rebuked the scoffing and doubting thief) and after commending his spirit into God's hands, Jesus gives up the ghost without any talk of God forsaking him. John's account is very Spartan: Christ says little at the crucifixion. At the end, he says to Mary, "Woman, behold thy son!" and to his disciple, "Behold thy mother!," so he takes Mary home as his mother.[45] Then Jesus says, after he sees all things accomplished and that the scripture might be ful-filled, "I thirst," and after tasting the vinegar, "It is finished," then bow-ing his head, he gives up the ghost.[46] John provides interpretations of signs that Jesus has typologically fulfilled the scriptures. He then repre-sents the resurrection of Christ.[47] Doubting Thomas comes to belief and serves as an example against skepticism. Jesus says to him: "Thomas, because thou hast seen me, thou hast believed: blessed are they that have not seen, and yet have believed."[48] The unseen recognition, a mystery of belief, is part of the legacy for a post-crucifixion world.

Jesus transforms the world and becomes part of the recognition of God's way. On the road to Damascus, Christ speaks to Saul, who has been persecuting Jesus's followers, and a light blinds Saul. He hears and changes, sees through his blindness. He realizes his error and is con-verted to a new life. Christ sends a vision to a disciple, Ananias, who is to prepare the way for Saul, who is to be Jesus's vessel amongst the Gentiles. When Ananias lays hands on Saul, a kind of miraculous vision appears, a new sight that follows upon his recognition: "And immedi-ately there fell from his eyes as it had been scales: and he received sight forthwith, and arose, and was baptized."[49] Recognition is part of con-version: the person recognizes the errors of the past and sees in a great moment the right course for a future life.

In Revelation, recognition becomes an aspect of prophecy, a vision of the present through future projection and the last of the typologically related prophecies. Despair descends in the Christian community. At prison in Patmos, Christ appears to John. In a book, John is to represent what he has seen, what is, and what will be. Jesus creates a revelation in John, who has a vision of heaven, where he sees Christ as the Lamb of God who takes away the sins of the world, and Jesus opens the book of redemption as a great chorus sings of him as the redeemer. John recog-nizes the triumph of God, through Jesus, over Satan and evil: he sees the end of the fallen world and the advent of the redeemed world, a new heaven and earth. For John, this vision is the recognition of the end of exile, pain, and death and the finding of home, peace, and eternal life. This Holy City dwells in John's desire. Jesus promises to come soon. John's book has Jesus address controversies amongst Christians of the time, but also contains the book of seven seals and the vision within. Revelation mixes ideological containment—John reports Jesus's unhap-piness with specific cases of heresy and adultery—and a great collocation of symbols or allegory. This prophetic vision is the future disciplining the present but is also a vision in that time of the hope for all time. Precept and *muthos* mingle in this book at the end of things.

The pattern of recognition in this final situation, which is to cure John's despair in prison and to be an example for his followers at that dark moment, involves a similar function for the entire Bible. The witnessing of the truth at that moment—the recognition—makes clear what blindness went before and what insight lies ahead. The momentary tragedies of the Bible—the fall of Adam and Eve, the tricks on Isaac, the betrayal and crucifixion of Christ, Saul's persecution of Christians, and John's imprisonment at Patmos—occur within the comic structure of the Bible. This structure, both in its general sweep and in its typology, means that the time of great recognition is at hand. The synchronic redeems the diachronic. This comic pattern of ultimate recognition is a relief for believers and an embarrassment for doubters. But another way of looking at this recognition in Revelation is that it resides in human desire, that the recognition of hope amidst despair is all too human. Whether the *muthos* in mythology is a kind of central story that is in our bones but is neither true nor false owing to its habitation of a putative space or whether it is a delusory ideology that projects the past into the future to control the present becomes an interpretative or even theoretical choice for the reader. The recognition of recognition resides in the reader: how determined and how free the reader is in interpreting insight depends on whether the text controls the reader with its rhetorical strategies or whether the reader resists and subverts them or whether a tension and play exists between writer and reader. It is difficult to say which model describes what happens, but I prefer the third one. Nonetheless, in Revelation, John invokes as much authority as he can— a Christ who having suffered for humanity at its hands rebukes it for sins against Christ and John and who signals that he is coming to fulfill John's, and humanity's, desires. John uses the voice and the vision of the son of God in his recognition in order to bolster his own authority and to convince the reader of his truth as mightily as he can.

1.4   Classical Examples: Epic, Tragedy, Comedy

Recognition, as Cave points out and as the illustrations from the Bible demonstrate, implies a tension between recovering something once known and a discovery of a new insight (a movement from ignorance to knowledge). In the Bible, a human discovery/recovery of God's way is the primary thread. There is, then, as Cave suggests, in anagnorisis, as in peripeteia, a movement toward the opposite, but this reversal or change in anagnorisis has to do with the degree of knowledge rather than the course of action.[50] Having set out Aristotle's discussion of anagnorisis as a beginning, I would like to discuss some key Greek instances of recognition: in Homer, Sophocles, and Menander. Together the Bible and the classics (along with the mythology the latter displaces into literature) provide a model for subsequent representations of recognition. Whereas elsewhere it might be suggestive to supplement Homer and Attic drama with Virgil, here, I wish to discuss a few moments in Greek literature. This choice is based on my emphasis on the variety of recognition, which includes similitude and dissimilitude, rather than a highlighting of similarities alone. If typology were my sole concern, I might discuss Virgil, who poets and critics, including Dante and C.S. Lewis, have seen allegorically as anticipating the Christian sense of time, which progresses with meaning toward a climax.[51] This sense of an ending, to borrow a phrase from Frank Kermode, occurs most emphatically when Virgil's Jupiter promises the *imperium sine fine*.[52] Rather than involve this argument in recognition in theology, hermeneutics, and criticism, I would prefer in this section to concentrate on some of the crucial poetic recognitions in Homer's epics and Attic drama.

Homer is the poet whose great influence on Greek education led Plato to attack poetry. The recognition of Odysseus's scar is well known and unavoidable, but an incident in *The Iliad* also deserves close attention. *The Iliad* is about love and honor but focuses these themes through siege and warfare. In Book 24, the final part of the epic poem, as the waste of time and life is nearing its end, Priam asks Achilles to think of his own father and to see similarities between his father's situation and Priam's, and kisses the great warrior's hand. Both gestures ask for Achilles's mercy. The result is a kind of recognition that Priam brings to Achilles, who does think of his father and takes the hand of the Trojan king. Their memories make them weep:

> Priam, crouching at Achilles' feet, wept bitterly for man-slaying Hector, and Achilles wept for his father, and then again for Patroclus. The house was filled with the sounds of their lamentation. But presently, when he had had enough of tears and recovered his composure, the excellent Achilles leapt from his chair, and in compassion for the old man's grey head and grey beard, took him by the arm and raised him. Then he spoke to him from his heart: "You are indeed a man of sorrows and have suffered much. How could you dare to come by yourself to the Achaean ships into the presence of a man who has killed so many of your gallant sons? You have a heart of iron. But pray be seated now, here on this chair, and let us

leave our sorrows, bitter though they are, locked up in our own hearts, for weeping is cold comfort and does little good. We men are wretched things, and the gods, who have no cares themselves, have woven sorrow into the very pattern of our lives.[53]

This recognition is one of the common humanity that survives the suffering of war and the knowledge that humans are wretched before the carefree gods. Victor and vanquished alike share this wretched suffering and must, as Achilles says, face this grim situation with tight-lipped courage. This epic recognition reflects the honor amongst soldiers that underlies a heroic vision, a view that is made to overcome the darkest hours of life. Unlike the biblical view, except perhaps with glimpses in Job's suffering, the epic represents a vision in which men are to accept their pain without hope in divine redemption or agency. In such moments, they are on their own. The tragic suffering of Achilles and Priam, which may contain within it the beginnings of a comic community and redemption, is not a matter of embarrassment, except, perhaps, for a culture, like ours, that is only beginning to tolerate the tears of men in private or public.

Increasingly, then, we are seeing that recognition cannot be one thing. It is as mobile as change and knowledge are themselves. It moves from situation to situation and genre to genre, mixing them. A case in point is Odysseus's scar, which Eric Auerbach meditated on in *Mimesis*. This scar, as Cave notes, involves, through flashback, a conflation of two times, the boar's wounding of the adolescent Odysseus and the recognition of his identity by way of his scar after he has returned home.[54] The recognition in Homer's second epic, which is interwoven with many threads, contains, in Aristotle's words, "*anagnôris diolou*" or recognitions throughout. In Book 1 Telemachus recognizes Pallas Athene and in Book 4 Helen and Menelaus recognize Telemachus.[55] The diffuse and various nature of recognition, which involves a scattering of its body until remembering, is similar to what I have called in narrative the Osiris effect, or the dispersal and recollection of story fragments into a mythical body or narrative whole.

In *The Odyssey* we can begin with the first recognition and follow the series to the end, but will concentrate on those from the homecoming to Penelope's recognition of Odysseus. In Book 16, Pallas Athene has had enough of Odysseus's love of dramatic irony and she tells him that it is time for Telemachus to find out the truth about his disguised father's identity so they can plot the death of Penelope's suitors. After she touches Odysseus with her golden wand, he returns to his son, who notices a transformation and thinks the stranger a god. Odysseus says: "Believe me, I am no god. But I *am* your father, on whose account you have endured so much sorrow and trouble and suffered persecution at men's hands."[56] Telemachus will not believe that this disguised stranger is Odysseus, so that his father has to appeal to the power of Athene to explain his protean nature and, more specifically, his transformation from stranger to godlike man. As Telemachus accepts the recognition, they both weep. But being Odysseus's son, full of intelligence and curiosity, Telemachus asks him how he got here. This appeal to the story, another narrative dimension, qualifies the great emotions of the recognition and the preparation for the homecoming. But the recognition that arises from the wily Odysseus, which includes how the Phaeacians brought him home, is one of prudence because that is the character trait Homer emphasizes in his description of Telemachus in this situation. The son does not think that he and his father can overwhelm the suitors. Odysseus reminds his son of the help Athene and Zeus will give them and asks Telemachus not to tell a soul of his father's return: "You and I alone will discover which way the women are heading."[57] Homer further qualifies the recognition with another of Telemachus's objections and their discussion of plans for revenge against the suitors. At the end of Book 16, in a discussion with Eumaeus, Telemachus shares with his father, and with the reader, the dramatic irony of the knowledge of Odysseus's return.

Odysseus appears to engineer the recognition scene in Book 19 of *The Odyssey*. In disguise as a beggar Odysseus tells lies to his wife, Penelope, about having seen her husband and then predicts that he will return home between the waning of the old moon and the waxing of the new. He sets up the situation, which wrings with dramatic irony, where he suggests that he will allow an old respectable woman to wash his feet if the house contains such a person, knowing full well that Eurycleia lives in his home. The old woman thinks that the beggar looks like Odysseus and so he should, but the disguised Odysseus diffuses her movement toward recognition by saying that so many people have said that before. This twinning is worthy of Plautus or Shakespeare in the *cognitio* of comedy. In fact, Odysseus enjoys the flirting with the danger of recognition but does not want Eurycleia to recognize him. Even amidst this dramatic irony, the reader is surprised to find out that Odysseus did not intend to lead his old nurse to recognition. He turns abruptly to face the dark after it had occurred to him that Eurycleia might see the scar and tell the secret of his identity. She does recognize the scar immediately, so that Odysseus, who had refused footbaths other female servants had offered him, has lost control. He thought he had controlled the dramatic irony of the disguised encounter with Penelope. Instead, the situation has become dangerous and unexpected. The cunning man is caught in his tricks. At the moment of greatest tension, Homer decides on a digression, an inset that recounts how Odysseus got his name and scar. This recognition is one of Odysseus's lies, how he hid his identity through disguise and fictions, which is not surprising when the reader learns in the flashback that his maternal grandfather, Autolycus, the greatest thief and liar in the world and therefore much resented, named the child Odysseus, or the victim of enmity. The grandfather tells his daughter to have Odysseus come back to claim a gift of goods when he is a man, which he does. Part of the coming of age ritual is the hunt, where in a dark thicket the boar turns on Odysseus and wounds him in the knee with its tusk while the hunter transfixes it with his spear. Odysseus had lost control of the boar but regained it: he does so with this sign of recognition. This control he achieves because as the nurse feels the scar and recognizes him in her speech, Athene distracts Penelope from recognizing the recognition with a look at the nurse's eyes and because he threatens Eurycleia with death. Odysseus, ever self-reliant, refuses his nurse's offer of help, and after she has refilled the basin, the conversation between Penelope and Odysseus resumes. The recognition takes place by means of a subplot, an aside, a digression. Its obliquity and brevity give it a sharp focus. Penelope then reveals Telemachus's view of her remarriage and asks her disguised husband to interpret her dream. The gates of horn and of ivory, of insight and blindness, are the places through which, Penelope says, dreams reach us, and each has its role, by analogy, in the narrative and the way the reader will come to recognition. He evades the request, as her dream prefigures his revenge on the suitors, but encourages her to set up the contest for her hand in which the winner will shoot an arrow through twelve axes. Penelope and her husband part, and she weeps upstairs for her lost Odysseus until Athene gives her sleep.

But this great recognition is multifold. It involves the recognition by nurse, by master-herd, by son and by wife and suitors in various momentary stages. With the master-herd, Homer repeats the near-recognition by the nurse. In Book 20, Philoetius sees a resemblance between the beggar and Odysseus, and once more the crafty king, absent for nineteen years, prophecies his own return. The suitors show their blindness. For instance, before the disguised Odysseus, Agelaus tells Telemachus that his father will never return home. The seer informs Eurymachus that he and his fellow suitors are doomed, but, once again, they respond with laughter and ridicule. Telemachus meets with silence the jibes that the suitors have for him and for his disguised father: his patience arises from a focus on his father's plan for revenge.

In Book 21, Penelope brings out Odysseus's great bow in order to test her suitors to see which among them should win her hand. The winner will string the bow and shoot an arrow through twelve axes. While the suitors are failing at the task, Odysseus follows his cowman and swineherd out of the hall and, after testing their loyalty, reveals his identity by way of his scar. They weep and kiss. Odysseus puts an end to the emotional reunion by orders that make them part of his plan. He does not want their crying to alert the suitors and to allow them to discover his identity. Just when the suitors are going to postpone the remainder of the test to the next day, the disguised Odysseus suggests that he try the bow. This suggestion causes the uproar he predicted. Telemachus rebukes his mother for suggesting that the beggar have a chance to string the bow, and she retires to her tears for Odysseus and the sleep Pallas causes to descend on her. Homer is masterly in suspense, in effecting those delays in narrative that allow pressure to mount to the climax of the story, which is the revenge and the ultimate recognition—Penelope's discovery of Odysseus's return. While the suitors jeer at him, Odysseus strings the bow, and Zeus gives a sign with a thunderclap: the suitors recognize something indeterminate as the color fades from their faces and they are confounded. Odysseus recognizes Zeus's support with the thunderclap, and he does not miss an axe. He speaks to his son: the bloodbath will start.

The battle in the hall in Book 22 begins with Odysseus's slaying of the worst offender amongst the suitors: Antinous. The victim never knows what is happening and who the avenger is. The suitors think the beggar has killed by accident the greatest nobleman in Ithaca: "It had not dawned upon the fools that every one of them was marked for slaughter too."[58] With his revenge speech, Odysseus reveals himself to the suitors. In their discovery, Eurymachus pleads for forgiveness, first, by saying that Antinous was the leader of the plot against Odysseus's family and, second, by promising to make amends and to pay tribute. Odysseus gives them the option to fight or run. Eurymachus recognizes Odysseus' intentions, and calls upon the others to join him in resisting Odysseus. The killing begins again: Eurymachus is the first to die. Two men are spared: the minstrel Phemius and Medon the herald find the mercy of Telemachus and Odysseus. The returned king asks to see his nurse, checks her jubilation over the revenge, and asks her to say which of the women in the household were loyal to him. Eurycleia wishes to tell

Penelope but Odysseus wants her first to summon the twelve disloyal women. On Odysseus's orders, the women who had slept with the suitors are conscripted into helping with the cleaning of the blood-soaked hall and then are led outside to slaughter by hanging. It is not said whether some of these women were the maids whom, Odysseus said at the beginning of Book 22, the suitors raped, something that was surely not their fault. The story seems to presume a justice that would not allow for those victims to be amongst the disloyal women but this presumption is never stated explicitly. Next Telemachus and the two herdsmen savagely torture Melanthius the traitor, including castration, till he dies. Odysseus orders that the house be fumigated and a fire lit before Penelope arrives. The nurse brings the loyal women to Odysseus: they shower him with hugs and kisses and hold his hands. This warm reunion makes Odysseus sob: "There was not one he failed to recognize."[59] Homer reunites all of the loyal members of the household, first the men and then the women, but leaves the most important reunion till near the last: that between Odysseus and Penelope.

This climactic recognition, which Homer represents in Book 23, is not direct. The nurse reports it, and it is received with skepticism. So Eurycleia has to retell the story of discovery: "Odysseus really has come home, just as I told you. He's the stranger whom they all scoffed at in the hall. Telemachus has known for some time that he was back, but had the sense to keep his father's plans a secret till he'd made those upstarts pay for their villainy."[60] At this report, Penelope's heart leaps with joy. Homer uses the obliquity of report not in the way Greek tragedy uses it for compression or for decorum, but as a means of representing the oscillation of Penelope's reaction. It would be harder for her to sustain her objections if Odysseus were standing before her. He would have only to show her his scar. Thus, Homer causes Penelope to return to her doubt. She now tells her nurse that the figure who is supposed to be Odysseus must be an avenging god: as for her husband, he will never return home. The nurse reports her discovery of the scar as evidence, and she recounts how Odysseus threatened her not to tell Penelope or anyone else. But, this being the final recognition, it is also the most difficult. Penelope humors Eurycleia but still doubts her word.

The reported scar is not enough to move her to recognize her husband. She still calls him "the man who killed them [the suitors]."[61] But when Homer reports Penelope's thoughts, she thinks of the man as her husband. Her thoughts mull over what she should do when she sees her husband. Penelope is the only one who does not weep and hug or kiss the returned king. She sits in silence opposite the man by the fire with the downcast eyes and watches him as she is overwhelmed in wonder. Odysseus, crafty as ever, stares at the ground so he can see how she reacts to him. Telemachus breaks the silence by berating his mother for being flint-hearted, but she replies by saying she is without words and questions and cannot look at the man's face. Penelope is a resourceful woman, and in a poem full of disguise and dramatic irony, she brings up a secret knowledge that only Odysseus and she possesses and that will underpin the recognition: " 'But if it really is Odysseus home again, we two shall surely recognize each other, and in an even better way; for there are tokens between us which only we two know and no one else has heard of.' "[62] Odysseus shows patience and tells Telemachus to leave his mother alone and reminds him that they have a problem on their hands with the kin of the members of the Ithacan nobility whom they have killed.

The final seal of the last recognition is further delayed. They put Odysseus's plan for retreat into practice: an apparent wedding feast is to keep the dead suitors' families at bay. After Odysseus changes from his beggar's clothes, Penelope and he call each other strange for their reaction to his homecoming. The tension arises over their matrimonial bed, which Odysseus had made secretly so it was fashioned from an olive tree around which he had built their bedroom. It is Penelope's turn to test her husband. But after he describes the tree and the bed in detail, he passes the test: her heart melts and she cries. She kisses and hugs him and explains why she refused to recognize him readily because she feared that an impostor would approach her and that the gods controlled fate in a way that even Helen, who began their miseries, and the daughter of Zeus, could foresee. The return of the impostor husband is the kind of mythical and folkloric fable behind stories such as *The Return of Martin Guerre*.[63] The dispelling of her disbelief melts Odysseus's heart and makes him cry. The recognition, after such delay and tension, leads to bliss. They will sleep together after nineteen years, but not until, at Penelope's request, Odysseus tells the story of his wandering. Odysseus and Penelope exchange their stories of the nineteen-year absence. The returned king talks himself to sleep. With the dawn they awaken and Odysseus makes provisions for them to cope with the reaction to the slaughter of the day before. Odysseus will go to see his father Laertes.

In the final book Homer includes, in the meadow of asphodel, the dwelling of souls, Amphimedon's account to Agamemnon of the slaughter in Odysseus's house, which involved his own death. Agamemnon gives a brief commentary on unconquerable Odysseus and virtuous

Penelope, which reinforces the theme of the recognition. Homer speaks of the simultaneous actions of Odysseus on his visit to his father, Laertes. Odysseus wants to see whether his father will recognize him after such a long absence.[64] Once more, Odysseus decides to take the oblique route toward this ultimate recognition. Rather than hug and kiss his father, he will draw him out with a brusque manner and yet another role. In the story he tells Laertes, Odysseus pretends to be someone who has befriended Laertes's son. After further conversation, Laertes loses hope of seeing Odysseus again and pours earth on his gray head. Not being able to take the pain of the consequences of his fictional narrative, Odysseus rushes to hug and kiss his father. The son proclaims that he has killed the suitors, but the father wants proof of his identity. As in a romance, a sign is needed. Odysseus offers his scar as evidence. As a supplement, Odysseus names the trees Laertes gave him one day in the garden. And father recognizes son. They see each other anew. They feast. The servants recognize Odysseus. Dolius is worried that Penelope does not know about her husband's return. Meanwhile, rumor about the death of the suitors flies through the town. At the assembly, Eupeithes, grieving over his dead son Antinous, speaks against Odysseus and calls for vengeance. Medon and the minstrel, survivors of the slaughter, appear at the assembly and testify that immortals, such as Mentor, had been at Odysseus's side during the battle. Ancient Halitherses, who could see past and present, warns the Ithacans that their own wickedness brought on these deaths. The Ithacans, listening to Eupeithes over Halitherses, take up arms. Athene, who had the idea of Odysseus's revenge, consults with Zeus, who says she can do as she wishes but suggests that a pact be made whereby Odysseus be made king in perpetuity. Pallas once again visits Odysseus as Mentor and the three generations of Odysseus's family and their few followers clash with the avenging Ithacans. In this disguise she tells Laertes to pray to Zeus and Athene and hurl his spear, which he does, and thereby kills Eupeithes. A battle ensues and Athene saves the Ithacans from slaughter at the hands of Odysseus's party. Athene brings peace to Ithaca. This recognition that peace is necessary is something that even Odysseus is made to see. It takes one of Zeus's flaming bolts to stop Odysseus from pursuing the Ithacan posse. The ambivalence of and toward the gods is something the reader has witnessed throughout *The Odyssey*, especially as the divine plays a role in the homecoming and the recognitions it fosters to the very end of this epic. The reunion of Laertes, Odysseus, and Telemachus cements the male world of honor, although Athene, with her father's help, defines its limits. There is a cumulative outcome of how the various narrative strands are made whole, as if recognition in this epic depends on the Osiris effect.

It is, however, in tragedy and not epic that Aristotle centers his views of anagnorisis: the tragic recognition of Oedipus is Aristotle's central example in *Poetics*. In this famous instance, Oedipus is blind to his situation until his knowledge actually moves him to blind himself quite literally. In the final move toward anagnorisis, the Herdsman who saved the infant Oedipus is ushered in and the Chorus recognizes him. As Oedipus cross-examines the Herdsman, the dramatic irony increases. The Messenger forces the Herdsman to tell his part in the revealing story, but not without resistance, for the Herdsman denounces the Messenger for Oedipus's sake: "He speaks out of his ignorance, without meaning."[65] Oedipus will resort to torture if the Herdsman will not tell the truth. A death threat makes the Herdsman uncover the actual story even as he tries to deflect the recognition to everyone else from the Messenger to Jocasta. But soon the revelation of the oracle—that the infant should grow up to kill his parents—and the words: "If you are / the man he says you are, you're bred to misery," bring home the recognition to Oedipus: "O, O, O, they will all come, / all come out clearly! Light of the sun, let me / look upon you no more after today!"[66] Oedipus recognizes his curse in being born, living and killing. Except for this brief reaction, we hear nothing from him.

The consequences of recognition occur through report. The Chorus, alone, speaks. The Strophe declares the lesson for the audience: "What man, what man on earth wins more / of happiness than a seeming / and after that turning away? / Oedipus, you are the pattern of this."[67] The Antistrophe talks about Oedipus's "happiness complete" and how he defeated the Sphinx and became king. Both Stophe and Antistrophe lament how low fate has brought Oedipus: the latter cries: "O child of Laius, / would I had never seen you. / I weep for you and cry / a dirge of lamentation."[68] The Second Messenger enters and announces Jocasta's suicide, telling the story in detail as she laments her "infamous double bond" but breaking off his narrative with Oedipus's ravings about the womb of his mother/wife. After Oedipus rushes in and finds his mother hanging, he cuts her down, tears out the brooches that fasten her robe, and, with them, dashes his eyes, so they can never see the crime he committed. The Second Messenger reports Oedipus's words: "Dark eyes, now in the days to come look on / forbidden faces, do not recognize / those whom you long for."[69] The blinded Oedipus enters, which causes an ambivalent reaction in the Chorus, which says this is the most terrible sight "he" has ever seen and pities the king's madness: "Indeed I pity you, but I cannot / look at you, though there's much I want to ask / and much to learn and much to see. / I shudder at the sight of you."[70] If the Chorus wants knowledge of him, it also wishes to avoid Oedipus. The blind king, who thanks the Chorus for being the only soul left to tend him, says he can now use memory to call up his own evil deeds and that although Apollo helped to bring him to blind himself, he did it with his own hand. Both Oedipus and the Chorus wish Oedipus had not been spared to bring so much misery on the earth. Oedipus disagrees with the Chorus who says that the king would be better off dead and seeing, but Oedipus replies that he could not bear to encounter with sight his father and mother in death. His very blindness in life will prevent him from false visions and facing those he has brought a curse upon. Oedipus's recognition is that he does not want to recognize others and be recognized by them. He has lied to Creon, and now Creon arrives. He will take Oedipus in so only his kin will hear the evils of his past, but Oedipus wants to go where he may not hear a human voice. Like the Chorus, Creon wishes to recognize what should be done: "But in the present need we had best discover / what we should do."[71] Oedipus asks that he be sent to the mountain where his parents had intended him to die and that his sons be left to make a living, but that he would not touch his daughters whom Creon should grant special protection. The infamous double bond that Jocasta lamented before hanging herself is the theme of Oedipus's departure from his daughters, Antigone and Ismene: "O children, / where are you? Come here, come to my hands, / a brother's hands which turned your father's eyes, / those bright eyes you knew once, to what you see, / a father seeing nothing, knowing nothing, / begetting you from his own source of life."[72] After Creon and Oedipus go out to begin the exile, the Chorus speaks once more about this happiest of men brought to misfortune. The play ends with a moral the audience is supposed to recognize: "Come no mortal happy till / he has passed the final limit of his life secure from pain."[73]

Oedipus's recognition is a knowledge of his ignorance whereas the Chorus emphasizes pleasure and a humility before the limits of life. Although Oedipus's recognition is central to *Oedipus Rex*, there are other recognitions—those of Jocasta, the Chorus, Creon, the silent daughters. No woman speaks at the end, to take up the horror Jocasta felt or the feelings the daughters have. The multifold complexity of the recognitions creates some of the fear and pity Aristotle discusses and creates dramatic tension. It is left to *Oedipus at Colonus* for Antigone's suffering to be felt. The curse Oedipus fears, continues. The recognition of a blighted man in tragic isolation soon finds in its sequel an expression beyond the silence of the end of this great play.

Cognitio, an analogous term for anagnorisis but certainly not one mentioned in *Poetics*, is a form of comic recognition or an uncovering of the confusions, disguises, concealments that New Comedy represents.[74] In Menander's only complete extant comedy *Dyskolos* (translated as *The Curmudgeon* or as *The Grouch*), the killjoy Cnemon tries to thwart the lovers under the protection of Pan until this senex falls into a well. He is rescued—and after his cognitio, where he recognizes his error and changes his mind, he joins in the dance that celebrates a double wedding.[75] Gorgias, the stepson of Cnemon and stepbrother of the daughter Sostratus loves, helps to save the old man when he falls in the well, while Sostratus nearly kills Cnemon through negligence—the young man cannot take his eyes off Cnemon's daughter. The comic effect of Sostratus's report of these events is obvious. Cnemon then enters, supported by his daughter on one side and Gorgias on the other. In a comic spirit that has little to do with the recognition of tragic isolation, Gorgias says to Cnemon: "See how bad it is to cut yourself off from everybody? You almost lost your life just now!"[76] Cnemon is hurt and concludes: "It certainly looks as if the only way we learn is by bitter experience," a recognition that Menander qualifies when Cnemon overhears Sostratus saying that he is a lucky man that his daughter is holding him up.[77] Eight lines are missing after Cnemon's irascible retort to Sostratus's quip. Cnemon soon reveals the recognition he has gained as a result of nearly dying:

> I guess the big mistake I made was in thinking I was the one person who was completely self-sufficient, who'd never have need of anyone else. Well, now when I see how strange and sudden the end of a man's life can be, I realize how little I knew. A man has to have someone around who can look after him. [*Falls silent a moment, brooding. Then, passionately.*] But, as god's my witness, what ruined me was seeing how everybody lived, the ways in which they went grubbing after money—I was convinced the person didn't exist who had a kind thought for anybody else. This was what blinded me. [*Dropping his voice and speaking with deep feeling.*] Only now have I gotten the proof, from one man—Gorgias. He did something that only the finest sort of person would have done. I never let him come near my door, never helped him in the slightest, never said hello to him, never exchanged a word with him—and yet he willingly saved my life.[78]

This recognition is the need for a human community and arises from the dangers of generalization and stereotyping. The grouchy killjoy laughingstock has, if only for a moment, come to some serious wisdom. The result of this cognitio is that Cnemon separates his daughter and Gorgias, whom he makes her guardian. When Gorgias says that Sostratus helped save Cnemon's life and has asked for the hand of his daughter, then the old man consents and the generational battle is over. Comic celebration, which includes community and harmony, represents a new order.

These are but a few of the types of literary recognition amongst the Greeks. The heroic, tragic, and comic dimensions suggest that the movement from blindness to insight brings with it many emotions and can be cast in many forms. Attendant and scattered recognitions, involving various characters and actions, often surround the central moment of recognition. It is as if recognition is a formal movement that can contain any kind of content and be contextualized and received in multifold ways. These few but crucial examples from the Bible and the Greeks serve as a general outline, which is by no means complete, by which we can observe recognitions in other fields beyond religion and literature. Whereas Frye and Cave distinguish recognition according to genre (something I have also done to this point), I now observe how these models of religious and literary recognition can be found in ancient and modern texts in philosophy, history, and other disciplines. In using poetics to find a rhetorical similitude between the disciplines or faculties, I am interested here in what these fields share rather than how they have too often, at least since Plato, concentrated on the contest between them.

1.5   Some Philosophical Instances

Rather than concentrate on Aristotle, where recognition is at the heart of his poetics, I want to begin with Plato, who denies the importance of knowledge through mimesis.[79] His argument against poetry depends in part on a world of forms behind words and on a downgrading of rhetoric into a verbal art of persuasion without the foundation of truth. Plato's visionary philosophy can be viewed in a way opposite to the one he intended. Even if Plato should be interpreted on his own terms, he can also be read against the grain. Such a reading should cast some light on the rhetorical nature of the Platonic enterprise and on the way in which his visionary philosophy shares much with visionary poetics. Although I could stress the differences between the disciplines, such as poetry and philosophy, as Plato himself did, and Aristotle effected to some extent based on the criterion of universality, I would like to emphasize similarities. In looking for likenesses, a shared ground of recognition, I continue to show the particulars of recognitions. The shared experience of recognition in a move from ignorance to knowledge unites the disciplines or faculties, but even within each work in each field there are simultaneous centripetal and centrifugal forces that render each discovery particular, complex, and ambivalent in the face of the need for overview or generalization. An ironic gap exists between theory and exempla. Each needs and refuses the other.

The matter Plato raises in *The Republic* is what kind of knowledge is to be desired. He favors philosophy as a means to knowledge, although his definition of the philosophical differs from that of the historians. Whereas Herodotus writes that philosophy first meant curiosity or the desire for new experience (i.30), like that which led Solon to travel and see the world, Thucydides envisions it as the pursuit of intellectual culture, as in Pericles's speech on cultivating the mind without the loss of manliness.[80] Plato's philosopher desires knowledge of all of truth and reality, the world of essential Forms as opposed to that of appearances. For Plato, the mind has two faculties: knowledge of the real and belief in appearances (*doxa*). Knowledge is infallible as it is of unique and unchanging objects: belief is true or false. The Forms have an absolute and independent existence from the human mind. The apprehension of changing things is doxa and resembles a dream, which is neither entirely real nor nonexistent. *Doxa* may be translated as opinion or belief. This is the ground of politics and the arts when not considered by philosophers, the world of appearances or phenomena, apparent truths or opinions, apparent goods such as legal decisions and conventional morality.[81] Plato assumes that his philosopher will go beyond the recognition of appearances through language and will find truth, for he loves wisdom and not belief (the *philodoxical*).[82] There is a religious dimension to Plato's philosophy, which also rests on what today we would call belief—the view that an immortal soul exists separately from the body before birth and after death.[83] Paradoxically, utopian vision or belief underwrites the reason that enables the wisdom of philosophy.[84] The ideal republic, realized in Plato's putative fiction or dialogue, will suffer dissolution.[85] Cornford summarizes the paradox that lies at the center of the philosophy of the Platonic Socrates: "wisdom begins when a man finds out that he does not know what he thinks he knows."[86] This self-knowledge, which occurs through a recognition of one's own ignorance, resembles dramatic irony that leads to discovery in the religious and literary texts we have examined.

The quarrel between philosophy and poetry, for Plato, means that he would distinguish between their recognitions because the philosopher recognizes Forms and the poet the appearances of opinion, sound, and sense. In Plato's view dramatic poetry injures the mind.[87] Dramatic poetry moves the audience to admire and enjoy bad behavior in the theatre that we would condemn in life. Poetry leads to pleasure and not an apprehension of truth and must defend itself before returning from exile to the republic.[88] And so the defenses of poetry begin, chiefly with Aristotle and including that of Philip Sidney, who argues that poetry moves people to virtue more than philosophy does precisely because of the concrete and universal language. The crux becomes: Is the apprehension of truth possible through language or must it occur beyond language? Like all philosophers and others who proclaim beliefs and truths, Plato must use language. Whether his myths transcend ideology or precede it or whether they are intertwined with it begins a long debate that has been taken up again by Nietzsche and postmodernist theorists. The religious impulse in Plato informs similar views of ideal realms of knowledge in the noumenal or utopian space, beyond this world of appearances, in thinkers as diverse as Augustine, Kant, and Hegel. The religious or metaphysical recognition often recedes but must be expressed in fallen language, the very symbols and icons that are earth-bound or are to be doubted or despised from their incomplete or imperfect state. In recognition a tension occurs between the medium used to express or represent the discovery and the discovery itself. Discomfort, suspicion, or theory intercedes as part of the experience of recognition. Story and argument, mythology and ideology cannot do without each other but are asked to do so. They are desired opposites.

An idealist philosopher who is more sympathetic to recognition is Hegel. Although in his theory of tragedy Hegel has made a contribution to modern expansions of Aristotle's anagnorisis, it is his philosophy of history that best serves the purpose of this argument. Plato's theory of language tries to distinguish between belief and truth and to devalue poetry's appeal to the senses and value philosophy's apprehension of truth while eliding their shared linguistic and rhetorical strategies. Poetry appeals to pleasure and not to truth. Like Plato, Hegel makes recognition difficult to discern. Both center on the progress of political action through dialectic. Hegel's philosophy of history enables a consideration of the mediation of particular examples in time in relation to the dialectical movement of history itself. Hegel's dialectic involves the dramatic irony that world history is not yet complete, so that human actors must necessarily be ignorant of the goal of human society. Ironically, people are agents of something they cannot fully recognize:

> The History of the World begins with its general aim—the realization of the Idea of Spirit—only in an *implicit* form (*an sich*) that is, as Nature; a hidden, most profoundly hidden, unconscious instinct; and the whole process of History (as already observed), is directed to rendering this unconscious impulse a conscious one.[89]

The hidden will be revealed in time and the unrecognized will be recognized retrospectively. Realization of the Idea, which is a social enactment in history, leads to individual recognition.

Hegel does not neglect the subjective. Rather, he sees it in the unconscious service of the objective:

> Thus appearing in the form of merely natural existence, natural will—that which has been called the subjective side—physical craving, instinct, passion, private interest, as also opinion and subjective conception—spontaneously present themselves at the very commencement. This vast congeries of volitions, interests and activities, constitute the instruments and means of the World-Spirit for attaining its object; bringing it to consciousness, and realizing it. And this aim is none other than finding itself—coming to itself—and contemplating itself in concrete actuality.[90]

The World-Spirit works through the subjective and comes to contemplate itself in actualization. Contemplation is essential to Hegel's discussion of this spirit because realization is nothing less than its reflection on itself in concrete form in the world. In the self-interest of a myriad of individuals there lies a greater goal:

> But that those manifestations of vitality on the part of individuals and peoples, in which they seek and satisfy their own purposes, are, at the same time, the means and instruments of a higher and broader purpose of which they know nothing—which they realize unconsciously—might be made a matter of question; rather has been questioned, and in every variety of form negatived, descried and contemned as mere dreaming and "Philosophy."[91]

Hegel is defending philosophy as that which allows for the recognition of realization through a reflection of spirit made concrete, a movement from unconscious welter to conscious pattern. Philosophy allows for recognition. It is for the philosopher to hypothesize a pattern to history or to assert a belief in the aim in history. The philosopher's recognition is something putative:

> I announced my view at the very outset, and asserted our hypothesis—which, however, will appear in the sequel, in the form of legitimate inference—and our belief, that Reason governs the world, and has consequently governed its history.[92]

Reason is the recognition behind the swirling movement of self-interest. The dialectic combines the subjective and the objective. Hegel denies that the subjective or psychological alone accounts for historical change, although he insists that the passions of individuals serve reason in history. The psychological reduction of the actions of world historical men to base motives arises from envy: "The Free Man, we may observe, is not envious, but gladly recognizes what is great and exalted, and rejoices that it exists."[93] This is the context for Hegel's famous gloss on the proverb that no man is a hero to his valet, not because the man is no hero but because the valet is a valet. Extrapolating from Hegel's comments, which include an allusion to the Homeric Thersites, this psychological criticism, this thorny and complaining envy, might be called the Thersites principle, whose condemnation, Hegel admits, has a dark side to it.[94] Freedom is the story of history that Hegel tells. By freedom he means something whose limitations enable it, something that limits impulse, passion, and desire not as a fetter but as a proviso. Society and state limit the individual and thereby free him.[95] Hegel's recognition is the dialectics of freedom: that is, what the philosopher sees in the unhappy theatre of history. If in the middle of things Hegel announces: "The History of the World is not the theatre of happiness," he returns to where he began: "The History of the world is none other than the progress of the consciousness of Freedom."[96] Thus Hegel recognizes the pattern of history while admitting that the structure of human time is not yet complete.

Hegel affects Marx and Nietzsche, but they do not always respond positively to his influence. Marx criticizes Hegelian history while turning its dialectical idealism on its head to serve a materialism in which material production enables ideas. The most trenchant of Marx's critique of Hegel's philosophy of history, *The German Ideology*, was published posthumously in 1932. Here, Marx emphasizes alienation. The materialistic conception of history

> has not, like the idealistic view of history, in every period to look for a category, but remains constantly on the real ground of history; it does not explain practice from the idea but explains the formation of ideas from material practice; and accordingly it comes to the conclusion that all forms and products of consciousness cannot be dissolved by mental criticism, by the resolution into "self-consciousness" or transformation into "apparitions," "specters," "fancies," etc., but only by the practical overthrow of the actual social relations which gave rise to this idealistic humbug; that not criticism but revolution is the driving force of history, also of religion, of philosophy and all other types of theory. It shows that history does not end by being resolved into "self-consciousness" as "spirit of the spirit," but that in it at each stage there is found a material result: . . . . It shows that circumstances make men just as much as men make circumstances.[97]

Marx is not simply a determinist because he balances determinism with agency. The recognition of revolution as being greater than mental recognition or self-consciousness of history informs Marx's philosophy of history. For Marx, the English and French follow the political illusion, which is moderately close to reality, whereas the Germans find their illusions in the realm of the pure spirit, thereby making religious illusion the force that drives history. Illusion blocks actual recognition. Marx explicitly attacks Hegel's concept of history:

> The Hegelian philosophy of history is the last consequence, reduced to its "finest expression," of all this German historiography, for which it is not a question of real, not even of political, interests, but of pure thoughts, which consequently must appear to Saint Bruno as a series of "thoughts" that devour one another and are finally swallowed up in "self-consciousness."[98]

The illusion that blinds Germans gives way to the recognition in reality and practical materialism in which the Communist revolutionizes the existing world and attacks and changes existing things. Marx's theory of ideology, which uncovers a materialist history of the world, is based on a practice in that world. He will not embrace Plato's forms, but he, too, warns of appearances and illusions that must be discovered and seen through. The communal world of each republic is social and utopian but Marx insists on the material reality of his vision at the end of things.

In the *Grundisse* (pub. 1941), Marx scoffs at the notion that free competition is the ultimate form of the development of productive forces and therefore of human freedom because this is a pleasant thought for the middle class, yesterday's parvenus, because such a vision of the end of world history would justify the domination of that class.[99] In this same work, Marx discusses self-knowledge in terms of free time from production and how that leisure changes the relation of the person to and in production. For the man who is already formed, this process "is practice, experimental science, materially creative and self-objectifying knowledge, and he contains within his own head the accumulated wisdom of society."[100] This self-knowledge involves a movement to wisdom from ignorance, a kind of transformation through leisure. In the *Economic and Philosophical Manuscripts* (1844, pub. 1932), Marx also discusses self-knowledge, this time in relation to Feuerbach and in the specific context of private property and Communism. Marx notes that sense experience is, for Feuerbach, the basis of all science. In Marx's extrapolation of Feuerbach, man is the direct object of natural science, and only through "his fellow men" does sense-experience become human for him: "man's first object—man himself—is nature, sense experience; and particular human sensuous faculties are only objectively realized in natural objects and can only attain to self-knowledge in the science of nature in general."[101] Although Marx departs from Hegel, he shares with Hegel a view that the subjective is expressed objectively. The experiential and the practical meet in this Marxian moment of recognition.

With Nietzsche an attempt at fracturing system and a dialectic philosophy of history occurs. He questions the quest for truth as Plato and Hegel see it. In a letter to his sister in 1865, Nietzsche calls into doubt the relation between faith and objectivity, something Hegel suggests, but while doing so he seems to agree with Plato that truth must be put before pleasure: "Faith does not offer the least support for proof of objective truth. Here the ways of men part: if you wish to strive for peace of soul and pleasure, then believe; if you wish to be a devotee of truth, then inquire."[102] The early Nietzsche envisages a truth that is extremely difficult to discern, and in this view he differs little from Plato and Hegel. Nietzsche emphasizes the differences from the Greek world and challenges the notion of a system in the philosophy of history. In a posthumously published fragment on Homer (1872), Nietzsche returns to Aristotle in order to interpret the contest between poetry and philosophy. Aristotle makes a list of agons or hostile contests that arise out of ambition and of envy or jealousy amongst the illustrious Greeks, including some in which the living wish to triumph over the dead: "That is how Aristotle describes the relationship of Xenophanes of Colophon to Homer. We do not understand the full strength of Xenophanes' attack on the national hero of poetry, unless—as again later with Plato—we see that at its root lay an overwhelming craving to assume the place of the overthrown poet and to inherit his fame."[103] This is the kind of psychological explanation that Hegel disdained and which Freud's Oedipus complex and Harold Bloom's extended analysis of the agon develop.[104] But Nietzsche is building his analysis of envy on the reputable philosophical source of Aristotle, and he is implying that one did not have to be Thersites amongst the Greeks in order to have a clash of envy and ambition. Nietzsche is also distinguishing between Greek culture and his own by saying how alien this agon is to moderns. The recognition that Nietzsche offers is a psychological insight based on a knowledge of Greek culture and a sense of history that allows for the discovery of difference. Nietzsche also focuses this personal fight on works of art. The modern looks for weaknesses in such a work, the Greek for its source of strength. Plato resides at the center of this Greek struggle to be the central work of art, to displace Homer:

> What, for example, is of special artistic significance in Plato's dialogues is for the most part the result of a contest with the art of the orators, the sophists, and the dramatists of his time, invented for the purpose of enabling him to say in the end: "Look, I too can do what my great rivals can do; indeed, I can do it better than they. No Protagoras has invented myths as beautiful as mine; no dramatist such a vivid and captivating whole as my *Symposion*; no orator has written orations like those in my *Gorgias*—and now I repudiate all this entirely and condemn all imitative art. Only the contest made me a poet, a sophist, an orator." What a problem opens up before us when we inquire into the relationship of the contest to the conception of the work of art![105]

Nietzsche suggests that the Greeks themselves at a social, as well as at a personal, level came to destroy themselves through such hostile contests and wars when they lacked envy, jealousy, and ambition. Without these emotions to fuel the contest, the Greeks descend into evil and cruelty, vengefulness and godlessness, a kind of self-destructive *hybris* reminiscent of the pre-Homeric Greeks. The individual example of this corruption is Miltiades, who uses his unparalleled success at Marathon to wreak vengeance and find personal gain. The collective collapse occurs when Athens destroys the independence of its allies and Sparta dominates Hellas. Nietzsche's recognition is that whereas Plato's agon with Homer was culturally vital, contests without that ambitious rivalry led to an obliteration of the legacy that Homer began and that Plato helped to continue. The contest of the faculties is a healthy rivalry in which all the participants have ambition to excel at the same game. The consequence of a lack of such a contest is historical degeneration.

The philosophy of history that Nietzsche advocates counters Hegel's. In his Notes (1873), Nietzsche criticizes the deification of success, which is a blasphemy against the good and the just: "This beautiful world history is, in Heraclitean terms, 'a chaotic pile of rubbish.' What is *strong* wins: that is the universal law. If only it were not so often precisely what is stupid and evil!"[106] Nietzsche is also critical of Hegel's views on the aim of history: the demand for stories with aims, the history of a people and of the world—the world process—all with a goal is a swindle. Life is accidental and has no aim; Nietzsche says that he can posit an aim for his life, "[b]ut a state has no aim; we alone give it this aim or that."[107] Hegel is involved in a mythology of the historical, as if history has as its aim the preservation of many wretched human beings so that a genius might arise and recognize in the swirl of history that he is like the hunter who fires hundreds of times until he hits a bird and thinks this accident an aim.[108] For Nietzsche, the German folk soul is another dangerous concept.[109] The state is a human construction and does not guarantee human freedom: it is, in Nietzsche's view, the individual who realizes the state and not the converse. This anti-systematic view of the philosophy of history is something postmodernists, such as Lyotard, adapt as part of their strategy against philosophical systems.[110]

These philosophers, as much as their religious and literary counterparts, play on the difference between story and argument, mythology and ideology. For each, reality is cloaked in illusions that the philosopher must look through to recognize the truth. There are as many illusions as there are truths, and each philosopher defines recognition, usually implicitly, in terms of the truth he is uncovering for the reader. Plato's philosopher searches for Ideas, Hegel's for social freedom expressed through spirit, Marx's in the freedom and classlessness that the shared benefits of production will bring, and Nietzsche's the difficult freedom that is part of an even more difficult individual quest. If there is argument in story, there is story in argument. Interpretations are built into narrative and theatrical mimesis that show or tell stories, and arguments have their mythoi or plots. Problems arise when these particular insights or recognitions claim their universal truth.

1.6   History: Exempla from Crossing Cultures

History is an inquiry into the truth of what happened and it is a story about the past. It is event and the representation of event. My discussion of recognition has to be highly selective, and the history I am examining here is about discovery of otherness, which is found from Herodotus through Columbus to Acosta and Montaigne, rather than the representation of world history.[111] The recognition in this kind of history, whether of the encounter with "barbarians" or "savages," is an account of strangeness and wonder. Mythology and ethnology mix in such historical narratives. The voyage out allows for greater self-knowledge, a sense of identity. In this history of otherness the reporter or historian catalogues the world and its inhabitants as matters of fact, but also impresses the reader with a travel narrative sometimes as fantastic as romance. This kind of history involves a recognition of difference that sometimes effaces and displaces that difference.

Herodotus crops up, even if momentarily, in Acosta's history and Montaigne's essay on cannibals.[112] In the Early Modern period, the Spanish and French sensed the continuities in this kind of history, where natural history combined with an incipient ethnology. Herodotus distinguishes between what he has heard and what he has seen, between hearsay and eyewitness report, and he says he will record what he will but it is not his business to believe what he sets down.[113] Herodotus made exploration and discovery of the world a central part of his historiography. One aspect of Herodotus's recognition lies in the reader who will find individuated scenes without vast generalizations, as a mirror set up to humanity.[114] In *Persian Wars*, Herodotus mentions cannibals.[115] A pattern that will later recur in Columbus's writings, the nation of the flesh-eaters is like their neighbors but is set apart as a threat: "The manners of the Man-eaters are more savage than those of any other race. They neither observe justice, nor are governed by any laws. They are nomads, and their dress is Scythian; but the language which they speak is peculiar to themselves. Unlike any other nation in these parts, they are cannibals."[116] Wandering and language are the differences often recognized in the maneaters or cannibals: they are not of civil society, which has a fixed address. It is not surprising that the Sythians become a type for Natives in the Americas, whose barbarity is made a central theme of

European representations of the New World, because Herodotus records Scythian customs in war in ways that become convenient, striking, and persistent forms of alterity: "The Scythian soldier drinks the blood of the first man he overthrows in battle."[117] After giving a detailed account of how the Scythian gets and cleans scalps as war trophies, including the softening of the skin by rubbing it between his hands until it is ready to serve as a napkin, Herodotus notes: "The Scyth is proud of these scalps, and hangs them from his bridle-rein."[118] Cannibals, cruelty, and Amazons are elements in Herodotus that erupt in the representation, the re-cognition, of the New World.

The manslayers (Amazons) are as much a cause of anxiety as the maneaters. From another source, Herodotus reports that when the Greeks fought the manslayers or Oiorpata, as the Scythians called them, they captured the Amazons and put them on three ships, but these women warriors rose up against the crews and massacred them. Afterward they plundered Scythian territory. The Scyths found these foes unknown in dress, language, and nation.[119] Their moment of recognition occurs when after a battle between Scyths and Amazons, the former find bodies of the slain, "whereby they discovered the truth."[120] The truth is that their foes were women. The Scythians would not fight women knowingly, so they sent young men to them, "on account of their strong desire to obtain children from so notable a race."[121] These wild peoples, having nothing but their arms and horses, could only support themselves from hunting and pillage. The Amazons scatter in ones and twos, and soon a Scythian attacks a lone Amazon: "she did not resist but let him have his way."[122] Through sign language, these two begin the trend of setting up friends for similar "trysts" until the Scythians "had intercourse with the other Amazons."[123] The Scythians marry those Amazons with whom they first had intercourse and the two nations join but have to go into Tanais, the men unable to understand the Amazons' language but these former manslayers quite able to comprehend the Scythian language. The marriage and exile are on the terms that the Amazons dictate, so even if there was original violence in war, and in that first sexual attack, the women prevail. In this new nation, the Amazons continue to hunt, fight, and cross-dress, sometimes alone and sometimes in the company of their husbands.[124] This recognition leads to the crossing of boundaries and the exploration of the taboo and difference. With signs they cross the boundary into a shared language. Herodotus begins his report of the Scythian account of the Amazons as "a marvel," another rhetorical dispensation that Columbus adopts. The wonders of the world are to be recognized.

The Spanish, French, and English recognize Natives in the wake of Columbus, who does and does not recognize the New World. He brings with him myths from his reading and culture while he looks at a land new to him. The Natives are seen as part of the land or as those who should be dispossessed of the land. In speaking about cannibals and Amazons in the Caribbean (named for those apparently fierce maneating Caribs), Columbus can demonize those Natives who oppose his claim of the land for Spain.[125] During the fourteenth century, the Portuguese use the legal fiction of *terra nullius* to dispossess Africans. The Portuguese and other Europeans take up the same strategy in the New World: they argue that the peoples there are nomadic and do not really occupy a civil society. Consequently, the Europeans can possess their lands because these people do not really occupy them. European practices of land use become the measure of ownership and the right for exploitation. It is difficult enough to recognize the Natives for who they are let alone recognize their rights. Columbus praises the good Natives, who inhabit a kind of paradise, for being like a pure blank slate ready for conversion.[126] Later, Bartolomé de Las Casas defends the Natives as being full of reason and as those who should be free and not enslaved. The Spanish crown wants them as vassals whereas the colonial landowners want them as slaves. Each category would, like the land, provide a public or a private form of wealth.

The French follow this pattern of ambivalence. Jacques Cartier in the 1530s and Jean de Léry in the 1550s represent the Natives in terms of mutual suspicion and trade. Cartier reports that the Natives he met in Canada "showed a marvellously great pleasure in possessing and obtaining these iron wares and other commodities."[127] When Cartier and his men set up a cross to take possession of the land, the chief seems to object, saying the land belongs to him. The French try to deflect their purpose with pleasant diversions about redemption and new trade.[128] They hide their signs and refuse to recognize the Natives and the right to the land. Signs mediate and become means to recognize whatever the French wish. The Cartier text implies that the Natives become a block to the exploitation of the land. Léry's first view of Natives in Brazil occurs in the ambiance of an already established mutual suspicion, in which the Margaia and the French experience enmity but dissimulate. When the Margaia assemble near the French ship, Léry's countrymen are wary: "since our people put no trust in them except for some express purpose, they stayed beyond an arrow's reach from land so as to avoid the danger of being seized and *boucané*— that is roasted."[129] Before Léry has seen the Natives, French and European views have affected his perception. The allusion to cannibalism yields to matters of trade. Léry calls attention to the novelty of his "first" sighting of Natives: "because these were the first savages that I had seen up close, you can imagine that I looked at them and studied them attentively."[130] He then says he will postpone this first moment of close inspection, but not without a passing description of how the men and women amongst the Margaia wear their hair and pierce their bodies (the men their lower lips, the women their ears, leaving gaping holes when their jewelry was taken out).

But the texts and the men who wrote them are often ambivalent if not sometimes critical toward France and Europe. Each recognition, although sharing certain properties, is different. These travel texts, as much as works of poetry, religion, philosophy, and history, themselves confound easy generalizations about European "discoveries" of themselves and others. Léry later sums up the difficulty of representing Brazil and its inhabitants, as if true recognition were something rare:

> During that year or so when I lived in that country, I took such care in observing all of them, great and small, that even now it seems to me that I have them before my eyes, and I will forever have the idea and image of them in my mind. But their gestures and expressions are so completely different from ours, that it is difficult, I confess, to represent them well by writing or by pictures. To have the pleasure of it, then, you will have to go see and visit them in their own country.[131]

He then ventriloquizes the reader by making him say that the plank is very long, which the author admits is true, so that if the reader lacks a sure foot and steady eye and fears stumbling, then this is not a path to venture down. Then Léry uses the authorial royal we, when he declares: "We have yet to see more fully" various domestic customs.[132] In closing the chapter on the bodily description of the Brazilians, Léry defends the women amongst them as not arousing wantonness through their nakedness. He says that the trifling clothing of French women causes more ills than the "crude nakedness" of the Brazilians. Although being somewhat of a backhanded defense and indicating something of a negative attitude toward his countrywomen, this passage serves as a reminder of how no simple opposition will suffice in describing the European discovery of themselves and others in the encounter with the New World. Another more famous instance makes the same point. Michel de Montaigne's "On Cannibals" (1580) suggests that when comparing American Natives and Europeans, the usual stereotype of barbarism is not so easy to sustain: "We are justified therefore in calling these people barbarians by reference to the laws of reason, but not in comparison with ourselves, who surpass them in every kind of barbarity."[133] Who is recognizing whom?

Like the French, the English could not escape Spanish textual influence when viewing the New World. Cabot had sailed to Newfoundland in 1497, but no journal or log is extant. Walter Ralegh is especially pertinent here. He wants gold and God as much as Columbus, but he says that England takes a higher road than Spain. He desires the land of Guiana, like a woman to be raped, but he does so on behalf of his virgin queen. In Ralegh the contradictions of moral aims and monetary goals lead to the exploitation of the New World and its inhabitants as outcrops of the land.

Ralegh's *The Discouerie of the Large, Rich, and Bewtiful Empyre of Guiana* (1596) shows ambivalence. In the Epistle Dedicatorie, Ralegh speaks of his goal, "*that mighty, rich, and beawtifull Empire* of Guiana, *and . . . that great and Golden City, which the Spanyards call* El Dorado, *and the naturalls* Manoa."[134] Here, Ralegh sounds like Columbus, although the latter mentions God as much as gold (often in conjunction), whereas the English explorer is more often silent about the divine. Ralegh takes his cue from Spanish legends as Columbus had from Marco Polo. The great reason England should be interested in Guiana is that Ralegh claims that it has more gold than the Indies or Peru.[135] The Natives support England's ambitions: "*All the most of the kings of the borders are already become her Maiesties vassals: & seeme to desire nothing more then her Maiesties protection, and the returne of the English nation.*"[136] In Ralegh's view the Natives await their true Lord whereas others may throw off Spanish domination: Spain is so rich and has so many cities, it will not miss this small area of America. He maintains that "*if it had not beene in respect of her highnes future honer & riches, I could haue laid hands and ransomed many of the kings & Cassiqui of the Country, & have had a reasonable proportion of gold for their redemption.*"[137] Long-term, rather than short-term, profit is Ralegh's goal for England.

Ralegh's *The Discouerie of Guiana* develops the need to observe the Spanish model of colonization while using its own methods to subvert it. This rivalry continues throughout Ralegh's book. Midway through the book, Ralegh exposes the dirty tricks of the Spanish, for instance, how they told the Natives on the way to Guiana that the English were cannibals. The myth that Ralegh is trying to propagate, especially by way of flattering Elizabeth, is that he puts her reputation before the sacking of towns and the hoarding of gold because this strategy will support the desire of the Natives of Guiana for England to liberate them from Spanish cruelty. If Elizabeth acts and takes Guiana and beyond, she will gain reputation and, as part of her secular cult of the Virgin Queen, she will be the virginal queen over the Amazons, who will help her invade other empires. Here, the sexual roles are reversed. Ralegh had described Guiana as a land who still had its maidenhead and needed to be entered, but now the virgins are to invade other, presumably male-dominated, countries.[138] Ralegh ends by appealing to God and Christ in royal imagery and implicitly conflates Elizabeth with the Virgin Mary as the "Lady of Ladies." All the men who would serve her in such an action would, with her grace and leave, be kings. And all these military plans and invasions would be done in the name of the "king of al kings."[139] The moment of recognition is that the Natives will yield gold in the glory of God and Christ through Elizabeth. The ghost of Herodotus and Columbus call forth cannibals and Amazons.

It is appropriate to end this section with José de Acosta, the Spanish Jesuit. In the same year that Ralegh's work on Guiana appears, Acosta's *De procuranda* is published in Cologne. In the preface Acosta notes that the nations of America "are very varied and diverse and very different from one another as much in climate, environment and dress as in intelligence and customs. It is a vulgar error to assume that the Indians are a single field or city, and because they are all called by the same name to ascribe to them a single nature and mind."[140] Acosta's recognition of cultural differences is part of his understanding of humanity.[141] The "shock of discovery" the Europeans experienced in sighting the New World and it inhabitants helped to contribute to a movement from relying on tradition and ancient texts as intellectual authorities to experience and observation themselves, although it is easy to underestimate the power of classical and biblical traditions to persist in European thought. Without calling it explicitly a moment of recognition, Anthony Grafton and his coauthors quote a passage from Acosta where he describes how on the way to the New World he reached the equator and did not burn up in the Torrid Zone, which made him laugh at Aristotle's *Meterology* and philosophy, and they observe: "Acosta's scene sounds dramatic—even Oedipal."[142] This paradigm shift almost takes the form, through its laughter, of a cognitio. The recognition scene is not so simple, and the reversal it helps to usher in is not always final or complete, except perhaps in the world of romance and comedy. People do not always behave like characters.

1.7 Psychology and Some Psychoanalytical Examples

But they have characters even if they do not always behave like characters. In this discussion of recognition we have looked at private and public instances, the worlds of mind and society. Psychological and political recognition affect each other. In earlier sections we observed differences manifested through descriptions of the body, but here we shift to those embodied in writing about the mind. Whereas earlier this chapter concentrated on texts from Homer to Marx, in this section, it begins where it left off, on the verge of this century. Psychology is also too vast to be explored here, but a few examples from Sigmund Freud, Jacques Lacan, and Julia Kristeva should suggest the importance of recognition to psychoanalytical theories. The exploration of the mind, especially as it relates to sex and therefore the body, becomes almost as great an obsession in the twentieth century as the New World became for Columbus and his contemporaries. The comment Grafton, Shelford, and Siraisi make about Acosta's Oedipal dramatic scene, what I would call his recognition or discovery on the way to the New World, demonstrates that in late twentieth-century interpretation, historical as well as literary, there is a psychoanalytical bent, explicit or implicit, that crops up even if the writer is trying to repress it. In refuting Freud, cultural critics and historians often reinscribe him, even in displaced ways.

Except for openings and end games, the moves in chess, Freud says, cannot be learned according to an exhaustive system but involve an infinity variety. In this limitation Freud finds an analogy between chess and the practice of psychoanalysis. He stresses that the rules of the game draw their significance from their relation to the general game plan, and, through this emphasis, he attempts to establish recommendations rather than a mechanical set of rules. Such is the rationale for Freud's "On Beginning the Treatment" (1913). One of the central aspects of psychoanalysis is recognition even if it is not called by that name. Freud poses a question that he frames in his discussion of principle in the treatment of a patient: "When is the moment for disclosing to him the hidden meaning of the ideas that occur to him, and for initiating him into the postulates and technical procedures of analysis?"[143] In this initiation into psychoanalytical hermeneutics, Freud warns that the analyst must build up a rapport with the patient as opposed, in the first interview, to thrusting guesses at the symptoms in the patient's face. In textual terms, Freud characterizes the relation between analyst and patient:

> It is not difficult for a skilled analyst to read the patient's secret wishes plainly between the lines of his complaints and the story of his illness; but what a measure of self-complacency and thoughtlessness must be possessed by anyone who can, on the shortest acquaintance, inform a stranger who is entirely ignorant of all the tenets of analysis that he is attached to his mother by incestuous ties, that he harbours wishes for the death of his wife whom he appears to love, that he conceals an intention of betraying his superior, and so on.[144]

Like a playwright, teacher, and a critic combined, the analyst leads his tutee/character to self-knowledge. But lightning intuition passed on to the patient leads to discredit in the patient's eyes "and will arouse the most violent opposition in him, whether one's guess has been true or not; indeed, the truer the guess the more violent will be the resistance."[145] The analyst should only give a patient a solution when he is a short step away from obtaining the explanation himself. Freud thinks the patient needs time for recognition and defends this view based on an argument for the meaning of knowledge. In the early days of psychoanalysis Freud and his fellow psychoanalysts rushed the patient and barely made any distinction between their knowledge of what he had forgotten and his. They met with resistance: "How could it be that the patient, who now knew about his traumatic experience, nevertheless behaved as if he knew no more about it than before?"[146] The recognition scene did not work as it might in a play. Freud continues: "Indeed, telling and describing his repressed trauma to him did not even result in any recollection of it coming into his mind."[147] Freud's explanation of this lack of knowledge in knowledge results in a distinction between psychology and psychoanalysis.

Freud's recognition scene becomes more complex because he explains that the unconscious accounts for a knowledge without knowledge:

> The strange behaviour of patients in being able to combine a conscious knowing with not knowing, remains inexplicable by what is called normal psychology. But to psycho-analysis, which recognizes the existence of the unconscious, it presents no difficulty. The phenomenon we have described, moreover, provides some of the best support for a view which approaches mental processes from the angle of topographical differentiation. The

patients now know of the repressed experience in their conscious thought, but this thought lacks any connection with the place where the repressed recollection is in some way or other contained. No change is possible until the conscious thought-process has penetrated to that place and has overcome the resistances of repression there.[148]

Conscious recognition is not enough. The resistance of the unconscious has to be overcome. By way of communicating repressed material to the consciousness of the patient, psychoanalysis begins a process of thought in which the influence of the unconscious recollection ultimately occurs.[149] The analytical treatment mobilizes the energies that are ready for the transference necessary for overcoming resistances and, by providing the patient information at the right time, it shows him the paths along which he should direct those energies. Only through intense transference that overcomes the resistances has being ill become impossible. This is the ultimate cure or recognition that the analyst enacts in the patient. The patient's understanding and intellectual interest are not as important as the other forces engaged in the struggle because these conscious recognitions are always in danger of losing their value owing to the clouding of judgment arising from resistances. The new sources of strength, which the patient owes the analyst, are transference and instruction. The transferences induce the patient to make use of instruction. The analyst should therefore withhold first communication until he has established a strong transference. He should wait until he removes the disturbance of the transference through the successive emergence of transference-resistances. In Freud's recognition, the analyst becomes part of the patient's cure or self-knowledge.

As Freud's "Observations on Transference-Love" (1915) testifies, this transference was reputed to lead male analysts to seduce female patients. Once again, Freud reminds the doctor that recognition is two-way, that a psychoanalyst's pride need not blind him to what is truly insightful in his work: "He must recognize that the patient's falling in love is induced by the analytic situation and is not to be attributed to the charms of his own person; so that he has no grounds whatever for being proud of such a 'conquest,' as it would be called outside analysis."[150] The gender of most of the patients becomes apparent here. The female patent's insight is swallowed up in her love for her doctor.[151] At a time when the analyst is trying to have her admit some particularly repressed and distressing part of her life history, her resistance uses her love to hinder the treatment. Freud then outlines his recognition about the motives of love and resistance: her love destroys the doctor's authority and her resistance uses this love to test the analyst's severity.[152] Freud avoids conventional moral advice to the doctor: psychoanalysts demand truth from their patients and should not depart from it.[153] The doctor must keep the counter-transference in check and remain neutral or abstinent physically and intellectually by means of surrogates, for the patient cannot obtain actual satisfaction until her repressions are removed. The analyst should neither suppress nor gratify the patient's "craving for love."[154] To gratify her wishes for love would allow for a physical expression of what should be a psychic event, which would then lead to an enactment of the patho-logical reactions and inhibitions of her erotic life without the possibility of correcting them until she felt remorse, which would then cause repression.[155] The doctor must make the patient feel safe "to allow all her preconditions for loving, all the phantasies springing from her sexual desires, all the detailed characteristics of her state of being in love, to come to light; and from these she will herself open the way to the infan-tile roots of her love."[156] This male authority and the infantalization of the female is a disturbing part of Freud's recognition. He classifies one kind of woman, those of elemental passion, as being incapable of accept-ing a psychic surrogate for the material man. In the face of this woman, who is neurotic and needs love intractably, the analyst must back away marveling at this combination while he admits defeat[157]

Freud supplies the doctors with arguments to show their patients that their love is not genuine. They are to use this dialectic to convince them into recognition. Female docility and respect for the male analytic procedure are part of Freud's view of genuine love and recognition: the woman must realize that her love involves resistance and that she should try harder to solve her problems because the man whom she loves wishes it. Freud criticizes the hypothetical woman for being rebellious and stubborn and for not respecting "the doctor's well-founded convic-tions."[158] Her resistance is under the guise of love. If the doctor will not accept her love, "as his duty and his understanding compel him to do," she can play the woman scorned and, out of resentment and revenge, withdraw from his therapy, which is exactly what her "ostensible love" is making her do now. The second hypothetical argument is that this love is not genuine because it involves copies and repetitions of earlier reactions, including infantile ones, and does not arise from the present situation. Before taking Freud to task for this typical situation of male authority, I have to consider his next textual move, which anticipates such an objection (in good chess, debating, or deconstructive fashion). Freud asks whether in putting forth such arguments "we" are actually telling the truth or merely resorting to desperate concealments and mis-representations. He sees the partial truths in what he has said about love-transference, especially the role of resistance, but he says that the second argument is much weaker than the first because all love, even if not with the same intensity, involves a repetition of infantile reactions. All love borders on the pathological. Transference-love, which resistance intensifies, arises from the analytic situation and possesses less regard for reality and the valuation of the loved person.[159] The doctor must not take advantage of a love arising out of analysis: it is like the exposure of the patient's body or the imparting of a secret. Freud admits that the male doctors have weaknesses and can find it hard to stay within the limits that ethics and technique prescribe. The use of the comic metaphor of throwing the dogs a sausage to throw them off the race is unfortunate because Freud has set up an analogy between dogs and women, the humorist (the thrower) and the doctor. Nonetheless, Freud recognizes the seduction of love even while advocating a male resistance to female seduction as resistance. The sensual desires are not the temptation, but "perhaps, a woman's subtler and aim-inhibited wishes which bring with them the danger of making a man forget his technique and his medical task for the sake of a fine experience."[160] Even after recognizing the power of love, Freud says the analyst must not give way: he must value curing the patient over loving her. From him, she will then learn to overcome the pleasure principle for a higher but less immediate and more uncertain social good. The doctor leads her through her primal mental development to the extra freedom that distinguishes the conscious from the unconscious mind.

There are, then, three recognitions: that of the patient, doctor, and reader. Ultimately, overcoming the perils of the psychoanalyst's profession relies on the recognition of three dangers: he must battle forces in his own mind that drag him down from the analytical level; those opponents outside psychoanalysis who dispute the role of sexual instinctual forces and hinder him from using them in his scientific technique; and his patients who overvalue the sexual life that dominates them and who would capture him with their "socially untamed passion."[161] Freud seeks objectivity, though his model sometimes betrays unfortunate hierarchical tendencies that privilege the doctor and the male. At least Freud has admitted the weaknesses of these male doctors even if he has played to the stereotype of the subtle woman. A social situation may repress the woman from expressing her desires to men, and can the doctor not be as oversubtle as the woman? Freud places himself as the ultimate authority but does so with some sensitivity to the difficulty of the situation. The recognition for the "postmodern" is that these are key texts in the debate on sexual harassment.

Recognition in Lacan is the recognition that the male discovery of truth is a fantasy based on the metonymy, standing in, or substitute of woman as a fantastic construction, as the negative of man, as the Other, for what is true. The male desire for unity and truth can be a fantasizing God. Lacan's psychoanalysis tries to uncover this mystification and thereby attempts a recognition in the reader. In reading there is a discovery of male self-knowledge and truth through female otherness, but Lacan denies the category of woman and therefore reveals the impossibility of such self-knowledge and truth. How then can a subject know or know itself? Knowledge and belief are, for Lacan, suppositions, myths that are false. Woman is used as a rescue or closure of male uncertainty, a pretext for knowledge and belief. The danger for Lacan, as Jacqueline Rose has implied, is that by relegating woman to the outside and denying her knowledge he is using the category of woman, which he has denied, as a means of defining his recognition or knowledge of, or belief in, uncertainty or the lack of knowing.[162] Lacan defines woman in terms of *jouissance*, which suggests a supplement and excess that signifies her as a desiring subject beyond the phallic order. Women, like mystics, experience a *jouissance*, but may know nothing about it. The woman does, however, experience it, a coming that combines the spiritual and physical (gives lie to this split), even if Lacan is speaking in paradoxes because he says the woman does not exist. Men have been misconstruing woman's *jouissance*, not surprisingly because it is beyond the phallus: for instance, courtly love and Freud have concentrated on petty considerations, which are as errant as equating *jouissance* with clitoral orgasm or intercourse.[163] Lacan is representing himself as a mystic of love. He leaves ambiguous his relation to the sacred, aligning himself with the mystics and pointing out the strangeness (potential otherness?) of Christians having Christ come (here he is referring to the end of Revelation) while leaving the existence of God as an open question. Perhaps there is a religious as well as an erotic recognition in Lacan's spiritual–physical experience of *jouissance*. If Christ can experience it, at least in John's male representation of it, is this another male fantasy (Christ as the bride whereas the church is his bride elsewhere) or is it a homoerotic or homosocial moment of discovery? Or is this simply a matter of gender bending? Lacan is a mystic who seems to be able to write about *jouissance* as John had. How strictly female then is this experience even if Lacan emphasizes the erring of men in its location? Possibly, Lacan is experiencing some Freudian Oedipal drama about the burden of the past or the anxiety of influence. Who is the best man to represent woman? Lacan understands women where his male predecessors have not recognized the truth about women. Like a man, Freud first attributed perversion to women, in a kind of narcissistic projection that serves to support him as a man. Aristotle refused to recognize perverts.[164]

Lacan builds on Freud even as he differentiates himself from the founder of psychoanalysis. This something more, or *jouissance*, occurs in Freud's concept of repetition, that is, woman is beyond the phallus because she is mystified as Other and owing to her *jouissance* as unsettling, of being more or less than, the male language that describes woman. It becomes difficult, as Rose has suggested, to recognize woman because Lacan, in the language of the phallus, even as he opposes it from within, has exposed her as a fantasy.[165] How do we recognize a fantasy in the language of the fantastic? The shift in sexual subject represents a shift in language: the give and play of woman is significance in language.[166] The difficulty here is whether the reader accepts any knowledge as a foundation for Lacan's assertions: can a male define a woman, except in a fantasy? Is this fantasy of doubt and uncertainty any more sound than the one of truth and self-knowledge? The premise may always be a conclusion. We have to start somewhere, but is that somewhere always doomed to have the foundation of a house of cards?

Aristotle's knowledge of the nature of things is not sufficient because Lacan wants to put some soul into it, to take into account sexual conduct not as perversion or amorality but, falling back again on his penchant for puns or etymology, soulmorality (a play on *âme* in *âmoralité*). The new male quest becomes, if it is new, a quest for what the female knows. Lacan points out the parallel here in the teaching of the unconscious, that somewhere within it, the Other knows. Here begins the confusion, as Lacan admits, casting off Aristotelian animism. Do we all know what we are doing? Is reality a fantasmic order? The speaking being or subject cannot use the unconscious as a model for the world but he "souls" for knowledge, which is the aspect the woman loves in him, but her *jouissance* makes it impossible to tell whether she can say what she knows about her *jouissance* (and perhaps her knowledge and his). Can the man as Other to the woman and the woman as the Other to the man know anything? But Lacan then, quite strangely (perhaps as an Otherness from his own subject/topic), bases his skepticism in, and of love on, hatred. Lacan reads Empedocles's fragment through Aristotle's reading of it. In this reading, Empedocles says that God is ignorant because he does not know hatred. Man should not, Lacan says, confuse woman with where she comes from—God—because the more he does so, the less he hates, the less he knows, the less he loves.[167] In a kind of symbolic or allegorical syllogism, which relies on a rereading of a reading of an ancient fragment, Lacan ends his love letter that asserts love through its denial. One cannot know love except through its opposite even though Lacan has acknowledged the evanescent or even impossible nature of love. The peril in these paradoxes is that men and women can become locked in oppositions, which may lead to misogyny and misanthropy rather than to understanding. In this recognition that recognizes what it is by what it is not, never certain of what it and the Other is, how can we be certain what hatred is? Quite possibly, it is not Christianity's emphasis on love that created problems, as Lacan says, but returning once more to its parody, a "knowledge of hatred." This suggestion might be an acknowledgment of hatred within all of us for the Other when it will not support us as ourselves, but questions still arise about this proposal. For instance, are hope and love any more fantastical than hatred? Even in a dialectic, hatred is a force difficult to rein in: a higher innocence, an embodiment of soul, moves beyond the hatred of songs of experience.

Julia Kristeva's analytical semiology owes something to Lacan and Freud. She is interested in the speaking subject underlying meaning and its structures and is mindful of the "discovery of the unconscious" and Lacan's breakthroughs in psychoanalysis when she sets out her semanalysis.[168] Rather than elaborate on Kristeva's intricate use of recognition (not by that name), I want to concentrate on a moment that reviews and renovates Freudian and Lacanian discovery. In discussing the novel as polylogue, she asks what is a materialist who speaks? The moment Kristeva chooses to define a subjectivity that can utter occurs when she is reading Sollers's *H* (1973) and *Sur le matérialism* (1974). This double reading allows her to see the fissures of the split "I" and to rescript the often rewritten Oedipal myth and the banishment of poets from Plato's utopian republic:

> It is a strange sort of incest where "Oedipus" comes out looking like Orpheus—singing—and where Jocasta remains blind. It involves a reversal of roles; the mother's power, engaged and directed towards refashioning a harmonious identity, is exhausted. Oedipus, made into a hero through the unconscious support from Jocasta, retraces his steps to a *before* all this happened—so as to know; his is a refusal to accept blindness, a demystification of the female sphinx, and a forsaking of Antigone.[169]

This knowledge becomes a form of demystification, a way of reading otherwise through the schizoid buckling of the "I." Kristeva's reading of Sollers' "Oedipus" allows for a novel recognition of recognition:

> The Greek myth is deflated, replaced by a non-Oedipal incest that opens the eyes of a subject who is nourished by the mother. The Phallic Mother—a blinding pillar of the *polis* and unconscious buttress of the laws of the city—is apprehended, comprehended, and thrust aside. The subject of this drama can in no way be a "citizen"—neither Orestes, murderer of his mother, nor Oedipus, castrated trustee of an invisible knowledge, occult wise man, tragic support of political religion. The "actor" subject, "poet" banished from the republic because he has shot through his maternal pedestal, abides in the margins of society by wavering between the cult of the mother and the playful, laughing, stripping way of its mystery. By the same token, he eludes all codes; neither animal, god, nor man, he is Dionysius, born a second time for having had the mother.[170]

The subject in this renovated myth moves from blindness to insight, acquiring an invisible vision at the social and political margins. The Dionysian eludes the Apollonian codes, taking Greek myth and Nietzsche into a new psychoanalytical realm, through a reading of Sollers. The oracular discourse that Kristeva finds in Sollers's "Oedipus," "split (signifier/signified) and multiplied (in its sentential and lyrical concatenations), carries the scar of not merely the *trauma* but also the *triumph* of his battle with the Phallic Mother."[171] We are asked to shift from Odysseus's scar to Oedipus's scar. Kristeva explores the way the man and mother do not exist in this desiring quest, which becomes a desire for appropriation by maternal language. The speaking subject is incapable of uttering the mother within herself. Puncturing "pure signification" deflates the signifier and its maternal support. The man is not the woman but neither actually is apart. Here, recognition is paradoxical, so that this family romance depends on the family becoming a signifying process that abolishes itself in its becoming, withdrawing, perhaps, before the contradiction of jouissance and work.[172] The quest for an identity that is and is not seems endlessly deferred.

The question of time and history follows from Kristeva's analysis of Sollers. She crisscrosses from *H* and *Lois* to *Drame* and *Nombres*. Kristeva discusses stratified time—history as infinitized totality. The dialectic she discovers in *H* and *Lois* totalizes all kinds of history into an infinite. The rhythm that scans this thesis is like a *Phenomenology of the Mind*, with chapters shuffled like playing cards, their piecing together revealing recursive determinations, trans-temporal causalities, and achronic dependencies that Hegel—a teleologist of the evolutionary finite who proceeded by closing cycles—could not have imagined. In *H*, there are no set cycles—they open up and crisscross.[173]

Kristeva sees time in *H*, and by implication the recognition of it, as revolutionary. It is a political temporality. This new stratified, multiplied, and recurring political topos, which has nothing to do with "classical, dogmatic, and merely linear political positions that incarnate a familial time within familial discourse," enables the polylogical subject.[174] Kristeva sees an unsettling of subject and history through the inextricability of politics and polylogue. The recognition that she summons is that we must transform the subject in his relation to language, the symbolic, unity, and history.[175] In this kind of dialectic, which turns Hegel on his head: "The negativity that underlies historical duration is the rejection of the other but also of the 'I,' of the altered 'I.' "[176] From reading *H*, Kristeva builds a utopian history that sacrifices the subject on this negativity-rejection-death, where all the continents are inextricably mingled and would be partners who, nevertheless, point out the shortcomings of one another: "Each one admitting of different semiotic practices (myths, religions, art, poetry, politics) whose hierarchies are never the same; each system in turn questioning the values of the others."[177] The subject who listens to this time could treat himself as a sonata. The writer and reader would be of the same rhythm, refashioning each other in the temporal music of splintered subjectivity. This novel, then, represents a new history that is enacted in a shared but differential rhythm in the minds of writer and reader. This global village involves a politics built on the recognition of the psychology of inclusive difference.

In the fictions of psychology and the psychology of fictions, the reader discovers a knowledge of the politics of authority and subversion, of family and state. In this politics, gender roles become mixed and problematic in a productive way. Psychoanalysis questions conscious authority, the realism of the world as it appears to us. The recognition of the undiscovered country of the unconscious allows Freud, Lacan, and Kristeva to question the authority of medicine, truth, family, and history. This kind of complication or irony takes hold with the German Romantics such as the Schlegels, Tieck, and Solger; develops among Victorians and modernists such as Kierkegaard, Freud, and Empson in different ways; and helps to support the celebration of the subversive and marginal in poststructuralist and postmodern questioning of conscious systems of truth in history, philosophy, and poetics. Irony, parody, and satire have long subverted and refocused the solemn pieties of Western societies. What is new with the idea of the unconscious is to build an ironic relation between the aware and unaware qualities of mind that has stuck in high and low culture. Plato's allegory of the cave and the many Christian explanations of sin cover some of the same territory, but the codification and recoding of the unconscious as well as exploring its relation to politics break new ground. Although a typology of recognition may be as possible as it is desirable, recognition experiences new contexts as well as new disciplines or subdisciplines. Psychoanalysis is an invention of the past century. Even if a typology is possible, each instance qualifies the last as texts read theory as much as theory reads texts. These few instances can only suggest aspects of recognition in Freud, Lacan, and Kristeva and the differences between them. A discipline may be an ever-changing, hypothetical space where related questions may be asked. It takes one discipline to know another. Soon they begin to cross boundaries, sometimes against our will, our desire to know, to keep knowledge possible, accountable, progressive, and tidy. That crossing might cross us into endless work.

1.8   Tentative Conclusions

General statements about recognition are possible, but as soon as they are made, instances qualify and embarrass the theory. Perhaps that is why Herodotus tried to stick to examples. But he could not avoid texts altogether. Specific detailed examples, as few as I have given, show up my theory of recognition as well as that of others. The scandal of recognition represents, perhaps through discovery itself, the scandal of theory. Recognition occurs in stories and arguments, myths and ideas, simultaneously erasing and discovering their mutual boundaries. An embarrassment for literature is the recognition of interpretation in the form of philosophy, history, aesthetics, criticism, and theory. Each wants to give a meaning or an argument to a story, make it conform to a world that it represents rather than presents, fictionalizes rather than realizes. An embarrassment for philosophy, history, aesthetics, and theory is that literature would remind the world of the stories or myths in their arguments or ideas, even those about literature. The danger is that people would notice the circularity in recognition between mythology and ideology. History would find itself in a circle between poetics and philosophy.

Perhaps this discovery, which I have set out from a few angles, would be a recognition of recognition. One might also note the difficulty in achieving recognition, the refractory nature, perhaps the possible impossibility or impossible possibility of knowledge itself, most especially self-knowledge.

Nonetheless, a few general and specific statements might reveal (uncover, discover) some insight in our blindness through the very tension between the putative universal and particular. In the Bible, a tension exists between the situational recognition of individuals, sometimes of tragic circumstances, and the structural recognition that leads to the triumph of God and his people over the fall into time. The classical sources explore recognition more discretely in terms of genre. Epic involves recognition of the hero as a central myth for the society. Tragedy represents the discovery of the protagonist's isolation from that community or nation. Comedy includes a moment of insight for the main characters that allows for their reintegration into a regenerated society.

Other disciplines, based on argument and dialectic, confront the problem of knowledge in terms of the recognition when not using the term. In philosophy this is true of idealists (Plato and Hegel) and its opponents (Marx and Nietzsche). Plato attacks poetry as the way to recognize self-knowledge and knowledge of reality: poetry sees appearances, philosophy discovers truth. Although, like Plato, Hegel finds truth and knowledge difficult to recognize, he sees that recognition as a possibility. It is possible by way of reason in History realized through the World Spirit, in a kind of incomplete dialectic of human freedom. Marx sees illusion in such a recognition just as Plato had in Homer's poetic recognitions. Although agreeing with Hegel that recognition occurs in history, Marx differs in defining that discovery: it is material, experiential, and practical. Nietzsche questions the social truth of Plato and Hegel as well as Hegel's systematic history based on success. Recognition, in Nietzsche, is that only the individual life has a recognizable meaning, and he gives to the state whatever significance it has. Perhaps in history we can recognize, as Kristeva suggests, a mutual understanding of people of different genders and backgrounds, the I and altered I without and within, admitting different semiotic practices and thereby recognizing the necessity that we transform the subject in relation to language. This utopian hope may split "I's" and "we's," not only reconfiguring them but also making some continuing attempt at seeing things as they are. This trial may, paradoxically, involve seeing things as they ought to be, something that Marx knew and practiced even if he did not like the way Hegel went about the same thing.

History, then, whatever Plato thought, is not without its forms of recognition. In the "discovery" of the New World, Columbus brings with him the truths and illusions of European culture, such as the recognition of the cannibals and Amazons just as Herodotus had in his history. This pattern of past myth and ideology versus present eyewitness or empirical evidence becomes a central issue as the Spanish attempted to distinguish themselves from the ancients and as the French and the English tried to differentiate themselves from the Spanish. In the building of empire what is illusion and what is knowledge? In psychoanalysis Freud represents the ambivalence between doctor and patient, male and female, in representation. The complexity of the recognition relies on the relation among doctor, patient, and reader and how they recognize the connection between the conscious and unconscious mind. Is such a recognition, especially in the relation between male and female, a fantasy, as Lacan suggests? How can Lacan's male language, even in its criticism of male projections about women, escape his own criticism that such language is fantastic? Recognition recognizes its own limits, an interplay of blindness and insight, a tension between situation and structure, where stability and instability vie as in the shadowy substance or substantial shadows in the dance of knowledge and wisdom, ignorance slips between them.

PART 2

Readings: History and Poetics

CHAPTER TWO

History and Empire

2.1 Texts and First Contacts

Interpretation of history is a key aspect of interpreting culture. Reading the past in its alterity and as a dimension of time that has instrumental value in the present and as a projection or prediction of the future has a long lineage. In the Western world, the shift from the Mediterranean to the Atlantic did not mean an abandonment of the classical antiquity of Greece and Rome or the biblical inheritance from Israel and beyond. The translation of empire from Greece to Rome to the Holy Roman Empire to the Spanish Empire and the rivalry of Western European empires until the British Empire and then the United States were dominant are not linear. Japan, China, the Mughal Empire, the Russian Empire, and other great powers also contributed to the intricate shifts in history in terms of culture, politics, and economics. For an English-speaking audience, the Atlantic world, particularly as it related to England (Britain), North America, and the Caribbean, is something that seems more immediate. It is an aspect of this perspective that I wish to interpret here. Canada is particularly of interest as it was a contested place for the various Western European empires and became a point of friction in the struggle between Britain and France and later Britain and the Thirteen Colonies. Later, the coexistence of various cultural elements in Canada was suggestive in the matter of cultural and historical interpretation.[1]

The textual underpinnings of English (later British) and French expansion to the New World, with a particular interest in Canada but in a comparative context within the Americas and imperial frameworks generally, suggest a significant context for an understanding of comparative imperialism. From the fifteenth century, the English and the French (centered in London and Paris respectively) were expanding their domain over the peoples adjacent to them while attempting to centralize their power in the Crown. Often concerns at home and in Europe affected and even nullified this effort to establish colonies or trading posts in the Western Atlantic. England and France, often using Italian mariners such as Giovanni Caboto and Giovanni da Verrazzano early on, were sometimes rivals in colonization and at other times friends.[2] The rivalry is well known, but the cooperation, particularly between Huguenots and the English in the late sixteenth century, is something often occluded in both national and imperial historiographies.

The textual background, rhetorical as well as legal, should complicate widespread notions of these imperial powers in Canada and the Americas. The meetings of cultures and "multiculturalism" in the Grand Banks, slavery in the West Indies, French efforts in "Florida," and alliances with, and representations of, Native and other groups all qualify notions of monological empires. Comparison helps to effect revisions of the views of the English and French empires in Canada and the New World. Although the French lost Canada in 1763 and sold Louisiana in 1803, they left cultural and political traces as well as still maintaining some colonies in the Western Atlantic, and Britain, once colonized by the Normans, lost its most populous colonies in North America in 1783. Canada and the West Indies then became part of a new kind of empire for France and Britain and their place in the imperial frameworks changed ineluctably with the American and French Revolutions.

From the 1490s into the 1520s, France was fighting to keep its Italian possessions.[3] England, which had lost most of its French possessions under Henry VI, got off to a good start in the exploration of the New World but began to lag behind Spain. The papacy continued to play a role in legitimizing exploration after Columbus's landfall in the New World. The English and French opposed the papal donation to Spain and Portugal even while they imitated these leading colonial powers. England preceded France in voyages that successfully reached the New World.[4] In the first letters patent granted to Cabot, citizen of Venice, and his sons, on March 5, 1496, Henry VII gave them and their heirs and deputies the right to sail to any foreign parts in the eastern, western, and northern sea at their own expense. In *Divers Voyages* (1582), which was meant to promote English colonization of North America in the reign of Elizabeth I, Richard Hakluyt printed for the first time the patent that Henry VII granted to Cabot.[5] Verrazzano, a Florentine, would make the first official French voyage across the North Atlantic in 1524.[6]

The Portuguese thought that the land Cabot encountered was quite possibly in their sphere as set out in the Treaty of Tordesillas (370 leagues west of the Cape Verde Islands). On October 28, 1499, King Manuel of Portugal issued letters patent to João Fernandez to make a voyage to discover new islands in the North Atlantic.[7] The Portuguese king issued similar patents to Gaspar Corte Real on May 12, 1500, and for a second voyage in 1501; to Miguel Corte Real in January 1502; for a fourth voyage in 1503. In 1501, from Bristol, merchants from the Azores and England joined together to petition for a patent to seek out the new lands in the northwestern Atlantic.[8] The Company of Adventurers to the New Found Lands was to serve as a model for later companies that helped to extend English trade and settlement to new lands. Newfoundland itself became a figure for the rivalry, cooperation, claims, and counterclaims of the European powers. Perhaps the most tenacious heirs to the elder Cabot were the French fishermen, later the men of the French shore in Newfoundland and of St. Pierre and Miquelon. Two decades before official French voyages to North America, French fishermen were involved in the fisheries near Newfoundland. This commercial fishing as a response to Spain and England was something France maintained by keeping St. Pierre and Miquelon at the end of the Seven Years' War (1756–63). In some ways the fishermen kept up contact with and interest in North America for the French between Jacques Cartier and Samuel de Champlain.[9]

2.2   Narratives of the New World

France was more active than England in exploring the northern reaches of North America from the 1520s to the 1570s. Even still, during the sixteenth century the French produced a small number of narratives compared to the Spanish and Portuguese.[10] Paulmier de Gonneville and Giovanni da Verrazzano were key figures in French expansion. Gonneville's relation of the voyage to Brazil in 1504 is the oldest account in French concerning an eyewitness report of the New World.[11] On one occasion, as much as François I seemed to ignore the papal donation dividing the "unknown" world between the Iberian powers, he sought to avoid the condemnation of Rome. On his behalf, through his relations with Cardinal Hippolyte de Médicis, archbishop of Montréal and nephew to the pope, Jean Le Veneur, bishop of Lisieux, approached Clement VII, who declared in 1533 that the bulls of 1493 applied to lands known to the Spanish and Portuguese before that date. The year before, when the French king had come on a pilgrimage to Mont-Saint-Michel, where Le Veneur was also the abbot, Le Veneur had proposed to the king that he back a voyage of discovery and presented Cartier, whose relative was a manager of the finances of the abbey, as his choice to lead it.[12] Apparently, the success of that mission helped to make Le Veneur a cardinal. Similarly, Paul III (1534–49), Clement's successor, did not intervene in the French colonization of America, a policy that troubled Charles V.[13] One of the most important aspects of the Cartier voyages was that they were official and financed by the crown. The goals set for Cartier were to find new lands full of riches, particularly gold, and to discover a passage to Cathay by the west.[14] Chief Donnacona's description of gold, according to Marcel Trudel, became the true motivation for French exploration, and this religious motive was a necessary façade to circumvent Portugal and Spain without offending the pope.[15]

In the course of discussions with the ambassadors of Charles V and John III of Portugal, François elaborated a new policy toward colonization. The doctrine was as elegant as it was simple: permanent occupation rather than discovery created possession.[16] He turned the Portuguese doctrine of *terra nullius*, begun in their exploration of Africa in the fifteenth century, against Portugal and Spain. In the fifteenth century the Portuguese had posts, instead of colonies, in Africa, so that the exact nature of this claim to possession there is not entirely clear, but for an argument for the Portuguese precedence in the use of *terra nullius* in Africa.[17] This legal doctrine of *terra nullius* came to affect the English colonies as much as those of the French: for instance, as late as 1971 Justice Richard Blackburn had confirmed *terra nullius* in Australia, and it took until 1992 for the High Court of Australia to reject it.[18] The French king issued formal orders to French seamen not to go to places in the New World occupied by the Portuguese and Spanish. The primary aim of France in Canada, besides the demonstrative one of religion and the underlying one of riches, shifted to settlement. Roberval's commission of January 15, 1541, showed settlement as part of the French policy for the New World, for in it François said that his deputy should not encroach on the property of any other prince, including those of Spain and Portugal.[19] In the 1550s in Brazil and in the 1560s in Florida (present day South Carolina), the French, especially the Huguenots, tried to establish colonies to challenge their Iberian rivals.[20] After the Reformation, France had been divided religiously in Brazil, Acadia, and New France more generally, as can be seen in the texts of Cartier, Champlain, Thevet, and Léry. This contestation, internal and external, strained France in its colonial expansion as it did the other Western European overseas empires at different points in their history.[21]

2.3 English Colonial Hopes

Humphrey Gilbert was an important figure in the renewed strategy of exploring a northwest passage as a route to China in order to challenge Spain. Composed in 1566 but printed in 1576, Gilbert's *Discourse of a Discoverie for a New Passage to Cataia* was an attempt to have the queen give him permission to sail in search of this passage and to exercise a monopoly over it. His efforts to that end were unsuccessful. When in 1572 he met Frobisher, a new scheme began when this sailor—taken with the learning of Gilbert and Michael Lok, a member of the Muscovy Company, which generally opposed the route to the northwest and preferred the one to the northeast—found favor with the earl of Warwick, who in turn was able to gain the approval of privy council for the plan.[22] Gilbert himself thought a northwest passage would lead the English to "ye East in much shorter time, than either the Spaniard or the Portingale doth" and in arguing for a great ocean in the north between Asia and America, he called on Jacques Cartier, Verrazzano, and Sebastian Cabot as well as Portuguese and Spanish sources, including the report of Salvaterra, a Spaniard who said the Natives in America thought there was a passage and who offered to accompany Gilbert on the search for it.[23]

In the meantime, England was attempting to circumvent the Portuguese and Spanish monopoly of the New World. Elizabeth I was also pursuing a policy initiated under Henry VII but which François I had begun in earnest in France—discovery, conquest, and settlement meant possession. Before Martin Frobisher's first voyage, the state papers included a document, a brief summa *avant la lettre* of Richard Hakluyt's "Discourse" that set out an English colonial policy sanctioning the discovery of lands that were unoccupied, the use of the commodities found there, and the spread of the Christian faith in that territory, all without offering "any offence of amitie."[24] This document suggested that the queen take up the lands toward the South Pole, which no other countries had possessed or subdued, so that Providence, which had given the Spanish the west, the Portuguese the east, and the English the south, would allow England to bring "in grete tresure of gold, sylver and perle into this relme from those countries, as other Princes haue oute of the lyke regions."[25] The riches of Spanish America still lured the English. A benefit of this enterprise would be to bring down the price of Spanish and Portuguese spices and commodities and to create a surplus in the English treasury.[26] England must have its place among the European colonial powers: "The Ffrenche have their portion to the northwarde directlie contrarie to that which we seke."[27] The queen did not act on these plans, but on June 11, 1578, she granted Gilbert letters patent of such scope that in Samuel Eliot Morison 's words, they "deserve the title of the first English colonial charter."[28]

The letter patent of June 1578 allowed Gilbert "to discover, finde, searche out, and view such remote, heathen and barbarous lands, countreys and territories not actually possessed of any Christian prince or people."[29] This legal ground was consistent with the attitudes of England in Henry VII's time and of France at least since François I: they do and do not recognize the papal donation to Spain and Portugal. On June 11, 1583, Gilbert sailed from Plymouth and, on August 5, took possession of Newfoundland for England, something Cabot had done in 1497. Edward Haie described how in St. John's harbor the fishermen greeted them in ships from Spain, Portugal, France, and England; how they all fired a salute of honor after Gilbert displayed his commission, and acknowledged that they were now under English sovereignty.[30] This scene is a reminder, at the commercial and unofficial level, that the cosmopolitan nature of European exploration of the New World, so evident before the Reformation, persisted in the Newfoundland fishery.

2.4   Permanent Colonies

In the first decade of the seventeenth century, France and England established permanent colonies in North America. From the aftermath of the Spanish Armada of 1588 to the founding of Montréal in New France in 1642, France and England, no matter how tentative their exploration and the establishment of permanent settlements would be, were transforming themselves from explorers and pirates to settlers and neighbors.[31] Paradoxically, at the peak of Spanish power, the English and French established their first permanent colonies, at Jamestown in 1607 and at Québec in 1608.

In France, the Crown's interest in New France lapsed after the completion of the last voyage of Cartier in 1544, although the fishery and the fur trade continued to grow. By 1578, the French ports that profited

from the fish and fur trade in New France asked for the protection of
Henri III, who appointed Mesgouez de La Roche, a Breton noble, governor of the lands in the New World.[32] Although this commission
achieved little, it did show a renewed royal interest in New France. In
1603, Pierre du Gua, sieur de Monts, was granted a monopoly in Acadia
for ten years and his main goal was to find rich mineral deposits. In 1607,
the French merchants who had opposed these monopolies in the New
World, succeeded in challenging the exclusive rights of de Monts and
others.[33] What distinguishes Marc Lescarbot from Hakluyt is that he
used the language of Christian republicanism and of a French preoccupation, which probably reached its greatest intensity under Louis XIV:
"la gloire."[34] Paradoxically, Spain caused France to be defensive, but, in
Lescarbot's rendition, the French should reclaim their past glory and go
into the New World as the Spanish had but in a manner that was inim-
itable.[35] Gabriel Sagard, a contemporary historian of New France,
recorded that for Port Royal, where some of the settlers were Catholic
and some Protestant, sieur de Monts, the leader of the colony, had provided a Huguenot minister and a Catholic priest, both of whom squab-
bled and came to blows until scurvy claimed them and the men buried
them in one grave to see whether they could in death rest in peace as
they could not when alive.[36] As W.J. Eccles says: "In America they [the
orders] had the example of the Spanish and Portuguese to challenge
them."[37]

2.5 British and French America:
Consolidation and Contestation

After the Glorious Revolution of 1688, France found that its ambitions
in Europe and America met with a more sustained English opposition.
French religious writing in and about the New World was also indebted
to Spanish influences even as, in some instances, the writers resisted
Spain or felt ambivalent about its colonization, particularly in its treatment of the Natives. In France, collections also helped to promote
colonies in the New World, and between 1632 and 1672, the Jesuits
published their annual relations, partly in order to promote their mission
to the Natives to patrons from the upper class. Whereas accounts of
America in French in the sixteenth century had been overwhelmingly
Protestant, in the seventeenth century they were Catholic.

John Oldmixon's *The British Empire in America* (1708) takes up the
continuing importance of the trope of *translatio imperii* in the context of

the preoccupation with Spain, the origins of European settlement in the Americas, the developing rivalry with the Netherlands, and the advantage of "our *American* Plantations."[38] Between 1713 and 1744, France and England, exhausted from war and attending to political problems at home, pursued peace at home and in North America. Observers from Europe, such as Peter Kalm, a professor of botany from Sweden who visited New France in 1749, the year the British founded Halifax in Nova Scotia, could not avoid seeing Canada stereoscopically, that is, with one eye on the colony and another on Europe.[39] These comparisons continued until the fall of New France and its life under British rule in 1763 onward. Louis-Antoine de Bougainville, a colonel serving under Montcalm in 1757, engaged in the now familiar typology of Old World and New World, when he compared the independence of the *habitants* or farmers in New France with dependence of the peasants in France.[40] Toward the end of French rule in Canada, some Canadians, as W.J. Eccles has pointed out, made significant contributions to the French empire in the royal administration: for instance, François-Joseph Chaussegros de Léry, son of a Canadian officer, was commander of the engineers in the Grande Armée and one of Napoleon's generals whose name is engraved on the Arc de Triomphe.

The peace allowed the French to expand their overseas trade considerably and in particular France's trade with its colonies increased over five times between 1710 and 1741. France's trade in sugar in the Caribbean, in fish in the north Atlantic, and in all sorts of goods through Cadiz to the Spanish colonies and with Turkey made the British nervous, particularly as Britain's overseas trade was stagnating in the 1730s and its contraband trade with the Spanish colonies was actively curbed by Spain. War began with Spain in 1739 and with France in 1743 over the Austrian succession. Throughout the war, the trade between the French West Indies and the British colonies on the American mainland flourished—the one exchanging sugar, molasses, and African slaves for lumber, flour, meat, and fish. Although the Royal Navy and forces from New England took Louisbourg in 1745, there was little lost in this war because the Treaty of Aix-la-Chapelle more or less maintained the status quo from the Peace of Utrecht. The French gave up their gains in the Netherlands and exchanged Madras for Louisbourg. France feared the loss of its slave and sugar trade in the West Indies above all. But the clash of the imperial powers resumed soon after. George Washington was sent to drive the French out of the region between Lake Erie and the Ohio River, where he ambushed a French party.[41]

2.6   British America: From Triumph
to Loss and Continued Tensions

In 1763 the French and British empires ceased to coexist in the territory that is now Canada, so that in one sense that is the actual end of comparative imperialism in this territory.[42] From that date onward, however, I concentrate on a few of many comparative strands, not simply between European powers now, but between British North America as Canada (including Acadia and New France) came to be known and the United States (thirteen former colonies of British America). The Royal Proclamation of 1763 seemed to mark the beginning of a British hold over much of eastern North America and the triumph of British institutions, but this was not to be. The Québec Act of 1774 restored French civil law and gave Roman Catholics religious and political equality but it also appeared to pen in the expansion of the English colonies into Native territories in the west. This act contributed to conditions that led to the American War of Independence. The great break in British North America had come with the American Revolution. This division—after the defeat of France in North America but only possible with the military help of France (perhaps owing much to Benjamin Franklin's prestige and the powers of persuasion after he had shifted from staying the course with Britain to choosing a way separate from the mother country)—has persisted through more than two centuries.

Within Canada itself there were lingering tensions between French- and English-speaking inhabitants of Canada, including divided loyalties to France and Britain and to Catholicism and Protestantism generally, although minorities in both linguistic groups, despite their relative neglect traditionally in school and official histories, did make Canada their home early on. In 1762, a year before the Royal Proclamation, John Gibson published a map of the British Empire in North America, an area that reached from Labrador beyond Lake Superior in the west and to Florida in the south. There was no officially recognized national border between Canada and the United States until twenty-one years after this map.[43]

On August 25, 1775, Thomas Jefferson wrote a letter to John Randolph in which he placed in a wider context the conflict between some in the British colonies and Britain: "Looking with fondness towards a reconciliation with Great Britain, I cannot help hoping you may be able to contribute towards expediting this good work. I am sincerely one of those, and would rather be in dependence on Great Britain, properly limited, than on any nation upon earth, or than on no nation."[44] Within weeks, however, the bond with Britain seemed not as secure, for George Washington, "Commander in, Chief of the Army of the United Provinces of North America," appealed on September 7, 1775, in French and English to the inhabitants of Canada—as a result of "The unnatural Conflict between the English Colonies, & Great Brittain"—to throw off tyranny and to take up "The Cause of America, and of Liberty."[45]

The leaders of the American rebellion enlisted the help of Spain and France. In Paris on October 6, 1778, Arthur Lee wrote to Gardoqui, saying that if driving Britain from North America and dismembering the British empire is an advantage to Spain, then "this is the moment for its monarch to decide and enforce these events by an immediate declaration of our independency and a union of force which must be irresistible."[46] Spain, as well as Portugal and later the Netherlands, were leading factors in the relations between France and Britain in the Americas. Now an independent United States would affect that rivalry and connection. After victory and independence, the American leaders kept up their relations with continental powers. Tensions with Spain arose over the western expansion of the United States in the region of the Mississippi, something James Madison noted concerning the debates of Congress in late 1786 and early 1787 and that also involved negotiations with Gardoqui [Guardoqui].[47] Writing from Mount Vernon to the Marquis de Lafayette on March 25, 1787, George Washington acknowledged his contribution and, by implication, that of France to the United States: "Your endeavors my dear Marquis to serve this Country are unremitted."[48] France had lost New France from its empire but had helped the Americans in the Thirteen Colonies to defeat Britain and win their independence. France and Britain had weakened each other and had suffered losses that would transform their empires, shifting their principal interests away from the Americas.

The Constitutional Act of 1791 followed on the Royal Proclamation of 1763 and the Québec Act of 1774. An unfortunate consequence of this act was it gave the governor and his appointed council control over revenues from Crown lands and so made them fiscally independent from the elected assemblies, something that helped in Lower Canada to divide the English minority from the French majority. This division began in earnest when in 1809–10 the governor, Sir James Henry Craig, imprisoned members of the Parti Canadien because he thought they were sympathetic to Napoleon, who was at this time expanding France and its empire. This tension would build until Louis-Joseph Papineau, having won a convincing electoral victory in 1834, led a rebellion in 1837. The

War of 1812, despite President Thomas Jefferson's assumption that Canada would be absorbed, ended with most French and English Canadians supporting the British connection or at least maintaining the status quo of their lives. Tecumseh and other Native leaders helped to preserve Canada for Britain. The American invasions failed and the Treaty of Ghent, signed as Christmas approached in 1814, returned boundaries to 1811.[49] In 1891, Martin J. Griffin wrote an extensive memorial for *The Atlantic Monthly* on John A. Macdonald, who had recently died. This article discussed Macdonald in terms of Canadian, North American, and imperial history. After describing the "wave of emotion" in Canada at the death of Macdonald, Griffin established a historical background: "Among the possessions of the British crown, Canada holds a peculiar place. For Canada, the empire made a great and costly struggle against France and against the United States. For the empire, Canada has thrice resorted to arms in 1775, in 1812, and in 1866 and turned the tide of invasion from the walls of Quebec and from the frontiers of Ontario."[50] In the wake of the American Civil War (where British commercial interests sometimes favored the defeated South) and the Fenian threat, Macdonald helped to unite British North America into Canada.

Other events, besides the American Revolution and the War of 1812, affected the survival and making of Canada. William Lyon Mackenzie, writing in Upper Canada in the 1830s, sounded like some British American writers, such as Franklin and Jefferson, in the 1760s and early 1770s. Mackenzie asserted that the British nation would not wish to perpetuate such a difficult situation in Upper Canada.[51]

His appeal to equal rights with the mother country and to the constitutional tradition and liberties granted in Britain was not unlike that made before the revolution that many in British North America had fled. Papineau led a rebellion the same year in Lower Canada and the legacy of the Rouges has informed Canadian politics, most especially among liberals and separatists in Québec, although the latter also took up a nationalist strain owing much to leaders such as Henri Bourassa. In two brief years a power shift occurred in the rhetoric of Mackenzie and his allies. On December 12, 1837, a group, chaired by Mackenzie, wrote a declaration on Navy Island, in which they praised the aid that General Van Renselaer and other Americans had provided, seeing what the citizens of Buffalo had done as support in proving "the enduring principles of the Revolution of 1776" and hoping that "emancipation will be speedily won for a new and gallant nation, hitherto held in Egyptian thraldom by the aristocracy of England."[52] In Nova Scotia, Thomas

Haliburton could represent a satirical agon between the Yankee
clockmaker Sam Slick and a Nova Scotian squire, the one upholding
Jefferson and the Declaration of Independence as examples for the
world, the other defending the British abolition of slavery and criticizing
the American institution of racial inequality: " 'Jefferson forgot to insert
one little word,' said I. 'He should have said "All white men," for, as it
now stands, it is a practical untruth in a country that tolerates domestic
slavery in its worst and most forbidding form. It is a declaration of *shame*,
and not of *independence*.' "[53] Joseph Howe, like Mackenzie, believed
strongly in responsible government and was an advocate of Lord
Durham's report in Nova Scotia and elsewhere. Writing an open letter
to Lord John Russell on September 18, 1839, Howe set out the remedy
for problems of government in Nova Scotia and other colonies: "Lord
Durham has stated it distinctly; the Colonial Governors must be com-
manded to govern by the aid of those who possess the confidence of the
people and are supported by a majority of the representative branch.
Where is the danger?"[54] The place of democracy in the debate on
empire and colony is central from the 1760s onward in the Thirteen
Colonies and in the remnant of British North America that became
known as Canada in 1867 and after.

2.7   Canada as and at a Crossroads

In the twentieth century, Canada has moved from the ideology of two
founding nations, English and French, to multiculturalism. Its French-
speaking minority has produced four prime ministers, some of them
among the longest serving in British parliamentary history; so the legacy
of French and British imperialism has melded into a new hybrid state
that has opened its doors to immigrants from every corner of the world.

Canada has shared the languages of three great powers—France,
England (Britain), and the United States—whose leaders have had
ambivalent attitudes toward empire, expansion, and contraction—and it
has sometimes been separated from these powers by a common culture
and language—similar but not the same. Whereas some in those centers
of power might have dismissed Canada over the centuries, others have not.
However marginal or not to European and American expansion, since
1497, Canada (with all its names until 1949 when Newfoundland joined
it) has been—in empire—a crossroads, a buffer, a beneficiary, a victim, a
byproduct, an aid, an ambivalent representation, and a collection of peoples. It has been comparative and multiple since the beginning—with

the meeting of Natives and Europeans, the rivalry and cooperation of Europeans, and immigration from probably every country. The Death of Wolfe, as Benjamin West's various versions of the scene and myth of the young general attest, and the Québec conference of 1864, the meeting of Churchill, Roosevelt, and King there during the Second World War, the Québec Referenda of 1980 and 1995 all show that the ancient center of the French Empire in America continued to play and still plays a central role in the making and translation of empire as well as the building of nations and their possible fracture. In Voltaire's "quelques arpentes de neige" [a few acres of snow], those waves of peoples have found the apparently inhospitable habitable and even, despite its very real flaws, a generous space, one kind of example to other countries, comparatively distinct despite its role in the imperial past, present, and future. The recognition of state, nation, and empire in past and present is a matter of shifting identities. It is difficult to discover these new worlds, especially in lands at once ancient to aboriginal peoples and new to the European newcomers. The old phrase, "voyages of discovery," is both apt and misleading because it is true that these other worlds were new to those discovering them but not to those who had long inhabited their shores. Point of view, then, plays a role in recognizing a time and place. Columbus might have thought he was discovering Asia, but Europeans came to see their errors, however slowly. Las Casas tried to defend the Indians against the long-standing framework of heretics in the Old World. He came to consider these peoples, as Columbus did, as blank slates, innocents who would be good vassals to the Spanish monarchs and pliable for conversion. They should not be slaves because they had no religion. European triumphalism, a celebration of their "discovery" of the New World, became in 1992 a commemoration of flaws, crimes, problems, and mistakes as opposed to the making of Columbus into a child of the Enlightenment and as the adoptive father of "America," as in the United States as a synecdoche and metonymy, as Jeremy Belknap saw him in 1792, or as the cultural icon and sign of American pride, know-how, and progress as in the Columbus of the Columbian World Exposition of 1893 in Chicago even if that triumph was delayed a year.

The "Canadian" experience was, after John Cabot's voyage in 1497, both central and peripheral to the Columbian legacy, central because Cabot's challenge in the wake of Columbus troubled the governments of Spain and Portugal and peripheral because Canada was at the edges of the great colonies that would form the United States. The very and varied interpretations of John Cabot (Giovanni Caboto), as of Columbus and other key European "discoverers" of places in the New World invoke interpretations in subsequent generations and discussions of discovery and misdiscovery. Even if we do not, in Caboto/Cabot's case, have any written interpretation by the captain or his crew of the voyage and encounter with Natives, interpretation and representation occur in the wake of the "discovery."[55] The word "Canadian" was a term applied to Natives, then to the French inhabitants of New France, and then to the English-speaking inhabitants as the French in the heartland of the Saint-Lawrence spoke of themselves as Québecois. Shifting identities, of which this is one shadow only, obscure and complicate recognition. As in Greek tragedy, such recognition is as much about seeing errors and flaws as about the power of seeing, the theory of the perspective that both eyes provide. Imperial pride has its fall. The rise and fall of Britain and France in North America provide this *de casibus* lesson. In the present as in the past it is not always easy to know what these eyes are looking at: in history the interpretations of the past as it recedes change. The recognition of misrecognition balances the misrecognition of recognition. There are many contexts for Canada as there are for Columbus.

In the interpretation of culture, history and historical texts are as elusive and challenging as literature and literary texts. The flawed anagnorisis and the anagnorisis of the flaw may well be a matter of the hamartia not just of the historical person but of the historian and the reader. Oedipus and Electra might never have made it to the shores of the western Atlantic, but just as Aristotle wrote about them Acosta could record a moment of recognition when Aristotle's torrid zone became for the Spaniards a joke in which experience trumped metaphysical speculation, a kind of cognitio in the comedy of learning. Sailors came to teach philosophers a lesson. Sometimes they needed historians to say so. But poets could also do so, as Philip Sidney understood, even in the face of classical authorities of the severe and poetic philosopher Plato, and his more poet-friendly student Aristotle. Ways of seeing were matters of the interpretation of culture for peoples as well as for individuals, although the relation between the whole and the part was not seamless and symmetrical.

CHAPTER THREE

Recognizing Canadian Women and Women in Canada

3.1 Seeing Double

A historical perspective can help us to understand literature in context. Canadian writing as much as Canadian history tells much about recognition. For a long time, Canada was not Canada: the name grew and shifted from village to colony to state, but not in any retrospectively neat and linear way. Newfoundland, New France, Acadia, Canada, and other designations were names Europeans attached to this northern part of the New World, or as Prospero reminds Miranda, what was new to them. And Miranda is a European, who cannot remember seeing other Europeans, except her father, until they land in a storm of his making. On her island in the Mediterranean—an adopted home that was unpeopled until Sycorax was exiled there and brought Caliban, her son, into the world—Miranda looks on these Europeans, some of them her own kin, as embodying a brave new world. Nature and nurture contend. In the naming of Canada the Europeans tried to name the ancient land in new ways. Canada itself shifted culturally as much as politically. Its women poets, and those who are attached to Canada but not technically Canadian by birth, suggest the ever-shifting identities of Natives and strangers in a familiar and strange land.

Many possible worlds affect Canadian writers, Native and settler (immigrant), male and female, so that an ambivalence or multiplicity pervades the literature of Canada. The poetry of women is no exception and in some ways multiplies the fictional worlds further. Seeing double is a stereoscopic or typological view of a place, being here and there (or various theres) in one moment, observing but crossing bounds in thought and imagination, primarily through language. Poets come to images and metaphors. Language is a tangle of stories and arguments. This duality or multiplicity (depending how fractured it is) can make the connection between here and there problematic. One of the key instances of the relation between here and there is home and exile: they are ancient concerns in writing, whether the exile from Eden in the Book of Genesis or Odysseus's or Aeneas's wanderings. To say that Canadian women poets are the sole heirs/heiresses to life east of Eden or west of Troy would be nonsense. To notice the preoccupation and persistence of the doubleness of here and there and the feelings of never quite being at home in the work of these poets is another matter. This exilic urge and division is something vital to boundary and immigrant writing and perhaps even today—when the vastness of Canada's back-yard extends from huddled and crowded cities often clinging close to the sea or to the border with the United States and is not the apparent emptiness of the land as it was earlier in Canadian history—such a vast land allows for the nostalgic, the elegiac, and the lonely words and representations of the writer.

This exploration begins briefly with some of the usual or expected male voices, who surface from time to time, but give way mainly to female voices, which should qualify and modify my own, instruct them and me. This dialogue should, with any luck, yield more than ventrilo-quy. The chapter has two points at its center—Elizabeth Bishop as a poet who was of but not of Canada and her mention of Natives in her mem-oir, and some Native and Black poets and prose writers in Canada who provide another example of the double bind of the first human inhabi-tants of the land and those often descended from slaves brought to North America against their will. This is a Nova Scotia and a Canada—until recently—not often represented, interpreted, or published from the van-tage beyond that of the "European" settler. The aspects of race and cul-ture, along with gender, will qualify the here and there of Canada and the actual and imaginary spaces found in the poetic geometry and music—the musings—of these writers. Sense of identity in a place in tension with a double or multiple space is something that will draw together these theorists, critics, and poets who have a connection with Canada—who came from it or to it, lived in it or from it, have a relation to it in body, spirit, and mind.

Over the course of decades, Northrop Frye said that the problem of Canadian identity appeared to him to be "primarily connected with locale, less a matter of 'Who am I?' than of 'Where is here?' "[1] Echoing

Earle Birney's poem "Can. Lit.," Frye proposed that Canadian poetry was haunted by a lack of ghosts. Frye implies the fallenness and alienation of Europeans in Canada: "The Christian, Baroque, Cartesian attitude that the white invaders brought from Europe helped to ensure that in Canada the sense of being imprisoned in the belly of a mindless emptiness would be at its bleakest and most uncompromising."[2] Perhaps the lack of ghosts is one of ancient European ones, but those of Columbus and his successors may have enough to haunt us for a very long time if not eternity. George Grant also noted, "the conquering relation to place" had marked Canadians and that in the Rockies the gods are not ours and because of what we are, we cannot know them, our memorial the immemorial treatment of "the environment as object."[3] Douglas LePan's "A Country without a Mythology" (1948) begins with "No monuments or landmarks guide the stranger / Going among this savage people" and moves through masks, "alien jargon," and other qualities of the land and the people in it to a situation where there is "not a sign, no emblem in the sky" and the final question of "some lust-red Manitou."[4] This poem builds on the legacy of explorers, coureurs de bois, and priests exploring the wilderness but also on a poetic theme in English Canada that Isabella Valancy Crawford and Marjorie Pickthall expressed in previous generations. Wandering in a vast land is, not surprisingly, something central to Canadian poetry: which is home and which is exile becomes a vexed question. Robert Kroetsch has also noted the theme of exile.[5] Frederick J. Turner's frontier thesis—that there is a perennial social rebirth on the American frontier—has its new counterpart in Canada's shifting cultural boundaries in the Technological Revolution.[6] During the 1970s, Marshall McLuhan, who did so much to advance the study of communications, explored the idea that Canada is a borderline case and also connected Canadian identity with location: "Canada's advantages of having no sharply defined national or private identity appear in the general situation where lands long blessed by strong identities are now bewildered by the growing perforation and porousness of their identity image in this electronic age."[7] Canada's multiple borders can be partly virtual as well, so there has been a shift in ideas of community, of home and exile over the past century.

Canadian poetry and literature have refracted some of these changes. The role of feminist critics and theorists and of women poets has been important in this era of great technological change. Doubleness, ambivalence, multiplicity, and multivalence are related elements that I first explored decades ago in Shakespeare, and certainly the German Romantics such as Tieck, Solger, and the Schlegels knew this well even before Coleridge and before Keats used the term "negative capability" in relation to Shakespeare.[8] Such relations are not bilateral: nor do they have simple vertical and horizontal axes. Jan Zwicky, a Canadian poet and philosopher, combines her kinds of writing in *Lyric Philosophy*, where, in the spirit of music that might bridge the dual rhythms of the poetic and philosophical, she suggests: "Polydimensional meaning might be pictured as being dependent upon a spray of possible axes of connectedness, whose relations to one another are neither necessarily symmetric nor orthogonal."[9] Leibnitz's possible world theory need not be read as his calculus, but it can also be viewed as a mother of invention (not solely in Frank Zappa's sense), as a putative or imaginative offspring of *inventio*, as a poetic space that can be interpreted. Space, as Gaston Bachelard recognized, has its own poetics, but Canada has and does not have its own space.[10] Zwicky, Atwood, and other Canadian women poets can suggest other ways—some related, some not—to see the space of poetry, Canada, the world of women, Canadian poetry, and other domains with shifting boundaries. When I was in school, I read Margaret Atwood's *Survival*, which had recently come out and which argued, as opposed to the frontier thesis of American culture, that Canadian literature was about survival—bare, grim, and cultural. Most basically, "For early explorers and settlers, it meant bare survival in the face of 'hostile' elements and/or natives: carving out a place and a way of keeping alive."[11] This motif of survival was something all peoples of the New World—Native and settler—had to face. The Pilgrims and other early settlers of New England and Virginia (a fair number of whose descendants live in English Canada) had to rely on Natives for food to survive. The Inuit especially had to cope with starvation. This harrowing experience of braving a harsh north occurs in "A Story of Starvation" by Marion Tuu'luq (b. 1910) as told to Susan Tagoona: at the time, "it looked as though we weren't going to survive. I will tell you some of those terrible events."[12] The tensions and bond between different peoples in North America and more particularly in Canada have been fear of starvation and a desire to survive: these emotions still have repercussions. Some literature was promotional—a means to or advertisement of the New World. Robert Hayman—in 1628—wrote a poem "To all those Worthy Women, who have any desire to live in Newfound-Land, specially to the modest & discreet Gentlewoman Mistris Mason, wife to Captaine Mason, who lived there divers yeeres," which opens with "Sweet Creatures, did you truly understand / The pleasant life you'd live in Newfound-land"?[13] Europeans immigrants lived amongst Natives and Africans brought over originally on forced slaving voyages, and men and women faced each other in this new natural and cultural environment. For Natives and Africans, surviving also meant living through the ordeal of European mastery and dominance. Some contemporary Canadian women poets take up this theme. Survival cuts both ways at least.

3.2   Elizabeth Bishop

Here and there is about actual and cultural survival and is about the exploration and crossing of boundaries. Elizabeth Bishop crossed the boundary between Canada and the United States, traveled widely, and lived in places outside both countries. She is a poet who had her roots in New England and the Maritimes: she was an American poet who found her first stable home in Nova Scotia and also lived in Brazil and elsewhere. Some might argue with my attributions and geography, but I am one who sees open borders if the affiliation of and for the poet is enough. Although Bishop was born in Worcester, Massachusetts, on February 8, 1911, she lost her father, William Bishop, to Bright's disease eight months later and ended up in Nova Scotia. Bishop's mother (née Gertrude Bulmer), whose parents were from Nova Scotia, suffered from mental illness, was hospitalized, had a final breakdown in 1916—the last time Elizabeth saw her—and died in 1934 in a sanatorium. "The first real home Elizabeth knew," according to her editor Robert Giroux, "was the coastal town of Great Village, Nova Scotia, where her widowed mother returned to be with her parents, the Bulmers." Giroux adds, "Elizabeth's portrait of the Bulmer grandparents in her poems and prose is that of unpretentious country people, whom she deeply loved."[14] This time in Nova Scotia did not last long as her wealthy paternal grandfather, John Wilson Bishop, himself from Prince Edward Island originally, brought her back to Worcester when she was six.[15] The Bishops and Bulmers had migrated from the Maritimes to New England (a familiar two-way pattern over the centuries) and Elizabeth herself was a migratory soul—caught between here and there, home and exile.

In "Primer Class" she describes her school in Nova Scotia, whereas in "The Country Mouse" she represents her shift from Nova Scotia back to Worcester. Bishop's stories supplement her memoirs: during the early 1950s she wrote "In the Village," set in a Nova Scotian village much like Great Village, where her Bulmer grandparents lived. In her imagination, as well as in her life, Elizabeth Bishop dwelt in the borderlands, crossing boundaries in imagination, whether through autobiography, fiction, or poetry. I find her work attractive for many reasons as someone with roots in New England and the Maritimes, who has also experienced swimming at Wellfleet on Cape Cod but with thoughts less on the Assyrian Wars then, and when a child I remember going to Cape Breton among the mists.[16] Such border crossings between the Maritimes and New England with occasional stays in Britain, sway between royal and republican images—which is home, which is exile? how much is the past with us? Although born in New England, Bishop could write a poem about Elizabeth I, "Britannia Rules the Waves" (1935).[17] In "Questions of Travel," one of the sections or books that constitutes *The Complete Poems 1927–1979*, Bishop included "First Death in Nova Scotia," in which the speaker's cousin Arthur lies in the parlor beneath chromographs of King George, Queen Mary, the Prince of Wales, and Princess Alexandra and in which the speaker likens Arthur to a doll beginning to be painted the way Jack Frost "always painted / the Maple Leaf (Forever)."[18] This speaker, perhaps this poet, seems to be representing from the inside a private Canadian scene in a public imperial context. Still, this is the same poet—like Whitman, she contains multitudes—who writes "View of the Capitol from the Library of Congress" in which "the little flags / feed their limp stripes into the air," a poem that comes immediately after "Cape Breton" in "North and South."[19]

Bishop also stretched and circumvented the border between Canada and the United States: her story, "Memories of Uncle Neddy" transports this relative, who only went "possibly two or three times as far as Boston after his daughters had moved there and married, into his childhood when he is made to journey from Nova Scotia to Rio de Janeiro.[20] Bishop bends time and space, life into art. Moreover, Bishop's anthology of Brazilian poetry is another example of this wider geography that involves English and her experience in North America but transforms it. She opens the collection with her translation of Manuel Bandeira's "My Last Poem," which contains the apposite line in which the poet wishes the last poem to be thus: "That it be gentle saying the simplest and least intended things."[21] What is not intended in travel and identity is the fluid tension between here and there, home and exile, the search the poet takes as part of something beyond the quest of her speakers and characters.

Another traveler between Nova Scotia and Massachusetts, Deborah How Cottnam (pseudonym "Portia") was born in Canso, settled in Salem, and returned to Nova Scotia in 1775 as a Loyalist refugee. Cottnam could write in "On Being Asked What Recollection Was," that "Recollection whispers while I write."[22] The use of memory as a means to write of a calm place of identity or home, between Nova Scotia and Massachusetts, or other points, is something poets—and Canadian women poets—have long addressed.

Nor is the representation necessarily about the poet or her own family or cultural background. In Bishop's "Primer Class" there were in the classroom "two little Micmac Indian boys, Jimmy and Johnny Crow," whose "dark bare feet" she stared at, herself compelled to wear sandals whereas most of the children went to school barefooted.[23] This Nova Scotia, this Canada, was not homogeneous. Indians or Natives were also there in the class.

3.3 Native Poets and Poets and Natives

Native and settler writers have represented the indigenous peoples of Canada. Rita Joe (b. 1932), a Micmac (Mi'kmaq) poet, sees other dimensions to students such as those Bishop described. He opens "Today's Learning Child" with "I see the bronze hue of skin / The dark eyes flashing."[24] The tensions, frustrations, and intricacies in Joe's representation are less about a pastoral and naive childhood than found in Bishop's description.

Before Bishop, women of European descent represented Natives in their writing, sometimes in a minor key, sometimes as a major theme, and Native women found voices of their own to give their own point of view on their experience. Even though the focus of this discussion is a few key works by twentieth-century Canadian women poets, the double vision explored here in this time is something that began early and was repeated often. Isabella Valancy Crawford (1850–87) imagined in "The Camp of Souls" (1880) a vision of whiteness and a Native world. At one point in the poem, the speaker says, "When I paddle back to the shores of earth / I scatter them over the white man's hearth," these "flowers"— "Immortal smiles of Great Manitou."[25] This cultural empathy, representation, or ventriloquy—depending on one's point of view—is something that has become controversial but was less contested then. In "Ojistoh" (1912), Pauline Johnson, a Mohawk poet, represents the tensions between Huron and Mohawk and leaves the Europeans out of the conflict.[26]

Marjorie Pickthall's speaker is the French Jesuit Father Lalemant, so an English-speaking female poet imagines a French male and puts his thoughts about Natives into words. In "Père Lalemant" (1913), the priest says of the Natives, probably Ouendat or Huron, who would take him on the long journey between Québec and Sainte-Marie:

> My boatmen sit apart,
> Wolf-eyed, wolf-sinewed, stiller than the trees.
> Help me, O Lord, for the very slow of heart
> And hard of faith are these.
> Cruel are they, yet Thy children. Foul are they,
> Yet wert Thou born to save them utterly.[27]

The poet is not necessarily the speaker and Pickthall and Lalemant might diverge on this equation of Natives with nature—they are like wolves and trees—or the attribution of cruelty to them. Jean de Léry, writing of Brazil during the sixteenth century, was able to point out that the French could themselves be cruel in their own civil war, and how much the historical Lalemant, quite possibly a convert from Protestantism, would have mediated on or considered this is something for suggestion and speculation and not for proof.[28] The Iroquois did manage to destroy Ouendake or Huronia (Pays des Hurons) in 1649, killing Native and French alike.

Native women poets over the past hundred years and more have been creating their own images of here and there.[29] When Pauline Johnson's (Tekahionwake's) speaker exclaims in "Shadow River": "O! the pathless world of seeming!" she was exploring what is ideal and real in the speaker's life.[30] The movement of the poet refracts the poet on the move. Buffy Sainte-Marie, a Cree born in Saskatchewan but raised by foster parents in Maine and Massachusetts (her foster mother was part Micmac) and was adopted at a Cree powwow when she was eighteen, wrote in the 1960s about concerns that were central to the debate on the Vietnam War for Natives and for many other groups.[31] Her popular success as a singer, songwriter, and poet made her famous in Europe, North America, and beyond. In "Universal Soldier," she explores how without soldiers the abuse of power and wars could not be enacted and that "His orders come from far away no more / They come from here and there and you and me," when "he's fighting for Canada and he's fighting for France / He's fighting for the USA."[32] Here and there are nearby and are a space where we take responsibility. What is also suggestive is that when listing countries Sainte-Marie mentions Canada first and then France (a large part of Canadian historical consciousness and key to Métis culture on the prairies where she was born—her own surname is apparently French) and then the United States, her adopted country where she grew up, before proceeding to Russia and Japan. Sainte-Marie gives a local habitation and a name to this universal soldier. In "My Country 'Tis of Thy People You're Dying" satire and irony are directed toward American attitudes to, policies for, and treaties with the Indians and stress the miseducation and disinformation of the schools that forbid the Indians their languages. Although Sainte-Marie is focusing on the United States, she could have mentioned similar abuses in Canada. Of this schooling, the speaker notes that the Indians are made "to despise their traditions" and the American settlers—the "you" addressed in the poem—tell Natives "That American history really began when Columbus set sail out of / Europe! / And stress that the Nation of leeches that's conquered this land / Are the biggest and bravest and boldest and best!"[33] This poem also examines the root of Native poverty and frustration, something Rita Joe expresses more indirectly.

In "Now That the Buffalo's Gone," Sainte-Marie appeals to members of the population, those who might even have Indian grandfathers or great grandfathers, to realize that even the losers in a war, such as the Germans, have been able to keep their lands, but not the Natives, whose lands the victors continue to take. Although earlier in the lyric the speaker says that "Oh it's been written in books and in songs / That we've been mistreated and wronged," she wants action: the poem ends with a reminder: "It's here and it's now you must help us, dear man, / Now that the buffalo's gone."[34] This poem is again about the United States but has its implications for Canada and the Native land claims that have occurred in the past few decades. The disappearance of the millions of buffalo, something Sainte-Marie's Cree ancestors would have witnessed, embodies the rapid, careless, and full exploitation of wildlife during European expansion westward. Sainte-Marie was born Native, was raised in a white society, and has crossed borders between Canada and the United States, where she lives. Her here and now was and is a place of urgency and responsibility. There is no sense of escape about dreaming of another place only something practically utopian about making the future better now and here. There may be more than one now and here for the Seneca and Cheyenne, but the multiple points of view are rooted in lives and in making a difference. Words make a difference and are not spoken or put in books to be filed away to then and there.

History is also a concern of Jeannette C. Armstrong, an Okanagan born in 1948 on the Penticton Reserve in British Columbia. In "History Lesson" she represents a parodic journey from Columbus to the present, a world full of violence, disease, alcohol, junk food, pollution, development, disrespect for the dead and for Native culture, ecological mutilation, remains of animals, "a long journey / and unholy search" for a power in a garden closed and lost for ever.[35] In "Indian Woman" Armstrong sets out stereotypes, but the speaker proclaims in the first person "Some one is lying" and then celebrates the beauty and glory that surrounds the woman as she walks.[36] The poem also characterizes the Indian woman as the keeper of the generations and strength of nations and the giver of life even in the face of "dangerous / wastelands," teaching songs and providing truth "among cold and towering / concrete."[37] The poem concludes: "I am a sacred trust / I am Indian woman."[38] The woman's seed in a waste is especially important as Native culture and lands are under threat from strange forms that threaten the landscape and Indian people.

To be exiled in one's own land is a concern in Native Canadian poetry. The legacy of Columbus and the attempts at healing find their expression in the work of Sainte-Marie, Armstrong, and others. The attempt to undo or extricate stereotypes from outside Native culture is one of the quests in these Native women poets and more widely in Native literature, having its roots in the earlier encounters and cultural representations from first contact. Natives in Canada and the United States do not recognize the border between the two countries in the ways settlers and immigrants do. Here and there are not always the same for Natives in North America.

3.4   African Canadian Writers and the Double Bind/Doubly Blind

Being in two places but not being able to be in two places is a preoccupation of many Canadian immigrant poets and writers as opposed to the doubleness of some Native writers, which involves the place of their ancestors and the scarring or pillaging of the landscape by invaders, newcomers, immigrants. The stereoscopic view of the settlers, from Africa, Europe, Asia, and elsewhere, might be of the place of origin and the place of adoption or arrival. One group that does not make an explicit appearance in Elizabeth Bishop's primer class is African Nova Scotians, who have lived in the colony and then province for centuries but have traditionally been occluded from or placed in a minor key in official or dominant cultural documents. Carrie M. Best (b. 1903) began the Foreword to *That Lonesome Road* with a bald statement of the hardships of her community: "The problems resulting from racial inequality and its limitations have weighed heavily upon me from my earliest recollections and increased with the years and the knowledge of the early history of black Nova Scotians."[39] There is a fallenness and alienation in the memories of individuals but most especially in groups who have been disadvantaged or ill treated.

There are sometimes tensions between Nova Scotian or Canadian-born Blacks and those from the West Indies—and not simply between the white and black worlds—even if the white society has been most responsible for exclusion of those of African descent. Sometimes a writer who returns home to the place of her birth or family from the exile of her new home describes other bifurcations and divisions of ground. In "return," Dionne Brand opens the poem with an address that embodies such a two-eyed view: "From here you can see Venezuela, / that is not Venezuela, girl, that is Pointe Galeote / right round the corner."[40] Another typology occurs between Canada and the other place of the speaker's youth and family. This typological supplement—one place is not enough in life or imagination—becomes explicit in the eponymous poem in *No Language Is Neutral*: "I did read a book once about a / prairie in Alberta since my waving canefield wasn't / enough."[41]

Brand's first novel, *In Another Place, Not Here*, as the title suggests, is about doubling worlds, about there being no here "here." Two examples show that there are different kinds of twoeyedness. The first is within Toronto:

> There are two worlds here in this city where she arrives years earlier with a shoe box of clippings. One so opaque that she ignores it as much as she can—this one is white and runs things; it is as glassy as its downtown buildings and as secretive; its conversations are not understandable, its motions something to keep an eye on, something to look for threat in. The other world growing steadily at its borders is the one she knows and lives in. If you live here you can never say that you know the other world, the white world, with certainty.[42]

Here is a new version of the two solitudes that Hugh MacLennan, who came from Nova Scotia and studied at Princeton, wrote about in Montreal over fifty years before. This is a division based on skin color—not necessarily language—that plays itself out through knowledge and power. Brand also alludes to the east end of Toronto where there were tensions between "the West Indian and the Nova Scotians."[43]

The second type of living in one place and imagining or dreaming of another is rooted in gender. Brand's novel represents that kind explicitly: "These women, our mothers, a whole generation of them, left us. They went to England or America or Canada or some big city as fast as their wit could get them there because they were women and all they had to live on was wit since nobody considered them whole people."[44] There seems to be no place like home.

Divided, people divide. They dream of another place. Home and exile occur wherever people write, but in Canadian literature women are often haunted by this friction and by their isolation or sense of not having been treated fairly.

3.5   More Dualities

Other dualities occur in the work of women poets in and from Canada. Even in the apparently more settled and established world of mainstream Canadian literature, there have long been differences, intricacy, and ambivalence. The politics of Canadian women writers is prismatic and resists the temptation of stereotypes. Even with an all-too-brief discussion of poets—for instance of Dorothy Livesay, whose poems spanned many decades and, even more briefly here, Margaret Atwood, Anne Carson, and Gwendolyn MacEwen—the interpretation of this aspect of Canadian culture suggests the recalcitrance of the double nature of recognition. Writers seek recognition and evade it in both senses.

Dorothy Livesay (1909–96) led an active life as a poet, teacher, journalist, organizer, and editor. She published books of poetry in every decade from the 1920s to and including the 1990s and won the Governor General's Award in Canada for poetry in 1944 for *Day and Night* and in 1947 for *Poems for the People*. Here is a poet who cared about the everyday. Having read her literary work over the years, I was pleased to see that Dean J. Irvine had brought out her uncollected and unpublished poems.[45] This collection allows for a widening view of her work, a kind of posthumous interpretation or recognition. While refracting her time and place, Livesay is a poet who speaks beyond her time and country.

Poems that were not collected or published might have fallen behind the radiator, got lost in a box or suitcase, were handwritten or typed without duplicate, or were not the best work in the eyes of the author, her friends, or her editors. We can all be wrong about what in our work can stick, and certainly I have lost my share of poems to moves, single copies afloat on the pre-computer ether or even on disk, Internet, and hard drive, some spent in email meltdowns, others handwritten on envelopes. Livesay moved about a good deal: she taught in Zambia from 1959 to 1963, and she was writer in residence in various universities across the vastness of Canada.[46] So it is difficult to say why these poems—which Irvine organizes according to the decades and whose sections are preceded with photographs of Livesay presumably from the decade in question—were lost or left. Rather than discuss the poems systematically, I go to the places from the 1920s onward that please me most, as if I had been reading them as found poems, as though in a study or attic, and turned to you to read out what struck my ear most. I try to find among these poetic strings the sweet spots.

The 1920s Livesay wrote with a lyrical directness. Her words could have a lovely suggestiveness beyond the poet's years. In "The Priest" the speaker says, when summoned: "There was nothing left in the universe / Save my desire to go."[47] This young poet had a gift for evocation: for instance, in "The Woman Who Lived Alone," she writes: "Sometimes I feed the sea / With faded petals / And old grey stalks / Nearly dead."[48] In "The Portraits," the speaker asks of the satisfied and smiling grandfathers what they knew that she did not: "Not the relentless morning, surely, / That tortures with the old taunt, / Urges the old certain quest / Into the long hours of the afternoon."[49] In these finely crafted lines gesturing beyond themselves through a well-defined concrete world is also a place defined as well by gender.

In the 1930s and later these questions take new directions. Livesay's power to describe physical surroundings and imbue them with a politics or a numinosity takes hold. The 1930s poem "At the Beach" begins with a typological scene of seaside and ominous events: "Even the headlines break upon / Our seaward gaze / And from the funnelled smoke of ships / Words shape and blaze / Of exodus, of mass arrest / (Here, sunlight quivers on your breast)."[50] Livesay dedicated "The Anarchist" to Bob Bouchette, who had drowned on June 13, 1938, and began the poem with a lyricism that once more yoked the political and the aesthetic, this time however reversing the technique of "At the Beach" because here there was a political title and a poem more apparently representing the physical world. The opening words are: "Cool cup of bay / Fern frosted— / Sand curled by waves— / Evergreens twitching winged shoulders / Blue clam shells in the tidal caves—."[51] The theme of loneliness returned to Livesay's poetry in "We Are Alone," which begins, "We are alone, who strove to be / Together in the high sun's weather," and ends "Each one ploughing a one-man clearing / Neither one alive to see" with a run-on into the last stanza: "In wider boundaries of daring / What the recompense might be."[52] In the beauty of these lines is the solitary walk and work each person has among others and in a

horizon beyond that life itself. What the reward is in such a life is difficult ever to know.

In the poems of the 1940s the theme of a sense of shelter in a hard
world, whether it is possible or not, persists in lyrical moments. The
speaker says—in "Motif for a Mural"—"In time of quiet / I lay under a
stone / Weeping / And the grass grew again."[53] The "I" of the poems
of the 1950s also has a lyrical gift expressed in a tension with the world.
According to the speaker of "Vancouver," "I was the one who, tensed
to northern air / Strode in one dimension through the plains."[54] Biblical
and mythological longings also inform Livesay's poems. "The Immortals"
starts with the simple and beautiful lines that gesture beyond themselves,
representing immortality through this mortal coil: "Those left behind,
who grieve / Hang on the living tree like fruit / Unripe for gathering; /
Those grieving seem to us / Thieves of the sap, the root."[55] Livesay
never really leaves the green rain of nature and the issue of gender (here
literally): in "Letter to My Daughter" the speaker says: "When you
began to talk, the world turned over: / The armies vanished into words,
the men / Returned to fathering. And once again / Lights flashed upon
the hill, / The leaning cherry tapped your window-pane / Washed its
green hands in the September rain."[56] Nature, war, and politics meet
here: the death of war and the birth of this girl coincide. Light and the
blossoms and greenness of nature revive the land. Always attuned to
typologies, Livesay presented another childhood in another poem of the
1950s, "In the Ward," this one much more painful and precarious:
"Around the corner / (Pale monk in a black cell) / The polio child / Lies
in his iron bell / Saying, with furtive fingers, / The beads of his hell."[57]
The rosary of suffering is far from cherry blossom and rain shimmering
on green leaves at the window.

Exile in this greenness is a theme that Livesay continues in the 1960s.
"Aliens All" she ends with "We are not at home here / being haunted by /
other music—/ green of another country."[58] Just as this exilic scene
shows a sense of place and the earth, so too does she in "Persephone,"
which despite its mythical aspect and concern with death and gender,
reveals a world literally rooted in nature and the everyday: "I feel affinities /
with cabbages / turnips and beets / all firm things / that hold their
roundness."[59] The speaker continues that these vegetables are "close /
to earth or under it / tasting the brown feel / of the turned-up autumn
soil / breathing the undercold," a lovely image of the fields after harvest and
a related descent into the "underworld."[60] This is the noumenal nature
of phenomenon that Livesay expresses with elegance and a delicate,
strong ear.

In the 1970s and 1980s, Livesay combined magic, myth, and gender in a natural world full of politics. For instance, in "Barometer Falling," written in the 1970s, the speaker records the fall of Churchill, Roosevelt, Stalin, and Mao—"The world's witches have concocted / no magical power / against the dissolution of man."[61] Earlier in the poem she evoked Eliot and Yeats, and here is another declaration that the center would not hold. Humankind was melting in the forces of a real power beyond magic. At a more domestic level, "Roomers" describes with some irony a scene of a tenant's love life: "when she cries out / too ecstatically / I rattle my dishes or move from kitchen to bathroom / and flush the toilet."[62] In an embrace of winter, the speaker in "January Snow: A Letter," a poem from the 1980s, contrasts herself with the Winnipeggers who escape Christmas and winter in warmer climates: "I need Christmas / and icebound New Year's trees / cushioned in whole reefs / of snow."[63] The use of "reefs" is apt as snow in drifts is configured like the reefs in the Bahamas but are ghostly, pale, and frozen figures of the warm ridges beneath the pellucid waters. The last poem of this posthumous collection, "Anything Goes," also written in the 1980s, begins with a fine turn, with an ekphrastic and synecdochic moment: "A poem can be many things / in miniature."[64]

A poet's world is smaller than the world it describes, but it sometimes seems greater and more enduring than the harsh and busy world that ignores it. These moments in Livesay's poems speak in and beyond her life and times with fictional spaces as tropic, as heated, turning and twisting, as the reefs she describes, as green as the rain she evokes when the abuses of politics threaten to eclipse nature itself.

Margaret Atwood (b. 1939) expresses intricate identities as Dorothy Livesay does, but with another kind of distinction. Like Brand's later representation of the distances that mothers and predecessors find themselves in, Atwood, in the third poem of "Five Poems for Grandmothers," has her speaker recall "The time you stood / in the nineteenth century / on Yonge Street, a thousand / miles from home, with a brown purse / and a man stole it."[65] Perhaps the grandmother came from Nova Scotia to the center of Toronto: she is from another time and place and faced dangers and disappointments long before the poem or the speaker existed. In "Northrop Frye Observed," Atwood mentions that whereas Frye had spent his youth in New Brunswick, she had parents from Nova Scotia, so that their irony might have Puritan, New England, and Maritime roots (as mine partly does).[66]

Although the Maritime–New England border is a subtheme of my chapter, it is not the same as the other ironies of doubling, for instance that expressed by Anne Carson (b. 1950), who explores the double traditions of Judeo-Christianity and classical antiquity. Carson has her speaker in poem IX of "The Fall of Rome: A Traveller's Guide," say wryly: "Now although I hate to travel / I go a lot of places."[67] Car rides and reading can be two solitudes in the same space. Carson's "On Reading" talks about how some fathers like trips but not reading whereas some children have opposite tastes but find themselves in the same car: "I glimpsed the stupendous clear-cut shoulders of the Rockies from between paragraphs of Madame Bovary."[68] This, then, is also another kind of clear-cut (logging practice that leaves the land bald). Flaubert's novel has much to tell about relations between male and female but is also a product of a nineteenth-century France far from the modernity of the car and the distance of western North America. By the end of the poem, the speaker does begin to meld the images of body and nature as in a natural erotic.

Dualities, doubleness, division, typology, and other forms of here and there can involve a blurring and crossing of borders between subject and object, home and exile. Sense of place might well be less predictable in the prophecy of words. Male and female might differ more than from the double helix, and women in Canada differ greatly as individuals and from cultural group to group. The concern with here and there, home and exile, while taking on distinct forms, plays a key role in the poetry of women with connections to Canada, whether they have come from or are going to it, having been born or arrived there. Some part of Canada might be a part of their here and there, lived and imagined. For Native and Black women poets, the ghost of Columbus and those who followed, who would work or enslave Natives or Africans haunts Canada and its borderlands. Quite possibly they haunt us all, consciously and unconsciously. These women find different threads and words and refuse to take one version of history and story to allow neglect, abandonment, isolation, and, above all, memory and the present to be in someone else's hands or mouths. The ruins and riches of the remembered as well as the doubleness and multiplicity of words and experience allow these women to write and act. Perhaps, as a favorite poet of mine at school, Gwendolyn MacEwen (b. 1941), might suggest: "here" is like Mancini, the escape artist, or, as the title of another poem says, "There Is No Place to Hide," or, as she ends "The Discovery," "I mean the moment when it seems most plain / is the moment when you must begin again."[69] The meaning of this and other discoveries is one possibility in this and other possible and fictional worlds. Fictional worlds can be counterintuitive and even counterfactual or they can reflect or refract the world. Discovery is as much a translation of study as a translation of empire. There are different kinds of discovery. This chapter and book hope to suggest some among many possibilities.

Recognition involves seeing and insight, but it can also be refracted and deflected through ideology, culture, race, and gender. Finding what is home and what exile might mean, what is there and what is here becomes something far more difficult and doubtful than might be first thought or imagined. Perhaps there are so many neurons and threads that it is hard to know what the relations among eye, brain, and hand might be. Our experimental and theoretical discoveries and findings are constantly shifting in this regard. Recognition is a metaphor and a metaphysics, but it is also physical and cognitive. Writers represent their own theories and findings that might confirm or be at odds with scientific work in the area. Written texts and fictions are a kind of evidence that might help bring a recognition of recognition or complicate the matter further still. What is the status of fictional evidence or evidence from fiction? The law has legal fictions but is no less the law for having them. The richness of the work of these Canadian women poets makes the images, ideas, and metaphors more intricate, more than a figure in a carpet or a thread in a labyrinth. The Minotaur may have gone and Ariadne writes more than weeps on coasts far from Naxos. Perhaps she has sent Theseus packing.

CHAPTER FOUR

Writing and History: T.E. Lawrence and Bernard and Charlotte Shaw

Some historical figures also write. Caesar, Hitler, Stalin, Churchill, and others have been actors in and writers of history. This was true of Lawrence of Arabia, although his fame was not of the magnitude of the leaders I have just named (infamy in some cases). T.E. Lawrence (TEL) was subtler than many public figures and struggled with his own identity as a person and writer. His groping to understand himself—taking up the Socratic dictum—led him to try to explore and discover his own personality and his own role as a literary, public, and political person. The relation between recognition and misrecognition is particularly unclear for TEL as for those who would subsequently interpret him. An icon of culture and politics, Lawrence of Arabia continues to fascinate long after the First World War. Recognition of TEL is at once personal and political. TEL's life and writing embodied a sometimes backward-looking privilege and empire with the ideals of self-abnegation and sacrifice as well as a leading edge, modern introspection, and self-exploration. To recognize TEL in search of his own recognition is fraught with paradox and contradiction. The layers are tantalizing, but sometimes TEL, those about him, and his readers lean toward interpretation in the vein of Tantalus. Like the early explorers in Western European expansion from the fifteenth century, who were sailors, soldiers, merchants, and priests, a tension between the spiritual and the worldly occurs in TEL. A key question remains in the figures in my book, whether in art, life, or the human sciences: What is recognition and what is misrecognition and can the two ever be entirely separated?

There was something about TEL that strongly affected people who met him. This was true of the Shaws. In death, years after, he continues to have an effect on the living. After reading and thinking about TEL's correspondence in the crucial period from when the Shaws met TEL by accident in March 1922 to December 1926, when the subscription to *Seven Pillars of Wisdom* was complete and TEL was leaving for military service in India, I considered his impact as writer and private and public person. This is a period in which TEL is particularly inward looking and one in which he reveals much about his desire to be a writer and his attitude toward writing itself. For TEL, who was such an important historical figure in Arabia during the First World War, writing was something more than it could be for most of us. Perhaps Caesar, as Bernard Shaw (GBS) said hyperbolically, or Winston Churchill, someone TEL worked with and admired, could understand TEL both as man of action and writer.[1] Most of us do not affect both events and readers: TEL has done both and with greatness in both. If that was daunting for GBS, then only a fool might think it commonplace. That action–writing axis that TEL brought to his life after the War puzzled or challenged those about him. He would not accept being a war hero or a great writer, but, instead, sought to be an enlisted man in the military. Money and power, just when he was offered them, were prizes on which he turned his back.

Most of us do not lead heroic lives and in an age of irony, which TEL himself did not shy from in his letters to the Shaws, we do not always know what to make of heroism. Rather than denigrate it, which is the easy thing to do, I think it best to concentrate on the doubts, uncertainties, restlessness of TEL who found the heroism to be an ill-fitting jacket. He is a thoroughly modern figure who tried to wrestle with his unease, with the abyss between action and words, with the experiences he had to describe even when he did not want to do so. I have come to see that part of TEL's power as a letter writer is that he takes the reader where he or she might not want to go: if the reader is also a writer, then that reluctance doubles. But as he takes us somewhere estranged and placed at angles, TEL most often leaves a trace of perception or turns a piercing and beautiful phrase that makes the self-doubt and the drifting sorrow too telling to turn from.

Before I thought much about TEL but had been asked to write something about him, I was somehow drawn to think about his relation with the Shaws in terms of experience and place. Somehow, without knowing why, I did not think I could write about TEL's writing without taking into account something of him and at least one place he liked to visit; I didn't know that TEL's introspection, his explorations of the tensions between life and writing, would take me to my own places as well as his.

During the summer of 2000, I traveled to Shaw Corners, the house of Bernard and Charlotte Shaw, and asked whether there were any documents relating to TEL there. My children and I were told that most of the papers relating to TEL and the Shaws were in the British Library and we were taken to see a picture of TEL with his motorcycle. This was not the color Lawrence of Arabia of my own childhood, the piercing blues eyes of Peter O'Toole looking out from the screen, but a black-and-white photograph of a sturdier figure. This was my twin's introduction to TEL, the apparent chiaroscuro realism of a photograph, and the inverse opposite of my first contact with him. They might some day work their way to the romantic and dashing Lawrence of the film. So here we were at Shaw Corners, which was not so easy to get to, even now, as GBS himself led TEL to believe—there is a cow path of a road leading to the house part of the way despite its proximity to Hatfield and London, unless, of course, one was riding a bicycle (GBS's preferred means of transport) or a motorcycle (TEL's).

In a crucial period of his life after the Great War, TEL corresponded with the Shaws, and in many letters, one of which I will get to in a minute, he tells about his motorcycle. TEL was made for a motorbike, as if he had stumbled painfully on modernity itself, like those who discovered in the Great War that tanks were replacing horses. In a letter of January 30, 1923, TEL, writing to GBS about leaving the Royal Air Force (RAF), describes his "motor-bike": "It goes 80 miles an hour, and it is a perfect thing. I hope to eat it shortly . . . or rather, when regretfully I have to eat it. I hope it will last me a very long time."[2] The context for this wry remark, after noting the sheer power of the machine, is TEL's coming to terms with life after the Great War, his enlistment in the RAF, his desire to make a living and to earn something from his writing, and his decision whether and how to publish *The Seven Pillars*, his account of the war in Arabia.[3]

The motorbike on the mantle in Shaw Corners was not, then, simply an emblem of a war hero but an insertion into a narrative about TEL as a writer. Without realizing it, I had stumbled on a Lawrence I did not know really existed: Peter O'Toole's Lawrence was not, for the child I was when it first came out, a writer but a hero on a motorbike under the deep blue of the desert sky. O'Toole's eyes were like that sky. My children were experiencing TEL and the Shaws differently: they saw the famous small rotating shed in which GBS wrote in search of the light. One of the reasons the Shaws were interested in Lawrence was because he was a writer of distinction with a distinct story to tell. Lawrence himself wasn't always as sure of his role as a writer, as he agonized over *The Seven Pillars*, to the Shaws. How much of this was a pose and how much involved serious self-doubts is at first hard to say.

What was being seen, elided, eluded, recognized in TEL as person, writer, hero? Here is a man who spoke of something that plunged him into the wind at eighty miles an hour in a world that did not move that fast but who worried about plunging himself into a life of words even as he saw himself as a historian and would be a writer, like GBS himself. In what follows, I would like to explore this indecision and decision to be a writer and his correspondence with Bernard and Charlotte Shaw in a crucial period when he was coming to terms with this ambivalence over writing. This hero might not have a thousand faces, but TEL reveals and conceals many sides, often in conflict, in his relation to the Shaws, who as writers and editors knew much about the professions of writing and publishing, which in turn were part of a dialogue on writing.

4.1   A Writer and Not

On July 22, 1922, TEL wrote to GBS asking him to read a long book he had printed but not published: *Seven Pillars of Wisdom*. TEL's ambivalent attitude toward his work—he realized its importance but was disgusted by it—comes out in the letter. TEL claims "I am not a writer, and successfully passed the age of 30 without having wanted to write anything."[4] But he portrays himself as feeling compelled to have written the book:

> I was brought up as a professional historian, which means the worship of original documents. To my astonishment, after peace came I found I was myself the sole person who knew what had happened in Arabia during the war: and the only literate person in the Arab Army. So it became a professional duty to record what happened.[5]

To some extent, I think it is right to take these words at face value. He did feel, at times, as if his writing were more of a duty than an opportunity. In his correspondence with the Shaws, in his dealings with publishers, and in his choice to turn his back on a fellowship at All Soul's, Oxford, for a life as an enlisted soldier, TEL repeatedly chose a route that was not opportunistic, comfortable, easy, or profitable.

What also arises in this first letter to GBS is TEL's forthrightness, modesty, and self-effacing nature that verges on self-denigration. TEL is rare: he knows how difficult it is to write well: "the job became too much for me."[6] There is, especially in TEL's correspondence with Charlotte Shaw over the next four years, a certain *agon* with GBS, the great writer of an earlier generation, an agon that is never far from the surface, even if that contest is most affectionate in tone. In this first letter to GBS, TEL wrote: "*Your* first book was not perfect, though it was a subject you had chosen for yourself, and you had an itch to write!"[7] TEL says that he himself has cut down to his own size and stitched together "second-hand words," "borrowed expressions and adjectives from everybody I have ever read," and has included "a lot of half-baked thinking."[8] While Lawrence is attacking his own writing, he also undermines his own military claims: "I'm not the least a proper soldier."[9] But paradoxically, in his correspondence with the Shaws in this crucial period, TEL again and again tries to establish himself both as a proper writer and soldier.

It is hard to imagine what GBS made of this letter, but, to give him credit, he ignored its convolutions and responded. But before I proceed to GBS, I wish to return to TEL's labyrinthine shifts in tone and syntax. He dwelt in doubt and in conditional clauses: "If you read my thing, it will show you that your prefaces have been written in vain, if I'm a fair sample of my generation."[10] In case GBS were to think that this "thing" were amusing, it is not: "it's long-winded, and pretentious, and dull to the point where I can no longer bear to look at it myself. I chose that moment to have it printed!"[11] TEL obviously understood irony and had some flair for the theatrical. Still, the self-criticism is striking; this tact is hardly the stuff of self-promotion.

And just when the convolution seems to be reaching a threshold, TEL adds a few extra twists, leaving such a maze that even GBS might have been perplexed. The letter bears reading whole, but here is a long paragraph that gives some indication of what TEL was building up to:

> You'll wonder why, if all this is true (and I think it is) I want any decent person (still more a person like yourself)* [*ambiguous: but I wanted to avoid expressing my liking for your work.] to read it. Well it's because it is history, and I'm shamed for ever if I am the sole chronicler of an event, and fail to chronicle it: and yet unless what I've written can be made better I'll burn it. My own disgust with it is so great that I no longer believe it worth trying to improve (or possible to improve). If you read it or part of it and came to the same conclusion, you would give me courage to strike the match: whereas now I distrust my own judgement, and it seems cruel to destroy a thing on which I have worked my hardest for three years. While if you said that parts were rubbish, and other parts not so bad, and parts of it possible (and distinguished those parts variously) then your standards might enable me to clear up mine, and give energy enough to tackle the job again. (If you say it

is all possible then I will reluctantly get rid of your own books from my shelves.)[12]

These shifts are dizzying. First, TEL returns to his reason for publishing the work: it is the only history of these events. He then attempts to bond with GBS as a reader but also to try to guess his reaction and almost to coerce it. Would he really be disappointed if GBS said that the book was all good? GBS is supposed to be TEL's "judgement" but TEL is almost coercing that judgment even as he gives him apparent freedom in a series of conditionals and concessive clauses. And even though he had already met the Shaws by chance at their London flat earlier that year, TEL seems to be wrestling with their reputation. Despite his shifts, however, TEL is also forthright: the book disgusts him, but it would be cruel to destroy something "on which I have worked my hardest for three years." If TEL is ambiguous, as he says, about GBS, that ambiguity and ambivalence extends to his view of himself and his labors. TEL is not hiding behind the more usual stance of the uncertain and unpublished writer: I just dashed this off and I don't really care what happens to it.

Poor GBS. But he could handle himself. He might have felt that he was on the front lines and Lawrence of Arabia had him in some intricate trap. The end of the letter closes in ever-smaller circles:

All this is very unfair—or would be, if you knew me: but deleting that twenty minutes with Cockerell we are utter strangers, and likely to remain so, and therefore there is no pressure on you to answer this letter at all. I won't be in the least astonished (indeed I'll write another of the same sort to a man called Orage whom I have never met, but whose criticism I enjoy): and my opinion of you will go up. Yours with many apologies.

T.E. Lawrence.

Incidentally: I don't want people to know the book exists. So whether you reply or not, I hope you will not talk of it.[13]

GBS is treated with great intimacy and then is told he is a stranger and does not need to respond and that besides TEL was going to contact a critic he had not met. TEL also says that GBS will go up in his estimation if he does not respond, but why write the letter in the first place? If TEL does not want anyone to know about the existence of his book, why is he writing GBS and is thinking about writing Orage? Perhaps TEL wants to try his luck with some influential readers without the public knowing about the project. This letter would leave most people, except GBS, breathless, exhausted, and speechless.

In his reply of August 25, 1922, GBS drops formalities and really ignores the multitude of shifts in TEL's letter. He makes two points:

> There is not the smallest doubt (within human limits) that any publisher would jump at your book on Arabia; and there is no doubt at all that the book, having forced itself from you, will be published with whatever imperfections its mortal lot may involve, whether you like it or not.
>
> Second, as man to man. It will be pure waste of *your* time for me to read your book before you send it to press; but it would not waste mine, as I shall read it sooner or later.[14]

Attempting to stick to the point and have TEL focus on the business of bringing his book out, GBS seems also to have tried not to become involved with the intricacies of TEL's emotional state. He built him up and urged him to use his time wisely. Moreover, GBS wanted to put TEL at ease. Near the end of his brief letter, he sets out a more informal relation (just as he did in his form of address—"My dear Lawrence (to drop ceremony)"—to begin the letter): "You need not stand on any ceremony with us. You are a privileged soul, and can deal with both of us as with old friends."[15] GBS spoke both for himself and for his wife, Charlotte, who was in Ireland and had only noted the meeting with TEL in her diary in March but had not corresponded with him.

Not surprisingly, TEL, on August 27, 1922, continued his contrary ways. He mimics GBS's "First" and "second" construction and under-lines the words. Then he quibbles about GBS's use of "privilege": "and as you say I'm privileged, I'll try it: though it's an unwholesome state to live in: and I don't think I won there on my own efforts."[16] His doubt about his massive manuscript precedes by a few sentences his skepticism over his status as a war hero. There is enough modesty and self-doubt to fill many vessels; and this doubling doubt persists.

But for all the dizzying and difficult shifts, TEL does show some admirable self-awareness and an ability to put together in suggestive ways war and peace, the poet and soldier, these aspects of his life and writing that pressed upon him. In this same letter he mentions that GBS was to be one of six people to read the book and why that was:

> You see the war was, for us who were in it, an overwrought time, in which we lost our normal footing. I wrote this thing in the war

atmosphere, and believe that it is stinking with it. Also there is a good deal of cruelty, and some excitement. All these things, in a beginner's hands, tend to force him over the edge, and I suspect there is much over-writing. You have the finest cure for flatulence, and I have great hopes that you will laugh at parts of what I meant to be solemn: and if I can get at you before you have forgotten which they are, then I'll have a chance to make it better.[17]

Except for the self-satire, which might be a little too self-conscious, TEL's attempt to make sense of the war through writing and revision is understandable. His self-critical stance here is laudable, for he did not blind himself with the glory of his reputation as a soldier or assume that writing was easy and a reward for his heroic actions. This passage is one of the key places in TEL's letters: he knew he was overwrought; he saw the cruelty in war; he suspected that the experience of the war had, in places, adversely affected his writing. Even his ironic and satirical laughter at his own pretensions, as awkward or maddening as it could sometimes be, suggested a person who was not interested in becoming pompous or in believing the myth that he had become. This humility was a quest for the marriage of his experience as a soldier and as a writer, sometimes achieved through the disciplining power of irony and satire directed toward himself. It was also something that he attempted to live as well as accomplish in his writing, revisions, and discussions of his experience as a soldier and as a writer. TEL did not accept the honors offered to him; instead, he sought be an enlisted man. This became, in all its complications, an attempt to be a plain soldier, an ordinary man. In his writing, TEL did not seek the riches GBS said he could have with *Seven Pillars*. This behavior, as puzzling as it was to GBS and other contemporaries and perhaps to some among us now, might have been owing in part to being overwrought and in part to being on a kind of spiritual quest for atonement. It is not easy to turn one's back on honors, position, wealth, and fame as TEL did. He could never quite escape them, however, and his correspondence with the Shaws shows his attempts to follow the daily routine of a soldier with one modest goal: to get his book out into the world in a form that pleased him.

In a letter to GBS of September 30, 1922, Lawrence tries to sound breezy about his leaving the Colonial Office and enlisting in the R.A.F.: "It's a cleaner living than Eastern politics, and I haven't a busman's wages of my own, so must do something."[18] TEL's aversion to Eastern politics is understandable, but that Winston Churchill dismissed him penniless is highly doubtful.[19] Lawrence seems rather to have chosen his lot: his ongoing quest to be an ordinary man in the armed forces.

This is where Charlotte Shaw enters the scene once again. GBS had given Charlotte *Seven Pillars* to read. In a letter to Sydney Cockerell of November 24,1922, Charlotte Shaw talks about "a wonderful MS that has been given to us to read by someone you brought to see us."[20] Although Charlotte says she was sworn to secrecy, she gives enough of a hint that it would not be hard for Cockerell to guess TEL's identity. This is just one indication of how hard it was for TEL to become obscure and why GBS thought that this was a perverse game, precisely because it was impossible.

In a letter of November 30, 1922, TEL says he was afraid that GBS was delaying because he did not wish to tell him that *Seven Pillars* is "rubbish," and that if GBS wished to think it "rot" then TEL would "agree with you and cackle with pleasure at finding my judgement doubled."[21] GBS replied, ignoring once more TEL's irony, and explained why he had not had a chance to read all of TEL's great tome: "My wife seized it first, and ploughed through from Alpha to Omega. It took months and months and months; but it carried her through."[22] A wit with his own store of irony, GBS acknowledges TEL's genius but admits his own bafflement before it. He also hints at the apparent high-mindedness and impracticality of TEL's own attitude toward *Seven Pillars* and its appearance in print:

> However, I know enough about it now to feel rather puzzled as to what is to be done with it. That, you may say, is your business; but the Life Force will take it out of your hands. Obviously there are things in it that you cannot publish. Yet many of them are things that WONT die. It would cost you too much to engrave the book on plates of gold, and bury it somewhere for somebody to dig up and start in business as a prophet.[23]

GBS suggests sealing the book so the Trustees of the British Museum can open it in a hundred years and supports his case with examples from Charles Dickens and Oscar Wilde, suggesting thereby that he considers TEL's work to be worthy of the best literary company. GBS leaves little doubt about how important he thinks *Seven Pillars* is: "It is one of the Cheop's pyramids of literature and history."[24] Clearly, GBS understands the significance of TEL as a writer and historian. GBS also sees TEL as a great man: "You are evidently a very dangerous man: most men who are any good are: there is no power for good that is not also a power for evil."[25] While suggesting that TEL also provide an abridgement for "general circulation," he compares him to Caesar.[26] In TEL's reply, on December 7, 1922, he states his admiration for Caesar's *Commentaries* but contrasts his own confessional style to its restraint: "They are the antithesis of mine: indeed I suspect that no successful general ever spilled so much of himself on to paper as I did."[27] TEL then mentions his enlisting in the ranks of the RAF, which he continues to maintain he did for money and that, should the abridgment be successful, he will abandon the service: "If so I'll become a civilian again. You have no idea how repulsive a barrack is as permanent home. It reconciles me to the meanness of the abridgement."[28] In fact, TEL often praises the service as a means to earn a basic wage and stay out of public view, a kind of monastic reflection on, or even penitence for, the war and the trying aftermath of working for the terms of peace. His enlistment as an ordinary serviceman is a contentious point for which TEL, even as here in the same letter, often shifts motives.

GBS continues discussing with TEL the publication of *Seven Pillars*. GBS tries hard to place the book with his own publishers, Constables, telling TEL about his meeting with the two senior partners there, and in his letter of December 17, 1922, quotes himself in this dramatic exchange: " 'Why in thunder didn't you secure it? It's the greatest book in the world.' "[29] Although GBS hears for the first time about Edward Garnett's abridgment, a draft of which was almost completed at this time, and would have known that this abridger was also a reader for the rival firm of Jonathan Cape, he nevertheless tries to change TEL's mind and have him shift it to Constables as part of an ambitious scheme:

> I then expatiated on the qualities of the work, and said that it really ought to be published in the good old eighteenth century style in twelve volumes or so to begin with, the abridgement coming afterwards. This is not at all so impossible as it would have been ten years ago; for people are buying very expensive books now on an unprecedented scale, whilst my early novels in Constable's shilling series have gone out of print for the moment because cheap books do not sell.[30]

GBS mentions Garnett and says that Otto Kyllmann, one of the partners to whom he had alluded, had found out that Garnett was acting privately as an abridger and not as a reader for a publisher already selected.[31] GBS pulls out all the stops in order to convince TEL to go with Constables. In fact, TEL was keenly interested in printing and publishing, almost so much so that they were as much a part of his interest in books as writing. For over a decade before TEL met the Shaws, he had had a particular interest in printing and the making of books. GBS and TEL discussed these bookish matters at length.

GBS's gentle and wry exasperation over TEL's new life in the military sums up how many, in Lawrence's lifetime and afterward, have been puzzled by his strange maneuver. As this is such a key aspect of Lawrence's life and mediates between the writer and the soldier, the hero and the man, its full rhetorical weight should be experienced whole:

> Your letter is more impressive than explicit. If I knew nothing else about you I should conclude that you were a depressed mechanic oiling up fuselages for profanely abusive pilots, and sleeping six in a bed with a hundred other such castaways. As it is, I can only pity the staff. Nelson, slightly cracked after his whack on the battle of the Nile, coming home and insisting on being placed at the tiller of a canal barge, and on being treated as nobody in particular, would have embarrassed the Navy far less. A callow and terrified Marbot, placed in command of a sardonic Napoleon after Austerlitz and Jena, would have felt much as your superior officers must in command of Lawrence the great, the mysterious, save in whom there is no majesty and might. The thing is ridiculous. Why in name of all that is sane did you not get £20,000 from parliament? It was yours for anybody else's asking, if you rule out your own; and you should have demanded it as your obvious right.
>
> You talk about leave as if it were a difficulty. Ask for three months leave and they will exclaim, with a sob of relief, "For God's sake, take six, take twelve, take a lifetime, take anything rather than keep up this maddening masquerade that makes us all ridiculous." I sympathize with them. If you must be Cincinnatus, go and farm. If you must be Garibaldi, live at Caprera instead of putting poor Aldershot out of countenance.
>
> Of course you know your own affairs worst; so I tell you how they strike me. Also, damn it, I want to know the other half of what you have told me. One can guess nothing about a man capable of anything, like Habbakuk. Are you a flying officer or a bloke in a military office? It would be so like you to be charading as an office boy. Distractedly,
>
> G. Bernard Shaw[32]

That TEL was able to answer this letter, even at times obliquely, is to his credit. Although there was bluster in GBS's flattering but penetrating satire, it would not be easy to respond to such a letter.

4.2   From the Shaws' Lawrence to the
Posthumous Film and Back Again

To have GBS bearing down on one's life and letters would be difficult for the most sturdy and accomplished writer. Considering what TEL had been through and how vulnerable he seems to have felt at the time, it is remarkable how strong and forthright he was with GBS. It is also telling that TEL addresses GBS's comments on his writing before those on his life.

In the film, "Lawrence of Arabia," the audience is witness to Lawrence's death and funeral, but not his youth, his days as an archeologist before the war, his negotiations at the Paris Peace Talks, or his years an enlisted man. There is no rising or falling action, only the climax of Lawrence in Arabia. There is no explanation about how he got there or what it did to him, only a suggestion that it changed him utterly and terribly, like the wound or *hamartia* that the hero sees in an anagnorisis, a Greek tragedy in the desert that the classically trained TEL, schoolboy and undergraduate in Oxford, would have recognized.

Cast a little differently, David Lean's story of Lawrence is like epic, romance, and the novel translated into film. The grand narrative of Lawrence's life is not unlike Lean's other movies based on the journey of a strong central character: "Great Expectations" (1946), "Oliver Twist" (1948), "The Bridge on the River Kwai" (1957), "Dr. Zhivago" (1965), and "A Passage to India" (1984). These are stories of coming of age, education, war, revolution, and empire, great sweeping tales where heroes live, even if ambiguously, in tangled gardens, streetscapes, or exotic landscapes. Lean's Lawrence is a great adventurer and soldier who is too sensitive or vulnerable to the conflict he so daringly mastered, a paradox of a liberator and avenger caught between freedom for the Arabs and British imperial ambitions, a great military strategist driven mad in war and by torture or rape, perhaps propelled even to war crimes, and spit out by politicians who no longer had any use for him. This is the Lawrence I knew as a child, from the movie, the tall blue-eyed O'Toole rather than the small but athletic historical Lawrence. This TEL of history had to answer GBS, something that the film, as epic as it is, does not attempt to represent. It is hard to put Doctor Faustus in a tale about Tamburlaine, or to mix Hamlet with Henry the Fifth.

In a letter of December 27, 1922, TEL seizes on GBS's phrase about *Seven Pillars*, that it's a "great book," which is actually TEL's moderating rendition of GBS's hyperbole: "it's the greatest book in the world."[33] Lawrence, whose long-standing interest in printing is manifest in the subscribers' edition of *Seven Pillars*, takes up his own version of GBS's description of the volume in terms of its layout and theme:

> But you say that it's a great book. Physically, yes: in subject, yes: an outsider seeing the inside of a national movement is given an enormous subject: but is it good in treatment? I care very much for this, as it's been my ambition all my life to write something intrinsically good. I can't believe that I've done it, for it's the hardest thing in the world, and I've had such success in other lines that it's greedy to expect goodness in so technical a matter.[34]

This is the core of the TEL I have come to know, or think I know. Whereas this Lawrence does not necessarily contradict the Lawrence of popular legend, which the film so aptly represents. It complicates this "Arabian prince" met in *medias res* as if the before and after barely mattered, as if the image of Lawrence could rob him of his childhood and his maturity.

TEL continues to GBS, taking up the matter of writing: "However your phrase makes me hope a bit: will you let me know your honest opinion as to whether it is well done or not?"[35] The phrase is TEL's downsizing of GBS's praise, even if he attributes the phrasing to GBS, as his earlier elision from "greatest" to "great" to "good" stressed the more. Humility and self-doubt are blended in this strategy of breaking down GBS's accolade. TEL then proceeds with a recreation of his technique of writing and the gap between desire and performance in the creation:

> When I was actually writing it I got worked up and wrote hardly: but in the between-spells the whole performance seemed miserable, and when I finished it I nearly burned the whole thing for the third time. The contrast between what I meant and felt I could do, and the truth of what my weakness had let me do was so pitiful.[36]

What TEL realizes is how difficult writing is, something that does not always occur to those with lesser expectations than his. His inability to reach his ideal was a "weakness," a "flaw" that was "pitiful." I am not suggesting that TEL had Aristotle's *Poetics* in mind when writing this sentence, but this recognition is a catharsis without a catharsis. TEL is both the character in the tale and the reader following the story of a flawed hero, a hero who suffers from pity if not terror.

The agon of writing is something that TEL says that he acknowledges but avoids. To GBS, he confesses:

> You see, there's that feeling at the back of my mind that if I really tried, sat down and wrung my mind out, the result would be on an altogether higher plane. I funk this extreme effort, for I half-killed myself as it was, doing the present draft: and I'd willingly dodge out of it.[37]

Here is someone who was an avid student before he was a soldier, and he is returning to his prewar aspirations to become a scholar and a writer. He who had faced so much danger now faced himself and found the specter of writing before him. The writing of history, especially through autobiography, had a hardship of its own.

Part of the unrest resides in the relation between the personal and the general in history: "Isn't it treated wrongly? I mean, shouldn't it be objective, without the first-person singular? And is there any style in my writing at all? Anything recognizably individual?"[38] The paradox is this: he desires objectivity through the expression of his own personality, through his own individual style. The autobiographical "I" rests uneasily with the third-person point of view of history.

Then there is in this letter TEL's move to printing and publication, which also suggests the intricate shifts of his motives, mind, and character. Printing, publishing, and the decision to take a profit or not from his writings on the Arab campaign are themes that recur through TEL's postwar correspondence. His view on the question of writing for profit is particularly convoluted and contradictory. We have already seen him deny to GBS any desire to make money from the Arabian writings, but here he considers it:

> About business. Curtis Brown—or rather Savage, his manager, served me in the war, and is doing my money-worries on the usual 10% terms. I hate business, and would be child's play for any publisher. I believe Cape, a new publisher of the respectable sort (he runs that divine book of extracts from yourself) is the first in the running for my thing: but I've told Savage that I want £300 a year, to live on, and have left it at that, with only two conditions, a. that I have the last word as to type, paper and format. b. that it be royalty, not an out and out sale. It's good of you to have worked up Meredith to the point of offering, and I'll tell Savage about it: but Garnett reads for Cape, and liked parts of the book: so that Cape has a special wish for it. I fancy film and serial rights are worth more

than royalties: and my only motive in publishing a scrap of the book is money: so that I'm as bad as Butterworth in the matter.[39]

He disclaims any interest in or knowledge of business, but seems keenly aware of it. So often in his letters TEL disclaims any profit motive for *Seven Pillars* or any of his writings about the Arab campaign, but here he offers it as a motivation. Usually coupled with this disclaimer about profit is his justification for enlisting because the armed services will pay him a wage, which he needs in order to subsist. Shaw was convinced that Lawrence had manufactured his own money problems by stubbornly deflecting and rejecting all honors and financial rewards, but TEL here denies this: "So far from getting £20,000 from Parliament I had the utmost difficulty in getting my gratuity of £110 from the War Office when they mobilised me. I'm not such a figure as you think."[40] TEL's army file, released in 1998, seems to bear TEL's claim.[41] As the letters between TEL and GBS bear out, GBS himself would go on a campaign to try to get TEL a war honor or pension. As generous as this was, nothing came of it. The British government did not always see the Caesar in TEL that the author of *Caesar and Cleopatra* did.

The armed forces were not simply a means of getting away from painful memories and an intruding press and of setting up a spiritual exercise in daily routine, although this is often the case TEL makes in his correspondence—implicitly and explicitly. In the next part of this letter of December 17, 1922, to GBS, TEL says "You ask for details of what I'm doing in the RAF. Today I scrubbed the kitchen out in the morning, and loafed all the afternoon, and spent the evening writing to G. B. S."[42] The deeper the reader gets into this paragraph, the more one sees the hero as penitent and wonders what is his relation to money and influence. The scene swings back and forth between the realm of ideas, motorbike rides, and conversations and details of menial chores: "Yesterday I washed up the dishes in the sergeants' mess in the morning (messy feeders, sergeants: plates were all butter and tomato sauce, and the washing water was cold) and rode to Oxford in the afternoon on my motor-bike, and called on Hogarth to discuss the abridgement of the Arabian book."[43] This is the prose of a skilled writer who has talent for the scene, historical, actual, and even novelistic. From butter and tomato sauce in cold washing water TEL moves to his motorcycle ride to Oxford and the Ashmolean Museum, where his old mentor and friend, D.G. Hogarth, was Keeper. This is a transportation from the mess to the museum, in which the one-time colonel and war hero, TEL, becomes a private because of some kind of need for atonement and serves men who would have served him, and travels back, probably riding swiftly as he liked to, on a motorbike, considering his past campaigns in Arabia through a future publication with a man he had met in 1910 at about the age of 22. Thus, TEL's journey to Oxford from the officer's mess, which he describes for GBS, was a journey backward and forward.

After describing this trip to Oxford to meet Hogarth, TEL then returns to his routine in the military:

> It being Christmas we do fatigues in the morning, and holiday in the afternoon. Normally I'm an "aerial photographer under training": it doesn't mean flying, but developing the officers' negatives after they land: and the "under-training" part means that I'm a recruit, and therefore liable to all sorts of mis-employment. For three weeks I was an errand-boy, I've also been dustman, and clerk, and pig-stye-cleaner, and housemaid, and scullion, and camp-cinema-attendant. Anything does for airmen-recruits: but the life isn't so bad, when the first crudeness works off.[44]

In his letter of September 30, 1922, TEL had told GBS of his enlistment and had claimed it was "a cleaner living than Eastern politics."[45] TEL had a good job but decided to resign and enlist; his decision was more than financial, whatever pretexts he offered. In some ways he seems to have taken pleasure in his life: "We have a bed each, and suffer all sorts of penalties unless they are 25 inches apart: twelve of us in a room. Life is very common, besides being daily. Much good humour, very little wit, but a great friendliness. They treat my past as a joke, and forgive it me lightly. The officers fight shy of me: but I behave demurely, and give no trouble."[46] Military training and monastic life are not that far apart: they are exercises of disciplining the will in order to make the body, mind, and soul fit; they are austere and communal; they can bring joy in hardship. In TEL's letters the reader can observe this life as something that keeps him sane and happy with its simple repetition and regulation, and that cleanses his mind and spirit by making him physically fit through wearying labor. He has to humble himself in order that the officers will leave him be. This letter, then, moves from TEL as writer to printer/businessman to serviceman: it brings him back to earth. Paradoxically, as that great self-publicist GBS would have noted, this very sainthood was a means of making TEL into a myth. As he denied the world, it sought him out.

The British Press Association's story of December 28, 1922 about TEL's enlistment reads as much as an advertisement as an apologia. Concerning TEL, it declares: "The reason given by him for the change is that he wishes to have quiet and rest to write the concluding chapters of his book of memoirs. The opening chapters of this book, which will tell for the first time many unrecorded incidents of his adventures in Arabia and Palestine, were written at the suggestion of an Oxford friend, Captain Raymond Savage, of Messrs. Curtis and Brown, and the complete volume will be published by Mr. Jonathan Cape."[47] This excerpt begins with what is probably a sincere motive on TEL's part, but it shifts, in recounting the genesis of the project, to a puffing of the book. The world would not let this "saint" alone anymore than it would Saint Joan, something GBS was probably already thinking about for his play on that soldier-saint.

4.3   The Shavian Belief in Lawrence

In response to that story GBS wrote TEL the same day: "The cat being now let out of the bag, presumably by Jonathan Cape with your approval, I cannot wait to finish the book before giving you my opinion, and giving it strong. IT MUST BE PUBLISHED IN ITS ENTIRETY, UNABRIDGED."[48] GBS still hoped that Constables would publish *Seven Pillars* whole and then produce an abridgement if Cape would not. Shaw also introduces his wife Charlotte: "My wife, who believes fanatically in your genius, wants to know why you withdrew your preface to Doughty's book."[49] It is clear from the beginning that Charlotte helped promote TEL to her husband. GBS returns to business, and offers TEL this warning: "The truth is I am anxious lest you should have committed yourself already. I had ten years on the managing committee of the society of authors, and learnt that there is no bottom to the folly and business incompetence of authors or to the unscrupulousness of publishers, who, being in a gambling business where one live book has to pay for ten duds, cannot afford to lose a single opportunity."[50] For whatever reason, GBS was too late. TEL either did not want to make any money on *Seven Pillars* or had been so impractical as to ensure that he would not make anything from it.

At this time, TEL was thirty-four years old and the Shaws were in their mid-sixties. Charlotte Shaw's response to TEL is strong. Her letter of December 31, 1922, considering her age and her standing, is touching in its modesty:

> If you've been "mad keen" to hear about your book I've been mad keen to write about it ever since I read it, or rather ever since I began to read it, and I simply haven't dared. I got from it an impression of you as an Immense Personality soaring in the blue (of the Arabian

skies) far above my lowly sphere, and that anything I could say in the way of admiration, or comment, or question, could only be an impertinence. But the latest developments of your career have been so startlingly unexpected, and your letters so human, that I take my courage in both hands and send you a word.[51]

From the grace and aptness of these words, it becomes clear that there were two writers in the Shaw marriage. The humane nature of Charlotte (or C.F.S. as she signs her letter) also comes out in this passage. She praises Lawrence sincerely, but she, like her husband with whom she had obviously been "communicating" concerning TEL and the letters he sent GBS, also wants TEL to settle down and realize how capable he is.

CFS actually picks up on the GBS–TEL exchange on *Seven Pillars* as a "great book." Like TEL himself, she is an active close reader and picks out phrases, as in pursuing an *explication de texte*, to interpret:

How is it *conceivable, imaginable* that a man who could write the *Seven Pillars* can have any doubts about it? If you don't know it is "a great book" what is the use of anyone telling you so. I believe (although he has never said anything of the sort) that G.B.S. thinks you are "pulling his leg" when you ask him. I devoured the book from cover to cover as soon as I got hold of it. I could not stop. I drove G.B.S. almost mad by insisting upon reading him special bits when he was deep in something else. I am an old woman, old enough at any rate to be your mother; I have met all sorts of men and women of the kind that are called distinguished; I have read their books and discussed them with them; but I have never read anything like this; I don't believe anything really like it has been written before. When I find in your letter such suggestions as "should it be without the first person singular?" "Is there any style in my writing?" "Anything recognisably individual"? I think—are you laughing at us! Why, foolish man, it *could* only have been written in the first person singular: it is one of the most amazingly individual documents that has ever been written: there is no "style" because it is above and beyond anything so silly.[52]

What more could Lawrence hope for: he had GBS and CFS, the Shaws, telling him his book was a singular wonder. CFS took up where GBS left off, saying, "Your book must be published as a whole," "*don't leave out the things an ordinary man would leave out*," and ending with a recommendation that Constables would do the whole book and do it right.[53]

CFS had not liked Cape's takeover of her selections of GBS, first given to her friend A.C. Fifield, who went out of business, and so she had her own motives for pushing Constables.

But Lawrence being Lawrence, or Ross, and later Shaw, was found out, and, in a letter of January 2, 1923, tells GBS that because the *Daily Express* exposed his enlistment, he was going to change tack: "I felt that to publish anything now might look as though I were using the RAF as an advertising stunt. So I've cancelled Cape's contract (fortunately not completed, and so I hope there will be no damages to pay) and have told him that nothing is to appear this year."[54] Signing himself, T.E.L., Lawrence presents an identity that is shifting at this point—as he tells GBS: "I'm going to wash out that old name, which has too many war associations to please me: and which isn't my real name, any more than Ross!"[55]

GBS will have none of this. Taking up where CFS left off, GBS uses his considerable talent for satire to awaken TEL to his own situation and identity:

> Like all heroes, and, I must add, all idiots, you greatly exaggerate your power of moulding the universe to your personal convictions. You have just had a crushing demonstration of the utter impossibility of hiding or disguising the monster you have created. It is useless to protest that Lawrence is not your real name. That will not save you. You may be registered as Higg the son of Snell or Brian de Bois Guilbert or anything else; and if you had only stuck to it or else kept quiet, you might be Higg or Brian still. But you masqueraded as Lawrence and didn't keep quiet; and now Lawrence you will be to the end of your days, and thereafter to the end of what we call modern history. Lawrence might be as great a nuisance to you sometimes as G.B.S. is to me, or as Frankenstein found the man he had manufactured; but you created him, and must now put up with him as best you can.[56]

Shaw underscores TEL's responsibility for self-promotion and myth making. TEL himself created Lawrence of Arabia and called attention to himself, so he cannot dodge his creation just because it is inconvenient or he is weary of the role. This self-conscious theatricality cannot be turned off once the drama has been produced on the public stage. Once the persona has been let out in the public domain and in history the creator cannot control it and must put up with the good and the bad.

As CFS did, in a letter of January 4, 1923, GBS also hammers at publishing the book unabridged and at "style" as something to put aside.[57] CFS and GBS both assure TEL that he is above worries over style and is a writer of the highest order. GBS faces the question of writing head on:

> As to style, what have you got to do with such dilettanti rubbish, any more than I have? You have something to say; and you say it as accurately and vividly as you can; and when you have done that you do not go fooling with your statement with the notion that if you do it over five or six times you will do it five or six times better. You set it up, and correct its inevitable slips in proof. Then you get a revise and go over your corrections to see they fit in properly and that you have not dropped one stitch in mending another. Then you pass for press; and there you are. The result has a certain melody and a certain mannerism which is your style, of which you are no more aware than you are of the taste of the water that is always in your mouth.[58]

So TEL finds himself debating style with one of the greatest stylists in the language who tells him there is no hothouse plant called Style. TEL is also engaged in an exchange with a person who sees writing in terms of the printing process, as he does, but from a jarringly different vantage. GBS actually uses the word "gibe" to characterize what he has done to disabuse TEL of his inflated illusions.[59]

GBS also has a knack for connecting the different aspects of TEL: war hero, writer, enlisted man, gifted publicist. He will not accept TEL's separation of these roles in time or by category. *Seven Pillars* provides GBS with a way into this analysis:

> Now as to the book just as it is. You will no more be able to get rid of it, or play about it with it, than with Lawrence. It is another Frankenstein monster; and you must make up your mind to do the will of Allah, in whose hand you were only a pen. You say that to publish anything now might look as though you were using the RAF as an advertising stunt. Considering that you have already used the whole Arab race and the New Testament and the entire armies of all the countries engaged in the war to advertize yourself (since you take that view of it), I do not see why you should have a sudden fit of bashfulness of the lady in reduced circumstances who cried laces in the street but hoped that nobody heard her.[60]

There is a great deal to what GBS says. GBS points the moral—publish the book straight away—and tries once more to land it for Constable.[61] This latter aim is instrumental but it does not take away from the good sense of GBS's argument. He is also probably right that the RAF would not necessarily mind the leak as it would advertise the force. But TEL has forgotten an important aspect of public spectacle that GBS, as a dramatist, could not: "And the people have their rights too, in this matter. They want you to appear always in glory, crying, 'This is I, Lawrence, Prince of Mecca!' To live under a cloud is to defame God."[62] TEL, like many later celebrities, wanted the celebration of his persona on his own terms, the notoriety without being notorious. He wanted to be famous with a great deal of privacy. This is like Oscar Wilde's well-known quip that there is only one thing worse than being talked about and that is not being talked about. Apparently, TEL wanted to be talked about but left alone. Sometimes. The complexity of TEL's personality, as GBS himself realized, makes any definitive interpretation difficult.

That complexity makes itself known in his response to CFS in a letter of January 8, 1923. Although TEL was obviously pleased by her praise, he will not yield. The letter opens:

> It's a wonderful letter, that of yours, and I've liked it beyond measure: though my doubts as to the virtues of the *Seven Pillars* remain: indeed I'd be an insufferable creature if I was sure of it, for to me a good book is the best thing that can be done. However I'd been thinking it possibly a bad book, and your praise of it makes me more hopeful. At the same time, you know, it's more a storehouse than a book—has no unity, is too discursive, dispersed, heterogeneous. I've shot into it, as a builder into his yard, all the odds and ends of ideas which came to me during those years: indeed I suspect that it's a summary of myself to February 1920, and that people who read it will know me better than I know myself.[63]

There is something apt in TEL's response. He is a writer who doubts himself, and self-doubt, when sincere, is something admirable in a writer. He does not seem entirely satisfied with *Seven Pillars* and seems beyond fishing for compliments. It is also telling that TEL shifts from his former life in the war and its aftermath to his current life in the RAF. Whereas once he complained about the possibility of remaining an enlisted man, he now seems to have found something in it: "It would be hard to remain inhuman while jostling all those days and nights in a crowd of clean and simple men. There is something here which in my life before I've never met—had hardly dreamed of."[64] That Lawrence spent about another thirteen years in the ranks means that there was probably something to this kind of companionship and *esprit de corps* that he is here describing to CFS.

TEL appears to have felt comfortable expressing his innermost thoughts to CFS. TEL addresses her comments on the publication of *Seven Pillars*. He now thinks that he is unlikely to publish the book, but that if he ever were, he agrees that "the whole is the only honest thing."[65] Very soon he returns to the personal. He has introduced CSF to his mother by way of her letter: "I showed my mother your letter. She likes you now, because you praised my work, and mothers have (privately) an inordinate pride in their sons. The horrors of the book strike her painfully, and she hates my having noted, or seen, such things."[66] This passage cuts to the heart of the burden of *Seven Pillars*. It is as much a confession as a memoir. It is TEL's heart of darkness: he was a great admirer of Conrad. This heavy load might explain in part his reluctance to publish and profit from the book and why he embraced the kind of quotidian routine he did in the RAF from 1922 onward. The very arguments that the Shaws had used to have him bring out *Seven Pillars* might have contributed to his sudden about face.

4.4   The Sack of a Hero

Another twist occurs in the story of TEL and the Shaws. On January 30, 1923, TEL opens his letter with an announcement to GBS that "I've now been sacked from the RAF, as a person with altogether too large a publicity factor for the ranks: and feel miserable about it."[67] At the time of this sacking, Cape agreed with Lawrence to a contract for a limited edition of 2000 of an unabridged *Seven Pillars*, which, owing to TEL's state of mind, he cancelled. TEL reiterates to GBS what he told CFS: "it's been a bad month, for the RAF was the most interesting thing I ever did (after the squalid difficulty of getting used to it) and I'll regret its loss for good."[68] After having lunch with the Shaws in London on February 1, 1923, TEL announces, in a letter of March 23 of the same year, that "after hesitating here and there eventually I joined the Army, and am now at a camp in Dorset being trained."[69] In a postscript, TEL tells GBS that he gave the Bodleian Library "at Oxford the manuscript of my Arabian effort."[70] The book would not be likely to be lost now.

GBS wrote to Sydney Cockerell on April 13, 1923, that *Seven Pillars* "is one of the great books of our time; and I must finish it to the last morsel."[71] According to GBS's letter to TEL on May 13, 1923, TEL had apparently asked Cockerell to have the Shaws return the book and GBS makes another plea for TEL to get on with publishing the volume quickly and at a fair price.

On May 31, 1923, GBS decided then to write Stanley Baldwin, the prime minister, to rectify Lawrence's complex situation. Of TEL, GBS says:

> This man kept the Arabs fighting for us instead of with one another until the way was finally clear for Allenby to enter Damascus. Allenby sent him a message to say that he should like to have the Arabs enter with the first troops if it could be arranged. The All Souls gentleman immediately marched his Arabs into Damascus; found it left in a horrible condition of anarchy and pestilence by the retreating Turks; organized the hospitals, the police, and the municipal services in a couple of days ready for Allenby's entry; and, when Allenby arrived, asked for nothing but to be let go about his business.[72]

That GBS would take this extraordinary step on TEL's behalf is remarkable. TEL actually went to Jesus College before the war and was a member of All Souls after, although this is not really significant to GBS's argument. This man of many names, which GBS lists as T.E. Lawrence, Luruns Bey, Colonel Lawrence, and later Ross and Shaw, needs to be saved from himself because it is honorable for the government and for TEL. GBS's Lawrence is shy or proud or both but he is also someone with scruples: "He was given an imaginary job in the Colonial Office; and when he threw it up as an imposture, he was left to fend for himself as best he could."[73] Nor does Shaw mince words in assessing TEL's unpredictability. Whereas TEL has placed the manuscript in the Bodleian and Shaw had offered him publication, "he had already realized that he had only to hold up his finger to get half a dozen offers from first rate firms. He prefers, however, to lend his five copies to selected readers, and to remain a mystery man with money and a new reputation within his reach."[74] Shaw then goes on to tell the whole story about how TEL deserved at least £20,000 for the services he rendered the nation but instead had trouble even collecting £130. GBS drives home his point:

> Clearly this is a bad case of Belisarius reduced to begging obols in an ungrateful country; and as the man, strange as he is, has a dramatic instinct that makes obscurity and concealment impossible for long in his case, to say nothing of this wonderful book, with its fuse burning up to a sensational literary explosion, it seems to me

that the Government should consider the advisability of making a decent and indeed handsome provision for him.[75]

Now TEL is one of Justinian's generals forced to beg in the streets of Constantinople. It is impressive just how highly GBS thought of TEL, as "strange" as TEL sometimes seemed. GBS dramatizes the other "Shaw":

> But the fact remains that he is serving as a private soldier for his daily bread; and however much his extraordinary character may be accountable for this, it strikes all who know about it as a scandal that should be put an end to by some means. They feel that the private soldier business is a shocking tomfoolery, and are amazed to find that Lawrence is not in the position of a pensioned officer in dignified private circumstances.[76]

GBS uses a kind of royal we to add weight to the plea for a pension for TEL; he feels "uneasy" about the situation and so wants to let the government know about it, and attests to the quality of TEL's "history."[77] By granting a pension to TEL, the prime minister can avoid a "scandal." TEL was, after all, a media magnet. Shaw refuses to see anything more than role-playing in TEL's enlistment.

A similar assessment of TEL's intricate character is made in a letter of June 4, 1923, to GBS by a person TEL much admired: D.G. Hogarth, to whom GBS had sent a copy of his letter to Prime Minister Baldwin. Hogarth corrects GBS on All Souls, which had granted TEL a fellowship of £300 a year from 1919 till 1926, and on the job at "the Colonial office, where his functions were more real, I think, than your phrase implies."[78] TEL had mentioned the magic number of £300 a year as being his desired income: he already had it and had not collected it. Hogarth continues: "The fact is that money weighs much less with him than mode of life. I cannot conceive of any government post, such as the P.M. could offer, which L. would accept, or if he accepted, retain. He begins at once to talk of 'moral prostitution' and quits!"[79] Hogarth was like a mentor to TEL, had known him for about thirteen years, and he is now trying to reconstruct TEL's motivation and way of life. In a postscript Hogarth adds: "Lawrence is not normal in many ways and it is extraordinarily difficult to do anything for him! In some measure, the life of letters is best suited to him. He will not work in any sort of harness unless it is padlocked on to him. He enlisted in order to have the padlocks rivetted on to him."[80] Here in brief is one of the paradoxes of TEL that puzzled many during his life and afterward. In his next letter to Baldwin (November 12, 1923), GBS makes use of Hogarth's information. GBS satirizes TEL while still asking for a pension to be offered to him or kept with the Public Trustee if, as is quite likely, TEL will refuse it. But before that, GBS's satirical portrait is masterful:

> Belisarius is still begging the obal for the sake of refusing it with dramatic gesture when it is offered. His fellowship bed and board at All Souls are still unoccupied, and his grant undrawn. He is still saluting sergeants as Private Shaw, and dashing up to London when he can get leave on his famous 80-miles-an-hour bicycle, and waits for him at Thomas Hardy's, where he is introduced solemnly as Mr Shaw, and addressed as Colonel Lawrence.[81]

GBS then shifts to *Seven Pillars* and its connections with Oxford and Cambridge:

> Hogarth of the Ashmolean and Cockerell of the Fitzwilliam are still the holders of the dead secret of his name and address, which he writes across the sky as before. Hogarth makes people (including myself) put themselves down for £10 to publish the great history of the Arabian campaign, which the author threatens to burn from time to time, having carefully presented the Bodleian with the original MS. The edition is to cost £3000; and it will be impossible for Lawrence to make anything out of it, as he insists on reproductions in colour, at great cost, of the pictures which he has commissioned from eminent artists. Cockerell declares he is fifteen different men, and that you never know which will be on duty in any given emergency. Hogarth's hair whitens when his name is mentioned.[82]

He returns to the theme with which he began this sketch and represents Lawrence as demanding the same amount he could have at All Souls:

> But all the time he wants £300 a year, and is reduced to serve as a common soldier for his bread. As far as anything can be predicted of such a man, it seems that he is determined that you shall confer this pension on him, but solely in order that he may refuse it with a wave of his panache in the manner of Cyrano de Bergerac. And always, of course, he shrinks from publicity in the middle of the limelight. In all this he is quite sincere and genuine; but he is a born actor of Protean personality, he might, for official purposes, as well be all the Seven Humbugs of Christendom rolled into one.[83]

GBS's TEL cannot help being an actor of many parts who has a genius for publicity even as he shuns it. What is to be done with him?

TEL then writes GBS on December 13, 1923, with a scheme to have yet another edition of *Seven Pillars*, this a limited edition at thirty guineas for "the ungodly rich."[84] GBS replies five days later by addressing TEL as "Dear Luruns Bey" and by recounting what he said in the letter to the prime minister and in his interview with him. In the middle of this rhetorical flourish of reiterated satire, GBS mentions that he said

> that you were a man hiding in the limelight, whispering secrets to a broadcasting loudspeaker, writing amazing Sibylline books that everybody has read, being introduced everywhere as Mr. Shaw and at once addressed as Colonel Lawrence, a man of various genius, but always an inveterate and incorrigible actor to whom ordinary reasonable action is insipid and nothing but striking gestures endurable, even a walk to the post being a meteoric rush on an 80 mph motorcycle.[85]

GBS mentions that the PM will talk with Hogarth in Oxford. GBS also warns TEL that the daily routine of a soldier is only healthy if he is moving on to new writing or a new campaign, "but if you are only acting, and devising superfluous ornaments for that old finished job of yours, you will presently find that you have lost the power of serious work, and that the end of pretending to be a common soldier is that you *are* a common soldier."[86] TEL replied on December 20, 1923, that the army is "an asylum for the little spirited" and says, "Your picture of my ending up to find that I am a soldier, by dint of playing much at it, comforts me: for it's the end I want, and am wanting with deadly seriousness. The peace of finding that my horizon was grown so near!"[87] As TEL explains earlier in the letter, he wants nothing to do with the Middle East again and so would reject such a political job; nor does he wish to become an officer because he does not want to give another order.[88] The question of the pension and TEL's motives for serving as a common soldier persisted in the correspondence between GBS and TEL. This exchange produced its own dramatic interest.

4.5   The Recognition of Charlotte Shaw

There is an imbalance: we have quite a few of TEL's letters to CFS but few of hers to him. It is difficult when we have his answers to her letters that are now as ghosts. TEL read the acting proof of GBS's *Saint Joan* and gave detailed comments on it. In a letter of March 16, 1924 to CFS, TEL makes a stylistic suggestion about dropping the word "pet" in one of Joan's speeches, and GBS seems to have adopted this change.[89] He comes to the representation of Joan at the climax and finds it wanting: "I have a prejudice against the writer who leaves the reader to make his top-scene for him . . . . I funked it, in the death of Farraj, my man: faced it, in the plain narrative of my mishaps in Deraa the night I was captured."[90] Having read this account of that night in Deraa in Chapter 87 of the 1922 edition of *Seven Pillars*, I can say that it is not as direct as this letter might suggest. It was difficult in the 1920s to speak openly about rape, all the more so of male rape. Even in the 1962 film, there is only a glancing sexual suggestion to the violence. So Lawrence's indirection is understandable, as is his pain in struggling to represent that event on the page. The horror at the heart of this magnificent book, this actual autobiographical event, would make the whole history all the harder to write. In another letter to CFS on March 26, 1924, TEL relates himself to Saint Joan:

> (vii) The trial scene in *Joan*. Poor Joan, I was thinking of her as a person, not as a moral lesson. The pain meant more to her than the example. You instance my night in Deraa. Well, I'm always afraid of being hurt: and to me, while I live, the force of that night will lie in the agony that broke me, and made me surrender. It's the individual view. You can't share it.[91]

However, TEL was able to share some of this with CFS, if not with GBS. The shame and pain at the heart of TEL's war experience was something he could not pronounce on publicly, so his behavior seemed odd to others. He sought a way to face his wound without descending into self-loathing or madness. Perhaps he gained some catharsis from confessing his feelings to CFS, who might understand and who would not be so close to him as his own mother:

> About that night. I shouldn't tell you, because decent men don't talk about such things. I wanted to put it plain in the book, and wrestled for days with my self-respect . . . which wouldn't, hasn't, let me. For fear of being hurt, or rather to earn five minutes respite from a pain which drove me mad, I gave away the only possession we are born into the world with—our bodily integrity. It's an unforgivable matter, an irrecoverable position: and it's that which has made me forswear decent living, and the exercise of my not-contemptible wits and talents.[92]

This wound, long before the terror of rape was discussed openly and widely, was a burden to TEL. How much confusion and anger and guilt arose from his experience, how it scarred him and how it affected his sexuality, is something that needs to be considered but cannot be gauged. In his confessions to CFS, this gloss to his own memoir, TEL offers that night at Deraa as the reason for his seeking out a secure life in the armed forces, a life as a private soldier doing routine tasks. This is the man who had a job at the Colonial Office and left it and who refused Air Chief Marshal Hugh Trenchard's invitation to continue the history of the air force in the war when Walter Ralegh died in 1922. Why did he not turn his back on the world straight away? Who can say? These shocks and horrors do not necessarily work directly and in a linear fashion.

Lawrence continues: "You may call this morbid: but think of the offence, and the intensity of my brooding over it for these years. It will hang about me while I live, and afterwards if our personality survives. Consider wandering among the decent ghosts hereafter, crying 'Unclean, Unclean!' "[93] On sex, TEL writes to CFS: "Perhaps the possibility of a child relieves sometimes what otherwise must seem an unbearable humiliation to the woman:—for I presume it's unbearable. However here I'm trenching on dangerous ground, with my own aching coming to life again."[94] The pain of his brutal rape never left TEL. His letters to CFS are his opportunities to revisit that pain, to cleanse an old wound. Over the course of their correspondence, however, there is no steady progress, no march toward reconciliation with his past. TEL, although full of wit and ideas, was prone to melancholy. His various roles were not, for him, a game but an expression of anguish about a ruined past he struggled to contain. In a letter of September 28, 1925, he revisits this relation between the change in the self and the shameful wound:

> I've changed, and the Lawrence who used to go about and be friendly and familiar with that sort of people is dead. He's worse than dead. He is a stranger I once knew. From henceforward my way will lie with these fellows here, degrading myself (for in their eyes and your eyes and Winterton's eyes I see that it is a degradation) in the hope that some day I will really feel degraded, be degraded, to their level. I long for people to look down upon me and despise me, and I'm too shy to take filthy steps which would publicly shame me, and put me into their contempt. I want to dirty myself outwardly, so that my person may properly reflect the dirtiness which it conceals . . . and I shrink from dirtying the outside, while I've eaten, avidly eaten, every filthy morsel which chance threw in my way.[95]

TEL finds himself converted away from his old self through a shameful and dirty past from which he cannot recover. To Winterton, an old comrade of the Arabian campaign, and to CFS, his conversion seemed more of a fall, the new testament of his life a degradation of the old. The outward show of his life "conceals" the filth of the rape, humiliation, and torture. And so TEL hopes to find in the filth of the ranks, if not reconciliation, at least consistency.

4.6 The Wound

On June 8, 1926, TEL wrote to CFS, setting out the process of his composition of what would become *Seven Pillars*:

> What were lost were my later notes: observations on the road, scribbled at random in the saddle, without much reference to place or time: they included sketch-maps, tribal notes, personal thumb-nails, complaints and things. Generally I wrote them on blocks of Army telegraph forms, which were limp, easily crushed into the fold of my belt. I have three or four of them still: (in Clouds Hill): and as many were lost.[96]

Some of these notepads were lost in 1919 when the original manuscript of *Seven Pillars* was stolen from TEL at Reading Station. It is telling that TEL felt close enough to give CFS two of these notepads, which she bequeathed, along with her other TEL papers, to the British Library.[97] In 1926, GBS helped work on the draft preface to *Revolt in the Desert*. But GBS was growing impatient with TEL's perverse advertising genius, which wanted to delay the book for ten years.[98] The final version, called a "Foreword," asks why TEL would abridge "an unsatisfactory book, instead of recasting it as a history," and answers, among other things, that to do otherwise he would need "an interest in the subject which was exhausted long ago with the actual experience of it."[99] TEL was tired of the book. But instead of publishing the whole and being rid of it, he created a limited edition of *Seven Pillars* that could not earn him a profit and published an abridgment.

The correspondence with GBS and CFS did help TEL to define himself. Here he muses with the categories of action and dream. In a letter of October 5, 1926, to CFS, TEL includes a comparison between his Brough Superior motorcycle, nicknamed Boanerges, or "sons of thunder," which was capable of rest and then running "furiously," and

GBS, who does everything hard without rest.[100] The order of the analogy between the motorbike and GBS and TEL (like his own motorcycle) and GBS leaves it a little uncertain as to which is given to dream and which to action: "He is like a Martha: whereas I'm like my bicycle in my capacity for sitting down, or lying down, vacantly and happily, for weeks on end. It's the difference between a man of action and a dreamer."[101] Is TEL the soldier actually claiming to be the dreamer whereas GBS, who never rests, is the active one? If so, how is GBS also like Martha?

Why TEL chose the RAF is a complicated matter, and a little like the motivation of Iago (Othello's shame) among Shakespearean critics: the ostensible motives do not always add up to the action. In a letter to CFS on November 1926, TEL takes claims ownership of his enlistment and absolves Winston Churchill of any responsibility:

> It is quite true that the RAF is my own fault: it is my deliberate and very happy choice. I should not leave it to become Prime Minister. And it is quite true that Winston would have given me Egypt, if I had been willing, early in 1922 when Allenby first came home.
>   (Egypt is a social job—£20,000 a year, much entertaining, a large house, a silk hat, dignity. Do you see me so?).[102]

Lawrence had made up his mind, at least for the moment. If he could not decide whether he had joined the RAF freely or out of financial necessity, at least he had decided that he would take no great public role, whatever the reward. Instead, he found life in the RAF to be good. In November 1926 he crashed his motorcycle and could not spend his last free Sunday with the Shaws before he went to India on a crowded troop ship.[103] This was a hardship and an exile, as TEL once wrote his mother, but one that would allow him to fade from the social scene in Britain.[104]

4.7 Publish and Perish

An indirection should help provide one more gloss on TEL: the correspondence with F.N. Doubleday, his publisher in New York. TEL wrote to Doubleday in the 1920s and early 1930s, and his letters shed some light on his correspondence with the Shaws. Indeed there are echoes of TEL's words to the Shaws in these letters to Doubleday. Concerning the abridgment of *Seven Pillars*, he proclaims in a letter of June 30 [1920?]: "I haven't any illusions about the rotten book it is, and will feel delighted if you find it below your standard: however perhaps its faults may help it sell, and I'm a well advertised person, so that the necessary money may be raised by it. If it fails I'll have to go and work, which will be disgusting."[105] At this point, TEL does not seem to think that the service is such a good prospect. But by September 17, 1923, TEL is telling F.N. Doubleday to tell his wife that "Cincinnatus was probably happy, for though farming is labour, & therefore beastly, yet it is irresponsible labour: and private-soldiering though beastly & laborious, is even less responsible: & so correspondingly happier."[106] Cincinnatus was a Roman patrician who, as legend has it, was called from his plough to lead the Roman army to victory over the Aequi. When he had triumphed, he laid down his office and returned at once to the plough. It was to this well-known classical figure that GBS also once compared TEL.

TEL's letter of November 15, 1923, to Doubleday sums up many of the concerns he expressed to the Shaws about being a soldier and a writer, about his sense of self, and about his ambivalence regarding the publication of his great book.

> I'm sorry. I didn't know you had lost sight of my insignificant person. Money troubles make me hide my head. One can't be "Colonel Lawrence" (not even so mild a celebrity) on nothing a year. So I became Private Shaw, in the British Army, instead, & am paid nineteen shillings and threepence a week in compensation for the loss of my liberty & the use of my mind & body by the state. My engagement is for seven years (till about 1928) and till its termination I will not be seen in London or elsewhere. Now I am in Dorset, camped near Hardy.
>
> Naturally such a life is not my choice: I like a solitary bed, & quiet meals, & leisure for books, & the opportunity of music and converse with experienced men . . . but I had to choose between enlistment & immediate hunger, & chose to go on living. You would probably have done the same in my case . . . and I am alleviating the barrack-conditions by making myself a book-corner in the ruinous cottage for the C.C.F.L. [Cape Cod firelighters]. So that all is well (or better) now. The translating of French books pays for this luxury.
>
> I'm glad you did not close with Savage, for he was not empowered to sell my book. Indeed it is not for sale. I have been very fortunate in my readers. Kipling, Shaw, & Hardy have read it. K. did not like it much. Shaw & Hardy praised it far beyond what I ever dreamed (beyond what I still dream) its merits. Encouraged by them I have coquetted with the idea of a reprint of its full text,

to accompany reproductions of the fifty pictures illustrating it; these pictures are by some of the best artists we have & I lean greatly to see them worthily done.

Of course I don't want the book published, or even circulated. So some friends of mine are enquiring:

  i) For a millionaire to put up £3000 for the privilege of owning the unique copy.
  ii) For a hundred rich men to put up £30 each for a copy of a subscribed edition of a hundred copies
  iii) For three hundred subscribers of ten guineas each.

The reproduction of the pictures & good printing of the text is estimated to cost exactly three thousand pounds, thus there can be no publisher and no book-sellers: and the value of a subscribed edition is that the copyright is not brought in question (either here or anywhere) & there are no reviews.

Whether any of i. ii. or iii. schemes is feasible only experiment will show.[107]

GBS makes an appearance in this letter in order to balance the reception of the book among great writers. And here again life in the armed forces does not seem to be a spiritual redemption, but an unfortunate necessity.

And of course TEL's ambivalence to publication shines through. There are a number of letters that explain TEL's intentions not to make any money from his books on Arabia. The way he frames the matter in these letters is very much like the way he frames the matter to the Shaws. To F.N. Doubleday on June 16, 1927, he writes from Karachi, India:

Your notion of an article from me, I'm afraid, won't do. I have decided never to use the name "Lawrence" again: in spite of its having a market value. Nor will I write about Arabia or any derived subject. My scruples on these points have made me refuse the profits of "Revolt in the Desert" which has sold well in England, I believe, whatever Doran may make of it and have made me keep the more valuable "Seven Pillars" out of circulation.[108]

TEL did translate French novels for a little money, but he stuck closely to this scruple: the profits from *Revolt* went to a RAF trust. Despite his refusal to earn profit, TEL was pleased that Doubleday liked the art of his great tome: "Your praise for the printing of the Seven Pillars pleases me."[109]

TEL's own shifting identity was tied up with the fate of his book. His ambivalence over the promotion of one fed his ambivalence over the promotion of the other. In a letter of August 25, 1927, after the period of the Shaw correspondence we have examined, TEL discusses with Doubleday his own assumed names and pen names and explains why he can never use the surname his was born with:

> So you see the name "Lawrence" bars itself. It is worth a lot of money, because of Arabia: whereas my father chose it for me because it meant nothing, to his family. The only authentic part of my name is the initials T.E. (They do not, I believe, translate into Thomas Edward . . . but that's no matter) and most people who know me write me as Dear TE! They feel safe with that. There aren't many things safe about what are beautifully called "natural" children![110]

Lawrence's illegitimacy now plays into his search for himself. The RAF gave him a routine, a safe haven, even an identity different from the one the world seemed to want for him. In a confessional mood, as 338171 A/C GBS at RAF Cattewater Plymouth, he writes to FN. Doubleday on April 4, 1929: "It does not seem to me, looking back at it, as though anything I've ever done was quite well enough done. That is an aching, unsatisfied feeling, & ends up by making me wish I hadn't done anything: and very reluctant to try anything more. Hence the RAF which is a routine that keeps me sane, & sometimes happy. A big word, that, happy: but I think it is sometimes true of me."[111] Years before he had told the Shaws that he had found happiness in the RAF. They were still part of his life in 1929, as can be seen in this letter to Doubleday from Plymouth, dated June 28 of that same year:

> Frere-Reeve wrote to me, two excellent letters, about good printing. I shall go to see him when, or if, I get leave in October. I have a design of sliding down some odd day (Dear, it *will* be an odd day!) if he permits it, & I achieve it, with Bernard Shaw and Mrs. Shaw. She is quaint & comfortable, and fresh, & kind. G.B.S. is exciting, per contra. Together they are like bacon and eggs, a harmony in blue & silver. I fear I talk nonsense.[112]

And in his letters to Doubleday, TEL could not avoid self-dramatization. On December 18, 1930, he describes to Doubleday a scene with a clerk in a bookshop in Scotland: " 'You *are* hard to please' she grumbled, offering me the Boys Book of Colonel Lawrence at a reduction, seeing I was in uniform and he now in the RAF. I told her I knew the fellow. And he was a wash-out: then I bought a Daily Express & escaped the shop."[113] The dramatic irony here has several layers, including TEL's toying with his own popularization. It seems that he can see himself as a character even when others cannot see him as a person.

Sometimes there is a sense that TEL had stock responses for his letters. Responses from the letters to the Shaws recur in his correspondence with Doubleday. His view of himself as a writer is a case in point. While inquiring about F.N. Doubleday's failing health in a letter of January 27, 1931, he comes to the theme of writing:

> Only this writing . . . honestly, you know, I can't write. The Seven Pillars was so long ago, and it did not rise to the height of its theme. I had better stuff than any writer has had—and botched it. Then some spring or other got tired (there is nothing broken) and the works stood still. Today there is nothing I want to write, and I will not try to write out of an empty mind. A book should burst out of a man, against his will, like a vomit into the sea.
>
> So it is not possible for me to write: and it would be false pretences for me to accept any brain-work: there is no will for it. Body-work—yes: that I can do, and do do, all day long for the Air Force, and I do it cheerfully & well just because there is no longer any fret of the brain or ambition left.
>
> Nor was I ever a good writer, technically considered.[114]

It seems that TEL needed more than one confessor in his life. Although he claimed that he had found happiness, for which we should take his word, TEL seems to have remained split between the writer and soldier, between the public figure and obscure everyman.

4.8   Seeing among the Pillars or a Genius of Publicity

CFS was perceptive to see just how important a writer TEL was and to interest her husband in him as well. GBS was right: TEL was a genius of publicity, and that genius lives on. Born late in the nineteenth century and dead a little after the first third of the twentieth century, TEL is still a figure in our collective imagination at the beginning of the twenty-first century. GBS saw in TEL's oscillation between fame and obscurity a paradoxical genius for making himself known. GBS also realized that although TEL might not have always wanted to be recognized, he could not avoid it. Take for instance this letter to Sir John Maxwell, who had inquired after the great book:

4.1.26

Dear Sir John Maxwell

General Weight has told me that you want a copy of the private edition of my war-book. I'm willing of course—but have they told you that it won't be ready for months, that it is very long and very dull, being discreet: and that it costs thirty guineas, of which fifteen have to be sent in advance to manager Bank of Liverpool and Martins 68 Lombard St. E.C. 3. Marked "Seven Pillars Account." If you wait till March 1927 one-third of the same text will be published for sale at a guinea. Few people will want to read more, after they have read that.

I've put my present name and address at the head of this letter in case you want to ask me any thing else about the book. I shall quite agree with you if you decide against it.

Yours sincerely

TE Shaw[115]

It is as if Alexander Pope advertised his wit by saying that he was Dullness, one of his dunces in his *Dunciad*, and somehow convinced people that he was the wittier for it. Maxwell would not be put off by all this talk of tediousness or by this undermining business maneuver, making a cheap edition available in order to undercut the subscribers' edition (not something Pope would have done in the eighteenth century when he set up a subscription for his Homer). Neither Maxwell nor the world would ignore TEL, despite his best, albeit ambivalent, efforts.

But that is TEL, man of the book. And then there is TEL, man of the film. I recently watched the film for the first time since its first incarnation in 1962. In the archives at Princeton University I found a book entitled *Columbia Pictures Presents The Sam Spiegel and David Lean Production of Lawrence of Arabia.*[116] Through its title page, Peter O'Toole's eyes look out through a rectangular cutout from his full picture on the next page. His face is framed by the lines "His name will live in" and "English letters."[117] In the unpaginated film book, A2 recto proclaims: " 'I deem him one of the greatest beings alive in our time. I do not see his like elsewhere. His name will live in English letters; it will live in the annals of war; it will live in the legends of Arabia.'—Winston Churchill." And GBS is twice invoked as part of this puffing of Lawrence: " 'With the single exception of myself, no man of our time has had such a power of tempting journalists and even diplomats to tell lies about him as Lawrence.'—G.B. Shaw." About *Seven Pillars* the book declares: "But George Bernard Shaw gave him enthusiastic encouragement in its preparation, H.G. Wells called it a great human document, E.M. Forster judged it a masterpiece but feared to tell Lawrence so lest he evoke a sarcastic reaction from a man whose friendship he treasured. Certainly it is unique."[118]

TEL's correspondence with the Shaws, who do not appear in the film, is one way to understand TEL as a writer who wanted to escape the past that he had created, a man who had to face a wound he would rather not. He could not turn to fiction in the face of a truth that was his heart of darkness. That darkness remains. The film makes a strong statement when it shows Lawrence meeting his death on the motorcycle he so loved. Danger was one of his idols, this man of shifting identities. Here was a man, Odysseus and not, with a wound that would scar but not heal, a mark that TEL himself looked for, hard as it was to identify, hardest of all to recognize, in one way at least. The death at high speed in the prime of life is something to remember. But the student and scholar before the war and the serviceman afterward, hard as TEL tried, could not be ordinary. Like the saint who has confessed and the sinner who has converted, like the soldier as court jester and holy man, Lawrence was more than of Arabia.

What kind of recognition was he seeking and what do we seek in him? This a hero with many faces who had a hard time facing himself. He wrote about himself and his circumstances: he wanted to write but found it wanting. The writer and his history—both story and story about the past—bore a difficult relation to each other. Here was a scholar and writer, soldier and statesman all wrestling in one tormented body. Here was a private man of great publicity, a public figure who wanted to be a private man. TEL recognized that somewhere in these tensions and the shadowlands of identity writing mattered, and he both affirmed and denied it.

CHAPTER FIVE

Poiēma, Theoria, and Tekhnē

The poet (*poiētēs*) is the maker of created things (*poiēma*) who shows skill and art (*tekhnē*) in this making. In the age of rapidly advancing technology—advancing is neither good nor bad but it is what is done with the advancement—it is tempting to forget the underlying relation between the making of things or creations in words and objects.[1] Both are in the world. Each has a symbolic and material presence in that world. A shoe can be an object of beauty and utility. What was considered to be a jug or vase or urn with a specific everyday use thousands of years ago can sit in a glass case in a museum or gallery to be admired for its beauty. Perhaps what is true for a carpenter can be true for a philosopher. *Thēoria* is a contemplation, a speculation that can be a representation, thought as a mirror for the world, or an idea apart from it, but a theorem is a proposition that needs to be proved or an idea that has been proven or is thought to be true. One is in the domain of formal logic or mathematics and the other in the realm of informal logic or verbal argument. The art lies in the symbols as mathematics or words and is in the world but is abstract from it. *Thēorein* means to observe. Seeing is believing the truth, although seeing is not necessarily the same as observing closely or understanding. Even though there are connections between the making of poetry and technology, it is not sure that they always involve the same kind of seeing.[2] The relation between making and theory, poetry and philosophy is difficult and can be oppositional, at least ideologically, as the discussion of poets in Plato's *Republic* illustrates.[3]

We still think about Euclid and Archimedes, but applied technology and theoretical explorations in science have led us from craft to industry and mass production. The poet as maker is dwarfed by the scale of the making, and the theories that tie the craft of art and science together can get lost or obscured in the sheer scale of economics and machinery. The repetition or assembly line of making consumer products, no matter how graceful the design, can overwhelm with parodic multiplication or a kind of misapprehension or even nausea from the vast number of duplications. Poets tend to avoid that mass production because their product is not usually mass produced, perhaps because it is generally thought to be useless or difficult to "use." Even with a computer the poet explores storytelling, symbols, and myths that seem to be partly in the brain stem and the unconscious than in the engineering of modernity and beyond.

The pace of change appears to have accelerated even if that sense of time may or may not be objective. Even decades ago the gap appeared to be growing between the classical world and the "modern" world. The Battle of the Books and the tensions between ancients and moderns from the Renaissance onward appears to have intensified. Classical learning and many of the tools of the humanist or maker in the human sciences have been pushed aside, subordinated, or scrapped. So what are we to make of poetry in the age of technology?

5.1   Poetics of Communication

About twenty-five years ago I was auditing some classes given by Marshall McLuhan, who was, more than one of his mentors, Harold Innis, a most poetic theorist of communication. He spoke in fragments, one-liners, dialectical turns as if a mixture of Socrates and Nietzsche, a provocateur well steeped in the modernists, particularly Joyce, a prophet new-inspired to some and an opportunistic charlatan to others. Some people outside the university asked me how I could understand McLuhan: whether I did or not, I cannot say (I wrote an essay on him, now lost, on his use of Shakespeare). What was apparent to me is that McLuhan liked to probe, tease, and question, which seemed to me then and now a good thing. Why not shake up a few young minds and see how they might question the electronic buzz and world of propaganda and theories in which they inhabited. Perhaps they might be free, and perhaps literature had something urgent and vital to teach among media. If television was McLuhan's mechanical bride, then poetry might be a way of grooming the mind and senses in the global village. Here was a medium, apparently archaic but oral and aural in the new orality, whose message would be different by definition.[4] Poets and those given to poetry, even if not formally considered poets, have an important role to play in an age of theory and technology that apparently ignores, occludes, and obliterates poetry and poetics expression while also giving it a potentially wider dissemination in different media.[5] Poetry might even be a means of preparing the mind in the fight against propaganda, something George Orwell warned against in "Politics and the English Language" (1946), a language and truth so battered by Nazi and Soviet regimes that it is hard to see how even some of the world slipped out from under its shadow.[6] Poetry, although feeble and fallible in so many respects, might have some power to resist lies and abuse in the world. Literature might have experienced a decay of lying in Oscar Wilde's sense, but it has also expressed what Goethe saw in Werther as an education and what Dostoevski represented in terms of psychology.[7] Poetry is an art, not of improvement but of endurance and reinvention: it recreates somehow the struggle between life and death, good and evil, innocence and experience no matter how ambivalently. Poetry purifies the spirit of language but is not entirely pure. Poetry has its politics, too.

Poetry, then, is an art that does not improve as science does. Whereas technology advances for better or worse, poetry may slide back and move forward but not in any progressive sense. That is why it is strange that something so opposite to science and technology could be its conscience or at least some dialectical other. Poetry might share with mathematics and physics forms of intuition and thinking like metaphor, logic, and analogy, but it cannot be checked with a proof. The possible and fictional worlds, such as dream and hypothesis, can be compared to this world and can tell us something about nature and human experience and their interpretation, but they do not have the mathematical precision of the binary language of computers. Leibnitz, the coinventor of calculus, was the founder of possible world theory, which has had implications for game theory, literary theory, and other disciplines.[8] Human wishes, aspirations, and frustrations are the truth of poetry. But Hamlet and Werther never die the way Shakespeare and Goethe do. Achilles lives in the text and mind of the reader whether Homer was one poet or many.

5.2   Theory

Literary theory begins in earnest with Plato and Aristotle and owes a debt to Longinus, Aquinas, and others.[9] It is a something between philosophy and history (as poetry is) and is and is not connected to literature. Beginning with works like Northrop Frye's *Anatomy of Criticism* (1957), literary criticism and theory declared its independence from philosophy and with Jacques Derrida theory seems to have made a break from literature.[10] Poetry was no longer an object of study as it might have been in Sainte-Beuve and I.A. Richards, but something to be moved aside or treated with the hermeneutics of suspicion.[11] Not all theory went this route, but some of the most influential theorists of the past two or three decades seem to have tended in this direction. Where did this leave poetry? Television and the Internet take up more and more time and reading in its conventional sense is probably not as much practiced as before, just as the printing press appears to have transformed reading at the end of the age where manuscript culture predominated. Poetry may be now more accessible than ever, through the Internet, but how robust is it? The power of words has always been both great and tenuous.

Poetry in an age of theory in technology is a situation that is an intensification of the contexts of earlier ages from ancient Greece onward. The etymology of "theory" contains within it the tensions that exist in it then and now. The *Oxford English Dictionary*, one of the on-line sources I have tried to use in this chapter as a testament to the fact that the electronic age also includes poetry and scholarship in its Internet resources, gives the origins of the English word, which derived from the Italian, which came from the Latin, which borrowed from the Greek, as well as its meanings: "[ad. late L. *theoria* (Jerome in Ezech. XII. xl. 4), a. Gr. a looking at, viewing, contemplation, speculation, theory, also a sight, a spectacle, abstr. n. f. (:*) spectator, looker on, f. stem—of to look on, view, contemplate. In mod. use prob. from med.L. transl. of Aristotle. Cf. It. *teoria* (Florio 1598 *theoría*), F. *théorie* (15. in Godef. Compl.).]."[12] John Florio, an Italian Protestant who translated Michel de Montaigne into English near the time Shakespeare was writing his greatest history plays and tragedies, helped to introduce the first meaning of the word as contemplation. About this time, theory also came into English as a spectacle: Christ's passion was a theory or sight. Richard Hooker, also writing in the years about the turn from the sixteenth to seventeenth centuries, understood in discussing the church that theory was a scheme to be done, or a method of doing it; systematic rules or principles to be adhered to.[13] From the 1630s, the word was given more to natural philosophy and later took on an important place in science. This sense of theory meant ideas or generalizations that explain or account for a body of facts or phenomena or a hypothesis to be tested by experiment or observation, or the general laws or principles of something observed or known. We are just having a glimpse into the complex world of theory, which can be dismissed as abstract, impractical, oblivious to the facts, hypothetical but unproven, and so we can leave off with two aspects of this intricate word. One subdefinition that the *OED* gives is: "That department of an art or technical subject which consists in the knowledge or statement of the facts on which it depends, or of its principles or methods, as distinguished from the *practice* of it." The theory and practice of poetry may be two very different things.

Some disciplines raise up theory whereas others do not. Even in the age of theory this has been so. This controversy over poetry has been, in this language, long-standing. It is not simply Jonathan Swift's natural philosophers who need a dose of reality on the floating island in Book Three of *Gulliver's Travels*. Thomas Sprat's *History of the Royal Society* and the accomplishments of natural philosophers such as Newton and scientists such as Charles Darwin show that theory had an exalted place in England then and in the English-speaking world since.[14] Theoretical physics was much prized in the English-speaking world: Einstein took refuge in the United States. Nonetheless, English has derogatory words for theory and theorists—perhaps even worse that poetaster or versifier. It may be that in English one has to excel in poetry and theory in order to achieve a certain respect: the discourse in the seventeenth and eighteenth centuries was far too political and satirical to respect talent always. Here are the combinations that serve as a qualifier even in the age of theory—which we might say is a post–Second World War phenomenon that really took flight from the mid-1960s—once again courtesy of the *OED* on-line: "*Comb.*, as **theory-making** adj. and n., **-building, -monger, -spinning**; **theory-bigoted, -mad, -ridden** adjs.; **theory-blind** *a.*, (*a*) blinded by a theory, so as to be unable to see the facts truly; (*b*) blind to a theory, i.e. unable to see or apprehend it (cf. *colour-blind*); **theory-laden** *a.*, applied to a term, statement, etc., the use of which implies the acceptance of some theory; contrasted with **theory-free, -neutral** adjs.; *theory-man* (*nonce-wd.*), a theorist; **theory-tailor**, contemptuously for a shaper of theories." Ambivalence, then, characterizes historical attitudes from the early eighteenth century to the late twentieth century. The poet, a maker, is the subject to the eye or gaze of the looker (also seer and thinker), but he or she has other perspectives to represent, a tension between images and words, imagination and thought.

But "poetry" is not so straightforward in its history and etymology. In English during the fifteenth century, poetry could also mean a treatise or theory or critical view of poetry. The *OED* records an instance: "**1.** A rendering of med.L. *poetra* in sense of an *ars poetica* or treatise on the art of poetry. *Obs.*" And cites an example: "O. BOKENHAM

Seyntys Introd. (Roxb.) 3 Galfridus Anglicus in hys newe poetrye."[15] Geoffrey Chaucer used poetry as a general fiction or fable: "c1384 CHAUCER H. Fame II. 493 When thou redest poetrie How goddes gonne stellifye Briddes fisshe best."[16] But Chaucer also used "poetry" in its modern English sense or "The art or work of the poet: **a.** With special reference to its form: Composition in verse or metrical language, or in some equivalent patterned arrangement of language; usually also with choice of elevated words and figurative uses, and option of a syntactical order, differing more or less from those of ordinary speech or prose writing." Poetry is then a kind of special writing different from the prose of contemporary theory, although Horace, Galifridus Anglicus, and others have written their arts of poetry—their theories—in verse.[17] Historically, poetry can mean literature and it can also be theory. In terms of intellectual history, it makes it hard to separate the terms "poetry," "literature," and "history"—in English—to talk historically of literature in the age of theory and technology.

5.3   Poetry and Poets

"Poetry" itself has, as a word, taken on new meanings in English, so that those of us comparing literature written in English would have to take the semantic shifts into account. From the Renaissance through the Romantics—in Philip Sidney, Shakespeare, and W.B. Yeats, poetry assumes the beauty and truth that John Keats saw in it, perhaps in recreating and transforming the poetic tradition in English and drawing on the Greeks and the instruction and delight that Horace made so famous.[18] Along with a number of suggestive examples, the *OED* gives the following definition, which embodies this shift from earlier definitions (although Longinus would not necessarily find it all that strange): "**c.** With special reference to its function: The expression or embodiment of beautiful or elevated thought, imagination, or feeling, in language adapted to stir the imagination and emotions, both immediately and also through the harmonic suggestions latent in or implied by the words and connexions of words actually used, such language containing a rhythmical element and having usually a metrical form (as in sense 3a); though the term is sometimes extended to include expression in non-metrical language having similar harmonic and emotional qualities (*prose-poetry*)." Poetry can also sometimes be in prose: those who read Plutarch, Montaigne, Virginia Woolf, or James Joyce know the poetry of thought and expression, not necessarily sublime, that biography, essays, history, and philosophy can embody.[19] Theory itself, then, can be poetic. This is not a surprise as Plato was a poetic philosopher and Aristotle is said to have written dialogues that have been lost: Jacques Derrida may have tried to turn Plato on his ear (aural as well as oral culture being looked at anew) but he, too, has his poetry. Nietzsche, McLuhan, and Roland Barthes use suggestive aphorisms and narrative to express their thoughts: their theory has a poetics and vice-versa.[20] Story complicates argument and poetics and theory read each other. Although there is a distinction between the two, there is a blurring here and there in ways that might suggest a reconciliation of the two in this age of theory or a false dichotomy or opposition that makes a hierarchy that tends to place theory above poetry in the academic discourse of the past two or three decades. Perhaps this is a move like Plato's subjugation or banishment of the poets in *Republic*. If Plato's priority of the oral over writing produced this attitude toward poetics, why would the opposite do the same?

I hope that it is not about a parochialism of knowledge, that one discipline or practice is considered to be better in the humanities than another. Just as we need physics, chemistry, and biology and all the interdisciplinary fields formed from them, we should have room for poetry, philosophy, and history no matter how Plato, Aristotle, Sidney, and others have ranked them. We need all the help we can get with understanding the natural and human worlds. Theories can help explain the work of these fields as they do in science. As I am discussing poetry in an age of theory and technology, it is good to consider a world or time without it. In the middle of the nineteenth century, one writer did just that: "Hence poetryless a., devoid of poetry. 1854 H. STRICKLAND Trav. Th. 28 A soulless, poetryless, utilitarian, money-making Englishman is bad enough." A world without history and philosophy would be the poorer, and many would say the same about theory and technology. The spiritual and later Romantic notion of poetry is something that contrasts with the utilitarian or instrumental view that if time is money then what time is there for poetry.

The word "poet" has its origins in Greek: as is often the case, it came to English through intermediary languages on the Continent. It has an interesting history, which the *OED* etymology encapsulates: "[ME. *poete, poyete,* a. OF. *poete* (12th c. in Hatz.-Darm.), mod.F. *poète,* ad. L. poéta (Plaut.), ad. Gr. ποητής, early variant of ποιητής maker, author, poet (cf. *MAKER* 5), f. ποεῖν, ποιεῖν to make, create, produce. (An early Gr. word in L.; if introduced at a later period, the form would have been pæta.)]." The poet could be someone who wrote poetry or

literature. This maker or practitioner could also be a theorist: Philip
Sidney is a good case in point. Even in Elizabethan London, in which
one of the great flourishes of literature occurred, Sidney could complain,
as the *OED* records, "1581 SIDNEY Apol. Poetrie (Arb.) 71 The cause
why it [Poesie] is not esteemed in Englande, is the fault of *Poet-apes,
not Poets." England did not, even at this great moment, esteem poetry,
so what then would happen when in the last decades of the twentieth
century universities in English-speaking countries generally raised up
cultural and literary theory above the practice of literature among its
professors and as a form of discourse in the culture in general. Was this
old news? Was it always thus?—even before the Industrial Revolution
(of William Blake's "black Satanic mills") or the Technological Revolution
of McLuhan's global village.[21]

5.4   Technology

Technology, like poetry, is a kind of art and making, and, like theory,
can be akin to an art or the method behind it. Technology and poetry
are practical arts. The *OED* gives scope to the connection I am making
here, and its etymology helps to support this connection: "ad. Gr.
τεχνολογία systematic treatment (of grammar, etc.), f. τέχνη art, craft:
see -LOGY. So F. *technologie* (1812 in Hatz.-Darm.)." Technology,
which comes into English as a term in the early seventeenth century,
combines the art and language of poetry with the systematic nature of
theory. The word has come a long way from its origin as a grammatical
system in English to the practical application of science through machinery and the software that now drives it. Science once more has taken up
where art left off, but in doing so, in the modern age and after, it threatens to eclipse or displace art itself. Technology is an art that would
occlude or submerge poetry just as theory is a way of seeing that would
do the same. Natural philosophy became science, something whose
power gathered strength from the Renaissance and has intensified in
the age of nuclear power, computers, and other things that Horatio try
as he might to imagine in his philosophy might have trouble doing so.
The apparent lack of progress in arts such as poetry is weak as a means of
understanding nature and harnessing its power beside the potency of
technology. Theory in the humanities could be said to be in a similar situation in relation to the pure sciences. Francis Bacon's adage that
knowledge is power leaves poetry and literary and cultural theory in the
shadow of science and technology.[22] Reading often gives way to

mathematics and the symbolic and visual world of computers. McLuhan's television as a mechanical bride would mean that the Internet has taken much of the mechanical out of the bride, although this metaphor has its own historical limitations in an age in which women are not as interested in being represented as brides and hand-maidens and are themselves shapers of technology and science in increasing numbers. In the face of Sputnik, high school students in North America were not being encouraged to study poetry more. The Cold War put the freeze on poetry, and the research university was not built around poetry readings and departments of literature, despite some of their persistent allure and the relative lack of resources and support given to them by government and corporations. Science and business became partners in what Eisenhower called the industrial– military complex: the wealth of nations supported the arts but often as an ornament or social lost-leader.[23]

Shakespeare, Columbus, Newton, and Marie Curie are partly cultural figures—acknowledged in one sense, resources from the past to negotiate the future. The history of art and literature involves no real supplanting for those considered most worthy (I will not go into the construction of reputations and myths of fame here), but science is more ruthless about what is old. It has to work. Whatever in Newton is archaic or had been modified is shed, except in the history of science, a changing museum of dead knowledge. The what if and once upon a time of literature, the putative space of poetry, means that the protagonists of Sophocles, the speakers in the poems of Louise Labbé and the characters in the novels of Margaret Atwood are no more or less true or real than they were when they were created. The realm of literature is not necessarily the same as the empire of science and technology.[24] Gutenburg's galaxy, as McLuhan saw, was not the last revolution: that revolution in printing made for cheaply mass-produced books printed on both sides of the sheets. The revolution of the Internet in music and poetry might well make books and other forms of publication cheaper and more accessible and whereas that does not necessarily appeal to those who would limit their definition of poetry to something spiritual or Romantic, it will continue the democratization of poetry. Walt Whitman's America has its own electric light in the age of technology. Neglected poets—if all poets are not forgotten or underesteemed as they were in one aspect of Sidney's rendition— might gain more of an audience, or a great electronic forest of poetry—a virtual green world—might create so much poetry that, like the surveillance cameras, there are not enough people to interpret the tapes in real time. What kind of lack of acknowledgment is this? Perhaps poetry and literature are better served by asking other questions of them. It may well be that there are zones of uselessness and profitlessness in culture that inhabit some kind of privileged, ludic, cathartic, and sometimes even sacred space. Quite possibly there is a way through the two cultures debate that C.P. Snow was involved in so many decades ago.[25] The general space of poetry, of one human speaking to another, might be something we need now as much or more than ever. Human values are needed in the face of technological potential, which is growing but can never quite get beyond questions of right and wrong, life and death. Perhaps people need to acknowledge as many forms of knowledge as possible and to express themselves through a multitude of expressions.

It is easier now to read some poets, writers, and theorists from all over the world and these "writers" are more diverse than ever. Class, race, gender, and other previous exclusions matter less now even if they still exist as impediments. V.S. Naipaul, Derek Walcott, Franz Fanon, Umberto Eco, Louise Erdrich, Toni Morrison, Thomas King, Nancy Huston, Günter Grass, Garcia Marquez, Joy Kogawa, and many other well-known writers in many languages find themselves distributed more quickly than ever and whereas English seems to dominate—for now at least—book and film distribution, some writers have seldom reached as many readers.[26] The danger is in branding authors and stereotyping audiences but it is also possible that there is more choice for more people than ever before in all the kinds of publication. There may be dreams of fame and riches for some, but for others getting their work out is what matters. Apparently, there is not one way to be acknowledged then or now.

Poets are now unacknowledged: they are seldom the legislators that Shelley envisioned. Literary education, once at the center of British and French education, and certainly important enough in classical Greek education that in *Republic* Plato represented an attack on Homer's predominant place, is now caught between science, which has become the most powerful tool in culture, and business, particularly as it has played out in the technological realm.[27] Few poets, since Alfred Tennyson, have earned a living by poetry. In the time of greatest wealth in history, we have seen Oxford University Press and many others drop or crop their poetry lists. Even criticism has taken a hit. But back to poetry.

5.5   Poetry Then and Now

I am not lamenting, elegizing, or making apocalyptic this state but want
to consider the role of poetry and poets in a time when ads, videos, and
MTV, the drive to practical education, have added to the weight of television and other media in flooding the world with images and words.
There have never been many readers of poetry and a scarcity of com-
monplaces and clichés, so I do not want to make a cliché of the embat-
tled poet any more than I would of the humanist under siege. For
decades I have written and published poetry and I have written about it,
and I will do so as long as such a pursuit is possible, even if it seems more
and more like the mass held amidst bombs in the film *Apocalypse Now*.[28]
Matthew Arnold's displaced secular religion is as much under stress as
religion was in his day. Just as he saw poetry as a substitute for religion,
there are many alternatives to poetry today.[29] The apparent choices are
overwhelming. In a torrent of human voices and machine noises that
would strain Mozart's ears, we have the quiet of poetry, or some poems
howling, as Allen Ginsberg might say, in order to be heard above the
din. Either way these kinds of poetic expression, the pastoral and the
howling not to mention others, are under strain.

Tension is not always a bad thing. There are, however, other tendencies in culture that make poetry fragile and threaten to overwhelm it.
Ideology, for instance, is something that poetry never quite escapes, but
it does frustrate a reduction to the ideological. "So much depends on a
red wheelbarrow" might be glossed as nostalgia and a pastoral urge to an
agricultural past, but even if this imagistic fragment from William Carlos
Williams could be left at that, it has a suggestiveness beyond slogan,
groupthink, social bond.[30] If the muthos of mythology is not unmixed
with ideology, then the reverse is true.

Poetry can be primarily political but to be poetry it has to gesture beyond
the politics it espouses. Although poetry is partly instrumental, it frustrates
that movement while it represents it. Mythology is expressed through the
imaginative and hypothetical nature of literature: it is like fairy tales and
nursery rhymes, which embody the times in which they were written but
have a concrete and symbolic expression that communicates across time in
what might be called a childlike or dream world. Young children are sur-
rounded by politics and may even embody the ideological values imbued
in the adult world that teaches and indoctrinates them, but there is something more, perhaps something noumenal, unconscious, or unacknowledged that informs the language they live in. If adults write these stories for
children or folktales, they do so sometimes with children in mind, the

"as if" of their youth, the remembered "other" of themselves. I have noticed with some young children that they have poetic powers early, expressing a language that is rich and strange but simple and strong until the adult world of practical education and conventions teaches them otherwise.

A poetry then falls in the shadows of the official Poetry. Paradoxically, poetry too much acknowledged by official sources can become ossified, so that if poets were legislators perhaps even unacknowledged ones, this would put a great deal of pressure on poetry itself. Poetry can in official education even be part of an aggressive indoctrination or nationalism, militarism or imperial expansion. That is why I said earlier that some tension is good between society and poetry—and I am not assuming that the only kind of poetry is written from the vantage of the Romantics. The fragility of the story or web of poetic images that is not an argument, its apparent uselessness, and the long odds of it ever bringing notice or profit, is perhaps the usual predicament of poetry. This usualness is accented because there are many other media now—radio, television, film, video, computers—to express images and narratives for the culture. There is a certain marginalization, irrelevance, or reduction in stature that has accentuated the unacknowledged nature of poetry.

Poetry is mythology translated in literature and explained to the culture in criticism or theory in such a way as to have a double movement that seems to embody and resist the power of dominant ideologies and the political pressures brought to bear on writers, scholars, and critics. Myth might be a hope against the desolate record of human history, the tyrannies that have oppressed so many in the previous century. Many academic critics and theorists in the past fifty years have aspired to science, sociology, history, politics, anthropology, psychology, and other disciplines but not to poetry.[31] Poetry could be enfolded into a system of signs or semantics or be rendered with a suspicion that was born of a rivalry of the disciplines, as if we were back in Aristotle, Plato, or Philip Sidney trying to rank philosophy, poetry, and history according to how universal or particular they were. Harkening back to the 1950s, when literary criticism or theory was trying especially hard to free itself from poetry or from adjacent academic disciplines, Northrop Frye considered myth in literature as the rising up of the proletariat into a classless society and the return of the repressed. Frye returned to Marx and Freud, as well as to William Blake and others, to help create his vision of hope and regeneration. The social function of literature, in Frye's view, was to create a human community that cares for the basic needs of its members—the desire to live, eat, love, create, and move about freely. Frye's theory was a later and important contribution in the tradition of defenses of poetry that Sidney and Shelley helped to build in English. Frye is part of a European tradition that defends against the attacks contra fiction—especially in poetry and in the theatre—that begins with Plato and Aristotle, gathers momentum with the Church Fathers, and continues through the closing of the theatres in England in 1642.[32] In this attack on the making or representation of fictions, poetry, theatre, or novels are not considered morally, theologically, or philosophically serious enough. Literature and drama were demonic and parodic—the work of the devil, or at least a class of lying poets. It may be, as Frye suggested, that it is worth defending the dignity, autonomy, and significance of literature in political, social, ethical, and semantic systems, which are crucial human constructions.[33] In this view, literature is a human construction that only needs defending because of human ignorance and ideology, because it offers us means to regenerate ourselves and our society.

At a time when literary readings of texts are not popular with publishers, even within the walls of the university presses, I do not like to shift from literary criticism and theory, which historically have been much less acknowledged than poetry, but criticism and theory were, for a while, eclipsing poetry. It is possible that both are on life support, but perhaps they are as necessary as the religion that is often represented in the Bible as being up against it and in the face of power. The difficulty with poetry, which already contains strong elements of interpretation, is that human beings, especially literary critics and theorists, are interpretive beings, and the more suggestive sometimes the better, so that, as in the ancient commentaries on Virgil as much as those on the Bible, a few paltry lines on a page begot or were subject to long notes of commentary. This commentary could readily ossify into a doctrine and could be part of a structure of formal education, power, or ideology. The very acknowledgment of poetry could sweep it aside or contain it in the very act of deference or exegesis.

Literary studies has its roots in editing, biblical hermeneutics, rhetoric, and philology, so that poetry, the center of those studies growing out of the aristocratic ideals of classical literature, found itself in a maze or an archeology of knowledge. The thread out of the labyrinth seems invisible, woven of words on the wind that disappeared in the distance from tongue to hand, word to world. To an instrumental world, even to the increasingly practical world in the university and in the surrounding community, poetry can seem useless or ornamental or an embarrassment to order, efficiency, common sense, and worldly success. Even within the realm of literary studies and the university, for some time theory questioned and displaced poetry, which was something that could arouse skepticism and even suspicion. This "unacknowledging" of poetry has positive and negative means—the first as a putative space of communication and gathering freed of or minimizing ideology and the second as a downgrading or a ridicule of the useless and the uncommercial.

Europe has long had a tradition of skeptical or indeterminate textual and rhetorical methods in addressing texts as well as one that integrates them. The pre-Socratics, the Sophists, the skeptical philosophers were precursors to Derrida and Paul de Man.[34] This skepticism, if received positively, can be a benefit to understanding poetry or giving it its due. These early skeptical or rhetorical readers did not overturn ontology, epistemology, and semantics, but invigorated and complicated the debates in these areas. And so have deconstructionists. They do, however, call into question the authority of the poet to construct, perhaps even to legislate, meaning. Textual concern can involve a reading that stresses unity and meaning or one that emphasizes disunity and a vexed semantics. Poets can also represent fragments of epics and traditions, T.S. Eliot breaking down Homer and Dante, H.D.'s imagistic fragments ensharding nineteenth-century narrative poets such as Tennyson.[35] Perhaps some theories in the past three decades, most noticeably deconstruction or poststructuralism, have made rhetoric and the rhetoric of philosophy a means of questioning poetry. This disintegration of poetry, which has been helpful in its skepticism, has also acknowledged poetry while calling into question the value of acknowledging it. Even those critics or theorists such as Frye, who in the 1940s onward, may have preferred unity and structure to the deconstructionists' later exposures of contradiction and their dismantling of structuration, share with them skepticism about ideology and the construction of meaning. Ideology pervades society and influences and affects literature. Like many postmodern oppositional theorists, these earlier literary theorists—some New Critics and others structuralists—were skeptical about the manipulation of meaning as an ideological force and sensed the vulnerability of the writer, critic, and texts before the ideological policing of the state and its special interests. Although language is opaque and problematic in making meaning and not as a pellucid reflection of an outside world and reality, it is possible to communicate across time but not above it, that is, transhistorically but not transcendentally. The hope that poets may find some acknowledgment still is that poetry is of the imagination, as troubling as that could be to the Platonic Socrates. Poetry does not always sing official hymns to the republic.

My position as a poet as well as a theorist or critic living in an age where technologies and theories abound is to give metaphor and myth a chance. These are figures that help to make the phrases and structures of the texts we decide to call literary. By giving metaphor and narrative (mythos, or story) a chance, I am giving the imaginative reconstruction of a world that recreates the unity of subject and object a chance. And by giving metaphor and imagination a chance, I am giving myth a chance. It is important to speak against prevailing opinion, or even doxa or anti-doxa that has become doxa while paying attention to changes in historical contexts. The doxy is not something effectively tested or proved but a set of ideological attitudes, which derives from the Greek δόξα, meaning opinion, originally in religious or theological matters but now more generally in political, cultural, and literary matters.

Perhaps poetry can show in its indeterminacy, its gnomic utterance, its qualities of parable that ideology can, to some extent at certain moments, be evaded or escaped and that reading a literary text, especially a poem, even if the notion of the literary and the canon changes over time, is not the same as, even if it is similar to, reading other texts. Poetry, in the eye of literature, can be a critique of critique as well as of life. Perhaps to some theorists such as Louis Althusser ideology; is everywhere, including literature, and there is no escape from it, no beyond ideology; but if poets are to be acknowledged, perhaps as authorities who are anything but authorities in this paradox, then something interesting can happen.[36] Poets are less and less acknowledged—they seldom run governments, universities, churches, or large corporations. They have lost the world, perhaps from the start. It was probably an exception that the ancient Irish bards could do what they wanted because others feared their curses. Poets today do not travel in packs—even in creative writing programs, readings, or at writers workshops, conventions, and congresses—and it would not necessarily be a good thing if they wielded more worldly power or that they were always front and center. Shelley's unacknowledged legislators might well have come to be too unacknowledged. It may be that there are still some things worth finding in the refractory and unseen quest between myth and metaphor that might help us in a life that seems brutally short on a road that is hard and long. It is important to distinguish the parodic and ideological use of myth from this putative and recreative kind: the totalitarian government of Nazi Germany was probably the worst case of ersatz myths used for propaganda, a kind of apocalypse of nineteenth-century racial theories gone awry and taken to ghastly conclusion. Shelley might have sounded too official in his pronouncement: I am not asking for legislation in a defensive posture but for an openness to the simple difficulty of beauty in the telling lies and refractory truths of words made in images and tales. Sometimes it is good to lose the world for a metaphor even if that is a myth of poetry. Recognition is a matter of the vision of the maker and the viewer of the thing made. There is a relation between them that might have the rhetorical aspect of persuasion and the instrumental, but that can also be like the urn or jug that had a use but is now an object of beauty. Nevertheless, poetry is both useless and useful at once. Division is as difficult as vision. There is something possible, fictional, and putative about the poetic, but it can be as political as that great sonnet by Shelley on tyranny or the beautiful politics of the ugly in some of the *Songs of Experience*. The black Satanic mills itself is a gorgeous and euphonious phrase about the scarring and wasting of a green and pleasant land. There is a time and place for the poem or the created thing and it has a history as well as a now and might be or will be. Poetry gestures beyond the pat and simplistic to something that tantalizes, challenges, and suggests. To see and hear it is to be between what is and seems, part of the world and a sign of it. No statement or resting place can stall or fix poetry, but a proclamation of mystery is probably not enough for our inquiring minds and souls and the body that moves in the world.

CHAPTER SIX

Poetry and Mythology: Coda

Poetry can approach but never attain the condition of mathematics, apparently an objective realm of symbols and abstractions.[1] Even instrumental music might be said to echo bird song and other sounds in nature more than poetry does and have properties of proportion and harmony that are more readily apparent than those in poetry. The reason poetry falls short of the formal paradise of the mathematical is that it is made of words, which have meanings assigned to them. For short, I might call this possible asymptotic realm that poetry can aspire to but not reach— the music of mathematics. The Muse of poetry may share certain aspirations and inspirations with that of music and that of mathematics but can never be identical with them. Content, then, gets in the way of a poetry of mathematics or even, more putatively and controversially, in abstract music (more and more in the past decades discussions of ideology in music have arisen).[2] The *mythos* or *muthos* of story has a hard time keeping clear of the argument of ideology.

6.1 Mythos

By mythos I mean—as in the root sense from ancient Greek—speech, narrative, fiction, myth, plot. Aristotle uses the term in *Poetics* (1449^{b}5, 1450^{a}4, 1451^{a}16).[3] Since then, mythos has taken on various meanings: in English during the eighteenth and nineteenth centuries mythos and mythoi often appeared in discussions of myths or stories in the Bible or classical poetry, such as Homer's. Long before George Orwell and Roland Barthes, in English and French respectively, mythos was used to mean a mythology—a body of interconnected myths or stories, in particular religious, political, or cultural tradition (that is, a personal or collective ideology or set of beliefs), political writers from the 1840s onward in the United States were using the term.[4] After the Second World War, Northrop Frye extended to any narrative form Aristotle's use of the word mythos with regard to drama, the meaning of a structuring of events in a text, particularly in terms of archetypal themes or patterns.[5] Although I am using this word in the original Greek sense and take it to be primarily about story rather than about ideology, I am not doing so with emphasis on archetypes. There may well be overlap between mythology as I use it and ideology as its opposite in everyday life, but the opposition between the mythological and ideological helps to clarify the relations between form and content. In the middle ground of dialectics, mythology and ideology clash and contend. So often as words move in speech or writing, they do not progress. So much of language is story-argument or argumentative story, both varying mixtures of the rhetorical imperative to move the audience to action in the world and the poetic practice to move in the putative world of fiction.[6]

6.2 Mythology and Ideology

The relation between mythology and ideology is a troubled one. Perhaps in a certain aspect of modernist poetics there was a sense that a poetic space free from politics existed, but in recent decades many theories of literature have emphasized the political and ideological bent of poetry.[7] It would be foolish to deny the political element of poetry, but I think it important to resist going completely to a sociology of poetry. Here, however briefly, I would like to discuss what distinguishes poetry as poetry, the *mythos* and music that might be intertwined with politics and history but are not identical to them. Poetry itself will suggest its own poetics and its own messiness and intractability in suggesting a theory of itself. Possibly it is the untranslatable in poetry—which we must try to translate in our cultural conversation even within a language and its literature, not to mention between languages and literatures—that constitutes what we desire poetry to be.

By ideology I mean the push to convince, to convert, to control: by mythology I mean the desire to enchant, to evoke, to sing. A parable by Christ is a story that suggests, whereas if the interpretation of that parable is codified and systematized, then it becomes doctrine and dogma. Religion turns to theology. Systematic knowledge is helpful and might even be necessary, but universals also need particulars. Criticism, a kind of secular hermeneutics, can also become, in its systematic form, a secular theology. Poetry seems to invite explication but that invitation to interpretation can turn the craft of words, the made poem, into a fetish. The encrustations of interpretation can become an allegory itself, a metonymy for the poem itself.

Political criticism cannot only seek to be a substitute for poetry but can also try to displace or squash poetics. This rivalry between philosophy and poetry is nothing new. It is played out in the tenth book of Plato's *Republic*. If only, Socrates argues in the climax of this great work of his student, poets would sing a hymn to the republic, then they wouldn't need to be exiled.[8] The most poetic of philosophers also had a penchant for ideological allegory. He embodied the mixing of story and argument. As I have said, poetry is never entirely itself. Nor, it seems, is philosophy. Criticism is also a split, having divided into criticism or hermeneutics and into theory or philosophy. In the past decade in the English-speaking world, theory has largely shed its philosophical side and has turned to sociology, cultural studies, and politics. While having gained something with this turn, theory has also neglected, and in some cases denounced, the formal properties of poetry. To pretend that poetry has no content is perilous but so too is it dangerous to reduce poems to their content. Some might hope for a reconciliation among philosophy, history, and poetry or among what—in the wider terms and practices today—might be called theory, historicism, and the literary. It might well be that the very tensions among them and the care for or concentration on poetry mean that arguments, ideologies, and interpretations cannot leave the mythos—the fictional images, movement and stories—of poetry alone. The utopian, putative, or mythological moment of poetry is often—perhaps constantly—being called or pulled into the fray.

I'm not suggesting that poetry is one thing, that there is one type of poetry. No hymns to the republic of poetry here. Nor do I mean that we should embrace the anti-intellectual world of an ersatz mythology. Ideology in its worst form is a pseudo-mythological performance. We have seen too much of this kind of political illusion masquerading as authentic truth. Some of this nostalgia has been brutal: myths have led to the worst crimes, the greatest abuses of human rights. The mythology I am speculating on—perhaps it doesn't exist except in dreams—is not the return to purity or the fear of the stranger but rather that speech and writing that have the power of openness over time, an expression that opens readers and audience to experience and thought. Here perhaps is Buffon's equation of the person and the style, something Alexander Pope and Matthew Arnold also struck on in their own ways.[9] But quality of expression is not the only measure of the words that are fortunate enough to survive as poetry. Form without content is vapid, and poetry too overburdened with overt meaning—that is, poems that lecture or hector, poetry that neglects form—is not long remembered. Like a firefly on a hot summer's night, poetry flickers and disappears, the distance catching up with us.

6.3   Some Possibilities for Poetry

Perhaps poetry, like literature itself, is too various and changing to be defined. This multiplicity challenges, suggests, calls forth ever-shifting and ever-combining possibilities. Poetry need not be a question of taste but it is one of tastes over time. In English, for instance, there has been a great variety over time and place. A little like historical geography, poetry involves changes even in the same place and apparently in the same culture. The vast changes in Europe and the world in the past hundred years, culturally, technologically, politically, linguistically cannot help but affect the poetry that has been written. A paradox of poetry may be that in all that mutability something in the music and story of poetry, which may not be true or false in the world, endures. It is possible that the essence of poetry is that it is useless. In a world that knows the price of everything but the value of nothing, to paraphrase Oscar Wilde, it may be that words, which can rarely pay the bills let alone raise capital or win elections, are a kind of privileged space, a type of verbal theatre, the reader enters for a time before returning to the more instrumental space of the world.[10] Everyday language occurs in poetry and poetry in everyday language. They prompt and echo each other. It gets harder to separate world and word, ideology and mythology.

It is not for me, one poet and critic amongst many poets and critics, to say what poetry is. It is not for me to give a general or universal theory of poetics, but what I can do is say what poetry is not for me. Only then can I reach a provisional conclusion about what I think poetry might be for me.

Poetry communicates across time and cultures for reasons that are difficult to know. It almost makes the case for the much-maligned sense of universals. That doesn't mean that there is no room for cultural difference. Germans, the English, and North Americans all use different ways to number floors in their hotels. It might be that the universality of poetry is something local to a language. Although I read other languages, I never quite feel at home in them in a poem. This has its advantages.

But it also suggests that something is lost in my reading. When I depend on translations, I realize that I have a new poem as well, a parallel text: the translator's poem. Even though poetic traditions cross-fertilize one another, they are by definition mutually exclusive. No crossing cultures, no translation, can ever be the same as functioning in a mother tongue. That doesn't mean that writing and reading in a mother tongue are true and pure, but suggests that, for most, language is the greatest cultural and poetic bond. Joseph Conrad, Frederick Philip Grove, and Nancy Huston all give this mother-tonguism the lie, yet, to some extent, the world of poetics is the burnishing of words from one language at a time but not only in one language.[11] Translation throws some of what I say into doubt.

Poetry, as I see it, is the core of poems and prose works, but few texts are unremittingly poetic. Poetry is a sheering away of the hectoring, lecturing, false, manipulating, demeaning. The poetic is a facing of the world and nature, others and self, relentlessly looking for the best way to cut out the dross, flab, fakery. By referring to the "poetic" I am once more suggesting that there are properties of poetry in other genres that constitute the literary as well as in philosophy, history, and other discourses. This I have said but will say it in another way from another angle, which allows for amplification. In the world, unlike in the putative space of poetry, the myths of Plato and Toynbee, whether one believes the truth in them, have a poetic aspect.[12] Nor is all poetry always poetic: the instrumental, argumentative, and ideological dimensions modify the execution of poetry. What distinguishes poetry most— what is its nub even if other discourses share this property to some degree but not usually in such a concentrated form—is its language. That language—when it is most being itself—often includes images and forms that involve concrete representations. The movement of poetry seldom attains sustained abstraction: it often suggests through and beyond the concrete. Poetry expresses this form and language through myth: it is not a logical argument about actual events in the world, a recitation or coherent interpretation of historical fact, or a political handbook.

Poetry is not a career or a hierarchy of flattery: its power is that it has none. Poets are unacknowledged and are not legislators even if they are of the world. Poetry is expression whose happy marriage of form and content means a word need not be changed. Poetry is, through the metaphorical urge, a recreation of the animistic urge. It makes the world alive again even if the reader resists this union of subject and object or leaves it for the fallen world of split subjects when the poem is over. It is a temporal union for writer and reader and not a totalitarian yearning for a world that has no diversity in unity. Poetry contains this feeling of unity of person and world, a momentary realm of beauty and truth. Poetry is not propaganda, the commercial urge and political urge to manipulate and control others for the controller's profit, ideologically and financially.

6.4   A Poetry that Moves, or through the Vanishing Point

Poetry moves in human language. It needs interpretation but when the moment of interpretation begins, perhaps even in the original writing, the poem has begun to fall away from itself. That falling away is the critical distance poetry needs so as not to degenerate into ersatz mythology, but fallenness also means that the form and music must function in a world of content. The medium is and is not the message: it is, because the form of poetry is what makes it different, but is not the medium, because the content matters. Poetry might approach the condition of music, but of choral music.

Poetry is mythological in the sense that Jack and Jill went up the hill cannot be true or false whereas Abraham Lincoln was shot and died can be. However, a sonnet by Shelley on the rottenness of English politics is not simply about poetry itself. Clearly, as Philip Sidney knew, poetry affirms nothing, but it also affirms something.[13] It is only when it affirms too much denotatively that it dissolves.

Personally, we talk about poetry, but if I talk about poetry too much, as interesting as that might be for me (and I hope not too dull for others), I am glad to return to poetry itself, which is quite different. No matter how much I talk about poetry, I don't think I have it in my hands until I make or read a poem worthy of the name of poem. The proof is in the making, a practical end in the vanishing world of the theory of poetry. And so I end, perhaps like a firefly, with my own vanishing act.

PART 3

Readings: Writers, Images, and Poets

CHAPTER SEVEN

Creating the Word: Northrop Frye and Writing

7.1 Finding a Context

The longer I've lived the more I realize that I belong in a certain context. The more completely I am that, I think the more I am acceptable to others. It's the law in literature, which I've often expressed of Faulkner's devoting himself to a county with an unpronounceable name in Mississippi and getting the Nobel Prize in Sweden.

Northrop Frye in Cayley, *Northrop Frye*, 215–16

In an interpenetrating world every community would be the centre of the world.

Frye in Cayley, *Northrop Frye*, 65

Northrop Frye attempted to achieve recognition and understanding from different points of view. As someone who tried to declare the independence of criticism from literature, he created his own anatomy of the critique of the literary, building magnificently on Plato, Aristotle, Longinus, and others who made criticism a branch of their philosophical observations. Their ways of seeing or theoria helped to make a part of aesthetics. Frye did much in this domain. In some ways, over a long time criticism grew distinct from exegesis and commentary (which had their roots in the explication of sacred texts such as the Bible and secular ones such as Homer's) and from rhetoric (oration; the art of persuasion; the relation between speaker and audience, writer and reader). Frye came along in a period when many human sciences (the humanities and social sciences) were developing as fields and academic disciplines partly as a result of, or as a response to, the developments in the natural sciences. Just as Frye was proclaiming criticism, it was changing into theory. The critic became the theorist—the Greek *kritikos* meant to be able to discern whereas *theōria* suggested contemplation and *theōrein* signified to observe. Two related means of seeing led to a shift in literary studies in the 1960s that left the critical path of Frye aside as the theoretical way became the most current and preferred choice, particularly from the early 1980s. Nevertheless, Frye's relation to textual and theoretical methods that tried to explain what the text meant and how the author constructed theme, character, and structure meant that others who advocated a hermeneutics of suspicion or a skepticism about the possibility of stable meaning in literary and other texts did not always give him his due.

Ways of seeing shift: this is one of the ways of culture. There is no going back even if the moving forward implicitly and surreptitiously mines the past. Frye borrowed from his predecessors and the classical past and others came to him to see what they could find and discover. Recognition takes on many forms. Frye expressed a theoretical imagination.[1] Like Brecht, I think that a pocketful of theories is best because world, image, and text are so complex. Over generations, we make adjustments in culture and the observation of nature. Recognition is something apparently over and beyond time but also of it. Anagnorisis seems both timeless and vulnerable to time. Frye, the critic, tried to see what he could, and so did Frye, the writer. His efforts at fiction and poetry as well as plans for writing were an aspect of his asymptotic approach to seeing the world and the literary.

Although having a gift for language and structure, Northrop Frye could not find a place as a novelist. In his notebooks, Frye is given to the invention of possible worlds of putative novels. Occasionally, he writes a paragraph, a sketch, or a fragment of a novel, but we do not have a novel by Frye in a finished and published form. Even though he published some poetry and short fiction and over twenty books of cultural, biblical, and literary criticism, Frye could not, or would not, complete a novel for a reading public. His desire to be a novelist haunts some of his notebooks. In the *Locust-Eaters*, the Kennedy-Megill novel that I have discussed elsewhere, Frye uses a contrast between Western Canada and English Canada, of alienation and the *civis* of the university as a means of expressing his own experience and world.[2] Frye, however, unlike Faulkner and Margaret Laurence, was not able to create a full fictional world of the place where he grew up. It is Frye's expression of the desire to create fiction while abandoning it that is the central paradox of his spectral career as a novelist and, therefore, of this chapter on Frye's fictions about making fiction. As someone with a theoretical imagination, Frye struggled with the novelist's craft. In search of that fictional Canada, he loses himself, to use a metaphor from *Locust-Eaters*, on the long straight prairie roads and turns the binoculars against himself. More generally, Frye's talk about novels seems to become a substitute for the novels themselves. Frye cannot sustain a fictional equivalent of *Fearful Symmetry* or *Anatomy of Criticism*, but his fiction and notes suggest that his unfinished business reveals much about his imagination and his road not taken. Fiction is Frye's blue guitar.

This chapter is concerned with how Frye approaches a fiction without ever attaining it, what might be called the asymptote of fiction or asymptotic creativity. The talk about a novel becomes more than "notes towards": it is metonymic and represents an interpretative or ideological substitute for *muthos* or mythology itself. The only hope Frye has of overcoming this slide into the entire necessity of ideology, which he recognizes, is to mitigate it by rendering the ideological partial through recreating the word, through the "theoretical imagination."[3] In this fictional space alone can fiction be redeemed as something that is theoretically in and of itself even when it is part of a practical continuum of discourse and signs, where boundaries blur? If Frye's desire for the novel is a description without a place, an ideological argument in search of a mythology unmoved by time, then it calls into question the possibility of the inandofitselfness of fiction or literature and the autonomy of literary criticism or theory, the central idea in *Anatomy of Criticism* and, perhaps, in Frye's career. In any event, this is the idea for which he was and is best known.

7.2   Looking for Self-Expression

The novel, for Frye, becomes the unofficial geography of his imagination, the private musings and representations in his notebooks, a counter-terrain to his public acts in lectures, interviews, and books. In this private fiction, like his published short stories and poems, Frye seeks a voice and a place, looking for the physical and spiritual markers of his life in Canada or his years as a student in England. At one level, he wrestles with the green and pleasant land of his mentor, William Blake, and the difference in the hostile environment of the Canadian prairies he experienced one summer as a student preacher.[4] *Locust-Eaters* contrasts the university town of Eastern Canada, an analogue for where Frye felt at home, with the alien landscape of the endless land under the big sky where outsiders, if not all humans, feel naked and watched. It is a good thing that Frye did not spend the winter in the Bench in Saskatchewan or he would have been more depressed than he reported in his letters to his future wife, Helen.[5] Frye, who like T.S. Eliot and Wallace Stevens sought to escape personality, could not do so in his fiction. It is sometimes raw and bare and autobiographical, despite the wit, irony, and dialogue of ideas. This aspect of the modernist writer, struggling to escape what cannot be escaped, might have put Frye off in a Canada where it was hard enough to find an audience. As my epigraphs might suggest, Frye's quest for creativity and fiction presented problems at the level of the local and personal as well as of the practical and theoretical roles of fictionality itself. Frye's struggle for and with the novel produces interesting fiction with significant problems, but not a novel. In some ways this lack of an actualized *telos* is more attractive, leading us to an anatomy of the desire of desire.

If literature is like the dark side of the moon that we know from inference or a black hole we recognize indirectly through the detection of a gravitational pull, then the asymptotic nature of Frye's work as a novelist, much of which was unpublished, unseen, private, incomplete, pointing to vast unwritten novels does not mean that at one level Frye is not a novelist. His notebooks might be considered one large serial modernist novel, a prose song of the self, a cross between the mythical fragments of Blake's marginalia and unfinished epic, Eliot's *The Waste Land* and its notes and the metafiction of Borges, in which the fiction calls attention to itself where an imagined archive is archive enough. The notebooks perform other tasks, but they are a parallel and unofficial muthos to the public tale of Frye's criticism and theory.

Frye's notebooks are full of comments on stories he is writing and publishing and on novels he never sees into print or never writes at all. During the late 1930s, while he was at Merton College Oxford and on his return to Canada, Frye wavers between confidence and doubt. In his letters to Helen Kemp, his future wife, he displays this contradiction and ambivalence: "I shall never write a novel until I reach maturity, which will be whenever the summation of my past experiences takes on a significant unity" (May 22, 1935) and "I want to get a novel written and published. I've got the stuff of an unusually good writer in me" (May 15, 1939). This double attitude can be seen in Frye's realistic assessment of his art on the verge of his twenty-third birthday and the genealogy of a great Menippean tradition he traces for his novel in sonnet form, which seems to be "Quiet Consummation."[6] The first claim about his novel Frye makes to Helen on June 28, 1935: "I rather think it will be either so bad I shan't do anything with it, such as showing it to my friends or re-reading it, or good enough to be accepted. Somehow I don't think I'll write an unreadable novel. I've got a fair idea of prose rhythm, a fairly decent literary education (for a novelist), a fairly good eye for caricature, and a fairly good idea of what comedy is about. Anyway, we'll see. Just another experiment."[7] The second claim, probably written a couple of years later at Oxford, sounds like the systematic genre critic turning his analytical gaze back on his creative work:

> The sonata-form novel will be my great anatomy, perhaps containing the whole *Summa* and *Cassandra* schemes. Its ancestry goes through *Ulysses*, *Sartor Resartus*, *Tristram Shandy*, *Gulliver's Travels* and *A Tale of a Tub*, *The Anatomy of Melancholy*, to Rabelais. Recalls from ancient history, fantastic romance & realist sketching, generalized character study, extracts from an unpublished book, will all be tucks, and the Protestant scheme recalls the anti-Catholic outlook of all the great anatomies, just as the sonata form recalls *Sartor Resartus* & the triple organization of Burton & Joyce, and the complete scheme of four parts of *Gulliver's Travels* and the musical schemes of Sterne.[8]

Frye is readable and does have a good ear and his fiction is often satirical. Whether he was the Canadian Rabelais, as Anthony Burgess once said of Robertson Davies, is another matter and that the anatomy is a Protestant form is something that denies its classical origins and might surprise Rabelais. Frye's doubting confidence contains enough truth to shed light on Frye's fiction. His talk about writing is not so quiet a consummation, which may have been a substitute for the novel itself, something that scholars will have to test as they search the Frye papers for a complete version of the sonata-novel. If and when it is found, that novel resembles *Locust-Eaters*; then, Frye's fiction, although accomplished, will be like Frye's noble Menippean genealogy more in wishfulness than in observance. *Anatomy of Criticism* becomes Frye's great contribution to the genre of the anatomy.

Frye's inventory of invention for fictional worlds shows a young writer searching for stories. He is ironic with himself, aware of his predicament: "A historical novel on the English 14th c. might be a possibility, when I find something out about the 14th c."[9] On the other hand, Frye's ideas in the notebooks are printed in related forms, although it is not always clear which came first. At Oxford, he writes a note about a ghost story that parodies fascist art: "Ghost story—when supernatural event strikes Lew his first feeling is enormous sense of relief & exhilaration—he can now throw away his belief in tiresome scientific exactness. Say, this has possibilities. Devil tempts him, & he rides off on a broomstick [cackling?] joyously: this combines End of World & Fascist novel parodies. Second study in the end of the world. Better in Chap. V."[10] Frye's fiction includes ghostly themes and parodies on fascism. In 1936, *Acta Victoriana* published Frye's story, "The Ghost," which is a koan or a story about the moments after death, and in 1940 *Canadian Forum* brought out "The Resurgent," a satiric parable about fascist art. In entry 79 of Notebook 4, Frye associates abstention with fascism: "Wine will be the ruin of France, is an actual temperancer's statement. The trouble is the Petain crowd agree." In "Affable Angel," Harry remarks, "Not bad chaps, Nazis. . . . But could I get them to drink? Not them."[11] Frye associated the Middle Ages with a life affirming drinking of beer.[12] The apocalypse of imminent war in the late 1930s appears to have informed Frye's notebooks and fiction. In "Reflections in a Mirror," a draft of which appears in Notebook 20, Frye sets out a fiction that involves parallels between the visible and invisible worlds:

> I have been struggling for some time to think of a new fiction formula, and all my ideas tend to revolve around Rilke's idea of the poet's perceiving simultaneously the visible & the invisible world. In practice that means a new type of ghost or supernatural story, possibly approached by way of some science-fiction development. The idea is a vision of another life or another world so powerfully plausible as to make conventionally religious & anti-religious people shake in their shoes.[13]

This visionary fiction parallels the visionary poetics of Frye's criticism. Frye was much taken with the visions of Blake, Yeats, and others.[14] Another instance of the parallelism and supplementarity is the relation between a note at Oxford and a story published a few years later. The note provides a sketch: "Two men walk along the Thames embankment in a fog, talking of unpredictable feelings from the dismal: Dickens & Eliot: surrealism. Work up to expecting supernatural: radiant angel appears: won't do as too cheerful & normal."[15] Over the center of this paragraph is the word "done." The closest story to this description is "Affable Angel," which appeared in *Acta Victoriana* in 1940. Megill and Mrs. Kennedy from *Locust-Eaters* are scattered throughout Notebook 4,

which is full of best-laid plans.[16] The young Frye is teeming with ideas
for novels. Whereas Frye's notations about fiction often acted as substitutes for the fiction itself, they sometimes adumbrated or supplemented
his published stories.

One of the most interesting interplays in Frye's writing is his talk
about writing a novel and the actual fragments of novels in a diary,
which constitutes a possible metonymy for his novelistic pursuits. Frye is
self-reflexive about the nature of his ongoing but discontinuous diary.
Near the beginning of his diary for 1949, he reveals the tension between
life and art, miscellany and narrative: "The thing is not to be alarmed at
the miscellaneous character of one's life & stylize the diary accordingly,
as I've tended to do. It should be a continuous imaginative draft, not
itself a work of literature."[17] Frye's diary, written over many years, is a
substitute for other writing, including novels, and an example of the art
of writing. The diary is like an autobiographical novel, but also resembles a draft that lists and reflects briefly on quotidian events. The entry
for August 20, 1942 gets to the nub of the tension in Frye's diary and
perhaps in all diaries between the shaping of muthos and the flow of
everyday life. Frye uses Samuel Pepys as a way of discussing the diary. In
Pepys, Frye cannot see his own reflection, hypothesizing that the gulf of
individualism and Romanticism separates them:

> I've been reading in Pepys, to avoid work. I can't understand him
> at all. I mean, the notion that he tells us more about himself & gives
> us a more intimate glimpse of the age than anyone else doesn't
> strike me. I find him more elusive and baffling than anyone. He has
> a curious combination of apparent frankness and real reticence that
> masks him more than anything else could do. One could call it a
> "typically English" trait, but there were no typical Englishmen then
> and Montaigne performs a miracle of disguise in a far subtler &
> bigger way. Pepys is not exactly conventional: he is socially disci-
> plined. He tells us nothing about himself except what is generic.
> His gaze is directed out: he tells us where he has been & what he
> has done, but there is no reflexion, far less self-analysis. The most
> important problem of the Diary & of related works is whether this
> absence of reflexion is an accident, an individual design, or simply
> impossible to anyone before the beginning of Rousseauist modes of
> interior thought.[18]

In planning fiction and observing daily routines, can Frye's systematic
mind, which was so often concerned with genre, conventions, and the

generic, escape a generalized *inventio*, listing, and gnomic utterance of laws? Although he aspires to the minute particulars of Blake, it is possible that Frye, like Pepys, gathers his strength through a general wit and structure that conceals as it reveals. Even if these are diaries not published by their authors, they are the work of practiced writers caught up in the drama of culture and ideas. Thomas Carlyle's image of clothing as a metaphor for culture perhaps provides the link between Pepys and Frye.

Language cannot escape its rhetorical surfaces even in the service of sincere self-revelation. For Frye, Pepys becomes a visionary who enables the reader to visualize clothes and cultural surface, a man who conceals as he confesses. Pepys tells of his life without being autobiographical:

> Pepys knew perfectly well what he was doing: he wrote a book which he well knew to be an art-form. His motive in doing so is not obvious, because his *genre*, the diary, is not a branch of autobiography, as [John] Evelyn's is. He was a supreme observer, making himself a visionary, *se faire voyant*, as much as Blake or Rimbaud. And he knew perfectly how effective & oracular the random is: his camera keeps on clicking after he gets in bed with his wife because he knows better than to shut it off. A real artistic passion for observation in itself with no attempt at a creative follow-through is rare, but it exists.[19]

Frye himself deflected the world from his personality. In his criticism he warned of the dangers of value judgments, but in his unpublished diary of 1949, he says of the diary: "I also hope it will be of some moral benefit, in passing a kind of value judgment, implicit or explicit, on whether I've wasted the day or not, whether my schedule is in shape, whether my unanswered letters are piling up, etc."[20]. The life and values of the critic are to be put aside in criticism, but in his diary, where he discusses life, writing, and criticism, lessons on values might be learned. Is Frye, the diarist and critic, as abstract as he accuses Pepys of being? Frye continues his entry on the great diarist:

> And there's a riddling, gnomic quality in the photograph absent from painting. When I try to visualize Pepys I visualize clothes & a cultured life-force. I have a much clearer vision of the man who annoyed Hotspur or Juliet's Nurse's husband. I feel that Pepys makes the dead eerie and transplanetary, not our kind of species at all. He does not observe character either: I can't visualize his wife

or my Lord. Even music he talks about as though it were simply a part of retiring for physic.[21]

This comment on Pepys' abstract chronicle of his times raises a similar question about Frye, who gives commentary about books and the body of criticism, sketches, and fragments for the concrete observation and description of whole and sustained novels. The paradox persists: the writer reveals the self to hide it.

Except for *Locust-Eaters*, Frye's fictional worlds do not develop a Canadian setting or a village life, like that in Austen, Faulkner, or Laurence, that paradoxically represents the world itself. Frye does not hide his Canadianness in his criticism, diaries, or fiction but expresses it.[22] He does not, however, build on it as he might have, working, perhaps, on the Maritimes he knew in his youth rather than modulating it in *Locust-Eaters* from a prairies he had lived in for a few months and the Ontario of his university years. In his fiction he attempted some internationalism, especially drawing on his experiences in England. None of this is said to fault Frye but only to qualify his observations in the epigraphs I have used to introduce this chapter. Early on, he did not embrace his Canadian identity in fiction as much as in criticism, possibly because it was a position that was far less acceptable internationally with readers of fiction than with arbiters in criticism. Sometimes in his schemes and theory Frye created such a village or a sketch of such country life as a microcosm, but he never wrote a full-length fictional study of this kind of place. Not until after 1960 did a body of Canadian writers, to paraphrase Frye, begin to write about a here that was here rather than there.

In the diaries Frye is ironic and hopeful in expressing his various motivations for wanting to write and publish fiction. In jest and earnest he gives money, distraction, fame, talent, and genius as motives and suggests schemes for detective, historical, domestic, religious, philosophical, historical, speculative, satirical novels and many other modes of fiction. On July 21, 1942, his diary entry discusses his book on Blake and ironically offers fiction as a compensation should that critical work fall on deaf ears: "If the public doesn't like it I shall write a novel which shall earn me a million tax-free dollars, exclusive of movie rights, & lose me my job. The Verlaine-Rimbaud story would make a swell novel, as I dare say two or three thousand people have thought before. It could be combined with the de Nerval one."[23] Here Frye is following up on his earlier entry of July 18, where he describes Marcus Adeney, a cellist who played in the Toronto symphony and edited a magazine. The poets E.J. Pratt, A.J. Smith, Earle Birney, and others opposed this magazine, and Frye says that Adeney's intellectual development was arrested in his teens. Such a conclusion leads Frye to the idea of writing a novel about such a person in a village: "I'd like to do a novel on a small-town genius *in vacuo*, by the way, ending up with a de Nerval finish: subjective apocalypse, objective collapse. That's really the kind of thing I've been trying to dope out all along."[24] In the entry of July 30, Frye explains why he would prefer to stick with a tough Rimbaud in his idea for a novel rather than Verlaine, who was bad but came back to the Mother Church and can only talk about the badness of his youth.[25] Between these entries on this possible novel, Frye analyzes detective and ghost stories: he is fond of both but prefers the latter because of it use of atmosphere. In his writing of the 1930s and 1940s, Frye condemns stereotypes, especially racial ones such as anti-Semitism, and he finds some of this stereotyping to occur in English detective fiction no matter how technically brilliant it is, especially with regard to social conventions. The difficulty with detective stories is that they are stereotypes. Obliquely, Frye suggests what kind of detective story he might write: "I think a story in symposium form, with a Marlow-narrator supplying clues and his auditors all guessing shrewdly & wrong, would have its points."[26] The listeners would be, as Frye describes himself, readers of detective stories.

7.3   The Paradoxical Visionary

Not surprisingly Frye also planned an academic novel. It seems to have been separate from the "Megill-Kennedy crowd" of *Locust-Eaters*.[27] As early as 1939, Frye had considered an academic element in one of his planned novels described in a notebook he calls a diary: "Novel on two brothers: one a direct-action revolutionary, [the] other a studious weakling who admires him & wastes his own time & talents in a futile effort to compete."[28] In Notebook 20, after considering the Bardo Novel, which is one of many novels in his inventory lists, Frye says: "Well, anyway, that's one idea. Another, and a much more immediate one, is my university novel. The theme of that is simple enough: I have the theme, but I need a matching (or rather a containing) plot."[29] From the plan for a speculative fiction on the relation between dream and waking, the spiritual and material, Frye shifts to a liberal arts college where the center of the novel is a dispute over curriculum reform and, therefore, more immediate in Frye's professional life. He says he will have to read Mary McCarthy, James Reid Parker, and others who have produced academic novels. For Frye, the situation and not the president of the college is malignant: university presidents in Canada are not totalitarian but are put in "dictatorial situations."[30] The dramatic tension is to come from the struggle between the president and a professor of English: "I think of the focus of the book as a vigorous agon between two highly articulate people. The relation between them is one of enmity but not one of hatred."[31] Of his two antagonists, Frye observes that "they fight with complete detachment" and Frye himself keeps some ironic distance from the fictional dreams of his fictions. In his detached mood he is willing to speculate on the relation between his two sides: fiction and criticism. The academic novel reminds him of his general views on that relation as well as bringing the Bardo novel back up:

> Every once in a while I get a fit of euphoria, probably induced by gas in the stomach, in which I feel that I'm capable of writing good fiction. The old superstition that fiction is creative & criticism second-rate & second-hand talking about creation dies hard, although I've lived to see most criticism, including mine, become more creative than most fiction. Finishing A and C left me willing to speculate about Bardo again.[32]

At various times over his career, Frye tries to describe the Bardo novel he wants to write. This is a type of ghost story that Frye thinks is an artificial form related to the afterlife, a literary convention for religions. This observation leads Frye to wonder whether there are parallel ways of conceiving of reality, such as the dead, ghosts, spirits, angels, or some new manifestation—the "new twist" he is seeking.[33] A new shape, which represents unconscious meaning, might be found in the romance and anatomy traditions. As in his criticism, Frye is interested in the relation between religion and literary convention and between the subjective and objective.[34] Frye, like his mentor Blake, explores the visionary, where poetry explores the supernatural, the realm of religion, but with infinite supposition, and where criticism looks upon the superhuman with a human eye.[35] It is not an accident that Frye, for the lectures at Emmanuel College, Toronto, which became the basis for the title of his posthumous book *The Double Vision* returned to a poem in Blake's letter to Thomas Butts on November 22, 1802:

> For double the vision my eyes do see,
> And a double vision is always with me;
> With my inward eye 'tis an old man grey;
> With my outward a thistle across my way.[36]

The Bardo story in particular and the ghost story in general appeal to this twoeyedness or parallelism between the physical and spiritual worlds.

This double vision is a humanizing of the world, a recognition that the senses are not sufficient, that a subject recognizes itself as part of what it perceives. Poet and critic recreate the word in different ways, the one with possible worlds including the supernatural, the other in giving human understanding to the superhuman. This represents the doubleness and tension in the spiritual Frye. He recognizes the otherworldly as something he wants to suppose in his fiction, but the critic in him reminds himself and whoever else might read his notebook that such suppositions are not actual knowledge of the afterlife or superhuman but are literary conventions. Blake holds out the challenge of seeing at once the thistle and the old man. Frye's dilemma is how to represent the inward and outward vision not just within his fiction but between his critical and fictional worlds. Perhaps Frye's longing for fiction in his notebook-diaries is a feeling that criticism is not enough. Although he declared the creativity and independence of criticism from literature, a productive and necessary fiction or move, Frye seems to have felt (and I use this word because it is almost a need or a surfacing unconscious recurrence) that writing fiction would give him something that criticism, as important as it was, could not. Creating the word in religion and "creating" it in a different and independent way in literature were not exactly the same forms of verbal "recreation" as criticism was. In seeking redemption, the *telos* of much of Frye's work, religion, "poetry," and criticism are three ways in a quest in a world strewn with double signs such as thistles and old men. The resurrection of the soul, the poetic spirit, and the critical understanding are distinct but related. The identity with God and nature through writing becomes one of Frye's primary goals. Recognition or epiphany through reading the signs and purifying them through writing is another way of stating the embodiment of this aim. This is why I have called Frye a paradoxical visionary, whose first and last books, *Fearful Symmetry* (1947) and *The Double Vision* (1991), are on vision. The wholeness and atonement of imagination in the separate but related realms of religion and literature are Frye's concern. He often thought of himself as a person of the metaphor. That self-image caused him some anxiety because when he wrote fiction he was expressing himself primarily through metaphor but when he wrote criticism, even if he is granted his wish to be a metaphorical thinker, he is still thinking, which involves analysis and the breaking down of wholes into their parts even if, like Humpty Dumpty, it puts them back together again. *Anatomy of Criticism* is not like Rabelais's fictional anatomies. At one level, *Anatomy* does have a metaphorical and fictional structure and its examples are often examples or metaphorical shards from other stories, but at another level it is a theoretical structure. Frye had declared the independence of criticism from literature but then wanted it to be creative in the same way as stories, poems, and plays—through metaphor. As Thomas Aquinas and others argued, analogies that tell stories and analogies that further arguments are related but are also distinct. The same is true about metaphor. It also probably applies to muthos in history, literature and criticism, and philosophy. The theoretical imagination is imaginative, and sometimes in ways similar to the poetic imagination, but they are not identical. All writing is worthy and all is rhetorical, but there are differences, if only theoretical and not practically provable, between the kinds of writing such as theory and literature, history and philosophy, physics and biology. The disjunction in Frye might have been a distinction intellectually between poetry and criticism (to use his terms) but a conflation or confusion of them unconsciously or emotionally. Metaphor is important to both but, even when functioning in a similar manner, it finds itself in different contexts with different conventions in fiction and theory.

7.4   Critic and Writer

The critic and the writer coexist sometimes uneasily in Frye's notes. In planning fiction Frye is often theoretical and in his theory he uses story and metaphor. His thematics overlap and oppose each other. In Notebook 20, Frye speculates that the formal principles of art are found within us, so that they are expressed subjectively; a heightening of the senses through light and darkness or a mental disturbance through mescalin would allow a person to "see the real formal principles: the apocalyptic world of metaphor, with its jewelled trees & the like, & its demonic opposite."[37] In speaking about a possible story involving "the luminously realistic," Frye turns the possibility into a negation of his dreams of writing fiction: "I've never written fiction because [Aldous] Huxley's novels are there to remind me how bad it would be."[38] After saying that he will not write fiction, Frye returns to a desire to write. And one type of writing that fascinates Frye is ghostly or occult fiction, something that treats the inside and outside: "The inward or extroverted energy is for dealing with the world as given or created—anyway, as it is. An inward-turned energy explores the powers that create it: that's always the first principle of all occultism."[39] This returns

Frye to his interest in invisible shaping powers through a recognition that arises through the unconscious until, from this subjectivity, a new type of objectivity arises. Huxley's luminous realism had made Frye think about a detective story, but this author also suggests this magical fiction and in the context of Tolkien and Le Fanu:

> I've been reading Tolkien, who has certainly come very close to the kind of thing I'd like to do. The magic ring, the talisman on which the story turns, is an evil thing: when you put it on you become invisible to the ordinary world (which in this book includes dwarfs and elves), but visible to evil spirits. Hence you gain great power over the ordinary world at the price of being enslaved by evil. In Le Fanu's *Green Tea* story green tea (cf. Huxley's mescalin) breaks down the barrier between ordinary & dark worlds & a hideous monkey appears as a hallucination to a respectable bachelor clergyman. The story is derived from Swedenborg, who says that evil spirits live in a man but can't see him because he can't see them. If he could, he'd be in for it, because they'd try to destroy him.[40]

Like Robertson Davies, who, as Master, told ghost stories at Christmas after the founding of Massey College in Toronto during the early 1960s, Frye is fascinated with the occult and the atmosphere of "spirit" fiction. Frye explores the possibility of a dead narrator in the land of the living, the opposite of Dante's living narrator in the land of the dead.[41] Still in search of new twists, Frye plots out the possible worlds of his fiction, but increasingly, it seems from what we know at this point, he sketched out notes and lists that became substitutes for the fiction whereas in his youth he wrote on related themes in fiction and criticism. Perhaps a demanding career as a teacher, critic, guest lecturer, and administrator devoured the time he once had to write fiction.

Mythology in criticism and in fiction was a persistent interest during Frye's career. His notes reveal the tension between Frye's longing to write fiction and his critical self-restraint that delays or arrests such a project. In 1962, Frye was still pursuing the idea of a Bardo novel. Fiction was not second words to Frye although something prevented him from making it a part of his published record or an equal half of his métier. In Notebook 2, he works for and against himself in his entries on the Bardo novel: "I don't want supernatural materialism either. The book's ideology would be a Bardo projection of my own: perhaps the deadee would not regret having developed my kind of outlook and would go back to get it. It wouldn't be quite as bald as that in presentation, but it would be in essential theory. God damn it. This kind of mooning isn't fiction-writing."[42] Frye presents interesting theory or ideas for a novel in autobiographical terms, or at least in relation to his intellectual biography, but then dismisses the possible fiction as mooning. In a similar vein but in reversing the structure from self-praise then self-criticism to detraction then compliment, he refers to his own "fictional reveries" as prophetic and sometimes showing up in the works of professional writers.[43] Frye then calls his Bardo novel a *koan* to think about and exercise the mind and in an ambiguous justification says that he should let someone else write such a novel who needs bread to eat more than he does.[44] The Bardo novel, then, represents a complex of ideas for Frye and is another example of the ambivalence and contradiction. This kind of fiction has a crisis that most often represents "a threshold scene, a plunge into another order of being" and includes a recognition that is a return.[45] The boundary between life and death, from ghosts through apocalypse to resurrection and redemption fascinated Frye, so that much of his fiction and many of his "fictional reveries" as well as his criticism on the Bible and on romance and comedy focused on this theme. Human and divine comedy, especially in the structural sense, from the u-shaped narrative of the Scripture to Prospero's magical resolution and restoration, can be found in the fictions and the metafictions of the notebooks.

7.5   The Road Not Taken

Even though these notes over the years contain various webs of fictions, of what I have called elsewhere, borrowing from Frost to give to Frye, the "road not taken," Frye is sometimes hard on himself as a novelist or aspiring writer. Sometimes he criticizes his style: "The idiom of what I have written seems to be wrong: I don't seem to be fundamentally interested in writing the way novelists write, collecting the sort of data they collect, or throwing myself into the novelist's attitude with any conviction. What I write, with all its wit, is still pedantic."[46] Frye thinks that he avoids the themes of novelists, the externals of the world like business and war and "that the novel is decidedly not my main interest, & so is hard to integrate to the rest of my activities."[47] Here is a young scholar who will become one of the greatest critics writing in English, someone who has written some interesting fiction, dreaming of writing great novels and stories but also being brutally honest with himself, perhaps too hard on himself. Recognizing his penchant for satire, Frye wonders whether he should write "intellectual slapstick" rather than novels, something Kurt Vonnegut might have said, except that he has made the novel, that Protean term, include a slapstick of ideas.[48] Of one of his largest novel-fragments, Frye declares: "I feel that the Locust-Eaters, though clever, is mediocre, fits a too-well-established pattern, & would embarrass my friends. It's crotch-bound: it hasn't the Frye swing & confident brilliance, & represents the sort of careful synthetic wit I should have been producing at twenty & couldn't. As a novelist I suffer from abnormally arrested development."[49] Once again, even after such self-excoriation (mingled with the self-praise of his own brilliance), Frye suggests what fiction he might write, something satirical like Waugh, more bookish than Rabelais but less so than Robert Burton, "something that strikes glancing blow at fiction but is fundamentally a reader's synthesis of life."[50] Frye thinks of his critical brilliance and sees his fiction falling short. He is also worried about what his friends, perhaps especially those at the university, might think of his fiction. In his fiction he has not written and rewritten over the years as he has in criticism, which was part of his training at university. For all his self-criticism, he now finds an affinity with Dickens and Charlie Chaplin because, being sardonic and not bitter, he is "genuinely sentimental."[51] All this doubt is in the middle of notes toward his novel *Locust-Eaters*. Critical undertow is pulling Frye under even as he tries to write fiction. He sees in his many plans for a novel the usurpation in fiction what was planned for nonfiction: "I think that, as I'm not essentially a novelist, I should disabuse myself of the dream of huge complex masterpieces, especially as my dream of eight has gone back to an original essay ambition which growing familiarity with the novel usurped."[52] This critique leads Frye to say that he will keep *Locust-Eaters* short, but does not make him abandon it. About twenty years later, Frye is still expressing his dream of being a novelist. Meanwhile during the 1940s and 1950s, Frye spins out an inventory of novel ideas. Here is a metafictional description whose style and ideas might find itself in a novel of ideas, such as Thomas Mann's *Magic Mountain*:

> When I think of myself as a fiction-writer, I feel that I could produce dialogue, characterization, & wit enough to pass muster in a good detective story, if I could write a good detective story, which I couldn't. That's why I feel the need of a containing formula, not a tight one; something that has run through Lucian & Rabelais, to give me something an amateur could work on in odd moments.

One idea I had a long time ago was a variant of the Jesus novel. Archeologists dig up a fifth gospel, which sheds a quite different light on the rise of Xy (more Gnostic, I should think): authenticity unquestionable. The churches can't absorb it, so their struggles are interesting experiences in doubletalk. If I cold invent a Gospel that *sounded* authentic it'd be terrific—a Grand Inquisitor *theme*.

I think also of a time machine that reconstructs the past but doesn't allow the viewers to be seen or take part in past ages. Such things are used like TV sets (except that they have to occupy the same Newtonian space as what they represent). They supersede history & do a lot of things—no good for the future. Reconstructing texts by inspecting authors, etc.[53]

The desire to write fiction persists in a Frye who is contradictory and ambivalent. He dreams, he calls himself short on his dreams. The drama in the notebooks, both in the fiction and in the comments on fiction, is whether Frye will attain his goal and whether the writing about fiction will take on the dramatic power of fiction itself and join Frye's published criticism as a displacement or metonymy for the fiction itself. In such a supposition, the supposed failure to produce a novel would become the success of the notebook-diary as a Menippean form of fiction-autobiography. The reinvention of a mode would be an appropriate form of success for the great critic of genre. He would cross some borders as he had wanted to and would, like Coleridge, be a spirit or genius (to assume one of Frye's favorite words) of the fragmentary, unfinished but brilliant talk overheard, even if in writing and, eventually, in print.

I end with an anecdote and a confession. Someone suggested that I was wasting space by including "The Critic as Writer" in my book on Frye, which I thought was wrong-headed and the very thing that made Frye worry about his friends' reactions to his fiction. Whereas theory is supposed to be so dominant today in departments of literature, many critics, such as George Steiner, write fiction and many more have dreamed or still dream of writing it. I was told years ago that Alfred Harbage, the accomplished editor of the *Pelican Shakespeare*, wrote detective fiction under an assumed name. Tolkien and C.S. Lewis were accomplished critics and writers. During the 1930s and 1940s, particularly in Canada, it would have been difficult to be a novelist and then to establish a career as a scholar. Today there is still some division between the creative and critical despite the efforts of Frye and Derrida to break down the old stereotypes. Theory has its independence but is not entirely a substitute for literature. Ways of seeing—recognition and theory—blur in the critical and creative functions of writer and reader. A Platonic seriousness about the dangers of poetry to intellectual well-being and a plutocratic concern with its peril to the pocketbook make it difficult to practice, rather than to theorize, writing as one great discourse. Frye's notebooks lead us into this temptation, though not all the way, and that makes them worth reading. After all, Frye knew his poetry and, for him, the reader was the hero, at least when he wasn't worried about becoming a novelist, and perhaps even then.

CHAPTER EIGHT

Seeing Inside Willy Loman's Head:
The Tragedy of the Commoner on Film

In speaking about anagnorisis Aristotle had in mind the tragedies of his own culture. The protagonists of those tragedies were great even if they were flawed (hamartia) and even if the audience moved toward catharsis in the theatrical experience. Despite the continuities that are appealed to in the construction of "Western" culture, which is part of intellectual history and the trope of the translation of empire, there have been great changes. Many of those transformations, especially since the Middle Ages, and, particularly since the advent of the Industrial Revolution, have been technological. Trains, planes, automobiles, film, television, and computers are just a few innovations that go beyond those scientific discoveries that drove navigation, manufacture, warfare, and artistic production. In *The Crucible*, Arthur Miller looked back to the witch-hunt in Salem, Massachusetts, at the end of the seventeenth century to create a typology between that hysteria and the recent outbreak led by McCarthy against Communists and those who would be smeared with that name. In creating *Death of a Salesman*, Miller addressed the idea that an ordinary person could be the focus of a tragedy. Democratic America—the brave New World—could usher in a new kind of hero. Moreover, film and television directors could produce plays with ethical and theatrical values that built on those of the Greeks but that also differed with them. If Willy Loman created a new twist on recognition, for himself and for his audience, then empathy for him, getting inside his head, would possess certain degrees of difference in the theatre.

8.1 A Kind of Tragedy

The debate on whether *Death of a Salesman* is a tragedy persists. Just as Shakespearean tragedy does not always comply with Aristotle's view of tragedy, which he founded on a study of Greek tragedy, Arthur Miller's tragedy of the common man is not the stuff of *Hamlet, Othello, King Lear,* and *Macbeth.* The values of tragedy appear bound up with the historical milieu in which it is written. Willy Loman is an American protagonist of the 1940s, but his appeal is much more universal. The problem for most critics has been Willy's death and the Requiem. Performance can often affect the critical interpretation of a text. Such an influential performance need not be solely in theatre or film but can also occur on television. I intend to examine the ending of an important production of Salesman on television, which based itself closely on a Broadway production, to see whether it can illuminate the critical problem of the conclusion of Miller's play and of its genre.

If Olivier's *Richard III* and *Henry V* served as a measure of interpretation for those plays a generation ago, Hoffman's *Salesman* will probably fulfill that role for this play in our time.[1] Whether the director, Volker Schlondorff, interprets the play, and the problematic ending, in an expressionistic or realistic way, will affect the long-standing debate whether the Requiem is merely sentimental and pathetic, in Miller's sense, or enhances the tragic experience of the play. As John Hagopian and Brian Parker have pointed out, Miller's critical comments on *Salesman* do not always illuminate the nature of the play.[2] Nonetheless, at times the playwright's views help to focus critical debate. Although Miller does not relate "Tragedy and the Common Man" to *Salesman*, he writes it about the same time as the play, and it bears upon the discussion of pathos or tragedy in *Salesman*. At the end of the article, Miller's exhortation and distinction between the pathetic and tragic imply that he thinks Willy is a tragic figure:

> The possibility of victory must be there in tragedy. Where pathos is finally derived, a character has fought a battle he could not possibly have won. The pathetic is achieved when the protagonist is, by virtue of his witlessness, his insensitivity or the very air he gives off, incapable of grappling with a much superior force.
>
> Pathos truly is the mode for the pessimist. But tragedy requires a nicer balance between what is possible and what is impossible. And it is curious, although edifying, that the plays we revere, century after century, are the tragedies. In them, and in them alone, lies the belief—optimistic, if you will, in the perfectibility of man.

It is time, I think, that we who are without kings, took up this bright thread of our history and followed it to the only place it can possibly lead in our time-the heart and spirit of the average man.[3]

Salesman has split critics on its pathetic or tragic nature just as Miller himself has both regrets and hopes for the tragedy of the play. According to Miller, he is "sorry the self-realization of the older son, Biff, is not a weightier counterbalance to Willy's disaster in the audience's mind," but he says "the tragedy of Willy Loman is that he gave his life, or sold it, in order to justify the waste of it."[4] In examining Schlondorff's interpretation, we should ask how tragic and how pathetic are the final confrontation between Biff and Willy, and the Requiem. An author cannot, and should not, control critical response to this work, and the contradictions in *Salesman* must be explored by critics and directors as well as by Miller himself.

8.2   The End of the Play and the End of Tragedy

The end of the play raises questions about the connection between expressionism and realism, the relation of Willy and Biff, and the role of Linda. Others have explored these aspects, but the way Schlondorff interprets them will facilitate a better understanding of the conclusion and determine whether its effect is tragic. Parker has aptly noted the dramatic excitement in Salesman that derives from "its apparent uncertainty in apportioning realism and expressionism."[5] This uncertain technique is in keeping with Willy's contradictory nature. In a well-known passage from the Introduction to the *Collected Plays*, Miller explains the gestation of the play:

The first image that occurred to me which was to result in *Death of a Salesman* was of an enormous face the height of the proscenium arch which would appear and then open up, and we would see the inside of a man's head. In fact, The Inside of His Head was the first title. It was conceived half in laughter, for the inside of his head was a mass of contradiction.[6]

Like Parker, Schlondorff treats this passage seriously as well as Miller's declaration that "I wished to create a form which, in itself as a form, would literally be the process of Willy Loman's way of mind."[7] The audience sees Willy's life and death, past and present, as if through

Willy's eyes. Schlondorff mixes realism and expressionism from the opening scene, where he shows the headlights of Willy's car, then the New York license plate, then the car and Willy from various angles and distances. The scene is almost colorless, or black and white, as if the viewer were back in the 1940s before the wide use of color film. It seems this rendition will be realistic, but just as Willy is going to have an accident, Schlondorff uses slow motion and a shuddering sound, and a door slowly appears through Willy's head. He soon comes through this door, and the story begins.

The door is an important image for Willy. Schlondorff shows the circularity of Willy's story by concentrating on the door. In his own head, Willy enters through the door; Ben leaves through it; and, finally, Willy makes his last exit through it. At the beginning and the end, the director makes the door shimmer in white—Willy's fog and hope. For Schlondorff, the accidents at the first and last meet in Willy's mind during the almost simultaneous sense of past and present the protagonist experiences. The accidents are the pretext for the coming hither and going thence of Everyman, of Willy Loman, through the door of life and death. And the door is also the gateway to Ben's world—the opportunity in Alaska (or was it Africa?)—Willy's mind conjures: the door to the room and bathroom in the hotel in Boston that cannot prevent Biff from discovering his father's adultery; the door to the yard, where the elms grow, where Biff, Willy, and Hap talk and play around the 1928 Chevy—the threshold, as Schlondorff interprets it, between the realistic present and the expressionistic past. This last distinction is too simple, but Schlondorff gives the past more color and a dreamy movement, whereas the scenes inside the house are more colorless and closed. Although different from Jo Mielziner's original set, where the walls were even more imaginary, and from his lighting, which made the memory scenes a leafy, spring green, Schlondorff's set and lighting still differentiate between the texture of the realistic and the expressionistic scenes. The double focus of past and present mingles as the sound of the car crash and the whiteness in this production round out Willy's life. If Schlondorff is not radically reinterpreting the beginning and end, he refuses to reduce the play to either realism or expressionism and, instead, brings out much of its complexity.

When the denouement of Salesman begins is uncertain, owing to the double view of the action, to the mingling of past and present. I take the conclusion to begin when Happy and Biff return home, after leaving Willy in the restaurant, and find Linda waiting for them. This scene is like the familial bloodletting at the end of *Long Day's Journey into*

Night—it is close and oppressive. But the scene in *Salesman* is not as realistic as the one in *Journey*, for Miller surrounds it with Willy, abandoned in the restroom (washroom/w.c.) of the restaurant, hearing the knock of the waiter and dreaming about Biff's knocking on the hotel door in Boston, and with the Requiem. This climactic scene exposes Willy in past and present: Biff deserts him in the restaurant and at the hotel. Willy is humiliated in a mixture of realism and expressionism—the sound and the image of the door haunting him. Schlondorff mixes the colorless present with the colorful past and fades in and out of both to show the continuum of time Willy experiences and the audience witnesses through Willy. The director keeps before him the idea that the play occurs in Willy's head.

Unlike the end of *Journey*, the final scene of *Salesman* is not restricted to a claustrophobic indoors. Biff moves outside, and Linda follows him. Willy is planting his garden in a set that, although different from Mielziner's, is unrealistic, especially because it is a stage set on film for television.[8] This conscious incongruity emphasizes the dream Willy is acting out when he plants his garden. To add to the expressionism, Ben appears, and Willy says, in a line I think Schlondorff kept in mind when interpreting the play: "A man can't go out the way he came in, Ben, a man has got to add up to something."[9] The director will show Willy leaving the door he entered, in both the fog and the purity of white. In the meantime, Willy discusses with Ben the insurance he will give Biff to make his son a success. As an embodiment of Willy's desires and conscience, Ben argues with Willy about the merits of his plan, including a discussion of Willy's foolishness and cowardice, and Willy's vision of his own massive funeral. Biff, who occupied the center of the conversation between Willy and Ben, makes his presence felt, and the confrontation between father and son begins. Once again, the director uses a mixture of realism and expressionism. The action moves back into the house, where the ambivalence and confusion Willy feels about Biff continue. In Act One, Willy tells Linda that Biff is lazy but, in a matter of lines, says that Biff is anything but lazy. Father and son fight when they are together.[10] The end of Act Two shows that although they are still fighting and contradicting, Biff is gaining self-knowledge, even if Willy calls him spiteful.[11] Close-ups reveal the anguish and bottled-up feelings of the characters, allowing no overview or panorama to give them perspective. Miller represents an emotional family encounter, so it is suitable that Biff's crying awakens Willy. The wonder on Hoffman's face as he turns to Kate Reid emphasizes this essential moment: "Isn't that—isn't that remarkable? Biff he likes me!" But after Linda and Happy reassure Willy, he is back to his old delusions: "That boy—that boy is going to be magnificent!"[12] Just then, Ben appears out of the blinding light, a paradox Schlondorff does not miss. If Willy has courage, he lacks self-knowledge, even if Biff's crying frees him. After Ben leaves through the door, Willy does. Amid the whiteness and Linda's anxious voice, Willy crawls unburdened toward death. Willy dreams about the past as he walks out the door into his future. He goes thither as he came hence—and Linda's voice, the door, and the whiteness show just that. Willy fades out as he had faded in, and the crash, the sound of which the audience hears again, is this time fatal.

8.3   Requiem

The Requiem, as Schlondorff interprets it, does not break with the previous action. Out of the blinding whiteness, the director orchestrates the voices of the mourners. When Linda asks, "Why didn't anybody come?" Schlondorff emphasizes the line by fading in, showing the dark figures of the mourners.[13] By using a technique similar to that at the first and last of the main action, he is almost presenting the funeral as if it happens in Willy's head. Miller, however, realizes that the main body of the play and the Requiem also represent other points of view: "while all roads led to Willy the other characters were to feel it was their play, a story about them and not him."[14] Schlondorff stages the many positions of the characters but, through his imagery, frames them with Willy's ideas. The audience has learned to see with Willy's eyes. The figures are almost in black and white, representing a severity that qualifies the possible sentimentality of the end of Act Two and of Linda's "elegy." It is as if Willy knew that no one but Charley and Bernard would show up at his funeral. In a clear moment, he had told Charley that he was his only friend, and Ben warned Willy that Biff would think him mistaken.[15]

The audience sees the five figures across the screen; then Charley and Linda; then Biff and Hap; then the five figures with Linda in the center; then Linda and Biff; then Bernard, Happy, and Charley moving to the right of the screen; then Biff moving left; then Linda; then Linda in the foreground while in the background Biff stands on one side and the other men on the opposite; then a close-up of Linda with the mound of Willy's grave before her. Schlondorff reflects the various points of view—from Bernard's silence, to Charley's praise of salesmen, to Biff's assessment that his father's dreams were wrong, to Hap's determination to live Willy's dreams, to Linda's lack of understanding and ironic (for Miller, the director, and the audience) pronouncement: "We're free . . ." Nonetheless, Schlondorff centers on Linda and disregards the playwright's stage direction for Biff to carry her off stage, and to darken the stage over the house while "the hard towers of the apartment buildings rise into sharp focus."[16] This subtle change shifts attention from Biff's knowledge and focuses it more on Linda's loyalty and bewilderment. By doing so, the director implies, I think, that Biff's knowledge does not complement Willy's gesture of self-sacrifice to create tragic recognition, but that Linda's loyal suffering makes the end especially poignant, if not tragic.[17] This controversy may be, as Miller says, irrelevant, as long as audiences value the play.[18]

Once I held a view similar to Orm Overland's: that "the 'Requiem' may also be seen as the embryo of the narrator figure who becomes so conspicuous in *A View from the Bridge* and *After the Fall*: after the play is over the characters stand forth and tell the audience what the play is about."[19] Now I see the subjectivity of Willy that Schlondorff uses as a filter for the audience, even in the Requiem.[20] Schlondorff's interpretation seems to rely on Miller's comments in the Introduction to the *Collected Plays* that *Salesman* originated in an image of Willy's head rather than on Miller's stage directions at the beginning and end of the main action. The positions of the characters cannot be the playwright's, for the dramatis personae are dramatized and do not simply state the opinions of their creator. Rosalind's Epilogue is not Shakespeare's view at the end of *As You Like It*. The Chorus in *Henry V* does not make straight, factual statements and is clearly not Shakespeare's unironic representative because the action of the main body of the play modifies the words of the Chorus. If Linda borders on pathos, to use Miller's sense of that term, it is not the playwright who does but a limited character to whom he has chosen to give such language. The neoclassicists would have understood this principle of rhetorical decorum. In the Requiem, Schlondorff balances successfully the dark severity of the visual representation with the emotion of the words. *Salesman* need not be pathetic as a play even if some of its characters indulge in pathos.

8.4   Can Films Get Inside of This Salesman's Head?

Is this version of *Salesman* unsuccessful? Perhaps it is wise of the director not to use a green filter for memories to imitate Mielziner's technique, as the scene in the hotel room, for instance, might have been reduced to absurdity rather than have created a delicate balance of guilt, laughter, loneliness and disappointment. One medium must translate another. Schlondorff should have given more overviews of the set, for having avoided doing so, he may have repeated some of the faults Miller noted in the first film of *Salesman*. Even though Miller says the play was "sometimes called cinematographic in its structure," the failure of the original film occurred because "the dramatic tension of Willy's memories was destroyed by transferring him, literally, to the locales he had only imagined in the play."[21] If film can make these mistakes easily and turn an expressionistic doubleness of time into a single narrative, television can do so even more easily by the use of close-ups, so that even if the same set and locale are used, the audience loses an overview of the set. As is common knowledge, television drama can become a theatre of talking heads if the director is not careful. Schlondorff may neglect overviews a couple of times—in Charley's office and in the restaurant proper—but he redeems these "realistic" scenes with the fading techniques and the premise that the action may be occurring in Willy's head. The playwright warns about the limitations of film in representing *Salesman*:

> The movie's tendency is always to wipe out what has gone before, and it is thus in constant danger of transforming the dramatic into narrative. There is no swifter method of telling a "story" but neither is there a more difficult medium in which to keep a pattern of relationships constantly in being. Even in those sequences which retained the real backgrounds for Willy's imaginary confrontations the tension between now and then was lost. I suspect this loss was due to the necessity of shooting the actors close up—effectively eliminating awareness of their surroundings. The basic failure of the picture was a formal one. It did not solve, nor really attempt to find, a resolution for the problem of keeping the past constantly alive, and that friction, collision, and tension between past and present was the heart of the play's particular construction.[22]

If Schlondorff does not eliminate the problems Miller criticizes in the first film version, he goes a long way toward making the past and present clash in their contemporariness. This director gets inside Miller's head as well as Willy's, and makes the Requiem work. Even though Schlondorff may not go far enough with his expressionistic techniques, such as fading at the beginning and end of the play, he gives the audience a production that is worthy. He does this against the odds of the small screen and by consciously using a theatrical set in a different medium to show the theatricality of the play itself (as Olivier did with *Henry V*). If Schlondorff fails to decide for us whether *Salesman* is a tragedy or not, he is in good company. The inside of Willy's head is full of contradictions, giving rise to many critical contradictions.

This contradictoriness is not simply a matter of genre but is also suggestive as a way of seeing. Tragedy and art change as life changes but not necessarily in a direct and tangible relation to the world. Television and film represent, supplement, and displace theatre and literature. Representations in words and images of the world, as in a theatre, are multidimensional and intricate even if they are slices and refractions of the world. Culture and nature, theatre and society have an interplay that makes it difficult to see the world as it is: Plato's cave had one kind of shadow—film and television make another use of darkness and light. The chiaroscuro of painting is not that of film on a big or small screen. Miller did not think that the two films of his play were equal. The illusions of expressionism are not the same as those of naturalism. Everyman and Mankind, perhaps those medieval precursors to Willy Loman that were part of the tradition of the English morality play, were representative figures of all classes. Willy has this dimension, although his name suggests that he is low man on the totem pole.

Class and classlessness, those great topics of the nineteenth and twentieth centuries, are part of the tragedy of the common man. The changes from the Peasant Revolt of 1381 and the English Revolution of the 1640s, the American Revolution of the 1770s and 1780s, the French Revolution of the 1780s and 1790s, the Revolutions of 1848, the Russian Revolution of 1917, and the Chinese Revolution of the 1940s all place "common" people front and center. Film became a key part of historical events, such as great wars and revolutions, in the twentieth century.

There is a mythical as well as a historical aspect to motion pictures, so that the iconic and the documentary work together and contend. In telling a story with words and images there is a tension between the linear and the circular (perhaps even the recursive helix), the singular story and the doubleness of time. Perhaps in film there are even more kinds of doubling than in theatre. In film we try to recognize the changes not simply in Willy Loman and his world but in ourselves and the society in which we have lived, live, and will live.

CHAPTER NINE

Placing Ireland: Some Lyric Poets

The relation between theory and poetry, the critical and creative word, is the focus of this section of my study. Interpretation and recognition are key concerns through this book. The writers and figures have grappled with what it means to write in the experience and thought of modernity. Who can sign and interpret signs in an industrial and technological world? In the Atlantic world, Northrop Frye wrestled with his theoretical imagination, exploring the borderlands between the creative and critical. His quest in print is in the framework of interpretation and recognition. The film version of *Death of A Salesman* also attempts to represent the tragedy of the common man between dream and actuality, expressionism and the apparently realistic or everyday medium of film. Willy Loman's realization and self-realization find many interpretations, even among his family members, such as Linda and Biff. This section is built on an examination of wide-ranging texts in the opening section on recognition and a discussion of history in New France, the Thirteen Colonies, and Canada as well as women of different backgrounds writing in and about Canada and the relation between T.E. Lawrence and others, such as the Shaws, in his quest for and against recognition. Framing these discussions of those mainly in the North Atlantic basin— from Canada, the British Empire, the United Kingdom, the United States, and Ireland—I have centered much of the discussion on poetry and poetics, theory and practice, on the ways and means of recognition and the role of blindness and insight from Greek, whether it be the language, philosophy, literary criticism, and various genres. The poet, prophet, and philosopher are never far from the matter.

Here, the setting, natural and otherwise, is a key to the poet's way of seeing—from whatever blindness and insight he or she might experience.

A gap between poet and speaker or character can well create dramatic irony when the readers themselves seem to know they are not blind. Recognition and misrecognition haunt poet, speaker, character, and reader alike.

The land before the poet is something beheld and to which he or she is beholden. This is the place in which the poet is born into or which he or she has sought. In each place there is home and exile, as if the poet recalls a wholeness or atonement (atoneness) before being expelled. The poem can be an attempt to heal or to bridge the gap between the nostalgia for Eden or the golden world and what is there—the fallen or postlapsarian place into which poets and the people about them are misplaced and displaced. This is only one way to say that mythology—the words and plot of lyric and narrative—is used to make sense of the world, a kind of recognition of what was, is, and will be there or what might have been and might be still. As a poet and reader, who happens to write history and criticism as well, I respond to the recognition and misrecognition of place, perhaps a little differently from the Europeans looking upon the New World for the first time and Natives looking upon them. A few readings of Irish poets, caught themselves in the tangle of English and English history, coming to terms with the politics of colony, state, and empire, might help with the seeing and seeming of place. The lyric is a song, sometimes without music, and words bear some strange relation in and to the world. Texts have a texture and poems are made by a maker. Here, I try to see some of the ways these admirable Irish poets respond to the world before them with the words they have between their tongue and thumb. This response is one recognition by a poet reading.

Something about the evocation of place and the physical world has long drawn me to poets, and this descriptive impulse that suggests beyond the nature and the everyday objects evoked is something that some Irish poets have done so well. Yeats is skilled in this regard. And so I begin with him and move to Seamus Heaney and others, Protestant and Catholic, from north and south, and set out what I like most about these poets who write in English about Ireland whether they are there at the time or not. A sense of Ireland as a place, culture, or identity is intricate, ambiguous, and ambivalent. Physical nature has political aspects. My starting point is what as a poet do I find most admirable and intriguing in these poets. Rather than approach them and their poems with critical suspicion or the hermeneutics of distrust, where one discipline misunderstands or is rivalrous in some imagined agon for the hearts and minds of readers, I am seeking out what I find most positive in the aspects of the poetry I have chosen to explore here. Instead of reading against the grain, which is useful but has been done so much and increasingly in the past three decades, I would like to read with empathy, with an eye and ear to beauty, truth, and all the difficulties and astonishment that lie between. This truth and beauty may well be in a dialogue with the lies of fiction, an art that might not be decaying as much as Oscar Wilde said it was, even in the face of earnestness. Places, like Helen, cannot be taken at face value. They are and are not the world—settings people have lived in and *topoi*. To some implied textual intentions that the words yield up, with all the difficulties that time gives to the eternal now of the lyric, I turn. Places and nature can and cannot escape politics. Poetry turns toward and away from the ideological pressures in which the poets live. Their words embody and flee history.

Ways of seeing the land and the scene can be evocative, a suggestion of a descriptive, psychological, political, or symbolic landscape, something diachronic and synchronic, all within the *poēisis* of time and space. This Ireland also has a typology among then, now, and to come as well as here and there. Placing Ireland, it turns out, even in this shard, this one possible refraction, suggests no one sense of place. To recognize a place, as T.S. Eliot writes in *Four Quartets*, is and is not arriving there for the first time, perhaps even again and again. Part of the landscape Eliot found in poetry in English, when he arrived on the scene, was the work of W.B. Yeats, whose great example, consciously or not, has affected all those, after him, who write in English, especially those who write in and about Ireland. Poets see through language as well as looking directly at their setting. The description of place involves observation, translation, and evocation in a poetic drama of recognition and interpretation. How much can a place be recognized and interpreted and what identity is tied to the land? There is no one way to this, but this brief look at Yeats, Heaney, and others may suggest a few ways some key Irish poets of the past hundred years or so evoked place.

9.1 W.B. Yeats

The evocation of place and identity has many dimensions among these poets. Yeats wrote in English and is part of an English-speaking tradition of poetry even as he speaks about and learns from a Gaelic Ireland. The first line of "The Song of the Happy Shepherd," the first poem in *Crossways* (1889), is quite consciously in this English tradition, even as it drew from a wider European context: "The woods of Arcady are dead."[1] The death of Arcady or Arcadia, is a revolution in the grove and amid the laurel. Although this pastoral is more revolutionary than cold, it proclaims the death of the bower of bliss. The speaker says, "To the cracked tune that Chronos sings, / Worlds alone are certain good."[2] The lyric maintains with an early example of that deft Yeatsian musical syntax: "And dead is all their human truth."[3] Yeats's happy and sad shepherd, who appears in the next poem, is a recast version of the shepherds of Ralegh and Marlowe. Yeats's mythology has as much room for India and Greece as for Ireland. He begins "The Indian upon God" with the fine line: "I passed along the water's edge below the humid trees."[4] It is the surprising but apt "humid trees" that completes the line. "The Ballad of Father O'Hart" uses Irish diction like "Sleiveens" and "shoneen" and Irish place names to create a local and legendary narrative.[5]

In *The Rose* (1893), Yeats anchors the mythical in the physical, for instance, the opening lines of "Cuchulain's Fight with the Sea" providing a setting that gives a context but gestures beyond itself: "A man came slowly from the setting sun, / To Emer, raddling raiment in her dun."[6] The surprise and vigor of "raddling" bolsters the more archaic, formal, and distant "raiment" through the yoke of alliteration. Yeats's pastoral, his Irish georgic, combines the everyday in the first stanza of "The Lake Isle of Innisfree" with the more abstract notions of peace and the "glimmer" and "purple glow" that lead to the speaker listening to the "lake water lapping" until he hears "it in the deep heart's core."[7] Before this sublime feeling, the poet begins the poem with what might be an Irish version of Thoreau's Walden: "I will arise and go now, and go to Innisfree, / And a small cabin build there, of clay and wattles made: / Nine bean-rows will I have there, a hive for the honey-bee, / And live alone in the bee-loud glade."[8] This combination of stress in the rhythm and syntax and echoing in the diction makes this beginning apt and deft and haunting. The repetition of "go" and "there" connect the action of going to the distance of the place that is not here with the urgency of "now." The half-rhymes of "hive" and "live" bring together the teeming life of the bees and connect with the "have" of the poet, who will set out "nine bean-rows" that in turn chime inversely with "bee-loud glade," which is in turn linked with "honey-bee." The inversion that places "made" at the end of the line is not strained and allows for an end-rhyme with "glade," which ends the stanza with the suggestion of the pastoral. The uses of alliteration, particularly of "b" and "l" not just at the beginning of words but as a form of internal consonance builds a web of the emphasis of sound and sense, something that might have been stretched under New Criticism but have been a staple of poetics and rhetoric from the beginning and helps to form the language of poets, whether one embraces it, rebels against it, or is ambivalent about the connection between rhythm and meaning. "When You Are Old" combines physical description of the beloved's face with the describing of books and mountains and stars and with the personification of Love and a kind of hiding apotheosis.[9] This is a kind of oblique answer to Marlowe's lines on Helen: "Was this the face that launched a thousand ships?" There is a domestic pilgrimage in love that outlasts the love of youthful beauty "But one man loved the pilgrim soul in you, / And loved the sorrows of your changing face."[10] There is more to this book than some other elements that Yeats emphasizes, for instance, when in "To Ireland in the Coming Times," the speaker says: "Ah, faeries, dancing under the moon, / A Druid land, a Druid tune!"[11] The faeries have a political as well as a mythological aspect.

Some of these techniques of yoking the physical world with a symbolic realm carry through to *The Wind among the Reeds* (1899). Besides Yeats's return to the explorations of the rose and mythological yearnings, his keen sense of physical description persists. "The Host of the Air" begins with a setting that prepares the way for a narrative that gestures beyond itself: "O'Driscoll drove with a song / The wild duck and the drake / From the tall and the tufted reeds / Of the drear Hart Lake."[12] The first stanza of "The Song of Wandering Aengus" combines a sureness of physical detail with a noumenal sense. The opening four lines of that stanza concentrate this doubleness: "I went out to the hazel wood, / Because a fire was in my head, / And cut and peeled a hazel wand, / And hooked a berry to a thread."[13] The surprising logic of the first two lines—that someone could have a fire in the head that would lead them to a hazel wood—yields to the practical details of the next two lines in which the speaker sublimates or contends with the metaphorical fire in his mind by making something of the hazel wood.

In the Seven Woods (1904) begins with an eponymous poem, which starts with a physical world that joins the speaker's hearing and emotions with the sounds in a wood: "I have heard the pigeons of the Seven Woods / Make their faint thunder, and the garden bees / Hum in the lime-tree flowers; and put away / The unavailing outcries and the old bitterness."[14] There is an ancient human rancor that suggests politics here amid the sounds of nature, a kind of violence in waiting that make the "thunder" of pigeons "faint." "Adam's Curse" yokes poetry and beauty with labor: poems and the beautiful are worked on in a language that is palpable and concrete: "Better go down upon your marrow-bones / And scrub a kitchen pavement, or break stones / Like an old pauper, in all kinds of weather."[15] "The Old Men Admiring Themselves in the Water" describes these elders in memorable terms: "They had hands like claws, and their knees / Were twisted like old thorn-trees / By the waters."[16] This is a poem in which change leads to death and the beautiful drifts away and in which the pivotal half-rhyme of "alters" and "waters" in lines 2, 6, and 9 (the final verse) stress this connection.

"No Second Troy" in *The Green Helmet and Other Poems* (1910) uses descriptions of the body to ask questions about a typology between Troy and a present state like Troy: the speaker asks what made her noble mind peaceful "With beauty like a tightened bow, a kind / That is not natural in an age like this, / Being high and solitary and most stern."[17] Yeats threads a metaphor of the colt to play out the weariness of flesh and spirit over "The fascination of what's difficult," the burden of diurnal chores, and "Theatre business."[18] The colt, rather than have "holy blood / Nor on Olympus leaped from cloud to cloud," must "Shiver under the lash, strain, sweat and jolt / As though it dragged road metal."[19] At the center of the poem, Yeats places the rhymes "colt/jolt/dolt/bolt." Before the next dawn the speaker swears against business and management that "I'll find the stable and pull out the bolt."[20] This young horse becomes an emblem of a new nativity and of Pegasus against the everyday affairs of the modern world. Yeats's speaker would be identified with a colt rather than deal with "every knave and dolt" and would weather the "jolt" with the freedom of pulling out the "bolt." The symbolic possibilities and energy of the colt wear out in dramatic fashion the weary business of the theatre.

In *Responsibilities* (1914), Yeats uses natural setting in political poetry. For instance, in "September 1913"—with its well-known chorus, "Romantic Ireland's dead and gone, / It's with O'Leary in the grave"—Yeats begins the third stanza with "Was it for this the wild geese spread / The grey wing upon every tide."[21] Yeats also continued to devote his gift for physical description to other concerns, such as love in the title poem of *The Wild Swans at Coole* (1919). It opens, before the swans are introduced, with "The trees are in their autumnal beauty, / The woodland paths are dry, / Under the October twilight the water / Mirrors a still sky."[22] The poem is a meditation on change for the speaker, how the freedom, mystery, love, and beauty of the swans might vanish one day when he awakens to find them gone.

The multiple suggestiveness of nature in Yeats's evocations continues to find striking expression in *Michael Robartes and the Dancer* (1921). "Easter 1916" takes up where "September 1913" left off. The variations before the choral "A terrible beauty is born" plays on transformation itself.[23] The opening of "Easter 1916" sets out the everyday in a poem that is a more general political incantation of Irish martyrs and a people terribly born: "I have me them at close of day / Coming with vivid faces / From counter or desk among grey / Eighteenth-century houses."[24] Next with physical details commemorating the dead without naming them, Yeats proceeds to connect "Hearts" with images of animals in a natural landscape, and he stresses that "The stone's in the midst of all" and then asks "Too long a sacrifice / Can make a stone of the heart. O when may it suffice?"[25] The speaker suggests listing names of the martyrs as a possible response to the heart becoming like the stone he had described in the middle of the natural scene, and so Yeats does name them before the choral lament and defiance about change and the terrible beauty to which Easter 1916 has given birth. In "The Second Coming" the image of the gyre, with all its private visionary emblematics for Yeats, is anchored in the ancient practice of falconry. More literally, the turning falcon turns and flies out from the falconer, which is the first in a series of amplifications in imagery, each standing alone but also apparently standing as glosses of the image or images that went before. For instance, the brilliant image of the falcon is a doubling of a natural image but also flying in the movement of a gyre that is part of Yeats's visionary poetics or schema. Like William Blake, someone he much admired, Yeats may have thought he had built a system to escape being a prisoner in someone else's. The typology is made evident with images of natural disaster that also have an apocalyptic dimension: "Things fall apart; the center will not hold; / Mere anarchy is loosed upon the world, / The blood-dimmed tide is loosed, and everywhere / The ceremony of innocence is drowned."[26] In this "some revelation" or "Second Coming" the ancient revelation and coming is anew and different from this new incarnation through the body of a rough mythological beast that "Slouches towards Bethlehem to be born?"[27] A new epoch will be born in a terror perhaps but not as specifically political as at the end of "Easter 1916." The outward gyre of the new age will replace the inward gyre at the time of the birth of Christ? "A Prayer for my Daughter" is a meditation on beauty and innocence before arrogance and hatred, especially "intellectual hatred."[28] The poem lands in the confused middle of a comic structure like the storm at the beginning of Shakespeare's *The Tempest*, where Prospero, another father, worries about his daughter, Miranda. The chaos and confusion of the storm yield to the banquet and harmony of the promise of a marriage ceremony as well as to the learning of poetry and art, "the spreading laurel tree."[29] In both works the father tries to protect his daughter from ignorance and hatred, from the fierce schemes and ideologies of the world; although Prospero's daughter has come of age and is awake but sometimes inattentive, the child in Yeats' poem is a sleeping infant. Both Shakespeare and Yeats use classical mythology to lend another eye to the present. The whole poem is splendid and the first stanza is particularly beautiful, the first few lines begin *in medias res*: "Once more the storm is howling, and half hid / Under this cradle-hood and coverlid / My child sleeps on."[30] The rhymes of "half lid" and "coverlid" as well as the half-rhymes or off-rhymes of "cradle-hood" and "child" fall between the two balanced phrases before and after—"the storm is howling" and "My child sleeps on"—as if the cradled, half-hidden, and oblivious child persists by defying the loud howls of the tempest. Yeats also knits an assonance especially of "o" and consonance of "h," "l," "d," "c," and "s." Sleep defies storm.

The opening stanza of "Sailing to Byzantium," which itself begins *The Tower* (1928), is as good as modern poetry gets in English, and the poem itself—which weaves the past of Byzantium with the present of Yeats's Ireland and beyond, the trees and animals in nature with human nature, soul and body, dying and eternity— achieves a beauty and a generating and regenerating force seldom matched. The well-known "That is no country for old men" begins a series of reminders and challenges for the collective, the old men of this first line, and the individual, " An aged man" at the start of the second stanza. The young, the birds, they are all regenerating while the old are left out, "The salmon falls, the mackerel-crowded seas, / Fish, flesh, or fowl, commend all summer long / Whatever is begotten, born, and dies."[31] Even in this teeming and breeding, the speaker reminds the reader of "Those dying generations" and all this "dies" and their ignorance of more eternal matters: "Caught in that sensual music all neglect / Monuments of unageing intellect."[32] The old men become an old man that turns to the "I" of the poem who in his age sails to Byzantium in search of such monuments. He addresses the "sages standing in God's holy fire / As in the gold mosaic of a wall" as if they were divine and in art and not.[33] What the speaker addresses is not defined singularly and he does not know quite who he is or the person apostrophizing and asking them to gather him "into the artifice of eternity."[34] In the previous stanza, the speaker had tried to overcome the paltriness of age, which is "A tattered coat upon a stick," with "Soul clap its hands and sing, and louder sing / For every tatter in its mortal dress."[35] The "singing school" of the second stanza becomes "the singing-masters of my soul" in the third stanza. The tension between body and soul is amplified when the speaker says: "sick with desire / And fastened to a dying animal / It knows not what it is."[36] Yeats returns the melding of "God's holy fire" with "the gold mosaic" in the desire to be gathered "Into the artifice of eternity."[37] The poet is a maker like God but the speaker is all too mortal. The fourth stanza is such a gathering where the speaker sees himself as not taking his "bodily form from any natural thing" but being a form hammered out in gold or on a golden bough singing to an audience in Byzantium "Of what is past, or passing, or to come."[38] The oxymoronic tensions of beyond nature through natural description—of singing (perhaps like a bird?) of temporal matters, even in prophecy of the future, but yearning for eternal artifice—help to give the poem its dramatic quality. In a sense and desiring beyond the senses this is a different kind of *psychomachia*. "A sixty-year-old smiling public man" is the speaker the students face in "Among School Children," which is another variation on Yeats's theme of the aging and aged among youth.

The tower where Yeats lived is as symbolic as it is actual, and the poet refines its emblematic significance in *The Winding Stair and Other Poems* (1933), something especially apparent in the first part of "Blood and the Moon" in which the speaker says, "More blessed still this tower" and claims that "in mockery I have set / A powerful emblem up."[39] In the second part, the poet catalogues and elaborates on different towers: Alexandria's, Babylon's, Shelley's. In a typology of towers Yeats sets out the analogy explicitly and specifically: "I declare this tower is my symbol; I declare / This winding, gyring, spiring treadmill of a stair is my / ancestral stair; / That Goldsmith and the Dean, Berkeley and Burke have / travelled there."[40] The rest of this part amplifies and characterizes Swift and the other Anglo-Irish predecessors who are part of the place and the mythology of Yeats's tower. Yeats stresses "The purity of the unclouded moon" that lights the floor of the tower, which, over seven centuries, has witnessed so much and where "The blood of innocence has left no stain."[41] While musing about "abstract hatred" and "odour of blood on the ancestral stair" and then on "Tortoiseshell butterflies, peacock butter-flies / A couple of night-moths," he wonders: "Is every modern nation like the tower, / Half dead at the top?"[42] The stain of power is of blood, "But no stain / Can come upon the visage of the moon / When it has looked in glory from a cloud."[43] The moon is a world of wisdom found in death free of ideology: whether this is an illusion or a dream that can-not be realized or sustained in life is something the poem raises. The physical stair and the tower become a multitude of symbols lit by emblematic light in a world caught between eternity and change, violence and peace.

In *New Poems* (1938), Yeats seizes on the physical and symbolic aspects of the stone in "Lapis Lazuli." The apocalyptic predictions of the first stanza combine with Yeats's interest in carved figures later in the poem: "For everybody knows or else should know / That if nothing drastic is done / Aeroplane and Zeppelin will come out, / Pitch like King Billy bomb-balls in / Until the town lie beaten flat."[44] The typological pun yokes William III and Kaiser Wilhelm. "Every discolouration of the stone" or "accidental crack or dent" appears to be "a water-course or an avalanche, / Or lofty slope where it still snows."[45] The Chinese figures in stone have, through the poet's imagination, eyes that glitter as they come alive in a personified scene described in a way to make the matter sensible.

In *Last Poems* (1938–39), Yeats brings together land and mythology, for instance, in "Under Ben Bulben" and especially apparent in the opening stanza that connects various figures and landscapes with Ireland including Shelley's Witch of Atlas. Later in this poem, the speaker implores: "Irish poets learn your trade / Sing whatever is well made."[46] The poem moves, in part one, from the mythological context of Ben Bulben to, in part five, the familial and personal realm of Yeats himself: "In Drumcliff churchyard Yeats is laid, / An ancestor was rector there."[47] On local limestone Yeats has had an epitaph cut: "Cast a cold eye / On life, on death. Horseman, pass by!"[48] This allusion may well bring the reader back to the immortal horsemen of the first part of the poem, whose meaning Yeats glosses in the second part, including life and death between the "two eternities" of race and soul.[49] Yeats ends "The Circus Animal's Desertion" with another meditation on old age, using the image of climbing and of lying down or being laid to rest: "Now that my ladder's gone / I must lie down where all the ladders start / In the foul rag and bone shop of the heart."[50] The images, themes, the plays, the mythology in which the soul might take flight are begun in the old kettles, bottles, iron, bones, and rags—in the physical world and the body.[51] The collection ends with "Politics," which has for its epigraph a quotation from Thomas Mann: "In our time the destiny of man presents its meanings in political terms."[52] Yeats, so interested in fate and prophecy and so taken with Helen of Troy, muses about politics and the possibility of an imminent war. This poet, who sung so well of love and war, longs for the love of his youth: "And maybe what they say is true / Of war and war's alarms, / But O that I were young again / And held her in my arms."[53] This is a typology of youth and age, Helen and perhaps Maud Gonne. Yeats yearns still for something beyond age and politics. The ideology of death wish holds little joy compared to the generation and regeneration of a lover's touch.

9.2   Seamus Heaney

Seamus Heaney was born in the year Yeats died: 1939. Heaney also has a gift of enlivening a landscape, of giving phenomena a noumenal quality. The earth and land he chronicles are sometimes strained in the stresses of politics.

In "Digging" and "Follower," which appeared in *Death of a Naturalist* (1966), Heaney shows a sureness of description. By describing the father and grandfather in digging potatoes and cutting turf, he recreates the realm of the farm. The father digs: "The coarse boot nestled on the lug, the shaft / Against the inside knee was levered firmly."[54] The grandfather drinks milk then digs, "Nicking and slicing neatly, heaving sods / Over his shoulder, going down and down / For the good turf. Digging."[55] The son / grandson is the chronicler of digging but cannot follow suit: "The cold smell of potato mould, the squelch and slap / Of soggy peat, the curt cuts of an edge / Through living roots awaken in my head. But I've no spade to follow men like them."[56] Instead, he digs with a "squat pen" "snug as a gun," an image of potential violence and power.[57] In "Follower," which picks up on this theme of inheritance and aftermath, of the work of farming and writing, the first stanza embodies well Heaney's early descriptive power: "My father worked with a horse-plough / His shoulders globed like a full sail strung / Between the shafts and the furrow. / The horses strained at his clicking tongue."[58] The use of "globed" and the precision of the scene provide an almost hyper-realism that matches the aptness of the diction with the evocation of a "world."

"Thatcher," from *Door into the Dark* (1969), continues this marvelous expression of the physicality of this rural world: "He eyed the old rigging, poked at the eaves, / Opened and handled sheaves of lashed wheat-straw."[59] The internal rhyme of "sheaves" with "eaves," which compliments the half-rhyme of "knives" in line 3, supplements the strong verbs and the precision of the diction of the thatcher's trade, all of which lead the reader into the apparently actual world of this kind of work through the poet's possible world. Heaney shows an analogous "Midas touch" to that which he attributes to the thatcher in the last two words of the poem.[60] A later poem, "The Milk Factory," from *Hailstones* (1984), creates another kind of world in which "the factory / Kept its

distance like a bright-decked star-ship."[61] Such a movement among the
real, superreal, and surreal arises from apt but disparate details yoked
together, perhaps in a kind of magical realism but not quite of the Latin
American type. In "The Sandpit," from *Station Island* (1984), Heaney
creates such a scene in the following lines of the first part of this poem:
"Worms and starlight, / mould-balm on the passing cyclist's face. / The
rat's nose in the plastered verge / where they walked to clean their
boots."[62] Vision but not necessarily the visionary is the subject of "Field
of Vision," from *Seeing Things* (1991). The opening stanza creates a
world of vision in a poem that suggests the strangeness in the familiar
nature before her eyes and, by extension, the reader's who sees with her
while reading: "I remember this woman who sat for years / In a wheel-
chair, looking straight ahead / Out of the window at sycamore trees
unleafing / And leafing at the far end of the lane."[63] The field beyond
the television, window, gate, hedge is seen anew. Heaney's ability to
provide a setting that creates a world in the first stanza is admirable. In
XXV of *Sweeney's Flight* (1992), the speaker says: "Every night I glean
and raid / and comb the floor of the oak wood. / My hands work into
leaf and rind, / old roots, old windfalls on the ground."[64] The terminal
and therefore reverse "alliteration" of the "d" of "raid," "wood,"
"rind, " and "ground" at the end of these lines provides a kind of off-
rhyme (particularly the "nd" of the last words of the third and fourth
lines) that works more effectively than some of the stretches for rhyme
that happen too often in rhyme-poor English. The use of assonance, the
"o"s in these lines, and the apt diction for this work world primarily set
out in monosyllabic Anglo-Saxon words, the repetition of "old," establish an atmosphere and actuality of someone who works with his hands
and speaks with a simple lyric beauty that brings the reader into the
poem and gestures to the subsequent verses. This gift of making a world
of nature for the reader seems natural—of creating an invitation and a
world so right and real that the fiction often slips away in the precision,
rhythm, and beauty of the poetry—also occurs in the opening of "A
Drink of Water" in *Field Notes* (1979), so that Heaney has sustained this
ability throughout his life as a poet: "She came every day to draw water /
Like an old bat staggering up the field: / The pump's whooping
cough, the bucket's clatter / And slow diminuendo as it filled, /
Announced her."[65]

The bog of Ireland has typological affiliations with the bog in
Denmark. By including "The Bog Oak" and "The Tollund Man" in
Wintering Out (1972), Heaney makes this connection.[66] These poems
also have an affinity with "Bogland" from *Door into the Dark* (1969). The

bog, which is at the heart of some of Heaney's most effective earlier poems, appears in a new context, but the speaker knows his bogs. The poem begins: "Some day I will go to Aarhus / To see his peat-brown head, / The mild pods of his eye-lids / His pointed skin cap."[67] The aptness of the description leads to observations of how the bog man was dug out, how he was a "Trove of the turfcutters' / Honeycombed workings."[68] The end of the poem creates a diptych between Denmark and Ireland and implies human violence in these beautiful scenes of nature: "Out there in Jutland / In the old man-killing parishes / I will feel lost, / Unhappy and at home."[69] Heaney ends *Wintering Out* with "Westering," a poem that represents the double image of California and Ireland at its finale. Earlier in the poem, the speaker says, "Good Friday / We had started out," and in the final lines moves from "the studded crucifix" and light falling "On shining waters" in California to an imagined scene in Ireland: "Under the moon's stigmata / Six thousand miles away, / I imagine untroubled dust, / A loosening of gravity, / Christ weighing by his hands."[70]

An overt political stance in the refusal of being identified as "British" occurs in *An Open Letter* (1983), which ends with "But British, no, the name's not right."[71] Although not strictly a lyrical poem, *Sweeney Astray* (1983, rpt. 1984) represents the figure of Sweeney through an imagined history that has mythical and literary implications in a way that Cymbeline and Lear interested Shakespeare.[72] Earlier sources are reworked and amplified in poetry. In "Clearances," which appeared in *The Haw Lantern* (1987), Heaney uses physical setting to join personal history with the religious past of his country: "A cobble thrown a hundred years ago / Keeps coming at me, the first stone / Aimed at a great-grandmother's turncoat brow. The pony jerks and the riot's on."[73] The stone has a presence past and present in a typology between ancestor and descendant: it is palpable, a part of nature that is hurled as an element of the religious divide at the heart of Ireland's troubles. Private and public history collide.[74]

9.3   Paul Muldoon and Mary O'Malley

Other Irish poets make good use of physical description in their lyrics. This aspect of the depiction of the physical world and of the body gesturing beyond themselves is something that occurs in Paul Muldoon's poetry. Setting becomes atmosphere, outer life made inner. Plants, animals, buildings, fields—city and country—adumbrate a domestic and political space related through typology. Muldoon's poetry represents the doubleness of private and public: human nature and nature contend; tenderness and violence coexist. As I have discussed this aspect of Muldoon in detail elsewhere, I speak briefly about it here. He makes politics and history present through the physical world. In "The Boundary Commission," from *Mules* (1977), he uses nature to illustrate arbitrary political boundaries as political and cultural problems.[75] Apparently, the rain obeys this arbitrariness: metaphor and dilemma intertwine, and, at the end of the poem, the speaker has something before him that he needs to consider: "He stood there, for ages, / To wonder which side, if any, he should be on."[76] With a spare allusiveness, the title poem of *Meeting the British* (1987) is a historical lyric that evokes lavender, snow, frozen streams, historical allusions, and fragments. The speaker is an anonymous Native who ends the poem by yoking together the positive and the negative, the practical and the deadly: "They gave us six fishhooks / and two blankets embroidered with smallpox."[77] Once more, natural description and political history meet. In "Hay," the title poem of *Hay* (1998), a poem rooted in the countryside, the speaker itches "to cut the twine" of "a bale of lucerne or fescue or alfalfa" desires to speak about "something that takes flight" from this "hay."[78] Like Yeats and Heaney, Muldoon represents a nature that would be beyond ideology but that so often comes to be the physical environment for politics and a waiting violence.

A few more instances should suffice. Mary O'Malley begins "The Otter Woman" with assurance: "Against the wisdom of shorewomen / She stood on the forbidden line too long / And crossed the confluence of sea and river. One shake of her body on O'Brien's Bridge / And the sea was off her."[79] Animal and human, natural and mythological domains intertwine, and the reader enters into a scene that is remarkable and distinctive. Besides the tradition of poetry in English that haunts the Irish making and remaking of that tongue, some of the ghost poetry is Gaelic and the transfigurations and translations of it into English. A note below and to the right of the title of Brendan Kennelly's "The Hag of Beare" says "(from the Irish)."[80] As Yeats found poetry in the Irish past, so too have his successors. As great as Yeats and some other Irish poets writing in English have been there is a residual feeling that some of the haunting beauty of the Gaelic sources are in the ur-text of Irish mythology. The opening of Kennelly's poem is haunting in that primal and mythological way that *King Lear* is: "The sea crawls from the shore / Leaving there / The despicable weed, / A corpse's hair. / In me, / The desolate withdrawing sea."[81] The parallel worlds of modern Irish and

English meet in translations. Medbh McGuckian's translation of Nuala Ní Dhomhnaill's "An Mhurúch san Ospidéal" ("The Mermaid in the Labour Ward"), which appears in parallel texts in a special issue of *The Southern Review* (1995), brings this point home. The past and present meet in the diction and create a kind of typology of the mythical and actual, the imagination and science. The translation begins: "Something stirred in her: / not the swishing meteor of her fin, / but in the pit of the bed, / a body-long split of ice, / languid as dulse tentacles, / flaccid as fishbait."[82] The power of this translated poem is such that it seems its own original. Even for those Irish poets who did not or do not speak or read Gaelic, this language haunts Irish English and poetry, a ghost text, the bones it dreams with.

9.4   Some Further Meditations

There are other Irish lyric poems and poets I would like to discuss. This meditation on some poets and poems is not systematic and thus the title of my chapter. Some thoughts are not exhaustive or even representative. When I set out, I had meant to examine more poets but, beginning with Yeats and Heaney, I did not get very far. I adumbrate a few other poets who deserve more attention, perhaps in future work and shamelessly leave out important poets who deserve long, close readings. I present these thoughts unmediated by other readings because, as a poet, I wanted to face the poems directly. In a longer work I would go to other readers who have made their way through these and adjacent poems. I switch to discussing prose as I close out. This has been a chapter about the "physics of poetry," whether place attempts to get to its natural or mythical sense, or whether it suggests a political aspect. Yeats speaks of place in a way far from the flat suburban language of industrial England that he swerved from: "In a little time places may begin to seem the only hieroglyphs that cannot be forgotten, and poets to remember that they will come the nearer the old poets, who had a seat at every hearth, if they mingle their own dream with a story told for centuries of some mountain that casts its shadows upon many doors, and if they understand that the beauty they celebrate is a part of the paradise men's eyes shall look upon when they close the world."[83] Like Yeats, Heaney, Muldoon, and others have remembered the importance of place. I have concentrated on lyric poetry in English in Ireland. Seamus Heaney goes to Joyce's Stephen Daedalus in calling attention to this tradition: "What Stephen called in the diary entry 'our own language' is, after all, the

English language modified by its residence in Ireland."[84] In his Nobel speech, "Crediting Poetry" (1995), Heaney remembers his childhood in a thatched cottage in rural County Derry. Perhaps, as Wordsworth seems to have known, images of nature go deep into the mind of a child and feed the poet in later years. Heaney describes this place of his youth: "It was an intimate, physical, creaturely existence in which the night sounds of the horse in the stable beyond one bedroom wall mingled with the sounds of adult conversation from the kitchen beyond the other. We took in everything that was going on, of course—rain in the trees, mice on the ceiling, a steam train rumbling along the railway line one field back from the house—but we took it in as if we were in the doze of hibernation."[85] The sleep and dream of this physical world around him are at the heart of some of the greatest lyrics. These images come from the lives of poets. In the 1970s, I read Yeats and Eliot together in a course devoted to their published works. In 1985–86, I met Paul Muldoon in Peterborough, Ontario, and in 1986 Seamus Heaney at the English Institute in Cambridge, Massachusetts: I have heard them both read and talk. Perhaps it is no accident that these Irish lyric poets, whose words I read or heard, would become so central when I came to write something on this topic. It is for another place for me to look at other shadows from the mountain and other paradises that other poets celebrate from the places they lived as children and journeyed to afterward. The poems of the poets discussed here have an imaginative geography great enough for many readers of many kinds. This poetry creates a sense of place through and between the shadows and the hieroglyphs.

This mediation of seeing places might be also about listening to voices. Like Bottom in *A Midsummer Night's Dream*, people can find it easy to confuse the senses. Like lawyers before judges, critics look for evidence to make their case to their own readers. Philip Sidney thought poetry more universal than philosophy, thereby reversing Aristotle's hierarchy, because it could move readers to virtuous action. Somewhere between a will to believe and a reason to doubt, poems represent people and the places in which they dwell. We are apart from and a part of nature. Whether words can repair the ruin or prevent it is an open question. The visions and voices of Ireland hold a pride of place in one person's heart—mine—as he shuttles from one side of the Atlantic and back. There are different old riggings on land and sea that we eye.

CHAPTER TEN

Being Novel, Almost and Not

This is a matter of fiction, history, and European colonial expansion and after, but whether these elements of form, writing, time, empire, and the looking back of a later age that also looks forward hang together might be a convenient wish rather than something coherent. Sometimes it is difficult to know who is recognizing and what is being recognized. What is real and what is not became and becomes a matter of life and death. What is novel and what is old-hat is not always as simple a proposition as it sounds. Legal fictions and fictions are and are not alike. The lines between fiction and history, which were always blurred, were delineated with the rise of science, but fact came under siege in the return of rhetoric and the constructiveness and sometimes obscurantism of the postmodern and poststructural. Not that obscurity was anything new. Perhaps there were new recognitions to be made in the art of writing and reading. The novelty of the novel, which had a penchant for devouring other forms, seemed something new. Did the novel expand as the Western European empires expanded? That would probably be too neat and direct. The novel was born and reborn, but that implied some kind of death even if it were in the ways novels were being read, interpreted, and codified in a wider literary and cultural critique.

The death of the novel is something that has been proclaimed from time to time, but I do not think that the novel is in any danger of expiring. By "death" perhaps people mean change, transformation, shifts from what we know and where we have been to where we are going. The novel as it developed from epic and romance and grew from the Renaissance until it flowered in Western Europe from the eighteenth century onward has been a remarkably flexible genre that has allowed novelists and those who might be writing something different but related to the novel to explore what Gottfried Wilhelm Leibnitz (1646–1716) called possible worlds.[1] The world is not enough, as the family motto that James Bond's coat of arms took up from a much more ancient source—non sufficit orbis—attests. The insufficiency of this life means in the case of fiction that it supplements the world as well as reflecting and refracting it.[2] In Satura or Satire 10, Juvenal writes, "Unus Pellaeo inveni non sufficit orbis; / aestuat infelix angusto limite mundi / ut Gyarae clausus scopulis parvaque Seripho" or "One globe is all too little for the youth of Pella; he chafes uneasily within the narrow limits of the world, as though he were cooped up within the rocks of Gyara or the diminutive Seriphos."[3] Juvenal is talking about Alexander the Great—the youth of Pella, where he was born in 356 B.C., who died in Babylon in 323 B.C. He entered this latter city only to end in a sarcophagus. There are limits to empire. Alexander found that the world was not enough, but with some irony in this tenth satire about the vanity of human wishes. In literature we can see that the world is not enough or, as G.G. Ramsey renders it, the globe is too little, but the desire of literature is, like desire in life, not enough before death. The character might be a little more immortal than the author and reader. This ongoingness for the character has its limits. Sometimes we might wish for seven lives to live because one life is not enough.

10.1   Some Fictions

Reading and writing provide those multiple lives even if only as a possibility. The possible worlds of the novel, whether of Henry Fieldings's *Tom Jones* or Milan Kundera's *The Unbearable Lightness of Being*, whether ancient or contemporary, allow us to think, imagine, empathize, recoil from life, sometimes in parallel and almost simultaneous lives. In the world of imagination we do not bleed, but these worlds made of words permit catharsis, addition, subtraction, and other relations to our lived experience of flesh and bone. These books are part of our mental and spiritual worlds and have a material and physical dimension. The life of the book, like the technology of the book, is a wonder that is always under threat from those who might banish imagination. Even the ever-imaginative Plato and the master of word and argument—Socrates—wanted poets to sing hymns to the republic.[4] If novelists had been a bigger force then, they, too, as poets in a wider sense, would have suffered that banishment from Plato's possible and utopian world of philosophy as the guide to life and good government. The serious and real forces of economic production, science, and technology threaten to push aside the contemporary novel as a traditional book. In a time when the medium becomes the message, as Marshall McLuhan argued, the very texture and changeability of the technology becomes a mark of meaning and importance.[5] To look back at a world before planes, trains, and automobiles is hard enough, but one before computers and the almost world of nontechnology makes it seem primitive even in the place of our own culture. The virtual and e-book, the film that is no longer on film, the remixed music of technologies beyond the DVD presents the illusion of progress. The arts are not science, so that Shakespeare does not really make gains on Sophocles, or Virginia Woolf on Sappho, but in the empire of technology on a political and economic imperium based on the technological, this equation of technical prowess with moral wisdom and aesthetic power might even be made unconsciously or without adequate examination. Games are faster, special effects more gruesome, so that anything that went before was something lesser and not different. A silent film becomes the absence of words as if it were a movie that was always moving toward words but could not. Novels in such a world need to assimilate to television, film, video, perhaps even to write for them rather than for readers in and of themselves.

In a world like this, novels can be blamed for not having been born in the world of motion pictures. Novels were hatched from narrative, romance, history, and many other oral and written "texts" that extend back into the barely historical and the apparently primitive. Certainly, there is no denying, even for those who read poetry and prose in the putative world of fiction, that novels, so much a product of the rise of the middle classes, have to jostle in that bourgeois marketplace with a thousand technological entertainments that flesh is heir to. This competition and cross-fertilization can become debasement but can also spur innovation. Nothing is good or bad but in the execution.

Imagination, as Plato well knew and as the Romantics insisted on, helps to distinguish the work of the poets, and, by extension, that of its less aristocratic bards—the novelists.[6] It is a verbal art that might well be translated into scenes from painters or filmmakers, but only through translation. The novel translates and is translated: experience and various vernaculars—some verbal and some not—are involved in an economy of translation. This carrying across fields, cultures, and modes of expression is effective for many reasons, but one is the mutual transport of actual and fictional worlds. The one carries the other. To imagine is to dream in another dimension. However precarious the novel is (and poetry is even more so) as education continues its move from the historical, humanistic, and literary to the contemporary, efficient, and scientific, the novel and the literary will survive and flourish. The possible real death of the novel would be that the imaginative realm would have shrunk so much that there was no economic, political, or poetic space for the literary. I am more optimistic.

The power of the mythological is part of the motivation of poetry and all literature. The literary moves people. Part of that power to move can be negative and positive, so that literature is neither good nor bad but thinking and acting make it so. It depends on how we embody the literary as writer, reader, and audience. There is a multiplicity to literature as it reflects, refracts, denies the world with alternative worlds. There is an ethical as well as an aesthetic imperative in what novelists do. Characters are so much at the heart of novels even as they are eaten, obscured or denied in avant-garde or postmodern novels that also work against the story-world of conventional plots and structure. In *Poetics*, Aristotle had made plot the driving force of poetry, which included drama, giving structure primacy over character, but the novel, although building on that world, also, as if it could make Hamlet writ large, developed the psychological motivations of characters.[7] Flaubert, Henry James, James Joyce, and Virginia Woolf—and even Chekhov in the drama—use the language of displaced soliloquy, associative and extended anecdote, or stream-of-consciousness to explore the human mind and personality. This might be an amplification on Homer, Aeschylus, Sappho, and Plautus, but the degree of the elaboration is so great that it is as though it had shifted the very ground of literature from structure to character. In fact, the interplay of plot and character through language and gesture (action) was where the creative tension lay. It is not a matter of deciding between what is done and who is doing it: both are important in the rhetorical relation between the person and those about him or her. What is said and done in relation to what others say and do is the basic connection in literature and, most probably, in the world. That world and the world of literature are full of illusions as writers, as much as philosophers and historians and the religious, have warned. In the story, which is a parallel world with its own true nor false or not, there is and is not mortality. That Jack and Jill went up the hill is neither true nor false as it is when Jack and Jill are people and not characters. The novel, like other forms of art and of theory, gives an alternative way of seeing or speaking about the world that cannot compete with science, but that can represent that part of us that does not make progress. Perhaps the primitive is primary and cannot be repudiated so readily. The ethical and aesthetic may lack the power of scientific explanation and experiment, but without human values as expressed in novels as well as in religious, philosophical, and other texts, then science could be used—without debate—for whatever ends were expedient.

The rootedness of fiction, even if it involves innovation as well as perdurable convention, is a kind of unconscious, a store of values or even a return of the repressed. This latter alternative would arise from the novel as the embarrassment of history or the eruption of the primitive or the time when science was not born in the increasing fullness of its power and prestige. The novel is rooted in many things, including the wanderings of Odysseus and Aeneas, and in the historical travels of those visiting other cultures. In this brief space, I would like to discuss texts from this European expansion in connection with a few modern, post-modern, and contemporary novels. The expansion of Europe and the travel narratives that came before and after contributed indirectly and directly to the growth of the novel, which developed with capitalism and the industrial revolution. Such travel and narratives are now driven by a technological revolution based on air travel, computers, miniaturization, and other techniques. The desire for otherness in fictional or possible worlds is closely related to historical descriptions of other cultures far away in time and space. Sometimes, the fictional and the historical shared techniques in narrative, rhetoric, and even imagination. The word "history" in English meant story and story about the past, so that the blurring of the historical and the fiction was something implied in the language just as the relation between romance and the novel was expressed in other languages. In French, for instance, *roman* represents that connection. More specifically, I wish to talk about the European expansion of empire and travel with these historical and fictional texts.

10.2   Traveling Mimesis or to See or Not to See

The problem of representation (mimesis or imitation) of the world found a new critical point when the Western European countries, beginning with Portugal, began to expand in earnest in the fifteenth century. Although Russia also expanded from the fifteenth century, the Western European countries did sooner and faced cultures, on a large scale, that were not Jewish, Christian, or Islamic, so that, whereas the Russian experience is important, it will not be included in the confines of this chapter.[8] Many travel accounts—with their mix of ethnology, history, and narrative (sometimes bordering on fiction)—and essays represent cultural contact and colonial relations. Satires, such as Jonathan

Swift's *Gulliver's Travels*, which calls colonialism and the ethnocentrism of the English up short, are novels and are not. Gulliver, after his journey to Brobdingnag, reports on how Captain Thomas Wilcocks, his rescuer, takes Gulliver's report of his life among giants: "The Captain was very well satisfied with this plain Relation I had given him; and said, he hoped when we returned to *England*, I would oblige the World by putting it in Paper, and making it publick." Gulliver is a naïve who is not. His response builds on that ambiguity: "My Answer was, that I thought we were already overstocked with Books of Travels: That nothing could now pass which was not extraordinary; wherein I doubted, some Authors less consulted Truth than their own Vanity or Interest, or the Diversion of ignorant Readers." Having told a tale that was as fantastic as anything on the market in travel literature, or, for that matter, in the novel, Gulliver—unaware of this situation whereas the author, Swift, is fully aware of its ramifications—continued: "That my Story could contain little besides common Events, without those ornamental Descriptions of strange Plants, Trees, Birds, and other Animals; or the barbarous Customs and Idolatry of savage People, with which most Writers abound." Swift gives to Gulliver other kinds of fantastical detail. Gulliver, who sways between politeness and a frank annoyance or even repugnance with regard to his fellow humans, especially after his journey among the rational horses, concludes: "However, I thanked him for his good Opinion, and promised to take the Matter into my Thoughts."[9] Swift, to be sure, has already recorded the book that Gulliver might write if he could. Like Swift, Defoe also played with the mixing of genre, in this case more specifically blending the literature and historiography of British and European expansion. *Robinson Crusoe* has romance elements but is also a novel about culture and empire.

What I am most interested in this chapter is translation—literally—as well as the translation of study and empire. Columbus extends the earlier European tradition, which Marco Polo and others represent, of travel writing using romance elements. In Columbus's *Letter*, he represents a new situation and peoples unknown to the Europeans. Such writing, through recognition and misrecognition, attempts to come to terms with new experience or to tame it. In a sense, although the phrase "voyages of discovery" has fallen out of favor because of political sensitivities—indigenous peoples insist, quite aptly, that they were not discovered from their own point of view—the notion of discovery has to do with anagnorisis, or recognition, that is sometimes called discovery. As in a play, in which the protagonist, like Oedipus in *Oedipus Rex*, comes to some knowledge, clarity, or self-knowledge, the write of travel narratives or the explorer can also come to this understanding. This recognition or discovery often applies to novels, and is particularly a part of the Bildungsroman, or novel of education or coming of age, or the adventures of the hero on travels or in an exotic locale. Some recognitions are tragic and others are comic (*cognitio*), although many seem to have elements of tragedy and comedy.[10] How much Columbus recognized early on that he had not reached Asia is a matter of debate. He sought help to gain the knowledge he needed through the mediation of the Native peoples. Sometimes these explorers were both author and character in their writing even as they struggled with the shapes of fiction and history in recording or having the events recorded. After having said how timid the Natives were, Columbus admitted that he had taken some of them by force "in order that they might learn and give me information of that which there is in those parts, and so it was that they soon understood us, and we them, either by speech or signs, and they have been very serviceable."[11] Although Columbus then reiterated that the Natives still treated him like a god and said that they inclined to Christianity, he did not stress why he had thought it necessary to use force to take potential Indian interpreters as captives. Almost like Swift or Borges, Columbus mixed with fantastic descriptions precise measurements and details of the land. For example, after having given the measurements of the island Juana, which he said is larger than England and Scotland, Columbus stated that one of its provinces, Avan, contained people that were born with tails.[12] Whether Columbus, or those who brought the Columbian texts into print, possessed the irony of Swift or Borges is an open question. The stakes beyond Columbus's text were matters of life and death, especially for the Natives. When in his first letter Columbus speaks about the speech and signs he must interpret in the new lands in the Western Atlantic, he was not the first to do so among peoples beyond the pale of the Western European worldview.

One example will provide an illustration of this point of translation of culture and empire. Alvise Cadamosto's narrative—which has a complex textual history and seems to have been begun in 1463, completed by 1468, first appeared in the collection *Paesi* in 1507, translated into Latin in Milan and into German in Nuremburg both in 1508, and into French in Paris in 1515—claimed that he sighted the Cape Verde Islands in 1456, which led to their colonization, although many authorities credit Antonio da Noli with the discovery in 1458 or 1459. Cadamosto seems to have left Portugal for his native Venice in 1463 or 1464.[13] The popularity of Cadamosto, who described the Atlantic islands and West Africa, derived from Giovanni Ramusio's *Navigazioni* in Venice in 1550.

In English, neither Richard Hakluyt the Younger nor Samuel Purchas included Cadamosto's voyages in their collections: Hakluyt had asked John Pory to translate Leo Africanus, and this translation and amplification was supposed to appear in Hakluyt's compilation *Principall Navigations*, but a translation of Cadamosto into English, an abridged version of the text in Ramusio, did not appear until 1745 in the first volume of Thomas Astley's *New General Collection of Voyages*.[14] This text, like others concerning travel, exploration and geography, had distinct histories of translation and transmission in each country in Western Europe. Cadamosto's work is of particular interest because it is earlier than the "travel" texts that are better-known today—those of Columbus and Vespucci—but he describes before they do a sense of wonder and strangeness over a world new to Europeans and because he represents Black Africa, a region that was so crucial in the slave trade for Islamic North Africa, for Europe, and for the Americas. His *Voyages* begins with a chapter that appears in *Paesi* but not in the two earlier manuscripts, so that some ideological or interpretive editing or amplification might well have occurred here.

So when we approach colonial and postcolonial novels, we can see that Cadamosto, Columbus, and others have provided narratives of travel and ethnology beforehand. The multicultural and multilingual nature of the spreading out of Portugal, and of other European powers, is something that is readily noticed when examining the early texts. In 1508 there appeared, for instance, a Dutch edition of an influential work by Amerigo Vespucci—an Italian, who sailed for Portugal and encountered Natives in Brazil, including Guanabara Bay and the site of what is now Rio de Janeiro. It was full of woodcuts and Vespucci's narrative that told of the good health and long lives of the Natives as well as their incest, polygamy, and anthropophagy.[15] Later, the Netherlands would take a direct political and economic interest in the Portuguese colonies in Asia, Africa, and America. In Venice, in 1534, Benedetto Bordone gave an account of the charting and settlement of the islands to the south and west of Portugal and Spain, including Madeira (from ca. 1425), the Azores (from ca. 1427), and the Cape Verdes (from 1455–56).[16] A German soldier in the service of Portugal, Hans Staden was among the Tupinambá, who had captured him in 1554 and kept him prisoner for nine months, just before Jean de Léry, who, owing to the circumstances of his travels and the French Wars of Religion, was unable to publish his work until years later. Both Staden and Léry, whose books contained illustrative woodcuts, described the customs and manners of the Tupinambá and did not shy away from the question of cannibalism.[17]

These works show affinities to those of well-known figures such as Michel de Montaigne—whose essays on cannibals and coaches concentrate on the typology of Old World and New World, European and Native—and Shakespeare (whose play *The Tempest* was so seminal in early colonial and postcolonial representations), and those texts by writers such as Aphra Behn, Swift, and Defoe.[18] In John Florio's translation of Montaigne (1603, second ed. 1613) the Natives visiting France become a way of contrasting their innocence with European decadence: "Three of that nation, ignorant how deare the knowledge of our corruptions will one day cost their repose, securitie, and hapinesse, and how their ruine shall proceed from this commerce, which I imagine is already well advanced."[19] Montaigne also has the Natives question the following of a king who is a boy and observe how the poor should rise up, take the rich by the throats, and burn down their houses. Behn's *Oroonoko* also uses this familiar turning of the tables in order to enact a critique of European culture through representatives of the cultures with which it comes into contact. For instance, like Bartolomé de Las Casas, Léry, Montaigne, and others before her, Behn turns the ethnographical and critical lens back on Europeans. Behn's narrator tells of an English governor who did not keep his word: he teaches the Natives the term "*Lyar*," when they describe behavior similar to his without naming him, only to have it thrown back in his face: "Then one of 'em reply'd, *Governor, you are a Lyar, and guilty of that Infamy*." Behn has insisted that this entire story about the royal slave, Oronooko, whom an English captain kidnaps from Africa to their colony of Guiana, is true and not a fiction. The author wants this narrator to be her in a history and expresses her own opposition from within. This scene shows the innocence and superiority of the Natives vis-à-vis Europeans long before Jean-Jacques Rousseau's "noble savage": "They have a Native Justice, which knows no Fraud; and they understand, no Vice, or Cunning, but when they are taught by the *White Men*."[20] A blurring occurs, in a text published in 1688 as much as in 1493 (as in Columbus's *Letter*) or 1726/1735 (as is the case of the different versions of *Gulliver's Travels*), among eyewitness account, true "history," travel narrative, and fiction. The novel can express a critique of European society as much as representing its contradictions and ambivalence.

The colonial has epic affiliations as in Homer and Virgil, but wanderings also occur in narratives with romance elements such as the travels of Marco Polo.[21] While in prison Polo is said to have dictated his account of his journeys to the East to a French writer of romance. Centuries later, adventures still marked important travel texts and novels that make use of this genre and its wanderings. *The Life and Strange and Surprising Adventures of Robinson Crusoe* (1719), perhaps a late English prose romance or one of the first English novels, was based on the experiences of Alexander Selkirk. Crusoe ends up on an island where cannibals live and where he saves a Native, who becomes his servant, Man Friday. This novel had two sequels: *The Farther Adventures of Robinson Crusoe* (1719) and *The Serious Reflections of Robinson Crusoe* (1720), a collection of essays. These novels, almost novels and not novels, are "histories" in both senses of the word (stories and stories about the past). When we encounter postcolonial novels about conflict between what is Native and what is European, in the cultural tensions, mediations, and mixing in former colonies, these narratives or accounts, written in the colonial period, provide a suggestive framework with which to understand them. In *Imaginary Homelands*, when Salman Rushdie speaks about translation and the translation of people, he says he clings, "obstinately, to the notion that something can also be gained" in translation. The postcolonial and colonial read each other.[22] The translation of empire is full of ambiguities and whereas the traveling histories of colonization have their mobile tropes and contiguities, they never quite repeat themselves with exactitude.

10.3   Expanding and Moving Fictions

Expansion and movement do not have to be directly imperial or colonial. Fictions can also question or render uncomfortable the metropolitan centers. The novel has interior and psychological aspects as well as political elements. The reworking of classicism and the remaking of the past often occurs even in the most groundbreaking novels. James Joyce reworked the myth of Ulysses into the everyday life of Dublin: the wanderings became less physical and more mental, less exalted and more domestic, less sweeping and more quotidian. Virginia Woolf used stream-of-consciousness as Henry James turned to psychology to represent the inner life of outward events—the mental muddle and progress and motivation that history could not address or at least to the same extent. *Hamlet* was an important text for Goethe and its motivation through soliloquy might well have contributed to birth of Young Werther. The novel can go on for pages about a moment or a day. History, and even drama and poetry, does not usually have that kind of scope. The novel and its wanderings have their own niche that should encourage the survival of this genre.

The journey can also be one of satire and political outrage in the face
of dystopias and totalitarian states, such as George Orwell's *Nineteen-
Eighty Four* and *Animal Farm* and Mikhail Bulgakov's *The Heart of a Dog*.
Kurt Vonnegut, a favorite author of my early youth, was able to write
satiric postmodern exposés and, in *Slaughterhouse Five*, about the spiritual
and actual journey of Billy Pilgrim, the quintessential American but also
the essential man who had to come to terms with the bombing of
Dresden during the Second World War. The assault on Dresden is an
exploration of revenge, violence, war, and the desecration of humanity
and art. The spirit of Juvenal's savage indignation and Jonathan Swift's
questioning of the anti-human in the human continued well into
the twentieth century. The English morality plays of the fourteenth
century, such as *Everyman* and *Mankind*, showed long ago the lonely
course of the individual before the temptations of life. In the same century, Geoffrey Chaucer used satire to represent his pilgrims on the way
to Canterbury, but in our age similar moral problems are amplified by
the great changes to machinery and the technology of war and destruction. Recognizing the human in such a world becomes an immense
challenge.

Exile, travel, and spirit are some aspects that surround the trauma of
the world wars for Europe and beyond. Bernard Shaw wrote his great
play *Heartbreak House* as a kind of requiem for Europe over its collapse in
the First World War. Solzhenitsyn has explored the ravages of these
traumatic wars and of the Gulag (see *August 1914, The Gulag
Archipelago*). This is the wound at the heart of the twentieth century and
of European civilization. This is the wound, like the abuses of imperialism, that contemporary novelists must face or flee from like the blood of
a ghost. If Umberto Eco in *The Name of the Rose* (1980, Eng. trans. 1983)
writes about murder in the quest to secure Aristotle's lost treatise on
comedy, Bartolomé de Las Casas in the sixteenth century had to argue
against Aristotle's theory of natural slavery. Las Casas defended the
humanity of the American Native peoples in the face of extermination
by the Spaniards.[23] The death wish, the will to power and genocide are
old and tragic matters almost beyond speech as hard as historians, religious writers, philosophers, poets, filmmakers, novelists, and others try
to represent them. French and English pamphleteers and others used Las
Casas's account to warn Europe that Spain would do to Holland what it
did to the Natives in the Indies.[24] The murderous exploitation of the
human whether in the first years of European expansion to the Americas
through the holocaust and prison camps spawned by Germany and the
Soviet Union to massacres in Cambodia, Rwanda, the former

Yugoslavia, and beyond is still with us and with contemporary novelists and audiences. Novelists still report, refract, and warn.

In *A History of the World in 10 1/2 Chapters* (1989), Julian Barnes used legal cases and travel narratives to help in his writing of a fictional history of the world that is touched by the tone and fragmentation of satire. This novel begins with an unofficial version of the story of Noah's ark. Timothy Findleys's *Not Wanted on the Voyage* provides another interpretation of the story surrounding Noah. Fictional worlds can be a different kind of voyage. They can be a secular scripture that reinterprets the Bible or a rediscovery of the epic specifically or the classical past generally. The journey and the exploration are never over.

The different ways to express the expansion of the human positively can be measured in the multiplying voices of men and women of all countries and backgrounds that have come into a global literary world. Smaller or poorer countries and languages with a small group of speakers can find this expansion or world literature problematic. The development of human consciousness has had difficult material conditions. Still, more variety among writers means more points of view. Writers and novelists such as Simone de Beauvoir, Marilyn French, and Margaret Atwood have taken up with their own gendered names where two great women novelists, George Sand and George Eliot, left off. Atwood's *The Handmaid's Tale* has its share of dystopian elements, but its satire calls attention to cultural trends that would subjugate, efface, or obliterate women. Novelists and writers who have stressed issues of skin color, alternative cultures, and racism that vary as much in ideology as do Frantz Fanon, V.S. Naipaul, and Toni Morrison. Louise Erdrich and Jeanette Armstrong are Natives from North America who write contemporary novels about a world from a point of view different from that which the Europeans brought to their shores.

I would like to end with Thomas Mann commenting on a novel that was a favorite of my youth: *The Magic Mountain*. The end of that novel is the narrator's farewell to Hans Castorp, which finished with a question about whether love will rise out of and above "this universal feast of death."[25] At the end of his essay, "The Making of the Magic Mountain," Mann speaks about Castorp's "dream of humanity . . . before he is snatched downwards from his heights into the European catastrophe."[26] All this returns us to what might be in the quest or journey that the epic, the romance, and the novel has pursued for hundreds and thousands of years. It is not to succumb to slavery, torture, violence, and death but to seek out something much more positive and much greater in humans. According to Mann's commentary, Castorp's dream "is the idea of the human being, the conception of a future humanity that has passed through and survived the profoundest knowledge of disease and death. The Grail is a mystery, but humanity is a mystery too. For man himself is a mystery, and all humanity rests upon reverence before the mystery that is man."[27] It is not surprising that Mann uses the language of the Arthurian romance to describe the dream at the heart of his great novel written so many years after. For novelists today, the task of preserving humanity while representing it might sound too grand, but there is a heroism in words and imagination. To survive we must make a true beauty and beautiful truth, however ravaged in the world of death and disease, that crosses cultures and thinks of the human being made whole across the world, a human with a local habitation and a name but one that is of the entire world. The novelist might shore up fragments in the wasteland and make a garden that is at once then, now, and to come, something familiar and strange, something that heals through the exile of its art.

10.4 Recognition and Misrecognition Once More

Seeing is not always recognizing as eyewitness reports and cognitive experiments prove. The attempt to recognize is something critical. Making sense is a tricky business. The ideal and the actual give and take in a kind of play. The archeology of the translation of study and empire from classical antiquity to modernity and of European expansion and contraction is suggestive in its archive of recognition and misrecognition. Culture needs many ways of interpretation. No one kind of writing is enough. The loose ends of travel narratives, novels, and other genres might allow a space that enables a multitudinous recognition and reading. No one culture and no one way of writing is world enough. Perhaps imagination and a sense of possibility and otherness provide a slender thread to pass to the other side of disease, tyranny, and death.

Conclusion

The interpretation of culture often involves various types of recognition in literature, religion, and the human sciences that allow for a greater awareness of moments of ignorance and knowledge. Perhaps a paradox of insight is that it admits blindness. The meeting of text and reader, image and audience, culture with culture suggests ways we can see a strangeness or otherness in ourselves. This estrangement effect can be internal and external but within it an implied or explicit comparison occurs. Instances from various sources provide the means of coming to terms with recognition. Interpretation is a central human activity: this book is also an example. Here, one person, who has read signs from many sources, has sought to bring out the richness in instances where recognition and interpretation play a significant role. This study is not an overt theory of culture, interpretation, and recognition but an exploration of these terms through concrete contexts.

At the beginning of this study I set out the basis for key terms. The examples explored later should have reinforced aspects of these underpinnings. Interpreting suggests spreading or spreading out (perhaps dissemination) and comes from roots that convey the idea of expounding, translating, explaining, and understanding. The etymology of culture points to cultivation. To interpret culture is to read the signs of what is cultivated in various communities with their continuities and discontinuities. Sacred and secular images and texts are part of that culture that I have sought to interpret. Etymologically, recognition involves a thorough acquaintance with something, investigation, or getting to know once more. The original senses of the verb "read" meant taking care or charge, but also signified having or exercising control over something. Moreover to read could mean taking or giving counsel. Shedding light on something obscure is basic to various Germanic languages, and reading is an interpretation of texts, ordinary speech, and everyday works. This study, then, is built around moments of coming back to knowing, thinking, and seeing what texts, speech, and images grow up over time and what they might suggest. Culture, interpreting (interpretation), recognition, and reading are all contested and suggestive terms.

Beyond setting out the key terms and providing a framework generally, I have examined recognition from various points of view. Although my discussion of recognition is general, it should be suggestive about the comic and historical aspects of "discovery" and suggest how recognition crosses generic and disciplinary boundaries. All too briefly, I discuss the different kinds of blindness and recognition in literature and literary theory and investigate whether they occur in philosophy, history, religion, psychology, and other fields. A central question of the first section of my book, which should have some resonance throughout the study, is whether there is a poetics that applies to the different ways of discussing culture. Recognition—a moment that involves an apparent, possible, or actual movement from ignorance to knowledge or self-knowledge—can represent all kinds of experience from the comic through the absurd to the tragic. A moment of recognition or "discovery" can bring about many different effects from relief through terror to suspicion.

In practice and not in theory, the movement from religion to theology would constitute a move from story to argument. Biblical stories yield various interpretations, so that theological differences arise from hermeneutical variations. Theological recognitions are sometimes contrary and have offered pretexts for battles in Europe and its empires. The relation of mythology and ideology, story and argument, and the blurring of these terms into story-argument is an important point of departure. Instances from the Bible show a rich range from Creation to the Last Judgment. The power of these moments in this sacred muthos involves pain, ambivalence, and glory. In this part of my analysis, I concentrated on recognition in the stories in the Bible as opposed to the array of interpretations that comprises commentary and dogma. As I have argued, the primary thread in the Bible is a human discovery and recovery of the way of God. I have concentrated on recognition in the stories in the Bible as opposed to the mosaic of recognizing and recognizable interpretations, which make up commentary and dogma in Christian theology. Recognition in the Judeo-Christian tradition is one of revelation (even if we have to reason to make sense of the revelation). Many kinds of recognition occur in the Bible. However, there are two principal kinds of blindness and recognition in it—structural and situational—and, in both, knowledge exists in true and parodic forms. In exploring these recognitions, I found that the structural myth of a fall into knowledge, sin, and death informs the situations that comprise that myth. I also realized that from the Fall through Christ's crucifixion to the Last Judgment, the comic structure of the Bible shows various comic subplots of blindness and recognition in addition to this larger structure of bliss lost. The emplotment of narratives occurs as much in religious and historical texts as in literary ones. In this superplot of the Bible, happiness is restored through a recognition of disobedience in the quest for knowledge and a regaining of paradise after Christ enters human history and experience through the crucifixion and then ascends to make possible once again an atonement between human and divine. Other key moments or events of seeing and not seeing contributed to the great movement of the biblical superplot. For instance, in the Bible we experience the different blindnesses of Eve, Adam, Cain, Jacob, Job, Judas, and others and the recognition of error or ignorance at various stages in a series of u-shaped or "comic" narratives. In these moments of recognition between the tragedy of the situation and the comic structure of the larger recognition in the Bible a friction happens. That comic structure is not much different from other comic structures, for instance those that occur in literature. The divine comedy of the Bible is a movement from an old order through chaos to a new order, from innocence through experience to a higher innocence, from one happiness through exile and misery to a new happiness. As in literature (and perhaps in life), whether a recognition is tragic or comic depends on how short or long a view of the plot or *muthos* one takes, so that recognition is as temporal as it is spatial. Some of the connections between the biblical and classical inheritance are emplotment, genre, and the notion of recognition.

Classical instances of recognition are found in literature and in philosophy. The literary examples are foundational. In epic and comedy, as well as tragedy, which was the focus of Aristotle's discussion of recognition, characters are involved in ironic moments when they see what the reader or audience knows, the gap between their blindness and insight. This new moment of insight comes to dwell in the reader or audience but also dissolves when the book is closed or the performance ends. Word and image are in the world, yet they are staged in poetry and drama and so dissolve with the closing of the book or the emptying of the theatre. One of the recognitions in Homer is the ambivalence of and toward the gods. The reader witnessed this throughout *The Odyssey*. For instance, the divine plays a role in the homecoming and the recognitions it fosters to the very end of this epic. Even though Athene helps to define the limits of the male world of honor, the reunion of Laertes,

Odysseus, and Telemachus cements that realm. The poems build to a cumulative outcome: the various narrative strands are made whole. Recognition in this epic appears to depend on the Osiris effect, a scattering of parts, while trying to reassemble the broken narrative limbs. Aristotle's central example in *Poetics* is the tragic recognition of Oedipus, who is blind to his situation until his knowledge actually moves him to blind himself. Cognitio is an analogous term for anagnorisis yet not one mentioned in *Poetics*. It is a form of comic recognition—an uncovering of the confusions, disguises, concealments that New Comedy represents. An example arises in Menander's only complete extant comedy, *Dyskolos* (translated as *The Curmudgeon* or as *The Grouch*). In this play, the killjoy, Cnemon, attempts to thwart the lovers under the protection of Pan. This senex, however, falls into a well and is rescued. After his cognitio, he recognizes his error and changes his mind. Cnemon then joins in the dance that celebrates a double wedding. A new order or harmony occurs after the resistance of the blocking figure, but whether comic endings are wish fulfillments that fill in for the shortcomings or harshness of the world is an open question. Does this comic recognition represent a lack in actuality or an artificiality and convention that the audience and readers accept because such a recognition is unlikely to happen or that problems are so suddenly and harmoniously resolved?

Recognitions go beyond religious and literary texts. Even if Plato and Socrates would not want to equate philosophical texts—even dialogues, a dramatic genre as well—with poetry, they both share devices, schemes, and tropes. Rhetoric binds together various written texts. Recognition happens at a key moment in an argument as well as in a story. Whereas Aristotle places recognition at the heart of his poetics, Plato denies the importance of knowledge through mimesis. Plato argues against poetry by appealing to forms behind words and by downgrading of rhetoric into a verbal art of persuasion without the foundation of truth. This visionary Platonic philosophy can be questioned as much as admired for its interest and beauty. A reading against the grain can cast light on the rhetorical nature of the Platonic enterprise. Plato's visionary philosophy has common ground with visionary poetics. Hegel is an idealist philosopher who is more sympathetic to recognition than Plato is. Even though Hegel's theory of tragedy has contributed to expansions of Aristotle's anagnorisis, Hegel's philosophy of history was most instructive for the argument of my study because it allows for an examination of the mediation of specific instances in time in connection with the dialectical movement of history. Furthermore, Hegel's dialectic involves dramatic irony: as world history is not yet complete, human actors must necessarily be ignorant of the social telos. In other words, people are agents of something they cannot completely recognize. Blindness is part of Hegel's insight. Philosophers interpret and "recognize" other philosophers and their work. Although Hegel affects Marx and Nietzsche, they sometimes resist his views. For instance, Marx owes much to but criticizes Hegelian history. Marx turns Hegel's dialectical idealism upside down to serve a materialism in which material production enables ideas, something with which Hegel would hardly agree. Interpretation and misinterpretation, recognition and misrecognition, as my book has suggested, are sometimes hard to distinguish and may be part of each other. Early in his writing, Nietzsche speaks about a truth that is difficult to discern and here differs little from Plato and Hegel, Nietzsche challenges the notion of a system in the philosophy of history and thereby differs from Hegel. It was interesting to see that in his discussion of Homer, Nietzsche returned to Aristotle. This way he was able to interpret the contest between poetry and philosophy. The use of Aristotle is instructive as he made a list of agons or hostile contests that arose out of ambition and of envy or jealousy amongst the illustrious Greeks. One of the themes of this envy was the desire of some, like Plato, to displace Homer, to replace poetry with philosophy. This is the kind of psychological explanation that Hegel disdained. My study sees recognitions in poetry, philosophy, and psychology and each is framed rhetorically.

Psychological and political recognition affect each other. Descriptions of body and mind have important implications for recognition. A few examples from Freud, Lacan, and Kristeva suggested the significance of recognition to psychoanalytical theories. The exploration of the mind, particularly as it related to sex and therefore the body, became, as I have argued, almost as great an obsession in the twentieth century as the New World was for Columbus and his fellow explorers. At one point in Freud, we saw that there were three recognitions—of the patient, doctor, and reader—so that the multiplicity of interpreting or recognizing recognition becomes so intricate as to be as cautionary as it is fascinating. Who is seeing what and what is being seen? Freud begets interpretations, reinterpretations, or misinterpretations (the boundaries between them are not always easy to discern). His psychoanalysis affected many others including Jacques Lacan and Julia Kristeva. For Lacan, recognition was the recognition that the male discovery of truth is a fantasy based on metonymy. This metonymic impulse involved a standing in, or substitute of woman as a fantastic construction, as the negative of man, as the Other, for what is true. Lacan suggested that the male desire for unity and truth can be a fantasizing God. In Lacan's psychoanalysis, there is an attempt to uncover this mystification and thus an effort to enact a recognition in the reader. Kristeva's analytical semiology (semanalysis) owes something to Lacan and Freud. She is interested in the discovery of the unconscious and Lacan's breakthroughs in psychoanalysis. Kristeva has an intricate use of recognition by other names. Psychoanalysis and literature are closely connected for Kristeva, who asks, when discussing the novel as polylogue, what is a materialist who speaks. Each discipline is related to another and has a history of interpretation generally and recognition specifically that contributes to the contours of the interpretation of culture.

History also involves recognitions. It is an inquiry into the truth of what happened and it is a story about the past; it is event and the representation of event. The history examined in my book was about discovery of otherness. This kind is found from Herodotus through Columbus to Acosta and Montaigne. Whether of the encounter with "barbarians" or "savages," the recognition in this kind of history is an account of strangeness and the marvelous. The voyage out allows for greater self-knowledge, a sense of identity or the questioning of that identity. This history of otherness often involves a reporter or historian who catalogues the world and its inhabitants as fact but also as fantastic or aspects of romance (inadvertently or not). One reason I concentrated on this kind of history is that it differs significantly from Hegel's type and it involves a recognition of difference that sometimes effaces and displaces that difference. To some extent, there are stories in arguments and arguments in stories. Even in lyric there is often some kind of implied movement or argument and in syllogisms and the sparse and sporadic *Anglo-Saxon Chronicles*, there is some kind of implied story. Where does fact end and interpretation begin has been a key question, implied and otherwise, in much of my work. The range of philosophical texts that represent recognition is wide, so there is not one particular school or ideology that has a monopoly on recognition. The exemplarity itself disturbs ready generalizations about recognition. Are narratives and arguments ever entirely resolved or are they possibilities, fictional and otherwise, that must stage an answer or a process that acts as knowledge? Recognitions multiply one to the next. Is this a hall of mirrors, a kind of mimetic illusion and disillusion, or a progression toward a greater understanding? The array of recognitions—some comic, others epic and still others tragic, some philosophical, others historical, and some psychological or psychoanalytical—welcomes and begs such questions. In crossing cultures in history and travel accounts there are ethnographical and cultural differences that complicate this questioning. Is the other culture something to be recognized or another shroud for a blindness masquerading as recognition? In psychoanalysis, which borrowed from myth and literature, there is an especially narrative element to the argument about the composition of the self and the relation of I and other. Developmental stages and gender also complicate what that "I" is, does, and knows in the world. Perhaps recognitions are also tentative conclusions.

As hard as it is to make firm general conclusions about the multiple representations of recognition (misrecognition), the study made a few "uncoverings." In the Bible I found that a tension exists between the situational recognition of individuals, sometimes of tragic circumstances, and the structural recognition that leads to the triumph of God and his people over the fall into time. Genre affected classical literary recognitions. Epic represented recognition of the hero as a central myth for the society, tragedy the discovery of the protagonist's isolation from that community or nation, and comedy a moment of insight for the main characters that allows for their reintegration into a regenerated society. Other disciplines, based on argument and dialectic, confronted the problem of knowledge in terms of the recognition when not using the term, so that Plato attacked poetry as the way to recognize self-knowledge and knowledge of reality. For Plato, poetry saw appearances, philosophy discovered truth. Like Plato, Hegel found truth and knowledge difficult to recognize, but he saw that recognition as a possibility by way of reason in History realized through the World Spirit, in a kind of incomplete dialectic of human freedom. Just as Plato had in Homer's poetic recognitions, Marx saw illusion in such a recognition. Marx agreed with Hegel that recognition occurs in history, yet he differed in defining that discovery. For Marx, it was material, experiential, and practical. In addition to questioning the social truth of Plato and Hegel and Hegel's systematic history based on success, Nietzsche envisioned recognition differently. According to Nietzsche, only the individual life has a recognizable meaning. For Kristeva, we can recognize a mutual understanding of people of different genders and backgrounds, the I and altered I without and within. This recognition would involve an admission of different semiotic practices and thereby recognizing the necessity that we transform the subject in relation to language. There is a utopian hope as well as a historical view in this kind of recognition of an othering from within.

Religion, literature, philosophy, and psychology do not efface history, as hard as those who study them might try. History, as we have seen, is not without its forms of recognition. In the "discovery" of the

New World, Columbus brought with him the truths and illusions of European culture. Like Herodotus, Columbus expected a recognition of the cannibals and Amazons. Past myth and ideology, present eyewitness or empirical evidence take on importance. Just as the Spanish tried to distinguish themselves from the ancients, the French and the English try to differentiate themselves from the Spanish. One of the key questions in the historical element of my study is in the building of empire: what is illusion and what is knowledge? Representation also took on a psychoanalytical element. For example, Freud represented the ambivalence between doctor and patient, male and female, in representation. Recognition became complex because it depended on the connection among doctor, patient, and reader. How they recognized the relation between the conscious and unconscious mind also played an important role. Lacan suggested that such a recognition, especially in the relation between male and female, was a fantasy, but his expression is in "male" language. This is the slippery but intriguing world of recognition. In this book, I have made this a central point that recognition recognizes its own limits. Moreover, it is an interplay of blindness and insight, a tension between situation and structure. In recognition, stability and instability vie in which ignorance slips between knowledge and wisdom.

Discovery was a trope of the European expansion across the Atlantic. What was recognized and was not is a matter of debate. Canada is of particular interest as it was a contested place from the 1490s. The Portuguese and the Spaniards did not want English incursions there and the French tried to claim it. France and England (Britain) fought over Canada and the Thirteen Colonies (later the United States) and Britain experienced friction over Canada. In the matter of cultural and historical interpretation, Canada was always a place of interest and controversy. The interpretative frame of Europeans spread with empire only to be tested, overturned, and reinforced. In the twentieth century, Canada has moved from the ideology of two founding nations, English and French, to multiculturalism. Its French-speaking minority has produced four prime ministers, some of them among the longest serving in British parliamentary history, so the legacy of French and British imperialism has melded into a new hybrid state that has opened its doors to immigrants from every corner of the world. Canada has shared the languages of three great powers—France, England (Britain), and the United States—whose leaders have had ambivalent attitudes toward empire, expansion, and contraction. Moreover, Canada has sometimes been separated from these powers by a common culture and language—similar but not the same. Whether recognized or dismissed by some in those powers, Canada (with all its names until 1949 when Newfoundland joined it), since 1497, has been many things from a crossroads though an ambivalent representation to a collection of peoples. The Death of Wolfe, the Québec conference of 1864, the meeting of Churchill, Roosevelt, and King during the Second World War, the Québec Referenda of 1980 and 1995 are all much interpreted events. In Canada the recognition of state, nation, and empire in past and present is a matter of shifting identities. As I have mentioned, the old phrase "voyages of discovery" is both apt and misleading depending on the point of view of native and newcomer. Vantage is key in recognizing a time and place. The "Canadian" experience was, after John Cabot's voyage in 1497, both central and peripheral to the Columbian legacy. Terms show shifting significations, interpretations, and "recognitions." For example, the word "Canadian" was a term applied to Natives, then the French inhabitants of New France, and then the English-speaking inhabitants as the French in the heartland of the Saint-Lawrence spoke of themselves as Québecois. In this context I have suggested that shifting identities, of which this is one shadow only, obscure and complicate recognition. In Canadian history, as in Greek tragedy, such recognition is as much about seeing errors and flaws as about the power of seeing, the theory of the perspective that both eyes provide. The recognition of misrecognition balances the misrecognition of recognition. There are many contexts for Canada. It becomes an example for interpretation that has implications beyond itself. That is as true of its literature as of its history. Both are culturally suggestive.

An instructive part of that matter of culture and shifts in identity involves gender and that is why I discussed Canadian women and women who write about Canada. Double vision, seeing double or typology is an important matter of interpretation and complicates identities. As we saw in "Ojistoh" (1912), Pauline Johnson represented the tensions between Huron and Mohawk and left the Europeans out of the conflict. Boundary crossings are always part of this recognition and misrecognition, interpretation and misinterpretation. A celebrated American poet, Elizabeth Bishop, lived in Nova Scotia with her grandparents and explores the crossings between culture and family in Canada and the United States. Bishop's "Primer Class" represents her school in Nova Scotia and "The Country Mouse" includes her shift from Nova Scotia back to Worcester, Massachusetts. Bishop's stories supplement her memoirs. In the early 1950s, as we saw earlier, Bishop wrote "In the Village," set in a Nova Scotian village much like Great Village, where her Bulmer grandparents lived. Native Poets and poets who write about

Natives unsettle settler culture in Canada and beyond. One of the instances I discussed was Buffy Sainte-Marie, a Cree born in Saskatchewan but raised by foster parents in Maine and Massachusetts. Her foster mother was part Micmac. Sainte-Marie was adopted at a Cree powwow when she was eighteen. During the 1960s she wrote about concerns that were central to the debate on the Vietnam War for Natives and for many other groups. Sainte-Marie is associated with many different Native nations and with the United States and Canada. Jeannette C. Armstrong's "History Lesson" represents a parodic and terrible journey from Columbus to the present, including disrespect for Native culture. Carrie M. Best, Dionne Brand, and others have explored the legacy of slavery and prejudice and the wrestle with modern Canada for its Black inhabitants. In *Another Place*, Brand also alludes to the east end of Toronto where her characters lived between the West Indian and the Nova Scotians. Gender, as well as race, is another aspect of interpreting culture(s). Here are voices writing in English but with a difference. The interpretation of colonial and national identity can involve recognition and misrecognition. The double bind that African Canadian writers have found themselves in has made others doubly blind to their race and their role in the nation. These and other dualities complicate how we see, interpret, recognize, and try to understand. Jan Zwicky, Margaret Atwood, and other Canadian women poets of European descent can also suggest other ways to see poetry, Canada, women, and other domains with shifting bounds. Canada is a multiplicity of cultures that bring many different recognitions to their interpretations of culture.

The concern with history and writing is something I also explore in my discussion of T.E. Lawrence and his relation with Bernard and Charlotte Shaw. Lawrence of Arabia was a much recognized and interpreted figure who was a man of action and a soldier but had also been a strong scholar and became a sought-after writer. He was not comfortable in thinking about himself as a writer. Charlotte Shaw and he corresponded often and she recognized in him someone extraordinary. Bernard Shaw also exchanged letters with Lawrence and, with some prompting from his wife, championed Lawrence. The interpretation of character and writing is a key part of these textual traces of these relationships between Lawrence and the Shaws. The posthumous film portrays Lawrence in a different light, so that this cultural figure invites differing interpretations. Lawrence himself was subject to much attention as a hero and as a man of character. The Shavian belief in Lawrence could not allow him to accept the honors Britain might bestow, and Lawrence's complex character and circumstances led to the sack of a hero. Lawrence's public humility made it difficult for the armed forces to know what to do with him. The recognition of Charlotte Shaw, that is what she saw in Lawrence and he in her, could not spare him from living with a wound, another kind of Odysseus's scar. Lawrence was confident in his writing at certain times and could not see its worth at others. He wondered whether publishing was the right thing for the story of his life. Would he publish and perish? Lawrence was a genius of publicity who shunned the public eye and his *Seven Pillars of Wisdom* was painfully private in places but, by definition of being his work, an act of publicity. Would Lawrence allow a large publisher to bring it out or would he publish it by subscription or privately? The Shaws knew a great deal about writing and publishing and so this was part of the bond.

Discussing poetry and poets more generally, I then moved in the next chapter to an exploration of communication, theory, and technology, ways in which speaker and audience as well as writer and reader interact. In an age of technology what is the new rhetoric of signs? How do we see or hear anything in the wash of changing images and words and the media that carry or represent them? Does poetry matter in the age of the machine? Have the virtual and software worlds change the way we communicate, interpret, and know? From the First World War to the turn of this millennium, culture has changed with technology, but it is not certain that the underlying questions of interpretation and recognition have changed unrecognizably. I discussed how the poet (*poiētēs*) is the maker of created things (*poiēma*) who shows skill and art (*tekhnē*) in this making. In the age of technology, it is important to remember the connection between the making of things or creations in words and objects. Not only are both in the world but also each has a symbolic and material presence in that world. Making poems and interpretations can involve recognition. Ways of seeing are important. Theory is part of that. As we saw, theoria is a contemplation, a speculation that can be a representation, thought as a mirror for the world, or an idea apart from it. A theorem is a proposition that needs to be proved or an idea that has been proven or is thought to be true. The intricacies of these relations of making, recognition, and interpretation in culture imply that we are not going to discover a singular recognition. Recognition, as I suggested, is a matter of the vision of the maker and the viewer of the thing made. There is something possible, fictional, and putative about the poetic, but it can be political as well as aesthetic. Poems also have their historical contexts. Poetry embodies place and time while gesturing beyond. Moreover, I have suggested that to see and hear it is to be between what is and seems, part of the world and a sign of it.

Other readings also focus on writers, images, and poets. Northrop Frye talked about creating the word and, like T.E. Lawrence, thought a good deal about what it meant to be a writer. Frye, one of the great literary theorists of the twentieth century, was also a writer and someone who explored in his diaries and notebooks the metaphysics of being an author. The writing about writing, the interpretation of this kind of interpretation, is so suggestive that it is a hybrid itself, almost critical thinking as fiction or a Menippean satire that mixed many forms. In the Canada of his time, although Frye studied at Oxford and was a visiting professor in schools in the United States, Frye attempted to find a context for his own interpretative arts, critical and creative. In this precarious milieu, Frye seems to have been looking for the most effective means of self-expression. Frye himself was a kind of paradoxical visionary, both a critic and writer. Frye came along in a period when many human sciences (the humanities and social sciences) were developing as fields and academic disciplines partly as a result of, or as a response to, the developments in the natural sciences. One of the keys to Frye was that just as he was proclaiming criticism, it was changing into theory. The critic became the theorist. This seemed like a great shift, especially from the late 1960s onward, but these roles are very close indeed, especially if we examine their roots. The Greek *kritikos* meant to be able to discern whereas *theōria* suggested contemplation and *theōrein* signified to observe. Frye was significant in exploring the relation to textual and theoretical methods that tried to explain what the text meant and how the author constructed theme, character, and structure. Ways of seeing shift: this is one of the ways of culture. As Frye borrowed from his predecessors and the classical past, others came to him to see what they could find and discover. Here is another instance of recognition taking on numerous forms. Above all, in his literary and critical work, Frye expressed a theoretical imagination. His life as a writer of fiction and poetry beyond his youth was largely confined to entries in his private papers and unfinished works, all of which are interesting putative spaces of their own. They defy a ready framework for interpretation. They push back cultural boundaries. This is Frye's road not taken in a conventional sense. Lawrence, Frye, and Arthur Miller all explore democratic themes of the uncommon common "man."

It is no easy work to see inside Willy Loman's head. *Death of a Salesman* is not a straightforward naturalistic drama but is an expressionistic play on the senses and with an echo of words. Aristotle wrote about tragedy and recognition and this is a key moment in his treatise on poetics, which is about the art of writing and interpretation. By examining

Miller's tragedy of the commoner on film, I have tried to extend Aristotle's discussion of the noble person on stage. In the twentieth century, what is this kind of tragedy and how does it appear as a drama on television? It is also interesting to consider the end of the play as a possible end of tragedy and to ask what role the Requiem has to play in this kind of discussion. The end of the play raises the issue of whether Biff's knowledge does not complement Willy's gesture of self-sacrifice to create tragic recognition and whether Linda's loyal suffering makes the end particularly poignant, if not tragic. At one point, the playwright claimed that *Death of a Salesman* originated in an image of Willy's head rather than in Miller's stage directions at the beginning and end of the main action. In the Requiem, the director, Schlondorff, balances a dark, severe visual representation with the emotion of the words: the playwright also might have created distance even while characters indulge in pathos. Recognition and interpretation depend in part on point of view. Writer, director, actors, characters, audience, and reader all bring something to banquet of meaning. A further consideration is whether twentieth-century interpretation and recognition negate or build on Aristotle's framework for poetics. What continuities and discontinuities occur between the "classical" and the "modern?"

    In discussing some "modern" Irish lyric poets, most especially W.B. Yeats and Seamus Heaney but also briefly Paul Muldoon, Mary O'Malley, Brendan Kennelly, and Medbh McGuckian's translation of Nuala Ní Dhomhnaill, I explore a sense of place and, more particularly, the role of the land, landscape, and physical description. Each place suggests home and exile. The poet can write to try to fill the gap between nostalgia and prophecy in a vanishing present. Mythology is an attempt to make sense of the world, a kind of recognition of actual and possible worlds of past, present, and future. I am a poet and reader who also, though writing history and criticism, respond to the recognition and misrecognition of place. Among these poets, the evocation of place and identity has many sides. For instance, even while speaking about and learning from a Gaelic Ireland, W.B. Yeats wrote in English and is part of an English-speaking tradition of poetry. In a poem published not long before his death, Yeats represented a typology of youth and age, Helen and perhaps Maud Gonne, so that ancient Greece and modern Ireland were connected symbolically. Yeats seems to yearn for something beyond his age and its politics while representing so immediately this moment and that history. He explores the recognition of the ideology of death wish but also appears to reaffirm the generation and regeneration of a lover's touch. Like Yeats, Seamus Heaney also has a gift of enlivening a landscape: nature and politics can span the Irish land. In "Clearances," Heaney uses physical setting to join personal history with the religious past of his country. The stone has a presence past and present in a typology between ancestor and descendant. The religious divide at the heart of Ireland's troubles helps to make private and public history collide. Both sides misrecognize each other and the recognition in Heaney's poem, where the landscape informs the human world, might create from this desperate situation a hope. Like Yeats and Heaney, Paul Muldoon represents a nature that would be beyond ideology but often that the physical environment suggests politics and a waiting violence. Parallel worlds of modern Irish and English meet in translations: Medbh McGuckian's translation of Nuala Ní Dhomhnaill's "An Mhurúch san Ospidéal" ("The Mermaid in the Labour Ward") is a case in point. So close to England and with such a large diaspora across the English-speaking world and especially in the United States, Ireland is a land that takes on meaning much beyond its size and population. Ireland is also a focal point of Europe looking west and North America turning east. It is also within and against empire, a crossroads and a margin. In some ways it has affinities with Canada but with its own differences and ancient history and culture.

In discussing travel writing, encounter and exploration narratives from the early European expansion to the New World and novels, the book comes full circle (although such circles are never quite circles) and connects history and literature from the so-called discovery of America or a key moment, for Europeans and their descendents, of modernity. Such texts reaffirm one of the central points of this books that sometimes it is difficult to know who is recognizing and what is being recognized. In some cases, as we have seen, what is real and what is not can become a matter of life and death. Boundaries between fiction and history, which were always blurred, started to become more delineated with the rise of science. Nonetheless, this delineation was called into question with the return of rhetoric and the notion that discourse is rhetorical no matter what its truth claims and whatever its genre in science, social sciences, and humanities. Possibly, new recognitions have arisen in the art of writing and reading. One of the suggestive possibilities is that the novelty of the novel might have effected something new. Despite echoing the Italian and using a word for a long fiction that creates hope for something new, English also contains a body of criticism that shows an awareness of a long tradition of this kind of writing. This criticism recognizes that the novel developed from epic and romance and grew from the Renaissance until it flowered in Western Europe from the eighteenth century onward. Many Romance languages use *roman* or cognates to designate the novel, thereby embodying the connection with romance and the romance tradition. Even the Germanic *Bildungsroman* (novel of formation) and *Kunstlerroman* (novel of the growth of the artist) call attention to that lineage.

The novel has been a remarkably flexible genre that has allowed novelists and those who might be writing something different but related to the novel to explore what Leibnitz called possible worlds. As I have maintained, these fictional worlds—the possible worlds of the novel, whether of Henry Fieldings's *Tom Jones* or Milan Kundera's *The Unbearable Lightness of Being*, whether ancient or contemporary—permit us to think, feel, and imagine. We can experience distance or empathize, recoil from life or approach it in parallel and almost simultaneous imagined and actual lives. Recognition or discovery often applies to novels, particularly the *Bildungsroman*, which involves coming of age or education, or the adventures of the hero in an exotic place or on travels. As we have seen across genres of writing, some recognitions are tragic and others are comic although many combine elements of both.

Recognition can be a matter that is not entirely clear or without ongoing disputes or differences of interpretation. It is still a matter of debate how much Columbus recognized early on that he had not reached Asia. Columbus extends the earlier European tradition, which Marco Polo and others represent, of travel writing using romance elements. Alvise Cadamosto's narrative of Africa in the 1460s, Amerigo Vespucci's account, Hans Staden's and Jean de Léry's separate descriptions of the Tupinambá, Michel de Montaigne's essays on coaches and cannibals, Aphra Behn's *Oroonoko*, Defoe's *Robinson Crusoe* novels all represent various attempts at interpretation and recognition of other cultures in the Atlantic world and beyond. Jonathan Swift's *Gulliver's Travels* criticizes the colonialism and the ethnocentrism of the English. It is a satire, which is like and not like a novel. The novel had a penchant for devouring other forms and seemed something new. The journey, as I have noted, can also be one of satire and political outrage in the face of dystopias and totalitarian states, such as George Orwell's *Nineteen-Eighty Four* and *Animal Farm* and Mikhail Bulgakov's *The Heart of a Dog*. Furthermore, Kurt Vonnegut was able to write satiric postmodern exposés. In *Slaughterhouse Five*, for instance, he wrote about the spiritual and actual journey of Billy Pilgrim, an American who tried to come to terms with the bombing of Dresden during the Second World War. Julian Barnes's *A History of the World in 10 1/2 Chapters* used legal cases and travel narratives to help in his writing of a fictional history of the world. Barnes also drew on the tone and fragmentation of satire. Quite possibly, the novel expanded as the Western European empires expanded, although the kinds of interpretation and types of recognition these changes in representation involved have been intricate.

Do readers come to see something new or is there a translation of empire in the translation of study regardless of the apparent metamorphosis of genre? The nature and role of this traveling mimesis of these expanding and moving fictions leads again to questions of recognition and misrecognition. At the end of Thomas Mann's *The Magic Mountain*, the author bids farewell to Hans Castorp and the nagging question is whether Europe in its catastrophe can find humanity. Each recognition is part of a long trail of recognitions within and between cultures but each is new and distinct. The mount or mountain does not always allow for an overview for the *katascopos*. We are in the fray even as we try to rise above it in order to see better. We experience irony but that irony can be against ourselves. The capacity for interpretation and recognition helps to make us human even in a world in which nature can be harsh and humans can undo any wisdom and understanding that they or their parents, or human cultures over a long span, have gained. Recognition can be as much about knowing our flaws and frailties as about seeing clearly for the first time.

Interpreting culture involves a range of recognitions and misrecognitions (it is sometimes or even often hard to distinguish which is which). Argument is worldly, particularly in rhetoric but to some extent in dialectic. It makes uncertain the use and truth of *muthos* or the plot Aristotle discusses. The story of mythology that underlies literature also has its root in *muthos*. The mythological can also call into question the very claims of what is truth and seriousness. The ideological, as argumentative as it can be, also implies stories and can be turned into a pseudo-argument used in ersatz science and propaganda of which the Nazis employed some of the basic kinds. From classical drama through Early Modern "discovery" narratives to poetry, film, and novels by people of different cultures or genders representing the world, the interpretation of culture is something that suggests that ways of seeing, whereas sharing characteristics over time from place to place, can call into question as much as they resolve. Recognitions and interpretations are not stereoscopic or resolve the maze through twisting a childhood kaleidoscope into focus or a hall of multiple mirrors reflecting a singular world. Interpretation and recognition suggest the actual and the possible as cultures remake and break with themselves in tension between continuity and change. If Yeats asked how can we know the dancer from the dance, the same can be said about the seer and the seen and the hearer and the heard, which has implications for those who would interpret or recognize word, image, world.

NOTES

Notes to pages 2–4

Introduction

1. For a suggestive discussion of similar topics, see Clifford Geertz, *Available Light: Anthropological Reflections on Philosophical Topics* (Princeton and Oxford: Princeton University Press, 2000, rpt. 2001), 143–59. Geertz himself has had much of relevance to say in *The Interpretation of Cultures: Selected Essays* (New York: Basic Books [1973]). On the richness and on the debate of the nature of science, see, for instance, Bruno Latour, *Science in Action: How to Follow Scientists and Engineers through Society* (Cambridge: Harvard University Press, 1987); Richard Rorty, *Philosophical Papers* (Cambridge: Cambridge University Press, 1991). On subjectivity and objectivity in neurology, see Israel Rosenfeld, *The Strange, Familiar and Forgotten: An Anatomy of Consciousness* (New York: Knopf, 1992), a work whose title might invite comparison to Robert Burton, *Anatomy of Melancholy* (London, 1621) and Northrop Frye, *Anatomy of Criticism* (Princeton: Princeton University Press, 1957, rpt. 1973).

2. In this paragraph I am drawing on the *Oxford English Dictionary*, Second Edition, 1989. More particularly, the etymology of "read" is as follows: "[Comm. Teut.: OE. *raédan* = OFris. *rēda* using, OS. *rādan* (MLG. *raden*, MDu. and Du. *raden*), OHG. *rātan* (MHG. *rāten*, G. *raten*, *rathen*), ON. *ráða* (Sw. *råda*, Da. *raade*), Goth. *-rēdan*: OTeut. **raēdan*, prob. related to OIr. *imrádim* to deliberate, consider, OSl. *raditi* to take thought, attend to, Skr. *rādh-* to succeed, accomplish, etc."

3. Geertz, *Available Light*, 16.

4. Geertz, *Available Light*, 16.

5. *Brecht on Theatre*, trans. John Willett (New York, 1964), 15.

6. *Brecht on Theatre*, 34.

7. See Bertolt Brecht, *Vesuche*, 12 (Berlin, 1958).

8. Marvin Carlson, *Theories of the Theatre: A Historical and Critical Survey, from the Greeks to the Present* (Ithaca and London: Cornell University Press, 1984, rpt. 1986), 17; Carlson's survey is helpful in many ways and also suggests that the perception of theatrical performance and action has philosophical, ideological and historical variants; see also Gerald Else, *Aristotle's Poetics: The Argument* (Cambridge, MA: Harvard University Press, 1957), 322.

9. *The Republic of Plato*, trans. Francis MacDonald Cornford (1941; New York and London: Oxford University Press, 1945, rpt. 1968), 80 here and below.

10. Cornford, Notes, *The Republic of Plato*, 323–24, see Plato *Apology*, 22 B; see also T.B.L. Webster, "Greek Theories of Art and Literature down to 400 B.C.," *Classical Quarterly* 33 (1939), 166.

11. Jonas Barish, *The Antitheatrical Prejudice* (Berkeley: University of California Press, 1981).
12. *Aristotle's Poetics*, trans. George Walley, ed. John Baxter and Patrick Atherton (Montreal and Kingston: McGill-Queen's University Press, 1997), 87; for below, see 87–91.
13. David Hume, *A Treatise of Human Nature*, ed. L.A. Selby-Bigge (Oxford, 1928), 67–73. A helpful essay that frames the relation between the making and unmaking of meaning in interpretation is M.H. Abrams, "Construing and Deconstructing," *The Creating Word: Papers from and International Conference on the Learning and Teaching of English in the 1980s*, ed. Patricia Demers (Edmonton: University of Alberta Press, 1986), 30–65, esp. 32.
14. See, for instance, Hume, *Treatise*, 264–70 and Jacques Derrida, *Of Grammatology*, trans. Gayatri Spivak (Baltimore and London: Johns Hopkins University Press, 1976), 158–64; Abrams, "Construing," 33–36.
15. See Paul de Man, *Allegories of Reading* (New Haven and London: Yale University Press, 1979) and his *Blindness and Insight: Essays in the Rhetoric of Contemporary Criticism* (Minneapolis: University of Minnesota Press, 1983). Northrop Frye's double vision, Roland Barthes's double sign, and Derrida's double writing might well differ on the notion of the integration and disintegration of texts, but recognition and misrecognition through reading and interpretation concern them all. What is a double bind or double blindness and what is prophetic vision might be a question that goes back to Plato and carries on through philosophy and literary criticism or theory. For example, Derrida has attempted to shake up the way we see the world of texts and the textual world.
16. For one of my earlier discussions of doubleness, see Jonathan Hart, *Northrop Frye: The Theoretical Imagination* (London and New York: Routledge, 1994).
17. Roland Barthes, *S/Z* (Paris, 1970); in translation New York, 1974 and London, 1975.
18. Jacques Derrida, *Writing and Difference*, trans. Alan Bass (Chicago and London: University of Chicago Press, 1978), 293–95; for the original, see *L'Écriture et la différence* (Paris, 1967). Catherine Belsey summarizes this nexus nicely: "Common sense proposes a *humanism* based on an *empiricist–idealist* interpretation of the world." See Catherine Belsey, *Critical Practice* (London and New York: Methuen, 1980), 7.
19. For an insightful discussion of presentation and representation, see Jean Bessière, *Quel statut pour la littérature?* (Paris: Presses Universitaires de France, 2001), esp. 119–27.
20. For a discussion of the reading process (a phenomenological approach), see Wolfgang Iser, *The Implied Reader*, trans. David Henry Wilson (Baltimore and London: Johns Hopkins University Press, 1974).
21. R.G. Collingwood, *The Idea of History* (1946; London: Oxford University Press,1948, rpt. 1966), 282.
22. Collingwood, *Idea*, 282–83.
23. Erich Kahler, *The Meaning of History* (1964; Cleveland and New York: Meridian Books, 1968), 16–17; see Collingwood, *Idea*, 9.
24. Kahler, *History*, 19; Kahler also provides a discussion of comprehension and other philosophers of history (19n2 and 19 and 20n3), which I draw on here.
25. Theodor Lessing, *Geschichte als Sinngebung des Sinnlosen* [*History Seen as Imparting Meaning to the Meaningless*] (München, 1921), 10, 15, quoted in Kahler, *History*, 20n3.
26. Derek J. de Solla Price, "The Science of Science," *New Views of the Nature of Man*, ed. John R. Platt (Chicago and London: University of Chicago Press, 1965), 47–48.
27. For a punning extension of this phrase, see Marshall McLuhan and Quentin Fiore. Coordinated by Jerome Agel, *The Medium is the Massage* (New York, Random House [1967]).
28. John Fiske and John Hartley, *Reading Television* (London and New York: Methuen, 1978, rpt. 1982), 19.
29. Raymond Williams, *Drama in Performance* (1954; rev. 1968; Harmondsworth: Penguin, 1972), 179.
30. Richard A. Lanham, *The Motives of Eloquence: Literary Rhetoric in the Renaissance* (New Haven: Yale University Press, 1976), 1–9.
31. Clifford Geertz, "The Impact of the Concept of Culture on the Concept of Man," *New Views of the Nature of Man*, ed. John R. Platt (Chicago and London: University of Chicago Press, 1965), 96.

32. For a good discussion of tragedy, see Richard B. Sewall, *The Vision of Tragedy*, rev. and enlarged (1959; New Haven and London: Yale University Press, 1980), 1–9, esp. 5–6. Sewall speaks of such a vision but does not focus on recognition.

33. Erich Auerbach, *Mimesis: The Representation of Reality in Western Literature*, trans. Willard R. Trask (1946; Princeton, NJ: Princeton University Press, 1953, rpt. 1974), 554–57.

34. Terence Cave, *Recognitions: A Study in Poetics* (1988; Oxford: Clarendon Press, 1990), esp. 190–91, 489. See Frye, *Anatomy of Criticism* and Jonathan Hart, *Northrop Frye*.

35. E.H. Gombrich, *The Story of Art*, 12th ed. (1950; London: Phaidon Press, 1972, rpt. 1973), 224, see 223.

36. E.H. Gombrich, *New Light on Old Masters: Studies in the Art of the Renaissance IV* (Chicago: The University Press, 1986), 170.

37. Gombrich, *Story*, 170. See Plato, *Sophist*, L. 266c.

38. Thomas M. Greene, *The Light in Troy: Imitation and Discovery in Renaissance Poetry* (New Haven and London: Yale University Press, 1982), esp. 54–80.

39. Carlo Ginsburg, *Clues, Myths, and the Historical Method*, trans. John and Anne C. Tedeschi (1986; Baltimore: The Johns Hopkins University Press, 1989, rpt. 1992), xii.

40. *Aristotle's Poetics*, trans. George Whalley (Montreal and Kingston: McGill-Queen's Press, (1997) 81, 83 (1451a–b).

41. For discussions of their notions of tragedy, see Hayden White, *Metahistory: The Historical Imagination in Nineteenth-Century Europe* (Baltimore and London: The Johns Hopkins University Press, 1973, rpt. 1979).

42. See G.W. Bowerstock, *Fiction as History: Nero to Julian* (Berkeley: University of California Press, 1994, rpt. 1997), 16, 122–25. See Northrop Frye, *The Secular Scripture: A Study in the Structure of Romance* (Cambridge: Harvard University Press, 1976).

43. Frye, *Secular Scripture*, 183.

44. Lionel Gossman, *Between History and Literature* (Cambridge and London: Harvard University Press, 1990).

45. Northrop Frye thinks value judgments are not vital, whereas E.D. Hirsch, Jr. does. See E.D. Hirsch, Jr., *The Aims of Interpretation* (Chicago and London: University of Chicago Press, 1976), 3, 106.

46. See, for instance, *Explorations in Difference: Law, Culture and Politics*, ed. Jonathan Hart and Richard W. Bauman (Toronto: University of Toronto Press, 1996).

47. See Barbara Johnson, *The Feminist Difference: Literature, Psychoanalysis, Race, and Gender* (Cambridge: Harvard University Press, 1998).

48. See Evelyne Keitel, "reading as/like a woman," *Feminism and Psychoanalysis: A Critical Dictionary*, ed. Elizabeth Wright (Oxford: Basil Blackwell, 1992), 371–74.

49. See, for instance, Edward W. Said, *Orientalism* (New York: Pantheon Books, 1978); Tzvetan Todorov, *The Conquest of America: the Question of the Other*, trans. Richard Howard (1982; New York: Harper & Row, 1984); Michel de Certeau, *Heterologies: Discourse on the Other*, trans. Brian Massumi (Minneapolis: University of Minnesota Press, 1986); Gayatri Chakravorty Spivak, *In Other Worlds: Essays in Cultural Politics* (New York : Methuen, 1987); Henry Louis Gates, Jr., *The Signifying Monkey: A Theory of Afro-American Literary Criticism* (New York: Oxford University Press, 1988); Homi K. Bhabha, *The Location of Culture* (London and New York: Routledge, 1994).

50. See, for instance, Jonathan Hart, *Representing the New World: The English and French Uses of the Example of Spain, 1492–1713* (New York: Palgrave, 2001); *Columbus, Shakespeare and the Interpretation of the New World* (New York and London: Palgrave, 2002); *Comparing Empires: European Colonialism from Portuguese Expansion to the Spanish–American War* (New York and London: Palgrave/Macmillan/St Martin's, 2003); *Contesting Empires: Opposition, Promotion and Slavery* (New York and London: Palgrave Macmillan, 2005).

51. Miranda calls Caliban this at I.ii.351; the exchange and accusations occur between Prospero and Miranda on the one hand and Caliban on the other from lines 319 to 374 of this scene.

The island is contested. Prospero gives Miranda the history of their leaving Italy and their arrival on the island in Act One, scene two. Miranda describes the newly arrived Ferdinand: "I might call him / A thing divine, for nothing natural / I ever saw so noble" (I.ii.418–20). *The Riverside Shakespeare*, ed. G. Blakemore Evans, with J.J.M. Tobin, Second edition (Boston and New York: Houghton Mifflin, 1997). The First Folio (lines 2157–62) represents the crucial exchange between Prospero and Miranda: "*Mir.* O wonder! / How many goodly creatures are there heere? / How beauteous mankinde is? O braue new world/ That has such people in't. / *Pro.* 'Tis new to thee." For a detailed discussion of the play, see my *Columbus, Shakespeare and the Interpretation of the New World*.

52. R.C. Van Caenegem, *An Historical Introduction to Western Constitutional Law* (Cambridge: Cambridge University Press, 1995), 82–84.

53. Edmund Burke, *Philosophical Inquiry into the Origin of Our Ideas of the Sublime and the Beautiful* in *The Works of Edmund Burke* (London, 1906), I:101; see Terry Eagleton, *The Ideology of the Aesthetic* (Oxford: Basil Blackwell, 1990, rpt. 1991), 53.

54. Hayden White, *The Content of the Form: Narrative Discourse and Historical Representation* (Baltimore and London: The Johns Hopkins University, 1987, rpt. 1992), 185–213.

55. Jonathan Hart, "A Comparative Pluralism: The Heterogeneity of Methods and the Case of Possible Worlds,"*CRCL/RCLC* 15 (1988), 320–45, esp. 324. I draw on my article here. See Doreen Maitre, *Literature and Possible Worlds* (London: Middlesex Polytechnic Press, 1983), esp. 66–70. Although my article has a fairly extensive bibliography, I would like to point out, for our purposes here, two key books in the field, Jerome Bruner, *Actual Minds/Possible Worlds* (Cambridge: Harvard University Press, 1986) and Thomas Pavel, *Fictional Worlds* (Cambridge: Harvard University Press, 1986).

56. See Pavel, *Fictional Worlds*, esp. 55.

57. See Pavel, *Fictional Worlds*, esp. 144–48.

58. See Bruner, *Actual Minds*, 5–14.

59. See Jonathan Hart, "Stephen Greenblatt's Shakespearean Negotiations," *Textual Practice* 5 (1991), 429–48.

60. Bruner, *Actual Minds*, esp. 24–26.

1   Discovering Recognition

1. Umberto Eco, *The Name of the Rose* (1980, 1983; New York: Warner, 1984). Although this work on recognition was written at a time I was writing a paper for the Philosophy and Literature conference at George Mason University in 1996, I have, whenever possible and effective, updated its bibliography for this book. This is the longest version of this work and, owing to various circumstances, has not been published before now. Thanks to my hosts.

2. Plato, *The Republic of Plato*, trans. Francis M. Cornford (New York: Oxford University Press, 1941, rpt. 1968) and Aristotle, "On the Art of Poetry," in *Classical Literary Criticism*, ed. T.S. Dorsch (Harmondsworth: Penguin, 1965, rpt. 1975), 33–75. In chapter 11 of *Poetics*, Aristotle says that anagnôrisis or recognition is a change from *agnoias* or ignorance to *gnôsin* or knowledge. A recognition of one's or another's identity occurs. Taking a different tack, Patchen Markell says: "Tragic *anagnôrisis*, we might say, is the acknowledgement of finitude under the weight of a (failed) effort to become sovereign through the recognition of identity." Patchen Markell, *Bound by Recognition* (Princeton: Princeton University Press, 2003), 86, see 82–85. Much discussion of anagnôrisis occurs in relation to Greek tragedy, but Aristotle and the Greek dramatists have also influenced critics and playwrights in later periods. For a discussion of anagnôrisis in the film *The Fugitive*, see Ari Hiltunen, *Aristotle in Hollywood* (Bristol: Intellect Books, 2002), esp. 49–53. On anagnôrisis generally, see Roger W. Herzel, "Anagnorisis and Peripeteia in Comedy," *Educational Theatre Journal* 26 (1974): 495–505; Piero Boitani, "Anagnorisis and

Reasoning: Electra and Hamlet," *REAL: The Yearbook of Research in English and American Literature* 7 (1990): 99–136; Sherryll S. Mleynek, *Knowledge and Mortality: Anagnorisis in Genesis and Narrative Fiction* (New York: Peter Lang, 1999); Moon Won Lee, "Anagnorisis beyond Aristotelian Definition: A Study of Recognition Scenes in Electra," *Journal of Classic and English Renaissance Literature* 11 (2002): 105–34.

3. Philip Sidney, "An Apology for Poetry, " in *English Critical Texts: 16th Century to 20th Century*, ed. D.J. Enright and Ernst de Chickera (London: Oxford University Press, 1962, rpt. 1975), 3–49. On Sidney's defense of poetry as heroic diversion, as a kind of Horatian profit and pleasure, in a social context (with aristocracy under pressure of a rising middle class and of Protestantism), see Robert Matz, *Defending Literature in Early Modern Literature* (Cambridge: Cambridge University Press, 2000), esp. 56–58. On Sidney and his family and poetics, see Jacob Bronowski, *The Poet's Defence: The Concept of Poetry from Sidney to Yeats* (Cleveland, OH: World, 1966); A.C. Hamilton, *Sir Philip Sidney: A Study of His Life and Works* (Cambridge: Cambridge University Press, 1977); Andrew D. Weinder, *Sir Philip Sidney and the Poetics of Protestantism: A Study of Contexts* (Minneapolis: University of Minnesota Press, 1978); *Sidney in Retrospect: Selections from English Literary Renaissance*, ed. Arthur F. Kinney (Amherst: University of Massachusetts Press, 1988) (especially O.B. Hardison, Jr., "The Two Voices of Sidney's *Apology for Poetry*," 45–61); M.J. Doherty, *The Mistress-Knowledge: Sir Philip Sidney's "Defence of Poesie" and Literary Architectonics in the English Renaissance* (Nashville: Vanderbilt University Press 1991); Katherine Duncan-Jones, *Sir Philip Sidney, Courtier Poet* (New Haven: Yale University Press, 1991); Alan Hager, *Dazzling Images: The Masks of Sir Philip Sidney* (Newark: University of Delaware Press, 1991); Edward Berry, *The Making of Sir Philip Sidney* (Toronto: University of Toronto Press, 1998); Alan Stewart, *Philip Sidney: A Double Life* (London: Thomas Dunne Books, 2001); Elizabeth Mazzola, *Favorite Sons: The Politics and Poetics of the Sidney Family* (New York, NY: Palgrave Macmillan, 2003).

4. Jonathan Hart, "The Ends of Renaissance Comedy," *Reading the Renaissance: Culture, Poetics* and Drama, ed. Jonathan Hart (New York: Garland Press, 1996), 91–127.

5. Jane Harrison, *Themis* (Cambridge: Cambridge University Press, 1914); Gilbert Murray, "Excursus," in Harrison, *Themis*; Francis M. Cornford, *The Origins of Attic Comedy* (Cambridge: Cambridge University Press, 1934).

6. Northrop Frye, "The Argument of Comedy" (1948), in *Theories of Comedy*, ed. Paul Lauter (Garden City, NY: Doubleday, 1964), 450–60; Anne Barton, *Ben Jonson, Dramatist* (Cambridge: Cambridge University Press, 1984); Harry Levin, *Playboys and Killjoys: An Essay on the Theory and Practice of Comedy* (New York: Oxford University Press, 1987). Studies of comedy over the past fifteen to twenty years have continued to show a tension between humor and comic structure. See *Laughing Matters: A Serious Look at Humour*, ed. John Durant and Jonathan Miller (New York: John Wiley & Sons, 1988); Anne Barton, *The Names of Comedy* (Toronto: University of Toronto Press, 1990); T.G.A. Nelson, *Comedy: The Theory of Comedy in Literature, Drama, and Cinema* (New York: Oxford University Press, 1990); Patrick O'Neill, *The Comedy of Entropy: Humour, Narrative, Reading* (Toronto: University of Toronto Press, 1990); Susan Carlson, *Women and Comedy: Rewriting the British Theatrical Tradition* (Ann Arbor: University of Michigan Press, 1991); Barbara Freedman, *Staging the Gaze: Postmodernism, Psychoanalysis, and Shakespearean Comedy* (Ithaca, NY: Cornell University Press, 1991); Ejner J. Jensen, *Shakespeare and the Ends of Comedy* (Bloomington: Indiana University Press, 1991); Patricia Mellencamp, *High Anxiety: Catastrophe, Scandal, Age and Comedy* (Bloomington: Indiana University Press, 1992); Donald Perret, *Old Comedy in the French Renaissance 1576–1620* (Geneva: Droz, 1992); Audrey Bilger, *Laughing Feminism: Subversive Comedy in Frances Burney, Maria Edgeworth, and Jane Austen* (Detroit: Wayne State University Press, 1998); Marc Cogan, *The Design in the Wax: The Structure of the Divine Comedy and Its Meaning* (Notre Dame, IN: University of Notre Dame, 1999); Alexander Leggatt, *English Stage Comedy, 1490–1990: Five Centuries of a Genre* (London: Routledge, 1998); *Performing Gender and Comedy: Theories, Texts, and Contexts* (Amsterdam: Gordon and Breach,

1998); Mark Roche, *Tragedy and Comedy: A Systematic Study and a Critique of Hegel* (Albany: State University of New York Press, 1998); Glen Cavaliero, *The Alchemy of Laughter: Comedy in English Fiction* (London: Macmillan, 2000); Alan Dale, *Comedy Is a Man in Trouble: Slapstick in American Movies* (Minneapolis: University of Minnesota Press, 2000); Kirby Olson, *Comedy after Postmodernism: Rereading Comedy from Edward Lear to Charles Willeford* (Lubbock: Texas Tech University Press, 2001); Erich Segal, *The Death of Comedy* (Cambridge, MA: Harvard University Press, 2001); *Comedy, Fantasy and Colonialism*, ed. Graeme Harper (London: Continuum, 2002); Jill Levenson, "Comedy," in *English Renaissance Drama*, ed. Michael Hattaway (Cambridge: Cambridge University Press, 2003), 254–92. A suggestive although old study of the *commedia dell' arte* from its origins to its influences in French theatre is Pierre L. Ducharte, *The Italian Comedy* (1929; New York: Dover, 1966); Ducharte stresses the relation between the changing plots and the unchanging roles or masks of the comic actors in this Italian form (see 18). A wide-ranging discussion of comedy occurs in Michael Cordner, Peter Holland, and John Kerrigan, "Introduction," *English Comedy*, ed. Michael Cordner, Peter Holland, and John Kerrigan (Cambridge: Cambridge University Press, 1994), 1–11. Echoing Horace and drawing on Anne Barton's discussion of William Congreve, these editors observe: "Whenever comedy raises its voice—or puts its head over the parapet—it usually expects to be shot at for arrogantly rising above its literary station" (1).

7. Paul de Man, *Blindness and Insight: Essays in the Rhetoric of Contemporary Criticism* (1971; second rev. ed. Minneapolis: University of Minnesota Press, 1983); Terence Cave, *Recognitions: A Study in Poetics* (Oxford: Clarendon Press, 1988, rpt. 1990). On related aspects of Paul de Man, see, for instance *(Dis)continuities: Essays on Paul de Man*, ed. Luc Herman et al. (Amsterdam: Rodopi, 1989), which examines his rhetoric, literary history, theology, philosophy, and other elements; *Material Events: Paul de Man and the Afterlife of Theory*, ed. Tom Cohen et al. (Minneapolis: University of Minnesota Press, 2001), which discusses ideology, aesthetics, the lyric, materiality, and other matters. Other works of note, especially relating to ideology, aesthetics, or the controversy over De Man's wartime writings are Christopher Norris, *Paul de Man: Deconstruction and the Critique of Aesthetic Ideology* (London: Routledge, 1988); *Responses: On Paul de Man's Wartime Journalism*, ed. Werner Hamacher et al. (Lincoln: University of Nebraska Press, 1989); David Lehman, *Signs of the Times: Deconstruction and the Fall of Paul de Man* (New York: Poseidon Press, 1991); *Reading Paul de Man*, ed. Lindsay Waters and Wlad Godzich (Minneapolis: University of Minnesota Press, 1989). The influence of Cave extends beyond recognition in the literary. For instance, Wendy Doniger draws on his work in her discussion of seeing truth or power in sex in *The Bedtrick: Tales of Sex and Masquerade* (Chicago: University of Chicago Press, 2000), esp. 1–10.

8. On the difficulties of defining and discussing "recognition," see Cave, *Recognitions*, 1–9. Earlier, Terence Cave discussed "the conjunction of recognition with implausibility." See his "Recognition and the Reader," *Comparative Criticism: A Yearbook*, ed. E.S. Shaffer (Cambridge: Cambridge University Press, 1980), 49, see 49–70.

9. See Bertolt Brecht, *Brecht on Theatre*, trans. John Willett (New York: 1964); Jonathan Hart, "Alienation, Double Signs with a Difference: Conscious Knots in *Cymbeline* and *The Winter's Tale*," *CIEFL Bulletin* (New Series) 1 (1989), 58–78. For a more recent discussion of Brecht and the alienation or estrangement effect, see Melveena McKendrick, "Anticipating Brecht: Alienation and Agency in Calderón's Wife-Murder Plays," *Bulletin of Hispanic Studies* 77 (2000): 217–36.

10. See Gilbert Murray, "Excursis," in Harrison's *Themis*; Northrop Frye, *Anatomy of Criticism: Four Essays* (Princeton: Princeton University Press, 1957, rpt. 1973), 292.

11. Aristotle, *Poetics*, ch. 2.

12. Aristotle, *Poetics*, ch. 5.

13. Aristotle, *Poetics*, ch. 6.

14. Cicero, *On the Character of the Orator* (Bk. 2, lviii, 235–lxxi, 289), in Lauter, *Theories of Comedy*, 24–26.

15. Cave, *Recognitions*, 50.

16. Donatus, *A Fragment on Comedy and Tragedy*, in Lauter, *Theories of Comedy*, 30.
17. Donatus, in Lauter, *Theories of Comedy*, 27.
18. Cave, *Recognitions*, 1, see 2–9.
19. For a discussion of the politics of literature, see, for instance, Terry Eagleton, *The Ideology of the Aesthetic* (Oxford: Blackwell, 1990). Eagleton stresses the importance of aesthetics in European philosophy since the Enlightenment. In the pursuit of the recognition of otherness and autonomy in acknowledging someone else as a subject, it is important, in Eagleton's view, to realize this as a political goal and the contradictory nature of the concept of the aesthetic. Eagleton urges a use of dialectical thought and a transformation of discourses of truth, reason, subjectivity, and freedom in opposition to arrogant power rather than assumption that these are exhausted (see esp. 415). This is but one instance of the idea of the recognition of recognition is part of philosophical, critical, and theoretical discourse.
20. On story-argument, see Jonathan Hart, "Stephen Greenblatt's *Shakespearean Negotiations*," *Textual Practice* 5 (1991), 444 and *Theater and World: The Problematics of Shakespeare's History* (Boston: Northeastern University Press, 1992), 259.
21. See Northrop Frye, *Anatomy of Criticism: Four Essays* (Princeton: Princeton University Press, 1957, rpt. 1973); Roland Barthes, *Mythologies* (Paris: Editions du Seuil, 1957). See also Jonathan Hart, *Northrop Frye: The Theoretical Imagination* (London and New York: Routledge, 1994) for a more extended discussion.
22. See Hayden White, *The Content of the Form: Narrative Discourse and Historical Representation* (Baltimore: Johns Hopkins University Press, 1987).
23. Here I especially have in mind Etienne Gilson's *Reason and Revelation* (New York: Scribner's, 1938).
24. My scholarly interest in the structure of the Bible began when I audited Northrop Frye's Bible and mythology course (taught with Jay Macpherson) in the 1970s: some of Frye's ideas of the comic structure of the Bible have since remained with me. Frye's books on the Bible are all pertinent in the discussion of myth, metaphor, and vision as well as language and structure. See his *The Great Code: The Bible and Literature* (New York: Harcourt Brace Jovanovich, 1982); *Words with Power: Being a Second Study of the Bible and Literature* (San Diego: Harcourt Brace Jovanovich, 1990); *The Double Vision: Language and Meaning in Religion* (Toronto: University of Toronto Press, 1991). More recent introductory works in the area of the Bible as or and literature include: *The Bible as Literature; An Introduction*, ed. John B. Gabel, Anthony York, and Charles B. Wheeler (New York: Oxford University Press, 1986, rpt. 2000), which includes a wide range of topics such as the Bible and history (ch. 4) and interpretation (ch. 18); *The Bible and Literature: A Reader*, ed. David Jasper and Stephen Prickett (Oxford: Blackwell, 1999), see the editors' introduction, as well as Prickett's "Biblical and Literary Criticism: A History of Interaction," 12–43 and Jasper's "Literary Readings of the Bible: Trends in Modern Criticism," 44–64; this collection highlights Derrida above all recent theorists writing on literature and the Bible (see 90–93, 312–13); David Norton, *A History of the English Bible as Literature* (Cambridge: Cambridge University Press, 2000), which examines many topics, translators, and writers as well as the Geneva, King James, Revised, and New English Bibles. Norton's first volume (Cambridge: Cambridge University Press, 1993) covered the period from antiquity to 1700. Some other key works on the Bible and literature are Albert S. Cook, *The Bible and English Prose Style: Selections and Comments* (Boston: D.C. Health, 1892); J.H. Gardiner, *The Bible as English Literature* (New York: Charles Scribner's Sons, 1907); Laura H. Wild, *A Literary Guide to the Bible: A Study of the Types of Literature Present in the Old and New Testaments* (New York: George H. Doran Co., 1922); Charles Allen Dinsmore, *The English Bible as Literature* (Boston: Houghton Mifflin, 1931); Wilbur Owen Sypherd, *The Literature of the English Bible* (New York: Oxford University Press, 1938); C.S. Lewis, *The Literary Impact of the Authorised Version* (London: The Athlone Press, 1950); *Literary Interpretations of Biblical Narratives*, ed. Kenneth R.R. Gros Louis et al. (Nashville: Abington Press, 1974); Robert Alter, *The Art of Biblical Narrative* (New York: Basic Books, 1981), *The Art of Biblical Poetry* (New York: Basic Books, 1985), and *The World of*

Biblical Literature (New York: Basic Books, 1992); Robert M. Grant, *A Short History of the Interpretation of the Bible,* rev. ed. (Philadelphia: Fortress Press, 1984); *Feminist Interpretation of the Bible,* ed. Letty M. Russell (Philadelphia: Westminster Press, 1985); Meir Sternberg, *Poetics of Biblical Narrative: Ideological Literature and the Drama of Reading* (Bloomington: Indiana University Press, 1985); David Damrosch, *The Narrative Covenant: Transformations of Genre in the Growth of Biblical Literature* (San Francisco: Harper & Row, 1987); *Literary Guide to the Bible,* ed. Robert Alter and Frank Kermode (Glasgow: Collins, 1987); Robert Morgan with John Barton, *Biblical Interpretation* (Oxford: Oxford University Press, 1988); Amos N. Wilder, *The Bible and the Literary Critic* (Minneapolis: Fortress Press, 1991); *The Bible and the Narrative Tradition,* ed. Frank McConnell (New York: Oxford University Press, 1991); Walter L. Reed, *Dialogues of the World: The Bible as Literature according to Bakhtin* (New York: Oxford University Press, 1993); *A Complete Literary Guide to the Bible,* ed. Leland Ryken and Tremper Longman III (Grand Rapids, MI: Zondervan, 1993); Duane F. Watson and Alan J. Hauser, *Rhetorical Criticism of the Bible: A Comprehensive Bibliography with Notes on History and Method* (New York: E.J. Brill, 1994); John Rogerson, *Old Testament Criticism in the Nineteenth Century: England and Germany* (Minneapolis: Fortress Press, 1995); *Out of the Garden: Women Writers on the Bible,* ed. Christina Buchmann and Celina Spiegel (New York: Ballantine Books, 1995); Mark Minor, *Literary-Critical Approaches to the Bible: An Annotated Bibliography* (West Cornwall, CT: Locust Hill Press, 1992) and his bibliographical supplement, with the same publisher, in 1996; James E. Brenneman, *Canons in Conflict: Negotiating Texts in True and False Prophecy* (New York: Oxford University Press, 1997); Richard Harries, Of Little Faith—Influence of the Bible as Literature," *New Statesman,* October 16, 1998; *Revelation and Story,* ed. Gerhard Sauter and John Barton (Aldershot: Ashgate, 2000); Eryl W. Davies, *The Dissenting Reader* (Aldershot: Ashgate, 2003).

25. The Bible, Authorized Version [*AV*] Genesis 3:3. All quotations and citations from the Bible are from this version.
26. Genesis, 3:4–5.
27. Genesis, 3:7.
28. Genesis, 3:22.
29. Genesis, 25:3.
30. Genesis, 26:19.
31. Genesis, 27.
32. Genesis, 29:25.
33. Genesis, 31.
34. Genesis, 32:24–30.
35. Genesis, 33.
36. Matthew, 26:33–36, 27:69–75.
37. Matthew, 46, see 47–50.
38. John, 14:22.
39. Matthew, 26:24.
40. Matthew, 26:49.
41. Matthew, 27:3–5.
42. Matthew, 27:46.
43. Mark, 15:39, see Matthew, 27:54.
44. Luke, 23:34, see 43, 46.
45. John, 20:26–27.
46. John, 20:28, 30.
47. John, 21, see Luke, 24.
48. John, 20:29.
49. Acts, 9:18.
50. Cave, *Recognitions,* 33.
51. Thomas Aquinas's contribution is a fourfold typology of the literal, allegorical, moral, and anagogic. See Dante, *La Divina Commedia,* ed. C.H. Grandgent, rev. Charles Singleton

(Cambridge, MA: Harvard University Press, 1972); C.S. Lewis, *The Allegory of Love: A Study in a Medieval Tradition* (Oxford: Oxford University Press, 1936, rpt. 1976); See also Erich Auerbach, *Dante, Poet of the Secular World*, trans. Ralph Manheim (1929; Chicago: University of Chicago Press, 1961); Giuseppe Mazzotta, "Dante's Literary Typology," *MLN* 87 (1972), 1–19. In 1944 Auerbach wrote an essay in which he understood the importance of reading Biblical narrative for an understanding of Dante's *Divine Comedy*; see Erich Auerbach, "Figura" in *Scenes from the Drama of European Literature*, trans. Ralph Manheim (New York: Meridian, 1957); other studies on typology in the 1950s and 1960s also contributed to a better sense ot typology in literary studies; see Charles S. Singleton, *Dante Studies I: Commedia, Elements of Structure* (Cambridge: Harvard University Press, 1957); A.C. Charity, *Events and Their Afterlife: The Dialectics of Christian Typology in the Bible and Dante* (Cambridge: Cambridge University Press, 1966); more generally, see S. Bemrose, *A New Life of Dante* (Exeter: University of Exeter Press 2000). More generally, on typology and related topics, see G.W.H. Lampe, *Essays on Typology* (London: SCM Press, 1957); Paul Piehler, *The Visionary Landscape: A Study in Medieval Allegory* (London: Edward Arnold, 1971); *Literary Uses of Typology from the Later Middle Ages to the Present*, ed. Earl Miner (Princeton: Princeton University Press, 1977); *Typology and Medieval Literature*, ed. Hugh T. Keenan (New York: AMS Press, 1992); Jonathan Hart, "Poetics and Culture: Unity, Difference, and the Case of Northrop Frye," *Christianity and Literature* (1996), 61–79; Julia Lupton, *Afterlives of the Saints: Hagiography, Typology, and Renaissance Literature* (Stanford, CA: Stanford University Press, 1996); János Kenyeres, "Kerygma, Concern and Literature: Northrop Frye and the Bible," *AnaChronist* (1999), 177–200; David Jeffrey, "C.S. Lewis, the Bible, and Its Literary Critics," *Christianity and Literature* 50 (2000), 95–109; Gary Kuchar, "Typology and the Language of Concern in the Work of Northrop Frye," *Canadian Review of Comparative Literature* 27 (2000), 159–80; Phyllis Gilbert, "The Bible as Literature," *Inside English* 28 (2002), 20–21; Robert Alter, "Northrop Frye between Archetype and Typology," in *Frye and the Word: Religious Contexts in the Writings of Northrop Frye*, ed. Jeffrey Donaldson and Alan Mendelson (Toronto: University of Toronto Press, 2003), 137–50 and, in the same volume, Linda Munk, "Northrop Frye: Typology and Gnosticism," 151–63; *Northrop Frye's Notebooks and Lectures on the Bible and Other Religious Texts*, ed. Robert D. Denham (Toronto: University of Toronto Press, 2003); Joe Velaidum, "Typology and Theology in Northrop Frye's Biblical Hermeneutic," *Literature and Theology* 17 (2003), 156–69; Margaret Christian, "Academic and Personal Connections to the Text: The Bible as Literature," *Profession* (2004), 83–94; Phillip Donnelly, "*Paradise Regained* as Rule of Charity: Religious Tolerance and the End of Typology," *Milton Studies* 43 (2004), 171–97; Peter S. Hawkins, "Lost and Found: The Bible and Its Literary Afterlife," *Religion and Literature* 36 (2004), 1–14.

52. Frank Kermode, *The Sense of an Ending: Studies in the Theory of Fiction* (Oxford: Oxford University Press, 1967).

53. Homer, *The Iliad*, trans. E.V. Rieu (Harmondsworth: Penguin, 1950, rpt. 1977), 450–51. On the most recent English-speaking film adaptation of Homer's story of Troy, see Peter Green, "Heroic Style: Hollywood Pitted against Homer," *Arion* 12 (2004), 171–87. For the relation of Homer to Nietzsche, see John M. Lawless, "Homer, Nietzsche and the Heroic," *Providence* 6 (2001), 71–92 and James Porter, "Nietzsche, Homer, and the Classical Tradition," *Nietzsche and Antiquity: His Reaction and Response to the Classical Tradition*, ed. Paul Bishop (Rochester, NY: Camden House, 2004), 7–26. Barry B. Powell distinguishes between the philologist's, historian's and reader's Homer; his discussion of texts, editing, and textuality, the very appearance of print and Greek and how that differed more and more after A.D. 1000, from the presentation in classical and particularly Homeric Greek, is suggestive. See Powell's *Homer* (Oxford: Blackwell, 2004), 3–34, esp. 3–6. For a clear and succinct background to the *Iliad*, see Michael Silk, *Homer: The Iliad*, second ed. (Cambridge: Cambridge University Press, 2004), 1–27. On Homer more generally, see L.R. Lind, "The Uses of Homer," *Classical and Modern Literature* 10 (1989), 7–20; Suzanne Jill Levine, "Some Versions of Homer," *PMLA* 107 (1992), 1134–38; Maria Octavia Radulescu, "Remarks on the English Translations of Homer's Iliad," *Cahiers de*

Linguistique Théorique et Appliquée 29 (1992), 63–74; Mark W. Edwards, "Homer and the Oral Tradition: The Type-Scene" *Oral Tradition* 7 (1992), 284–330; James Heffernan, *Museum of Words: The Poetics of Ekphrasis from Homer to Ashbery* (Chicago: University of Chicago Press, 1993); Joseph Russo, "Homer's Style: Nonformulaic Features of an Oral Aesthetic," *Tradition* 9 (1994), 371–89; Richard P. Martin, "Homer's *Iliad* and *Odyssey*," *Teaching Oral Traditions*, ed. John Miles (New York: Modern language Association of America, 1998), 339–50; Simeon Underwood, *English Translators of Homer: From George Chapman to Christopher Logue* (Plymouth: Northcote House with the British Council, 1998); John Foley, *Homer's Traditional Art* (University Park: Penn State University Press, 1999). For a thesis whose title plays on recognition, a knowing again and remaking of the epic tradition, see Cynthia Dianne Wallace, "Toward Re-Cognition of the Epic Imagination: Uncovering the Legacies of Homer and Virgil in James A. Michener's 'Texas,' " Ph.D. dissertation, Texas A & M University, 1997. On alterity, see Wendy Olmsted, "On the Margins of Otherness: Metamorphosis and Identity in Homer, Ovid, Sidney, and Milton," *New Literary History* 27 (1996), 167–84. On Achilles, see Katherine King, *Achilles: Paradigms of the War Hero from Homer to the Middle Ages* (Berkeley: University of California Press, 1987). On disguise, see Franco Ferrucci, *The Poetics of Disguise: The Autobiography of the Work in Homer, Dante, and Shakespeare* (Ithaca, NY: Cornell University Press, 1980). See also Ann C. Watts, *The Lyre and the Harp: A Comparative Reconsideration of Oral Tradition in Homer and Old English Epic Poetry* (New Haven: Yale University Press, 1969).

54. Erich Auerbach, *Mimesis: The Representation of Reality in Western Literature*, trans. Willard Trask (original 1946, 1953; New York: Doubleday, 1957), esp. ch. 1 or 3–23; Cave, *Recognitions*, 22–23. For a comparative point of view, see Constance V. Tagopoulos, "Joyce and Homer: Return, Disguise, and the Recognition in 'Ithaca,' " *Joyce in Context*, ed. Vincent J. Cheng and Timothy Martin (Cambridge: Cambridge University Press, 1992), 184–200; Mario A. Di Caesare, "Recognition and Epic Tradition: The Motif in Homer, Vergil, and Milton," *The Western Pennsylvania Symposium on World Literatures: Selected Proceedings 1974–1991: A Retrospective* (Greensburg, PA: Eadmer, 1992), 87–105.

55. Cave, *Recognitions*, 41, 44.

56. Homer, *The Odyssey*, trans. E.V. Rieu (Harmondsworth: Penguin, 1946, rpt. 1976), 250. A dissertation examines the role of Penelope—see Dene Grigar, "Penelopeia: The Making of the Penelope in Homer's Story and Beyond," Ph.D. dissertation, University of Texas, Dallas, 1996.

57. Homer, *Odyssey*, 253.

58. Homer, *Odyssey*, 328.

59. Homer, *Odyssey*, 340.

60. Homer, *Odyssey*, 341.

61. Homer, *Odyssey*, 343.

62. Homer, *Odyssey*, 343.

63. Natalie Zemon Davis, *The Return of Martin Guerre* (Cambridge, MA: Harvard University Press, 1983).

64. Homer, *Odyssey*, 356.

65. *Oedipus*, 1152; all quotations and citations from Sophocles, *Oedipus the King*, trans. David Grene, in *Greek Tragedies*, Vol. 1., ed. David Grene and Richmond Lattimore (Chicago: University of Chicago Press, 1960), 107–76. For a suggestive and related comparison, see Martha C. Nussbaum, "Invisibility and Recognition: Sophocles' *Philoctetes* and Ellison's *Invisible Man*," *Philosophy and Literature* 23 (1999), 257–83. For anagnorisis in Greek tragedy, see Moon Won Lee, "Anagnorisis" (cited in note 2 of this chapter).

66. *Oedipus*, 1181–82 (first quotation); *Oedipus*, 1183–85 (second).

67. *Oedipus*, 1190–93.

68. *Oedipus*, 1216–19.

69. *Oedipus*, 1273–74.

70. *Oedipus*, 1303–06.

71. *Oedipus*, 1441–43.

72. *Oedipus*, 1480–85.
73. *Oedipus*, 1529–30.
74. As Cave notes, in the fourth century, Donatus-Evanthius's *De comoedia* assimilates New Comedy into the Aristotelian tradition (*Recognitions*, 50–51).
75. See Levin, *Playboys*, 36.
76. Menander, *The Grouch*, trans. Lionel Casson, in *Greek Comedy*, ed. Robert W. Corrigan (New York: Dell, 1965, rpt. 1973), 303. On Menander, see George E. Wellwarth, "From Ritual to Drama: The Development of Dramatic Form in Euripides and Menander," *Educational Theatre Journal* 17 (1965), 181–95; William Anderson, "Menander and Molière," *Molière and the Commonwealth of Letters: Patrimony and Posterity*, ed. Roger Johnson, Jr. and Editha Neumann (Jackson: University Press of Mississippi, 1975), 413–16; E.J.H. Greene, *Menander to Marivaux: The History of a Comic Structure* (Edmonton: University of Alberta Press, 1977); John Whitehorne, "Menander's *Dyskolos* as Detective Story," *AUMLA* 79 (1993), 87–105. See also Northrop Frye, "Old and New Comedy," *Shakespeare Survey* 22 (1969), 1–5.
77. Menander, *The Grouch*, 304.
78. Menander, *The Grouch*, 304.
79. Cave's perceptive and detailed discussion of Aristotle, which I read while I was completing this section (originally as a talk to a conference on Philosophy and Literature at George Mason University in 1996 and as a longer essay at the same time), has allowed me to avoid repeating that work and therefore to direct most of my attention elsewhere.
80. Plato, *The Republic of Plato*, trans. Francis M. Cornford, 179.
81. Plato, *Republic*, Cornford trans., 180–81. On Plato and related topics, see Douglas N. Morgan, *Love, Plato, the Bible, and Freud* (Englewood Cliffs, NJ: Prentice-Hall, 1964); *What Is Art? Aesthetic Theory from Plato to Tolstoy*, ed. Alexander Sesonske (New York: Oxford University Press, 1965); Peyton E. Richter, *Perspectives in Aesthetics: Plato to Camus* (New York: Odyssey, 1967); *Plato and Postmodernism*, ed. Steven Shankman (Glenside, PA: Aldine, 1994); Adriana Cavarero, *In Spite of Plato: A Feminist Rewriting of Ancient Philosophy* (Cambridge: Polity, 1995); M.J. Devaney, *"Since at Least Plato . . ." and Other Postmodern Myths* (London: Macmillan, 1997); James L. Kastely, *Rethinking the Rhetorical Tradition: From Plato to Postmodernism* (New Haven, CT: Yale University Press, 1997); Alexander Nehamas, *The Art of Living: Socratic Reflections from Plato to Foucault* (Berkeley, CA: University of California Press, 1998); Alvin Kernan, *In Plato's Cave* (New Haven: Yale University Press, 1999); Simon Brittan, *Poetry, Symbol, and Allegory: Interpreting Metaphorical Language from Plato to the Present* (Charlottesville: University Press of Virginia, 2003).
82. Plato, *Republic*, Cornford trans., 189.
83. Plato, *Republic*, Cornford trans., xxvii.
84. Plato, *Republic*, Cornford trans., xxviii. A text that plays on the utopian themes that Plato raises is Thomas More, *Utopia*, ed. Edward Surtz (New Haven: Yale University Press, 1964), which was first printed in 1516.
85. Plato, *Republic*, Cornford trans., 546A.
86. Plato, *Republic*, Cornford trans., xxix.
87. Plato, *Republic*, Cornford trans., 321.
88. Plato, *Republic*, Cornford., trans., x.605-C-608.
89. Georg W.F. Hegel, "Philosophy of History," in *History of Philosophy. Selected Readings*, ed. George L. Abernathy and T.A. Langford (Belmont, CA: Dickenson, 1969), 536. Hegel appeals to the poetry of philosophy, to the key nature of the aesthetic: "I am now convinced that the highest act of Reason, the one through which it encompasses all Ideas, is an aesthetic act, and that *truth and goodness only become sisters in beauty*—the philosopher must possess as much aesthetic power as the poet." To which Hegel adds: "The philosophy of the spirit is an aesthetic philosophy. One cannot be creative [*geistreich*] in any way, even about history one cannot argue creatively—without aesthetic sense." In case there is any doubt about the centrality of poetry, Hegel, who is basing his argument on the aesthetic and not the ethical as Plato and Sidney do,

declares: "Poetry gains thereby a higher dignity, she becomes at the end once more, what she was in the beginning—the *teacher of mankind*; for there is no philosophy, no history left, the maker's art will survive all other sciences and arts." See *The Hegel Reader*, ed. Stephen Houlgate (Oxford: Blackwell, 1998), 29. Hegel attempts to redeem the poet, who came under attack in Plato's *Republic*, with a recognition of his centrality. Sensory and pure knowledge have an intricate relation. What is the relation between recognition and consciousness. Once again, this is complex. One aspect of consciousness is ego. In discussing sensory certainty, Hegel asserts: "Consciousness is ego, nothing more, a pure This" [das Bewubtseyn ist Ich, weiter nichts, ein reiner *dieser*]; Georg Wilhelm Friedrich Hegel, *Hegel's Phenomenology of Spirit: Selections*, trans. Howard P. Kainz (University Park: Penn State University Press, 1994), 27. Like Plato, Hegel distinguishes between individual objects perceived and the idea of something: Hegel makes an intricate distinction between sense and idea, concepts and conceptions. What makes matters more complicated is the two types of conceptions, empirical and nonempirical, not to mention a distinction between thought and conception. See M.J. Inwood, *Hegel* (London: Routledge, 1983, rpt. 1998), 9–12. What is being sensed, what is being thought—moments of recognition, then, are not matters of one-to-one direct correspondence of individual subject perceiving individual object. On Hegel and related subjects, see Anne Paolucci, *Hegel: On Tragedy* (New York: Harper & Row, 1962); Daniel J. Cook, *Language in the Philosophy of Hegel* (The Hague: Mouton, 1973); Raymond Plant, *Hegel* (Bloomington: Indiana University Press, 1973); Walter Kaufman, *Hegel: A Reinterpretation* (Notre Dame: University of Notre Dame Press, 1977); *German Aesthetic and Literary Criticism: Kant, Fichte, Schelling, Schopenhauer, Hegel*, ed. David Simpson (Cambridge: Cambridge University Press, 1986); Jeanne Schroeder, *The Vestal and the Fasces: Hegel, Lacan, Property, and the Feminine* (Berkeley: University of California Press, 1998); Mark Roche, *Tragedy and Comedy: A Systematic Study and Critique of Hegel* (Albany: State University of New York, 1998); Jonathan Strauss, *Subjects of Terror: Nerval, Hegel, and the Modern Self* (Stanford, CA: Stanford University Press, 1998); Elliot L. Jurist, *Beyond Hegel and Nietzsche: Philosophy, Culture, and Agency* (Cambridge, MA: MIT Press, 2000); Allen Speight, *Hegel, Literature and the Problem of Agency* (Cambridge: Cambridge University Press, 2001); Dieter Henrich, *Between Kant and Hegel: Lectures on German Idealism* (Cambridge, MA: Harvard University Press, 2003). For suggestive contexts, see three books by Charles Taylor—*Human Language and Agency* (Cambridge: Cambridge University Press, 1985), *Sources of the Self: The Making of Modern Identity* (Cambridge, MA: Harvard University Press, 1989), and *Multiculturalism: Examining the Politics of Recognition*, ed. Amy Gutmann (Princeton, NJ: Princeton University Press, 1994).

90. Hegel, "Philosophy of History," 536.
91. Hegel, "Philosophy of History," 536.
92. Hegel, "Philosophy of History," 536.
93. Hegel, "Philosophy of History," 541.
94. Hegel, "Philosophy of History," 542.
95. Hegel, "Philosophy of History," 548–49.
96. Hegel, "Philosophy of History," 537 for the first quotation and 531 for the second.
97. Karl Marx, *The German Ideology*, in Karl Marx, *Selected Writings* (Oxford: Oxford University Press, 1977, rpt. 1987), 172–73.
98. Marx, *German Ideology*, 173–74.
99. *Grundisse* (pub. 1941) in Marx, *Selected Writings*, 373. In his headnote, Jon Elser writes, "This text is probably Marx's most important methodological contribution" and notes that although it was written in August 1857, it was not published until 1903. See *Karl Marx: A Reader*, ed. Jon Elser (Cambridge: Cambridge University Press, 1986, rpt. 1999), 3. In discussing Marx, Brecht (who sees modernist art as requiring different views from nineteenth-century realism) and Georg Lukás (who draws on Lenin's view that apprehension of the external world is a reflection of it in consciousness), Terry Eagleton appeals to Trotsky in complicating the reflectionist theory; see Eagleton, *Marxism and Literary Criticism* (London: Methuen, 1976), 48–54.

For more contextual material, see Raymond Williams, *The Long Revolution* (London and New York: Columbia University Press, 1961) and Malcolm Bradbury, *The Social Context of English Literature* (Oxford: Blackwell, 1971). On Marx and connected topics, see Fredric Jameson, *Marxism and Form* (Princeton, NJ: Princeton University Press, 1971); M. Lifshitz, *The Philosophy of Art of Karl Marx*, trans. Ralph B. Winn (London: Pluto Press, 1973); Karl Marx and Frederick Engels, *On Literature and Art*, ed. L. Baxandall and S. Morawski (St. Louis: Telos [1973]); Raymond Williams, *Marxism and Literature* (Oxford: Oxford University Press, 1977); Edward J. Ahearn, *Marx and Modern Fiction* (New Haven: Yale University Press, 1989); Walter A. Davis, *Inwardness and Existence: Subjectivity in/and Hegel, Heidegger, Marx, and Freud* (Madison: University of Wisconsin Press, 1989); Michèle Barrett, *The Politics of Truth: From Marx to Foucault* (Stanford, CA: Stanford University Press, 1991); Daniel Brudney, *Marx's Attempt to Leave Philosophy* (Cambridge, MA: Harvard University Press, 1998); Stathis Kouvelakis, *Philosophy and Revolution: From Kant to Marx* (London: Verso, 2003). On this particular text by Marx, see Thomas M. Kemple, *Reading Marx Writing: Melodrama, the Market, and the "Grundisse"* (Stanford, CA: Stanford University Press, 1995).

100. Marx, *Grundisse*, 384.

101. *Economic and Philosophical Manuscripts* (1844, pub. 1932), in Marx, *Selected Writings*, 94. On Marx and production, see Allen W. Wood, *Karl Marx*, second ed. (London: Routledge, 2004), 31–43, 63–81; Wood discusses Marx and ideology on 118–25, 143–62, and perhaps most germane here is the discussion of self-actualization, 22–25. He also underscores the complexity and sometimes diffuseness of Marx's use of estrangement and alienation (*Entfremdung*) and externalization and alienation (*Entäusserung*) (3–5). Marx suggests that actualization and recognition have certain obstacles before them and that humans can even create ideas and institutions that cause alienation. Marx and Engels also see language and consciousness in terms of society and both arise from "the need, the necessity, of intercourse with other men"; to which they soon add, "Consciousness is, therefore, from the very beginning a social product, and remains so as long as men exist at all." See Karl Marx and Friedrich Engels, "Primary Historical Relations, or the Basic Aspects of Social Activity" (1845–46), *Marx and Society: Key Readings and Commentary*, ed. Robert J. Antonio (Oxford: Blackwell, 2003), 58.

102. Friedrich Nietzsche, "Letter to His Sister" (1865), *The Portable Nietzsche*, trans and ed. Walter Kaufmann (New York: Viking, 1954, rpt., 1968), 30. All citations and quotations from Nietzsche are from this volume, including those from "Homer's Contest" (1872) and "Notes" (1873), 29–41. Nietzsche also discusses morality in terms of ways of seeing the world, so that, in transfiguration, the three ways in which Raphall divided the world were no longer the way the world is seen: "This is no longer how we see the world—and Raphael too would no longer *be able* to see it as he did: he would behold a new transfiguration" (see page 10). Morality, then, is subject to changes in ways of seeing, a kind of mutability in the ethics of recognition. In a later chapter, I refer to Nietzsche's style, which Lou Salomé, a philosopher with whom Nietzsche fell in love, called attention to when she proclaimed about Nietzsche: "And certainly, it must mean something when the premier stylist of his period says that 'I have written for myself,' for he has succeeded like no one else in finding the creative expression for each of his thoughts and their finest shadings." On this passage on "mihi ipsi scripsi," see Lou Salomé, *Nietzsche*, ed. Siegfried Mandel (1988; Urbana: University of Illinois Press, 2001), 4—a translation of *Friedrich Nietzsche in seinen Werken* (1894). Nietzsche saw in the aphorism not simply compression but a difficult invitation to careful and deep interpretation (*Auselgung*). See Christoph Cox, *Nietzsche: Naturalism and Interpretation* (Berkeley: University of California Press, 1999), 15–16. On Nietzsche and related topics, see R.J. Hollingdale, *Nietzsche: The Man and His Philosophy* (London: Routledge & Kegan Paul, 1965); Karl Jaspers, *Nietzsche: An Introduction to the Understanding of His Philosophical Activity*, trans. Charles F. Wallraff and Frederick J. Schmitz (Tucson: University of Arizona Press, 1965); Joan Stambaugh, *Nietzsche's Thought of Eternal Return* (Baltimore: Johns Hopkins University Press, 1972); Jacques Sojcher, *La question et le sens: Esthetique de Nietzsche* (Paris: Aubier Montaigne,

1972); John T. Wilcox, *Truth and Value in Nietzsche: A Study of His Metaphysics and Epistemology* (Ann Arbor: University of Michigan Press, 1974); Sander L. Gilman, *Nietzschean Parody: An Introduction to Reading Nietzsche* (Bonn: Bouvier, 1976); Carol Jacobs, *The Dissumulating Harmony: The Image of Interpretation in Nietzsche, Rilke, Artaud and Benjamin* (Balitimore, MD: Johns Hopkins University Press, 1978); Joseph P. Stern, *Nietzsche* (Hassocks: Harvester, 1978) and his *A Study of Nietzsche* (Cambridge: Cambridge University Press, 1979); Paul de Man, *Allegories of Reading: Figural Language in Rousseau, Nietzsche, Rilke, and Proust* (New Haven: Yale University Press, 1979); Michael Hamburger, *A Proliferation of Prophets: Essays on German Writers from Nietzsche to Brecht* (New York: St. Martin's Press, 1984); Alexander Nehamas, *Nietzsche: Life as Literature* (Cambridge, MA: Harvard University Press, 1985); Henry Staten, *Nietzsche's Voice* (Ithaca, NY: Cornell University Press, 1990); Laurence Lampert, *Nietzsche and Modern Times: A Study of Bacon, Descartes, and Nietzsche* (New Haven, CT: Yale University Press, 1993); Bernd Magnus, *Nietzsche's Case: Philosophy as / and Literature* (New York: Routledge, 1993); Gianni Vattimo, *The Adventure of Difference: Philosophy after Nietzsche and Hiedegger* (Baltimore, MD: Johns Hopkins University, 1993); Wayne Klein, *Nietzsche and the Promise of Philosophy* (Albany: State University of New York Press, 1997); Karl Löwith, *Nietzsche's Philosophy of the Eternal Recurrence of the Same* (Berkeley: University of California Press, 1997); Caroline Picart, *Thomas Mann and Friedrich Nietzsche: Eroticism, Death, Music, and Laughter* (Amsterdam: Rodopi, 1999); Tracy B. Strong, *Friedrich Nietzsche and the Politics of Transfiguration* (Urbana, IL: University of Illinois Press, 2000); David Wittenberg, *Philosophy, Revision, Critique: Rereading Practices in Heidegger, Nietzsche, and Emerson* (Stanford, CA: Stanford University Press, 2001); Joachim Köhler, *Zarathustra's Secret: The Interior Life of Friedrich Nietzsche* (New Haven: Yale University Press, 2002); Charles Bambach, *Heidegger's Roots: Nietzsche, National Socialism, and the Greeks* (Ithaca, NY: Cornell University Press, 2003); Andrew Bowie, *Aesthetics and Subjectivity: From Kant to Nietzsche* (Manchester: Manchester University Press, 2003); Mazzino Montinari, *Reading Nietzsche* (Urbana, IL: University of Illinois Press, 2003); Gary Shapiro, *Archeologies of Vision: Foucault and Nietzsche on Seeing and Saying* (Chicago: University of Chicago Press, 2003); George S. Williamson, *The Longing Myth in Germany: Religion and Aesthetic Culture from Romanticism to Nietzsche* (Chicago: University of Chicago Press, 2004). On particular texts, see Peter Fuss, *Nietzsche: A Self-Portrait from the Letters* (Cambridge, MA: Harvard University Press, 1971); Stanley Rosen, *The Mask of Enlightenment: Nietzsche's Zarathustra* (Cambridge: Cambridge University Press, 1995). Walter Kaufman's work most influenced me when I first read Nietzsche in my teens; see, for instance, Walter Kaufman, *Nietzsche: Philosopher, Psychologist, Antichrist*, fourth ed. (Princeton: Princeton University Press, 1974).

103. Nietzsche, "Homer's Contest," 35–36.

104. A related concept is W. Jackson Bate's burden of the past and Harold Bloom's anxiety of influence. See Bate, *Burden of the Past and the English Poet* (Cambridge, MA: Belknap Press, 1970) and Bloom, *The Anxiety of Influence: A Theory of Poetry* (New York: Oxford University Press, 1973). See also Bloom's agony or struggle in *Agon: Towards a Theory of Revisionism* (Oxford: Oxford University Press, 1982).

105. Nietzsche, "Homer's Contest," 37–38.

106. Nietzsche, "Notes," 39.

107. Nietzsche, "Notes," 40.

108. Nietzsche, "Notes," 40–41.

109. Nietzsche, "Notes," 41.

110. In discussing philosophy and painting, Lyotard questions the notion of system, especially as it now relates to ideology (181–82). He, too, uses the language of illusion as a trope. The works of Nietzsche he cites are *Thoughts out of Season* and *On the Future of Our Educational Institutions*, which assert that the progress of history exhausts the vitality and energy of style and art. Lyotard also discusses universal history in terms of cultural differences. See Jean-François Lyotard, *The Lyotard Reader*, ed. Andrew Benjamin (Oxford: Blackwell, 1989), 314–23. On

Lyotard, see, for instance, Geoffrey Bennington, *Lyotard: Writing the Event* (New York: Columbia University Press, 1988); James Williams, *Lyotard: Towards a Postmodern Philosophy* (Cambridge: Polity Press, 1998) and his *Lyotard and the Political* (London: Routledge, 2000); Alberto Gualandi, *Lyotard* (Paris: Les belles lettres, 1999); Gary K. Browning, *Lyotard and the End of Grand Narratives* (Cardiff: University of Wales Press, 2000); Keith Crome, *Lyotard and Greek Thought: Sophistry* (New York: Palgrave Macmillan, 2004).

111. Michel de Certeau, *Heterologies: Discourse on the Other*, trans Brian Massumi (Minneapolis: University of Minnesota Press, 1986), 68, 70; Anthony Pagden, *The Fall of Natural Man: The American Indian and the Origins of Comparative Ethnology* (Cambridge: Cambridge University Press, 1982, rev. 1986), 175, 195.

112. See, for instance, J. de Acosta, *The Natvrall and Morall Historie of the East and West Indies*, trans. Edward Grimstone (London: Sims for Edward Blount and William Aspley, 1604) and Michel de Montaigne, *The Essays of Montaigne*, trans. E.J. Treichmann (London. Oxford University Press, 1953). For a Native context for Acosta and his fellow Spanish chroniclers, see Gary Urton, *Inca Myths: The Legendary Past* (Austin: University of Texas Press, 1999), esp. 29. A recent translation of this text by Acosta is José de Acosta, *Natural and Moral History of the Indies*, ed. Jane E. Mangan and trans. Frances M. López-Morillas (Durham, NC: Duke University Press 2002). On Montaigne and knowledge, see Eric Aaron Johnson, *Knowledge and Society: A Social Epistemology of Montaigne's "Essais"* (Charlottesville: Rookwood, 1994). Montaigne focused on examining his life, self, and experience. See the editor's Introduction to Montaigne in *Moral Philosophy from Montaigne to Kant*, ed. Jerome B. Schneewind (Cambridge: Cambridge University Press, 2003), 37. On friendship, freedom, and tyranny in Montaigne, see *Freedom over Servitude: Montaigne, La Boetie, and "On Voluntary Servitude,"* ed. David Lewis Schaefer (Westport, CT: Greenwood Press, 1998), esp. 1–3. For useful and brief notes on the text of, and annotations to, Montaigne's *Essays*, see Michel de Montaigne, *The Complete Essays*, trans. M.A. Screech (London: Penguin Books, 1991), xlix–li. For some other relevant texts on Montaigne, see Philip P. Hallie, *Montaigne and Philosophy as Self-Portraiture* (Middletown: Wesleyan University Center for Advanced Study, 1966); Zoe Samaras, *The Comic Element of Montaigne's Style* (Paris: Nizet, 1970); Marko Papic, *L'expression et la place du sujet dans les Essais de Montaigne* (Paris: Presses Universitaires de France, 1970); Hélène-Hedy Ehrlich, *Montaigne: La critique et le langage* (Paris: Klincksieck, 1972); Alfred Glauser, *Montaigne paradoxal* (Paris: Nizet, 1972); Frederick Rider, *The Dialectic of Selfhood in Montaigne* (Stanford: Stanford University Press, 1973); Glyn P. Norton, *Montaigne and the Introspective Mind* (The Hague: Mouton, 1975); Richard L. Regosin, *The Matter of My Book: Montaigne's Essais as the Book of the Self* (Berkeley: University of California Press, 1977); Cecile Insdorf, *Montaigne and Feminism* (Chapel Hill: Department of Romance Languages, University of North Carolina, 1977); John O'Neill, *Essaying Montaigne: A Study of the Renaissance Institution of Writing and Reading* (London: Routledge & Kegan Paul, 1982); Gérard Defaux, *Marot, Rabelais, Montaigne: L'Ecriture comme presence* (Paris: Champion; 1987); François Rigolot, *Les Métamorphoses de Montaigne* (Paris: Presses Universitaires de France, 1988); Craig B. Brush, *From the Perspective of the Self: Montaigne's Self-Portrait* (New York: Fordham University Press, 1994); Hassan Melehy, *Writing Cogito: Montaigne, Descartes, and the Institution of the Modern Subject* (Albany: State University of New York Press, 1997); David Quint, *Montaigne and the Quality of Mercy: Ethical and Political Themes in the "Essais"* (Princeton, NJ: Princeton University Press, 1998); Philippe Desan, *Montaigne dans tous ses états* (Fasano, Italy: Schena, 2002); Ann Hartle, *Michel de Montaigne: Accidental Philosopher* (Cambridge: Cambridge University Press, 2003).

113. Herodotus, II, 99 on hearsay and eyewitness and VII, 152 on belief. All citations and quotations are from Herodotus, *The Persian Wars*, trans. G. Rawlinson (New York: Modern Library, 1942). On Herodotus, see, for example, Charles Fornara, *Herodotus: An Interpretive Essay* (Oxford: Clarendon Press, 1971); John Hart, *Herodotus and Greek History* (London: Croom Helm, 1982); Thomas G. Rosenmeyer, "History or Poetry? The Example of Herodotus," *Clio* 11 (1982), 239–59; R.A. McNeal, "On Editing Herodotus," *Antiquité*

Classique 52 (1983), 110–29; François Hertog, "Herodotus and the Historiographical Operation," *Diacritics* 22 (1992), 83–93; Donald R. Kelley, *Faces of History: Historical Inquiry from Herodotus to Herder* (New Haven, CT: Yale University Press, 1998); Rosalind Thomas, *Herodotus in Context: Ethnography, Science and the Art of Persuasion* (Cambridge: Cambridge University Press, 2000); Ivan M. Cohen, "Herodotus and the Story of Gyges: Traditional Motifs in Historical Narrative," *Fabula* 45 (2004), 55–68.

114. Arnaldo Momigliano, *The Classical Foundations of Modern Historiography* (Berkeley: University of California Press, 1990), 36–39.

115. Herodotus, *Persian Wars*, IV, 18.

116. Herodotus, *Persian Wars*, IV, 106.

117. Herodotus, *Persian Wars*, IV, 64.

118. Herodotus, *Persian Wars*, IV, 64.

119. Herodotus, *Persian Wars*, IV, 110.

120. Herodotus, *Persian Wars*, IV, 111.

121. Herodotus, *Persian Wars*, IV, 111.

122. Herodotus, *Persian Wars*, IV, 113.

123. Herodotus, *Persian Wars*, IV, 113.

124. Herodotus, *Persian Wars*, IV, 114–16.

125. Christopher Columbus, *Four Voyages*, ed. Cecil Jane (1932–33; New York: Dover, 1965), 14, 16. See my series on the New World and on colonization (four books so far); the books discuss a number of figures, including Columbus, Cartier, Acosta, Montaigne, Léry, and others. For instance, see *Representing the New World: English and French Uses of the Example of Spain* (London and New York: Palgrave, 2001) and *Columbus, Shakespeare and the Interpretation of the New World* (New York and London: Palgrave Macmillan, 2003). On Columbus, see, for example, Margarita Zamora, *Reading Columbus* (Berkeley: University of California Press, 1993); Frank Lestringant, *Cannibals: The Discovery and Representation of the Cannibal from Columbus to Jules Verne* (Berkeley: University of California Press, 1997); *Oviedo on Columbus*, ed. Jesús Carillo (Turnhout, Belgium: Brepols, 2000).

126. Columbus, *Four Voyages*, 6–11.

127. Jacques Cartier, *The Voyages of Jacques Cartier* (Toronto: University of Toronto Press, 1993, rpt. 1995), 21. For some work on Cartier, see Robert Melançon, "Terre de cain, age d'or, prodigies du Saguenay: Representations du Nouveau Monde dans les voyages de Jacques Cartier," *Studies in Canadian Literature* 4 (1979), 22–34; Richard M. Berrong, "The Nature and Function of the 'Sauvage' in Jacques Cartier's *Récits de voyage*," *Romance Notes* 22 (1981), 213–17; Guy Sylvestre, "Jacques Cartier et les letters," *Etudes Canadiennes/Canadian Studies* [*ECCS*] 10 (1984), 221–23 and, in the same issue, Daniel-Henri Pageaux, "Jacques Cartier et la France des Lumières," 155–59; in this same issue there are a number of other relevant essays on Cartier; Jean-Philippe Beaulieu, "La Description de la nouveauté dans les récits de voyages de Cartier et de Rabelais," *Renaissance and Reformation* 9 (1985), 104–10; Réal Ouellet, "De l'itinéraire au paysage: L'espace nord-américaine dans les textes de Cartier et Laudonnière," *Le Paysage à la Renaissance*, ed. Yves Giraud (Fribourg: Editions Universitaires, 1988), 91–99 and, in the same volume, Charles Bene, "Jacques Cartier et le paysage Canadien: Réalité et imagination dans les relations de 1534, 1535 et 1540," 63–75; Bernard Hue, "L'Histoire, substitut de la biographie: Le Cas de Jacques Cartier," *La Création biographique/Biographical Creation*, ed. Marta Dvorak (Rennes: Presses Universitaires de Rennes, 1997), 275–80; Catherine Broué and Gaston Desjardins, "A contre-courant: Le Saint-Laurent des récits de voyages, entre Cartier et Charlevoix," *Canadian Folklore Canadien* 19 (1997), 63–75; Marta Dvorak, "Thomas King's Christopher Cartier and Jacques Columbus," *Arachnē* 5 (1998), 120–39.

128. Cartier, *The Voyages of Jacques Cartier*, 26–27.

129. Jean de Léry, *History of a Voyage to the Land of Brazil*, trans. Janet Whatley (Berkeley: University of California Press, 1990), 26. On Léry, see, for example, Geralde Nakam, "Une source des Tragiques: L'Histoire memorable de la ville de Sancerre de Jean de Léry,"

Bibliothèque d'Humanisme et Renaissance 33 (1971), 177–82; Jean-Claude Morisot, "L'Histoire d'un voyage fait en la terre du Brésil de Jean de Léry," *Cahiers de l'Association Internationale des Etudes Francaises* 27 (1975), 27–40; Michel Jeanneret, "Léry et Thevet: Comment parler d'un monde nouveau?" *Mélanges à la mémoire de Franco Simone, IV: Tradition et originalité dans la création littéraire* (Geneva: Slatkine; 1983), 227–45; Frank Lestringant, "L'Excursion brésilienne: Note sur les trois premières éditions de l'Histoire d'un voyage de Jean de Léry (1578–1585)," *Mélanges sur la littérature de la Renaissance à la mémoire de V.-L. Saulnier* (Geneva: Droz, 1984), 53–72; Janet Whatley, "Food and the Limits of Civility: The Testimony of Jean de Léry," *The Sixteenth Century Journal* 15 (1984), 387–400; Marie-Christine Gomez-Geraud, "Du verbal au visuel: Sonnets liminaires à l'Histoire d'un voyage fait en la terre du Brésil de Jean de Léry," *Renaissance and Reformation* 12 (1988), 215–22; Irma S. Majer, "La Fin des voyages: Ecriture et souvenirs chez Jean de Léry," *Revue des Sciences Humaines* 90 (1989), 71–83; Frank Lestringant, "The Philosopher's Breviary: Jean de Léry in the Enlightenment," *Representations* 33 (1991), 200–11; Sara Castro-Klaren, "What Does Cannibalism Speak? Jean de Léry and the Tupinamba Lesson," *Carnal Knowledge: Essays on the Flesh, Sex, and Sexuality in Hispanic Letters and Film*, ed. Pamela Bacarisse (Pittsburgh, PA: Tres Rios, 1993), 23–41; Marie-Magdeleine Chirol, "Réalité, évidence et rhétorique: *Histoire d'un voyage fait en la terre du Brésil de Jean de Lery*," *Revista Letras* 12 (1993), 101–14; ; Marie-Christine Gomez-Géraud, "Le Détail et le décor: Description et illustration du Brésil chez Jean de Léry," *Op. Cit.: Revue de Littératures Française et Comparée* 13 (1999), 43–47; in the same issue, Frank Lestringant, " La Chorégraphie des Indiens ou le ravissement de Jean de Léry," 49–58; Frédéric Tinguely, "Jean de Léry et les métamorphoses du tapir," *Littératures* 41 (1999), 33–45; Frank Lestringant, "Léry-Strauss: Jean de Léry's *History of a Voyage to the Land of Brazil* and Claude Lévi-Strauss's *Tristes Tropiques*," *Viator: Medieval and Renaissance Studies* 32 (2001), 417–30; Andrea Frisch, "In a Sacramental Mode: Jean de Léry's Calvinist Ethnography," *Representations* 17 (2002), 82–106; Frank Lestringant, "Ulysse, l'huître et le sauvage: Giovanni Battista Gelli et Jean de Léry," *Rivista di Letterature Moderne e Comparate* 55 (2002), 117–28.

130. Léry, *History*, 26.
131. Léry, *History*, 67.
132. Léry, *History*, 67.
133. Montaigne's "On Cannibals," 114.
134. Walter Raleigh [Ralegh], *A Report of the Trvth of the fight about the Isles of Açores, this last Sommer. Betwixt The Reuenge, one of her Maiesties Shippes, And an Armada of the King of Spaine* London: William Ponsonbie, 1591[;] *The Discouerie of the Large, Rich, and Bewtiful Empyre of Guiana, with a Relation of the great and Golden Citie of Manoa (which the Spanyards call El Dorado) And of the Prouinces of Emeria. Arromaia, Amapapaia , and other Coun-tries, with their riuers, as-ioyning* (London: Robert Robertson, 1596, rpt. Leeds: The Scholar Press, 1967), A3v. For a recent general book on Ralegh, beginning with his biographical material, is Marc Aronson, *Sir Walter Ralegh and the Quest for Eldorado* (New York: Clarion Books, 2000), esp. 13–15. Ralegh's quest was partly one for recognition, a kind of restoration of his family's lost status, as well as seeking a recognition as an imitative example, but also in the shadow of Spanish conquest. See my *Representing the New World* (New York and London: Palgrave, 2001), esp. 125–26, 166–77, 22–23, 230–31. For an account of "Ralegh's discoveries," even those he was not at, such as those in North America, see Mary C. Fuller, *Voyages in Print: English Travel to America, 1576–1624* (Cambridge: Cambridge University Press, 1995), esp. 55–57. Ralegh depended in his search for El Dorado on the authority and experience of the Spaniards (even learning Spanish for the purpose) in order to use maps and texts for his discovery. See High Raffles, *In Amazonia: A Natural History* (Princeton: Princeton University Press, 2002), esp. 75–77. On Ralegh, see also C.F. Tucker Brooke, "Sir Walter Ralegh as Poet and Philosopher," *ELH* 5 (1938), 93–112; Pierre Lefranc, *Sir Walter Ralegh écrivain, l'oeuvre et les idées* (Paris: A. Colin; 1968); Stephen J. Greenblatt, *Sir Walter Ralegh: The Renaissance Man and His Roles* (New Haven: Yale University Press, 1973); Mary C. Fuller, "Ralegh's Fugitive

Gold: Reference and Deferral in the Discoverie of Guiana," *Representations* 33 (1991), 42–64; David Read, "Ralegh's Discoverie of Guiana and the Elizabethan Model of Empire," *The Work of Dissimilitude: Essays from the Sixth Citadel Conference on Medieval and Renaissance Literature*, ed. David G. Allen and Robert A. White (Newark: University of Delaware Press, 1992), 42–64; Karen Cunningham, " 'A Spanish Heart in an English Body': The Ralegh Treason Trial and the Poetics of Proof," *Journal of Medieval and Renaissance Studies* 22 (1992), 327–51; Maureen Michelle Heron, "(In)vested Interests: The Economy of Authorship in Columbus' 'Diario' and Ralegh's 'Discoverie,' " Ph.D. dissertation, Yale University, 1995; William M. Hamlin, "Imagined Apotheoses: Drake, Harriot, and Ralegh in the Americas," *Journal of the History of Ideas* 57 (1996), 405–28; Anna R. Beer, *Sir Walter Ralegh and His Readers in the Seventeenth Century: Speaking to the People* (Basingstoke, England; New York, NY: Macmillan; St. Martin's; 1997); William N. West, "Gold on Credit: Martin Frobisher's and Walter Ralegh's Economies of Evidence," *Criticism: A Quarterly for Literature and the Arts* 39 (1997), 315–36; Neil L. Whitehead, "Monstrosity and Marvel: Symbolic Convergence and Mimetic Elaboration in Trans-Cultural Representation: An Anthropological Reading of Ralegh's *Discoverie . . .*, *Studies in Travel Writing* 1 (1997), 72–95; Robert Lawson-Peebles, "The Many Faces of Sir Walter Ralegh," *History Today* 48 (1998), 17–24; Miri Tashma-Baum, "A Shroud for the Mind: Ralegh's Poetic Rewriting of the Self," *Early Modern Literary Studies* 10 (2004).

135. Raleigh [Ralegh], *Discouerie*, A4.
136. Raleigh [Ralegh], *Discouerie*, A4.
137. Raleigh [Ralegh], *Discouerie*, A5v.
138. Raleigh [Ralegh], *Discouerie*, 101, see 96.
139. Raleigh [Ralegh], *Discouerie*, 101.
140. Acosta, cited in Pagden *The Fall*, 162.
141. Pagden, *The Fall*, 162.
142. Anthony Grafton, with April Shelford and Nancy Siraisi, "Introduction," *New Worlds, Ancient Texts: The Power of Tradition and the Shock of Discovery* (Cambridge: Harvard University Press, 1992), 1, 5.
143. Sigmund Freud, "On Beginning the Treatment" (1913), *The Freud Reader*, ed. Peter Gay (New York: W.W. Norton, 1989), 375.
144. Freud, "On Beginning the Treatment," 375.
145. Freud, "On Beginning the Treatment," 375.
146. Freud, "On Beginning the Treatment," 376.
147. Freud, "On Beginning the Treatment," 376.
148. Freud, "On Beginning the Treatment," 376.
149. Freud, "On Beginning the Treatment," 377.
150. Freud, "Observations on Transference-Love" (1915), Gay ed., 379. For a discussion of Oedipus, which involves a topic I have discussed here in relation to recognition in Greek tragedy, see Peter L. Rudnytsky, *Freud and Oedipus* (New York: Columbia University Press, 1987) and Robert Bocock, *Sigmund Freud*, rev. ed. (London: Routledge, 2002), 49–56 (the original edition was out in 1983). Another topic related to recognition is myth. For the role of myth in Freud, see Robert A. Segal, "Psychoanalyzing Myth: From Freud to Winnicott," *Teaching Freud*, ed. Diane Jonte-Pace (New York: Oxford University Press, 2003), 137–64. This volume also examines Freud as an interpreter of religious texts. In "Teaching Freud in the Language of Our Students: The Case of a Religiously Affiliated Undergraduate Institution," Diane Jonte-Pace discusses the prejudices students bring to Freud and how they dismiss him as archaic, a reductionist sexist who was unscientific and how she tries to bring them to know different Freuds, what I would term a recognition in the students (in *Teaching Freud*, 19; see 17–33). A study that connects Freud with religion and philosophy is Douglas N. Morgan, *Love: Plato, the Bible and Freud* (Englewood Cliffs, NJ: Prentice-Hall, 1964). On Freud and literature and literary criticism and theory, see Claudia C. Morrison, *Freud and the*

Critic: The Early Use of Depth Psychology in Literary Criticism (Chapel Hill: University of North Carolina Press, 1968); Max Milner, Freud et l'interprétation de la littérature (Paris: CDU & SEDES, 1980); Malcolm Bowie, Freud, Proust and Lacan: Theory as Fiction (Cambridge: Cambridge University Press, 1988); Michel Arrivé, Linguistics and Psychoanalysis: Freud, Saussure, Hjelmslev, Lacan and Others Arrivé (Amsterdam: Benjamins, 1992); Jean Bellemin-Noël, La Psychanalyse du texte littéraire: Introduction aux lectures critiques inspirées de Freud (Paris: Nathan, 1996); Louis Althusser, Writing on Psychoanalysis: Freud and Lacan (New York, NY: Columbia University Press, 1996); Paul Verhaeghe, Does the Woman Exist? From Freud's Hysteric to Lacan's Feminine (New York, NY: Other, 1999); Edward W. Said, Freud and the Non-European (London: Verso, 2003). If the connections between Freud and Lacan are close, so too are those links between Freud and philosophers (some of whom, such as Hegel, Marx, and Nietzsche, are discussed in this chapter); see J. Preston Cole, The Problematic Self in Kierkegaard and Freud (New Haven: Yale University Press, 1971); Henry Sussman, The Hegelian Aftermath: Readings in Hegel, Kierkegaard, Freud, Proust, and James (Baltimore: Johns Hopkins University Press, 1982; William Beatty Warner, Chances and the Text of Experience: Freud, Nietzsche, and Shakespeare's Hamlet (Ithaca: Cornell University Press, 1986); Rainer Nägele, Reading after Freud: Essays on Goethe, Hölderlin, Habermas, Nietzsche, Brecht, Celan, and Freud (New York: Columbia University Press, 1987); Walter A. Davis, Inwardness and Existence: Subjectivity in/and Hegel, Heidegger, Marx, and Freud (Madison: University of Wisconsin Press, 1989); Angelika Rauch, The Hieroglyph of Tradition: Freud, Benjamin, Gadamer, Novalis, Kant (Madison, NJ: Associated University Press and Fairleigh Dickinson University Press, 2000). On comedy and Freud, see Richard Keller Simon, The Labyrinth of the Comic: Theory and Practice from Fielding to Freud (Tallahassee: Florida State University Press, 1985) and on Freud and aesthetics, see Sarah Kofman, The Childhood of Art: An Interpretation of Freud's Aesthetics (New York, NY: Columbia University Press, 1988). More generally, see Paul A. Robinson, Freud and His Critics (Berkeley: University of California Press, 1993); Pamela Thurschwell, Sigmund Freud (London: Routledge; 2000); Samuel Weber, The Legend of Freud (Stanford, CA: Stanford University Press, 2000); Lydia Flem, Freud the Man: An Intellectual Biography (New York, NY: Other, 2003); Susan E. Linville, History Films, Women, and Freud's Uncanny (Austin: University of Texas Press, 2004).

151. Freud, "Observations on Transference-Love," 380–81.
152. Freud, "Observations on Transference-Love," 381.
153. Freud, "Observations on Transference-Love," 382.
154. Freud, "Observations on Transference-Love," 383.
155. Freud, "Observations on Transference-Love," 383.
156. Freud, "Observations on Transference-Love," 383–84.
157. Freud, "Observations on Transference-Love," 384.
158. Freud, "Observations on Transference-Love," 384.
159. Freud, "Observations on Transference-Love," 385.
160. Freud, "Observations on Transference-Love," 386.
161. Freud, "Observations on Transference-Love," 387.
162. Jacqueline Rose, "Introduction," in Feminine Sexuality: Jacques Lacan and the École Freudienne, ed. Juliet Mitchell and Jacqueline Rose (New York: W.W. Norton, 1985), 50–51.
163. Jacques Lacan, "God and the Jouissance of the Woman," and "A Love Letter, " in Mitchell and Rose, Feminine Sexuality, 137–48 and 149–61. On Lacan, see Catherine Clément, The Lives and Legends of Jacques Lacan (New York: Columbia University Press, 1983); Lacan and Narration: The Psychoanalytic Difference in Narrative Theory, ed. Robert Con Davis (Baltimore: Johns Hopkins University Press, 1983); Jane Gallup, Reading Lacan (Ithaca: Cornell University Press, 1985), 45; Gary Handwerk, Irony and Ethics in Narrative: From Schlegel to Lacan (New Haven: Yale University Press, 1985); Juliet Flower MacCannell, Figuring Lacan: Criticism and the Cultural Unconscious (Lincoln: University of Nebraska Press, 1986); Ellie Ragland-Sullivan, Jacques Lacan and the Philosophy of Psychoanalysis (Urbana: University of Illinois Press, 1986);

Shoshana Felman, *Jacques Lacan and the Adventure of Insight: Psychoanalysis* (Cambridge, MA: Harvard University Press, 1987); Eve Tavor Bannet, *Structuralism and the Logic of Dissent: Barthes, Derrida, Foucault, Lacan* (Urbana: University of Illinois Press, 1989); Jonathan Scott Lee, *Jacques Lacan* (Amherst: University of Massachusetts Press, 1990); Mikkel Borch-Jacobsen, *Lacan: The Absolute Master* (Stanford: Stanford University Press, 1991); Malcolm Bowie, *Lacan* (Cambridge, MA: Harvard University Press, 1991); Sheldon Brivic, *The Veil of Signs: Joyce, Lacan, and Perception* (Urbana: University of Illinois Press, 1991); James M.. Mellard, *Using Lacan, Reading Fiction* (Urbana: University of Illinois Press, 1991); Michel Arrivé, *Linguistics and Psychoanalysis: Freud, Saussure, Hjelmslev, Lacan and Others* (Amsterdam: Benjamins, 1992); Carolyn J. Dean, *The Self and Its Pleasures: Bataille, Lacan, and the History of the Decentered Subject* (Ithaca: Cornell University Press, 1992); Jean-Luc Nancy, *The Title of the Letter: A Reading of Lacan* (Albany: State University of New York Press, 1992); Madan Sarup, *Jacques Lacan* (Toronto: University of Toronto Press, 1992); Slavoj Žižek, *Enjoy Your Symptom: Jacques Lacan In Hollywood and Out* (New York: Routledge, 1992); Marlene Müller, *Woolf mit Lacan: Der Signifikant in den Wellen* (Bielefeld: Aisthesis, 1993); Mark Bracher, *Lacan, Discourse, and Social Change: A Psychoanalytic Cultural Criticism* (Ithaca, NY: Cornell University Press, 1993); David Metzger, *The Lost Cause of Rhetoric: The Relation of Rhetoric and Geometry in Aristotle and Lacan* (Carbondale: Southern Illinois University Press, 1995); Elisabeth Roudinesco, *Jacques Lacan: Esbozo de una vida, historia de un sistema de pensamiento* (Barcelona: Anagrama, 1995); Henry Staten, *Eros in Mourning: Homer to Lacan* (Baltimore, MD: Johns Hopkins University Press, 1995); Henry W. Sullivan, *The Beatles with Lacan: Rock & Roll as Requiem for the Modern Age* (New York: Peter Lang, 1995); Ben Stoltzfus, *Lacan and Literature: Purloined Pretexts* (Albany: State University of New York Press, 1996); *Writings on Psychoanalysis: Freud and Lacan*, ed. Olivier Corpet (New York: Columbia University Press, 1996); Joël Dor, *Introduction to the Reading of Lacan: The Unconscious Structured Like a Language* (New York: Other, 1997); Elisabeth Roudinesco, *Jacques Lacan: Outline of a Life, History of a System of Thought* (New York: Columbia University Press, 1997); Henning Schmidgen, *Das Unbewußte der Maschinen: Konzeptionen des Psychischen bei Guattari, Deleuze und Lacan* (Munich, Germany: Fink, 1997); Hanjo Berressem, *Lines of Desire: Reading Gombrowicz's Fiction with Lacan* (Evanston, IL: Northwestern University Press, 1998); Shuli Barzilai, *Lacan and the Matter of Origins* (Stanford, CA: Stanford University Press, 1999); Christine van Boheemen-Saaf, *Joyce, Derrida, Lacan, and the Trauma of History: Reading, Narrative and Postcolonialism* (Cambridge: Cambridge University Press, 1999); Alain Vanier, *Lacan* (New York: Other, 2000); Tamise Van Pelt, *The Other Side of Desire: Lacan's Theory of the Registers* (Albany: State University of New York Press, 2000); Slavoj Žižek, *Enjoy Your Symptom! Jacques Lacan in Hollywood and Out* (New York: Routledge, 2001); Philippe Van Haute, *Against Adaptation: Lacan's "Subversion" of the Subject* (New York: Other, 2001); Jean-Michel Rabaté, *Jacques Lacan: Psychoanalysis and the Subject of Literature* (New York: Palgrave, 2001); Roberto Harari, *Lacan's Seminar on "Anxiety": An Introduction* (New York: Other, 2001) and his *How James Joyce Made His Name: A Reading of the Final Lacan* (New York, NY: Other, 2002); Marshall Needleman Armintor, *Lacan and the Ghosts of Modernity: Masculinity, Tradition, and the Anxiety of Influence* (New York, NY: Peter Lang, 2004); Karen Coats, "Looking Glasses and Neverlands: Lacan, Desire, and Subjectivity in Children's Literature" (Iowa City: University of Iowa Press, 2004); Alexandre Leupin, *Lacan Today: Psychoanalysis, Science, Religion* (New York: Other, 2004); Todd McGowan, *The End of Dissatisfaction? Jacques Lacan and the Emerging Society of Enjoyment* (Albany, NY: State University of New York Press, 2004).

164. Lacan, "A Love Letter," 157.
165. Rose, "Introduction—II," 50–51.
166. See Rose, "Introduction—II," 52.
167. Lacan, "A Love Letter," 158–60.
168. Julia Kristeva, "The Novel as Polylogue," *Desire in Language: A Semiotic Approach to Literature and Art*, ed. L.S. Roudiez, trans. T. Gora, A. Jardine, and L.S. Roudiez (Oxford: Blackwell, 1981), viii.

169. Kristeva, *The Novel*, 192. In her discussion of the system and the speaking subject, Kristeva discusses the nature of the discovery of semiotics and the parodoxes the semiotician finds herself in. For Kristeva, "what semiotics had discovered is the fact that there is a general social law, that this law is the symbolic dimension which is given in language and that every social practice offers a specific expression of that law." See Julia Kristeva, *The Kristeva Reader* (New York: Columbia University Press, 1986), 25. Noëlle McAfee argues that Kristeva drew on Hegel and Nietzsche, the former having argued against the self-conscious and autonomous individual and the latter having advanced this view by assuming that such a rational and unified being was an illusion. See McAfee, *Julia Kristeva* (London: Routledge, 2004), 2. As we have seen, recognition in Hegel, Nietzsche, and Kristeva has more twists and turns than this genealogy and reason and unity are more refracted than the strand. For some other work on Kristeva, see Janice Doane, *From Klein to Kristeva: Psychoanalytic Feminism and the Search for the "Good Enough" Mother* (Ann Arbor: University of Michigan Press, 1992); Kelly Oliver, *Reading Kristeva: Unraveling the Double-Bind* (Bloomington: Indiana University Press; 1993); Anna Smith, *Julia Kristeva: Readings of Exile and Estrangement* (New York, NY: St. Martin's, 1996); Martha J. Reineke, *Sacrificed Lives: Kristeva on Women and Violence* (Bloomington, IN: Indiana University Press, 1997); Sara Beardsworth, *Julia Kristeva: Psychoanalysis and Modernity* (Albany: State University of New York, 2004).
170. Kristeva, "The Novel," 192.
171. Kristeva, "The Novel," 193.
172. Kristeva, "The Novel," 194–200.
173. Kristeva, "The Novel," 201.
174. Kristeva, "The Novel," 203–04.
175. Kristeva, "The Novel," 204.
176. Kristeva, "The Novel," 206.
177. Kristeva, "The Novel," 207.

2   History and Empire

1. There are a large number of important contexts for the exploration and representation of the New World and of empire generally and concerning Canada specifically. For a suggestive discussion of Marguerite de Navarre, whose brother François authorized Jacques Cartier to colonize Canada, see Margaret Ferguson, *Dido's Daughters: Literacy, Gender, and Empire in Early Modern England and France* (Chicago: University of Chicago Press, 2003), 233–47. On Canada and empire, see Pierre Walter, "Literacy, Imagined nations, and Imperialism: Frontier College and the Construction of British Canada, 1899–1933," *Adult Education Quarterly* 54 (2003), 42–58; See also Thomas Richards, *The Imperial Archive: Knowledge and the Fantasy of Empire* (London: Verso, 1993); Jenny Sharpe, *Allegories of Empire: The Figure of the Woman in the Colonial Text* (Minneapolis: University of Minnesota Press, 1993); Deidre David, *Rule Britannia: Women, Empire, and Victorian Writing* (Ithaca, NY: Cornell University Press, 1995); Jonathan Rutherford, *Forever England: Reflections on Masculinity and Empire* (London: Lawrence & Wishart, 1997); Katie Trumpener, *Bardic Nationalism: The Romantic Novel and the British Empire* (New Haven: Yale University Press, 1997); Daniel Bivona, *British Imperial Literature, 1870–1940: Writing and the Administration of Empire* (Cambridge: Cambridge University Press, 1998); Saree Makdisi, *Romantic Imperialism: Universal Empire and the Culture of Modernity* (Cambridge: Cambridge University Press, 1998); John Willinsky, *Learning to Divide the World: Education at Empire's End* (Minneapolis: University of Minnesota Press, 1998); Jonathan Hart, *Representing the New World: The English and French Uses of the Example of Spain* (New York: Palgrave, 2001), esp. 37–45, 228–29. For an earlier version of this chapter, see my " 'English' and French Imperial Designs in Canada and in a Larger Context," *Imperialisms: Historical and*

Literary Investigations, 1500–1900, ed. Balachandra Rajan and Elizabeth Sauer (New York: Palgrave Macmillan, 2004), 187–202.

2. Early explorers mark the map, bridges, buildings, monuments, texts (literary, historical, and otherwise). For instance, in *Riot,* Gwendolyn Brooks, the African American poet, has the reader see the riot through the point of view of John Cabot, a prosperous white liberal who does not escape criticism. Even if this Cabot echoes the Cabot Lodges of Boston, they recall the name of the Italian-born explorer who set out for Cathay (China) and who "discovered"—from a European vantage—the mainland of eastern North America (at least this time round as the Vikings had been there centuries before). Gwendolyn Brooks, *Riot* (Detroit: Broadside Press, 1969). See James D. Sullivan, "Killing John Cabot and Publishing Black: Gwendolyn Brook's 'Riot,' " *African American Review* 36 (2002), 557–69. On the explorer, Cabot/Cabato, see Melvin H. Jackson, "The Labrador Landfall of John Cabot: The 1497 Voyage Reconsidered," *Canadian Historical Review* 44 (1963), 122–41; John T. Juricek, "John Cabot's First Voyage, 1497," *Smithsonian Journal of History* 2 (1967), 1–22; Samuel Eliot Morison, "Cabot: The Mysterious Sailor Who Gave England Rights to North America," *Smithsonian* 2 (1971), 12–21; Jake T.W. Hubbard, "John Cabot's Landfall: Cape Degrat or Cape Bonavista? Some Observations," *American Neptune* 33 (1973), 174–77; Allan Keller, "Silent Explorer: John Cabot in North America," *American History Illustrated* 8 (1974), 4–9, 47–48; David B, Quinn, "John Cabot and the 1497 Voyage to Newfoundland," *Newfoundland Studies* 15 (1999), 104–10. As this work suggests (as well as that in the final note to this chapter), Cabot/Caboto can appeal to the English as the beginning of westward expansion and modern empire, to the Americans as the foundation of English and American claims to North America, to Italians as part of the great Italian explorations on behalf of other European states, and to Canadians as the foundation of their country, especially the English-speaking part. Verrazzano, or Verazanus or Verazzanus as he referred to himself according to the Latin, was a Florentine who later had his name attached to a bridge in New York City. As Neil Ritchie notes, Verrazzano argued that the New World was a land mass neither connected to Europe or Asia, see Ritchie, "Verrazzano in America, 1524–8," *History Today* 22 (12) (December 1972), 847, see 843–49. See Norman J.W. Thrower, "New Light on the 1524 Voyage of Verrazzano," *Terrae Incognitiae* 11 (1979), 59–65; Camillo Menchini, "Il Canada di Jacques Cartier e di Giovanni da Verrazzano," *Il Veltro* 29 (1985), 115–25; Luca Codignola, "Another Look at Verranzzano's Voyage, 1524," *Acadiensis* 29 (1999), 29–43.

3. See Raymonde Litalien, *Les Explorateurs de l'Amérique du Nord 1492–1795* (Sillery: Québec: Septentrion, 1993), 52.

4. Original ms. (Latin) of William of Worcester's *Itinerarium* is at Corpus Christi College, Cambridge; printed in James Naismith, *Itineraria Symonis Simeonis et Willelmi de Worcestre* (Cambridge, 1778), 267, in James A. Williamson, *The Voyages of the Cabots and the Discovery of North America under Henry VII and Henry VIII* (London: Argonaut Press, 1929), 18–19.

5. The Second Letters Patent Granted to John Cabot, February 3, 1498, in Williamson, *The Voyages,* 22–24.

6. See, for instance, *The Italians and the Creation of America,* ed. Samuel J. Hough (Providence: John Carter Brown Library, 1980).

7. For a detailed discussion of the Cabots and the Portuguese, see H.P. Biggar, *Voyages of the Cabots and of the Corte-Reals and Greenland, 1497–1503* (Paris: [Macon, Protat], 1903) and also Williamson, *Voyages,* 119 ff., esp. 200–03. For treatments of the Cabots, see Henry Harrisse, *Jean et Sébastien Cabot* (Paris: Ernest Leroux, 1882) and John T. Juricek, "John Cabot's First Voyage, 1497," *Smithsonian Journal of History* 2 (1967), 1–22.

8. Williamson, *Voyages,* 204. For a study of the Corte Reals, including documents, see Henry Harrisse, *Les Corte-Real et leurs voyages au Nouveau-monde* (Paris: E. Leroux,1883). See also Eduardo Brazão, "Les Cortes-Reals et le Nouveau-Monde," *Revue d'Histoire de l'Amérique Françaises* 19 (2) (1965), 163–202; 19 (3) (1965), 335–49; Francisco Fernandes Lopes, "The Brothers Corte-Real," *Studia* 16 (1965), 153–65; Lucien Campeau, "Découvertes Portugueses

en Amérique du Nord," *Revue d'Histoire de l'Amérique Françaises* 20 (1966), 171–227; Richard Goertz, "João Alvares Fagundes, Capitão de Terra Nova (1521)," *Canadian Ethnic Studies* 23 (1991), 117–28; Mark Reynolds, "Land of the King of Portugal," *Beaver* 82 (2002–03), 13–15.

9. See Selma Barkham, "The Basques: Filling a Gap in Our History between Jacques Cartier and Champlain," *Canadian Geographical Journal* 96 (1978), 8–19.

10. See Jean-Paul Duviols, *Voyageurs français en Amérique (colonies espagnoles et portugaises)* (Paris: Bordas, 1978), 3–4.

11. Julien cites many French historians who agree with the claim that he makes: "The *Authentic Relation* of Gonneville represents the oldest testimony of the contact of the French with a territory and the American indigenes"; Duviols, *Voyageurs*, 5; my translation. For Michel de Certeau's interest in this topic from Gonneville onward, a project he never completed, see his "Travel Narratives of the French to Brazil: Sixteenth to Eighteenth Centuries," *New World Encounters*, ed. Stephen Greenblatt (Berkeley: University of California Press, 1993), 323–28.

12. For some recent work on Cartier, see Catherine Broué and Gaston Desjardins, "A Contre-Courant: Le Saint Laurent des Récits de Voyages, Entre Cartier et Charlevoix," *Canadian Folklore Canadien* 19 (1997), 63–75; Alan Gordon, "Heroes, History, and the Two Nationalisms: Jacques Cartier," *Journal of the Canadian Historical Association* 10 (1999), 81–102; Christophe Boucher, " 'The Land God Gave to Cain': Jacques Cartier Encounters the Mythological Wild Man in Labrador," *Terrae Incognitae* 35 (2003), 28–42

13. Charles-André Julien, *Les Voyages de découvertes et les premiers établissements* (Paris: Presses Universitaires de France, 1948), 115–17, 135–38; David B. Quinn and Alison M. Quinn, "Commentary," in Richard Hakluyt, *Discourse of Western Planting* , ed. D.B. and A.M. Quinn (London: Hakluyt Society, 1993), 187. In *Les Français*, Julien outlines Le Veneur's principal part in the Cartier expedition and the family connections and friendships behind this; see Julien, "Introduction," *Les Français en Amérique pendant la première moitié du XVIe siècle: textes des voyages de Gonneville, Verrazano, J. Cartier et Roberval*, ed. Ch.-A. Julien, R. Herval, and Th. Beauchesne and intr. Ch.-A. Julien (Paris: Presses Universitaires de France, 1946), I, 11. Also see Baron de La Chapelle, "Jean Le Veneur et le Canada," *Nova Francia* 6 (1931), 341–43.

14. Julien, *Les Français*, I, 11.

15. See M. Trudel, "Section One: Introduction to the New World," in *Canada: Unity in Diversity*, ed. Paul G. Cornell et al. (Toronto: Holt, Rinehart and Winston, 1967), 9.

16. Julien, *Les Français* (1946), I, 14.

17. See Keller et al., *Creation of Rights of Sovereignty*, 23–25, cited in Olive Patricia Dickason, "Concepts of Sovereignty at the Time of First Contacts," in *The Law of Nations and the New World*, ed. L.C. Green and Olive Dickason (Edmonton: University of Alberta Press, 1989, rpt. 1993), 221, 287. I have written about *terra nullius* in a number of my books and articles: for recent work on this legal idea or fiction, see the book review of Boyce Richardson's *People of Terra Nullius: Betrayal and Rebirth in Aboriginal Canada* (Seattle: University of Washington Press, 1993) in *North Dakota History* 62 (1995), 38–39 (as well as the book under review); Jonathan Bordo, "The Terra Nullius of Wilderness: Colonist Landscape (Canada & Australia) and the So-called Claim to American Exception," *International Journal of Canadian Studies* 15 (1997), 13–36; Monica Mulrennan and Colin Scott, "*Mare Nullius*: Indigenous Rights in Saltwater Environments," *Development and Change* 31 (2000), 681–707.

18. Tim Rowse, *After Mabo: Interpreting Native Indigenous Traditions* (Melbourne: University of Melbourne Press, 1993), 8, 21.

19. See "Roberval's Commission," January 15, 1540/41, in *A Collection of Documents Relating to Jacques Cartier and the Sieur de Roberval* (Ottawa: Public Archives of Canada, 1930), 180; my translation.

20. Nicolas Le Challeux, *Discours de l'histoire de la Floride* (Dieppe, 1566); Jean de Léry, *Histoire d'un voyage faict en la terre dv Brésil* (Geneva, 1580), corrected and augmented from the 1578 edition. For secondary material examining this French exploration, see Frank Lestringant, "Notes Complementaires sur les Sequelles Littéraires sur les Sequelles Littéraires de la Floride

Française," *Bibliothèque d'Humanisme et Renaissance* 45 (1983), 331–41 and his "Une Saint-Barthelemy Américaine" L'Agonie de la Floride Huguenote (sepembre–octobre 1565) d'après les Sources Espagnoles et Françaises," *Bulletin de la Société de l'Histoire du Protestantisme Français* 138 (1992), 459–73; John T.

McGrath, "Admiral Coligny, Jean Ribault, and the East Coast of North America," *French Colonial History* 1:63–76 and his "A Massacre Revised: Matanzas, 1565," *Proceedings of the annual meeting of the French Colonial Historical Society* 21 (1995), 15–29.

21. Although I have argued this point extensively in several places, it finds its most extended form in *Contesting Empires: Opposition, Promotion and Slavery* (New York and London: Palgrave Macmillan, 2005).

22. Humphrey Gilbert, *Discourse of a Discoverie for a New Passage to Cataia* (London, 1576), j ii recto–j ii verso.

23. Gilbert, *Discourse*, B iii verso–B iiii recto, D ii recto, F iii recto. On Gilbert and Newfoundland, see J. Steele, "Early Description of Newfoundland," *Newfoundland Quarterly* 63 (1964), 9–10.

24. Anon., "A Discovery of Lands Beyond the Equinoctial," in *The Three Voyages of Martin Frobisher*, ed. Richard Collinson (London: Hakluyt Society, 1867), 4. Whereas Hakluyt would look to North America, this advisor and promoter of colonization was apparently thinking about the southern end of South America. On Frobisher, his context and his legacy, see P.H. Hulton, "John White's Drawings of Eskimos," *Beaver* 292 (1961), 16–20; Eric Klingelhofer, "Three Lost Ceramic Artifacts from Frobisher's Colony, 1578," *Historical Archeology* 10 (1976), 131–34; *The Archeology of the Frobisher Voyages*, ed. William W. Fitzhugh and Jacqueline S. (Washington: Smithsonian Institute Press, 1993); Donald Dale Jackson, "Hot on the Cold Trail Left by Sir Martin Frobisher," *Smithsonian* 23 (1993), 119–30; Lynda Gullason, "Engendering Interaction: Inuit-European Contact in Frobisher Bay, Baffin Island," Ph.D. dissertation, McGill University, 1999; Thomas H.B. Symons, *Meta Incognita: A Discourse of Discovery: Martin Frobisher's Arctic Expeditions, 1576–78*, 2 vols. (Hull, PQ: Canadian Museum of Civilization, 1999); Robert McGhee, *The Arctic Voyages of Martin Frobisher: An Elizabethan Adventure* (Seattle: University of Washington Press, 2001) [reviewed by Wade A. Henry in the *Canadian Historical Review* 84 (2003), 103–05; Terry McDonald in the *American Review of Canadian Studies* 34 (2004), 156–57]. On Richard Hakluyt, the Younger, and his milieu and the encounter with Natives, see David B. Quinn and Jacques Rousseau, "Les Toponymes Amerindiens du Canada chez les Anciens Voyageurs Anglais, 1591–1602," *Cahiers de Géographie de Québec* 10 (1966), 263–77; Robert Detweiler, "Was Richard Hakluyt a Negative Influence in the Colonization of Virginia?" *North Carolina Review* 48 (1971), 359–69; David B. Quinn, "Stephen Parmenius of Buda: The First Hungarian in North America," *New Hungarian Quarterly* 15 (1973), 152–57; *The Hakluyt Handbook*, Second Series, vols. 144–45, ed. David B. Quinn, 2 vols. (London: Hakluyt Society, 1974); *Virginia Voyages from Hakluyt*, ed. David B. Quinn and Alison B. Quinn (London: Oxford University Press, 1973); Frank Lestringant, "Les Sequelles Littéraires sur les Sequelles Littéraires de la Floride Française: Laudonnière, Hakluyt, Thevet, Chauveton," *Bibliothèque d'Humanisme et Renaissance* 44 (1982), 7–36; Alfred A. Cave, "Richard Hakluyt's Savages: The Influence of 16th Century Travel Narratives on English Indian Policy in North America," *International Social Science Review* 60 (1985), 3–24; Gesa Mackenthum, "By Right of Narrative: American Beginnings and the Discourse of Colonialism," *Storia Nordamericana* 7 (1990), 3–23; Brigitte Fleishmann, "Uneasy Affinity: Strategies and Notions Behind the Old World–New World Analogies in Some Early English Reports from America," *European Contributions to American Studies* 34 (1996), 119–30; Philip Westwood, "Beyond the Western Horizon: Richard Hakluyt and the Colonization of Virginia," *Virginia Cavalcade* 47 (1998), 126–39.

25. Anon., "A Discovery," 5.

26. Anon., "A Discovery," 6.

27. Anon., "A Discovery," 7.

28. Anon., "A Discovery," 566.

29. "June 11, 1578. Patent granted to Sir Humphrey Gilbert by Elizabeth I," in *New American World: A Documentary History of North America to 1612*, ed. David B. Quinn, 5 vols. (New York, 1979), III: 186.

30. Samuel Eliot Morison, *The European Discovery of America: The North Voyage, A.D. 500–1600* (New York: Oxford University Press, 1971), 574–75.

31. On relations between France and Spain, what Philip II called "the principal thing" in 1589, see J.H. Elliott, *Europe Divided 1559–1598* (London: Fontana/Collins, 1968, rpt. Glasgow, 1974), 339–50 and for Spain's crisis in the 1590s, see J.H. Elliott, *Imperial Spain 1469–1716* (1963; Harmondsworth, 1990), 285–300.

32. For an account of Acadia, see Marcel Trudel, *Histoire de la Nouvelle-France*, Vol. 1, *Les vaines tentatives, 1524–1603* (Montréal: Fides, 1963). My discussion of New France is indebted to W.J. Eccles, *France in America* (1972; Vancouver: Fitzhenry & Whiteside, 1973), 12–15.

33. Marcel Trudel, *Histoire de la Nouvelle-France*, Vol. 2, *Le Comptoir, 1604–1627* (Montréal: Fides, 1966), 9–15. See Eccles, *France in America*, 14–15. On Gua, Champlain, and their associates and settlements, see Robert Le Blant, "Un Campagnon Blaisois de Samuel Champlain: Jean Rallau (5 janvier–après le 1er janvier 1628)," *Revue d'Histoire de l'Amérique Française* 19 (1966), 503–12, his "Les Premices de la Fondation de Québec, 16-7-08," *Revue d'Histoire de l'Amérique Française* 20 (1966), 44–45 and his "Henri IV et le Canada," *Revue de Pau et du Béarn* 12 (1984–85), 43–57; Ralph Smith, "St. Croix Island," *Beaver* 308 (4) (1978), 36–40.

34. Marc Lescarbot, *Histoire* (1609), b-iv-verso. In his address to Pierre Jeannin in the 1612 edition, Lescarbot used this language of republicanism; see Marc Lescarbot, *Histoire de la Novvelle-France . . .* (Paris, 1612), jx. On Lescarbot and his context, see LeBlant, "Premices;" Cornelius J. Jaenen," Images of New France in the History of Lescarbot," *Proceedings of the Annual Meeting of the Western Society for French History* 6 (1978), 209–19; Rick Bowers, "Le Théâtre de Neptune en la Nouvelle-France: Marc Lescarbot and the New World Masque," *Dalhousie Review* 70 (1991), 483–501; Guy Poirier, "Marc Lescarbot au Pays des Ithyphalles," *Renaissance and Reformation* 17 (1993), 73–85; Maureen Korp, "Problems of Prejudice in the Thwaites' Edition of the *Jesuit Relations*," *Historical Reflections* 21 (1995), 261–76; Alessandro Gebbia, "Marc Lescarbot, the Theatre of Neptune in New France e le Origini del Teatro Canadese," *Rivista di Studi Canadesi* 11 (1998), 103–11.

35. Lescarbot, *Histoire*, b-iiij-verso.

36. Sagard, quoted in W.J. Eccles, *The Ordeal of New France* (Toronto: Canadian Broadcasting Corp, 1967), 21–22.On Sagard, see Louise Côté, "Alimentation et Alterité: Autour du *Grand Voyage du Pays des Hurons* de Gabriel Sagard," *Canadian Folklore Canadien* 17 (1995), 63–83. In that same issue on pages 85 to 101, see Martin Fournier, "Paul Le Jeune et Gabriel Sagard: Deux Visions du Monde et des Amerindiens." Jack Warwick sees autobiographical elements in Sagard's *Histoire du Canada* despite the collective work and memory of Sagard's Recollet order; see "Gabriel Sagard et la Mémoire du XVIIe Siècle au Canada," *Etudes Canadiennes* 14 (1988), 7–14. Warwick has also called attention to the literary aspects of Sagard's writing; see Warwick, "Observation, Polemics and Poetic Vision in Gabriel Sagard's Narration," *University of Ottawa Quarterly* 48 (1978), 84–92. Along with discussing Sagard, a member of the Récollets or Greyfriars, Cornelius J. Jaenan examines the contribution of Father Louis Hennepin, who was on the LaSalle expedition to the upper Mississippi; see "Missionaries as Explorers: The Récollets of New France," *Journal of the Canadian Church Historical Society* 22 (1980), 32–45. Sagard, along with the *Jesuit Relations*, provides material for modern linguists and archeologists: see, for instance, John Steckley, "An Ethnolinguistic Look at the Huron Longhouse," *Ontario Archeology* 47 (1987), 19–32.

37. Eccles, *France in America*, 24.

38. John Oldmixon, *The British Empire in America* (London, 1708), xxxv. On Oldmixon, see Pat Rogers, "An Early Colonial Historical: John Oldmixon and the British Empire in America," *Journal of American Studies* 7 (1973), 113–23.

39. Peter Kalm, *The America of 1750: The Travels in North America by Peter Kalm*, 2 vols. (1937; New York, 1966), II:374–76. Also see Martii Kerkkonnen, *Peter Kalm's North American Journey*,

Studia Historica, I, Finnish Historical Society (Helsinki, 1959), 109–10 and Eccles, *France in America*, 134. Kalm took a comparative interest in the various groups in British and French America. For other studies of Peter [Pehr] Kalm and related topics, see Milton W. Hamilton, "Sir William Johnson: Interpreter of the Iroquois," *Ethnohistory* 10 (1963), 270–86; Tell Dahllöf, "Pehr Kalm's Concern about Forests in America, Sweden and Finland Two Centuries Ago," *Swedish Pioneer Historical Quarterly* 17 (1966), 123–45; Benôit Brouillette, "Quelques Observations Climatiques en Nouvelle-France au Dix-Huitième Siècle," *Transactions of the Royal Society of Canada* 8 (1970), 93–99; Risto Pikkola, "Delaware's Swedish and Finnish Immigrants in a New Ecological and Cultural Environment According to Israel Acrelius and Pehr Kalm," *Turun Historiallinen Arkisto* 46 (1990), 13–31; Paul Kelton, "Natural Historians: Scientists as Artists and Discoverers," *Gilcrease Magazine of American History and Art* 14 (1992), 10–19; Riku Hämäläinen, " 'We Are the mystic Warriors of Finland': Finnish Indianism," *European Review of Native American Studies* 12 (1998), 13–18.

40. *Rapport de L'Archiviste de la Province de Québec, 1923–1924*, 58, quoted in Eccles, *France in America,* 127 and 126.

41. Eccles, *France in America*, 133–34, 138–39, 146–47, 172–77, 181–82. On the controversy over Washington's ambush of a French force in the Ohio country on May 29, 1754, and his firing on French emissaries and the consequences of these actions on French-"American" and British relations, see Stuart Leiburger, " 'To Judge of Washington's Conduct': Illuminating George Washington's Appearance on the World Stage," *Virginia Magazine of History and Biography* 107 (1999), 37–44.

42. On the Seven Years' War, see T.R. Clayton, "The Duke of Newcastle, the Earl of Halifax, and the American Origins of the Seven Years' War," *Historical Journal* 24 (1981), 571–603. Clayton argues that George Washington's surrender to the French in 1754 in Ohio is a key event in the build-up to a war that spread from America to Europe.

43. J. Gibson, "An Accurate Map of the British Empire in North America as Settled by the Preliminaries in 1762," *The Gentleman's Magazine*, Vol. 32 (London, 1762), 602–03. See also *Library of Congress Geography and Maps of North America, 1750–1789*, 92. This map measured the longitude west from London and marked various types of names on the map: cities, bodies of water, and territories. These territories sometimes had different names, such as "Labrador Or New Britain," or overlapped as Canada, New England, and Nova Scotia had fluid borders that were not marked here; Pennsylvania and New York also seem to have different borders; the Adirondacks are north of Lake Huron here; the lands marked by "Six Nations" cross from lower Lake Michigan past Cadaraqui or Frontenac (modern-day Kingston, Ontario); whereas Georgia and Florida (which includes C. Canaveral) are curtailed, both Virginia and Carolina straddle or cross the "Allegany" Mountains. Although the map includes French and British settlements in Indian territory, the names of Native nations are prominent. This territory and the inset of "*A* CHART *of the* Entrance of the MISSISSIPPI," show interest in the contested territory with the French and what would become contested between Britain and the Thirteen Colonies or English or British America as it was known. There was no division yet between the northern colonies of Canada and Nova Scotia from the other American colonies.

44. Thomas Jefferson to John Randolph, August 25, 1775, *Thomas Jefferson Papers Series 1, General Correspondence, 1651–1827, Library of Congress*. After independence, British travelers, writers, and reformers expressed various ideas about Jefferson and American democracy; see S.W. Jackman, "A Young Englishman Reports on the New Nation: Edward Thornton to James Bland Burges, 1791–1793," *William and Mary Quarterly* 18 (1961), 85–121; Lucia Stanton, "Looking for Liberty: Thomas Jefferson and the British Lions," *Eighteenth-Century Studies* 26 (1993), 649–68. Jefferson himself changed his views of Britain after the War of Independence because he came to the position during James Munroe's presidency that an alliance with Britain was beneficial because Spain and France were threats in the New World; see Lawrence S. Kaplan, "Jefferson as Anglophile: Sagacity or Senility in the Era of Good Feelings?" *Diplomatic History* 16 (1992), 487–94. For more on Jefferson and Britain, see Merrill D. Peterson, "Thomas Jefferson and

Commercial Policy, 1783–1793," *William and Mary Quarterly* 22 (1965), 584–610 [this article also includes a discussion of European mercantilism and commerce with France]; Burton Spivak, "Jefferson, England, and the Embargo: Trading Wealth and Republican Value in the Shaping of American Diplomacy, 1804–1809," Ph.D. dissertation, University of Virginia, 1975, and his *Jefferson's English Crisis: Commerce, Embargo, and the Republican Revolution* (Charlottesville: University Press of Virginia, 1979). On the ground, Americans and their British North American cousins and neighbors traded in 1807 despite official policy; see Nicholas H. Muller, "Smuggling into Canada: How the Champlain Valley Defied Jefferson's Embargo," *Vermont History* 38 (1970), 5–21. See also Charles R. Ritcheson, "The Fragile Memory: What Really Happened When Thomas Jefferson Met George III," *American Heritage* 33 (1981), 72–77. Ritcheson argues that Jefferson's account of the king snubbing him when they met on March 17, 1786, is based not on evidence but on Jefferson's undying hatred of George III. For Jefferson in England at that time, see Ross Watson, Thomas Jefferson's Visit to England, 1786," *History Today* 27 (1977), 3–13. Thomas Jefferson compared the War of Independence with the English Civil Wars; see James C. Spalding, "Loyalist as Royalist, Patriot as Puritan: The American Revolution as a Repetition of the English Civil Wars," *Church History* 45 (1976), 329–40. The British actually were willing to cooperate in helping Jefferson acquire Louisiana for the United States and were cooperative in later arrangements for financing the purchase; see Bradford Perkins, "England and the Louisiana Question," *Huntington Library Quarterly* 18 (1955), 279–95. The American Revolution was the birth of British North America (later Canada) and the United States, one as the continuation of British colonies in North America and the other as an independent state. Jefferson had much to do with that War of Independence and continued to advocate the annexation of Canada, which was attempted once more during the War of 1812. This part of U.S. expansionism did not work. See Lawrence S. Kaplan, "Jefferson, The Napoleonic Wars, and the Balance of Power," *William and Mary Quarterly* 14 (1957), 196–217. There were dissenting voices against the War of 1812 and the attempt to conquer Canada: one of those was Matthew Lyon, a former supporter of Jefferson and a congressman from Vermont then from Kentucky, something that can be seen in a letter to James Munroe in 1811; see Donald R. Hickey, "A Dissenting Voice: Matthew Lyon on the Conquest of Canada," *Register of the Kentucky Historical Society* 76 (1978), 45–52. The competition among Russia, the United States, and Britain (British North America) for the West is something that James P. Ronda discusses in "A Moment in Time: The West— September 1806," *Montana* 44 (1994), 2–15.

45. George Washington to Canadian Citizens, September 7, 1775, *George Washington Papers at the Library of Congress, 1741–1799: Series 4, General Correspondence, 1697–1799.* For positive attitudes of the British toward George Washington, see Reginald C. McGrane, "George Washington: An Anglo-American Hero," *Virginia Magazine of History and Biography* 63 (1955), 3–13; In Britain, sympathy seems to have been directed toward Washington, especially in the British press, particularly involving praise of his character and military leadership. In Parliament, members on both sides praised Washington for the care he took of his troops and his placing of military matters above politics. For this view, see Troy O. Bickham, "Sympathizing with Sedition? George Washington, The British Press, and British Attitudes during the American War of Independence," *William and Mary Quarterly* 59 (2002), 101–22. Washington had close ties with Britain through trade and benefited from it, but later was not impressed by that dependence and the lack of profit in tobacco; see Bruce A. Ragsdale, "George Washington: The British Tobacco Trade, and Economic Opportunity in Prerevolutionary Virginia," *Virginia Magazine of History and Biography* 97 (1989), 133–62. Washington supervised the evacuation of the British in the autumn of 1783; see Nancy Dana Gold, "The End of the Revolution," *American History Illustrated* 18 (1983), 10–17. Whereas the King was criticized concerning the War of Independence on both sides of the Atlantic, George Washington generally received praise in Britain and the American colonies/United States; see Marcus Cunliffe, "The Two Georges: The President and the King," *American Studies International* 24 (1986),

53–73. On Washington's relation to the British, especially in regard to nationalism and anticolonialism and in social and psychological terms, see Philip L. White, "The Americanisation of George Washington," *History of European Ideas* 15 (1992), 419–25.

46. Arthur Lee wrote to Gardoqui, Paris, October 6, 1778, *1 Sparks' Dip. Rev. Corr., 518*. The *Revolutionary Diplomatic Correspondence of the United States, Volume 2, A Century of Lawmaking for a New Nation: U.S. Congressional Documents and Debates, 1774–1875, Library of Congress*. For more background on Spain and the American Revolution, see Thomas E. Chávez, *Spain and the Independence of the United States: An Intrinsic Gift* (Albuquerque: University of New Mexico, 2002). For some Spanish attitudes toward the English colonies in America, see Light Townsend Cummins, *Spanish Observers and the American Revolution, 1775–1783* (Baton Rouge: Louisiana State University Press, 1991). On Spanish policy, see Loliannette Emmanuelli, "Spanish Diplomatic Policy and Contribution to the United States Independence, 1775–1783," Ph.D. dissertation, University of Massachusetts, 1990. On the Spanish navy, particularly the Spanish attack on Pensacola, after the joint French and Spanish invasion of Britain was called off (Spain had broken off relations with Britain in April 1779), Enrique Fernández, "Spain's Contribution to the Independence of the United States," *Revista/Review Interamericana* 10 (1980), 290–304; René Quatrefages, "La Collaboration Franco-Espagnole dans la Prise de Pensacola," *Revue Historique des Armées* 4 (1981), 44–63; Carlos M. Fernández-Shaw, "Ayuda de Armada España a la Independencia de los Estados Unidos," *Inter-American Review of Bibliography* 26 (1976), 456–502 and his "Participation de la Armada Española en la Guerra de la Independencia de los Estados Unidos," *Revista de Historia Naval* 3 (1985), 75–80. More generally on Spain, see Victor Lezcano Morales, "Diplomacia y Politica Financera de España Durante la Sublevacion de las Colonias Inglesas en América: 1775–1783," *Anuario de Estudios Americanos* 26 (1969), 507–64; Carl J. Mora, "Spain and the American Revolution: The Campaigns of Bernard de Gálvez," *Mankind* 4 (8) (1974), 50–57; Overton G. Ganong, "Spain's Role in the American Revolution," *Escribano* 13 (1976), 51–56; James W. Cortada, "Rebirth of a Problem: Spain and the American Revolution," *Daughters of the American Revolution Magazine* 111 (1977), 212–16; Enrique Manera Regueryra, "Intervencion Española en la Guerra de la Independencia de los Estados Unidos," *Revista General de Marina* 209 (1985), 175–89; Ramón Clavijo Provencio, "España y La Conquista de Pensacola," *Historia y Vida* 19 (1986), 32–41. For instance, Morales discusses how the American Revolution allowed France and Spain to curb British hegemony, which had occurred since the Treaty of Utrecht in 1713, but how it exhausted all European treasuries. Mora says that Gálvez's role in the War of Independence led to his appointment as viceroy of New Spain. Fernández-Shaw argues that Spain helped the British American colonists even before the declaration of war between Spain and Britain in 1779. Ganong discusses the conflict between Spain and Britain, and the aid Spain offered the colonists between 1775 and 1780. Cortada examines relations between Spain and the English colonies in North America before and during the War of Independence. Regueryra maintains that from 1779 to 1883 the French and Spanish navies challenged British control of the seas and allowed for the land victories of Gálvez, Rochambeau, and Washington. Haarman also outlines Gálvez's success: see Albert W. Haarmann, "The Spanish Conquest of British West Florida, 1779–1781," *Florida Historical Quarterly* 39 (1960), 107–34. See also James Allen Lewis, "New Spain During the American Revolution, 1779–1783: A Viceroyalty at War," Duke University, Ph.D. thesis, 1975; Buchanan Parker Thomson, *Spain: Forgotten Ally of the American Revolution* (North Quincy, MA: Christopher, 1976); Light Townsend Cummins, "Spanish Agents in North America during the Revolution, 1775–1779," Ph.D. dissertation, Tulane University, 1977; *Anglo-Spanish Confrontation on the Gulf Coast during the American Revolution*, ed. William S. Coker and Robert R. Rea (Pensacola, FL: Gulf Coast Historical and Humanities Conference, 1982); Jesús Salgado Alba, "La Marina Española en la Guerra de la Independencia de los Estados Unidos," *Revista General de Marina* 207 (1984), 185–201. Some time ago, Eleazar Córdoba-Bello contrasted the English and Spanish modes of colonization in America (especially the absence of mixed marriages in English America, examined the influence of the American

Revolution on France, Belgium, and Spanish America and drew out the similarities between the revolutions in North and Latin America; see "Independencia de las Colonias Angloamericanas. Causas. Influencia que Ejercio en Otros Eventos Revolucionarios Europeos y Americanos," *Revista de Historía* 1 (1960), 57–95. For a discussion of relations with English Americans and the influence of the American Revolution on Spanish America, see Manuel Ballesteros Gaibrois, "Participacion de España la Independencia de los Estados Unidos," *Revista Cubana* 31 (1957), 29–48.

47. James Madison's Notes of Debates, March 13, 1787, *Letters of Delegates to Congress: Volume 24, November 6, 1786–February 29, 1788, A Century of Lawmaking, Library of Congress*. Later, Madison, as secretary of state and then as president (1809–17), also had much to do with Spain and Spanish-speaking America. For his time as secretary of state and the triangular relations with Spain and France, see Clifford L. Egan, "The United States, France, and West Florida, 1803–1807," *Florida Historical Quarterly* 47 (1969), 227–52. Thomas Jefferson was president during 1801–9 and Madison succeeded him and was in turn followed by James Munroe (1817–25). For Madison's relations with Spain before and during the Madison presidency, particularly in relation to the influence of Claiborne, from Tennessee but Territorial governor of Mississippi (1801–03) and Louisiana (1803–11), see Jared W. Bradley, "W.C.C. Claiborne and Spain: Foreign Affairs under Jefferson and Madison, 1801–1811," *Louisiana History* 12 (1971), 297–314. Peter J. Castor maintains that rather than ease tensions the Louisiana Purchase of 1803 actually exacerbated problems with relations with the Indians and with the Spanish Empire; see " 'Louisiana is Ours!' The Louisiana Purchase and the New Problems in American Foreign Policy, 1803–1815," *Consortium on Revolutionary Europe 1750–1850: Selected Papers 1997, 280–88*. Gene A. Smith argues that Jefferson and his successors, Madison and Monroe, thought it the right of the United States to secure a port near the mouth of the Mississippi River and to be able to navigate it; see " 'To Conquer without War': The Philosophy of Jeffersonian Expansion in the Spanish Gulf Borderlands, 1800–1820," *Consortium on Revolutionary Europe 1750–1850: Proceedings* 23 (1994), 415–22. See also Joseph Burkholder Smith, *The Plot to Steal Florida: James Madison's Phony War* (New York: Arbor House, 1983).

48. George Washington to Marie Joseph Paul Yves Roch Gilbert du Motier, Marquis de Lafayette, March 25, 1787, *The Writings of George Washington from the Original Manuscript Sources, 1745–1799*, ed. John C. Fitzpatrick in The George Washington Papers at the Library of Congress, 1741–1799. On the close relation between Washington and Lafayette, see René de Chambrun, "Washington, Second Père de Lafayette," *Nouvelle Revue des Deux Mondes* 12 (1981), 579–88.

49. See Graeme Wynn, "On the Margins of Empire," *The Illustrated History of Canada*, ed. Craig Brown (1987; Toronto: Lester Publishing, 1991), 209–17. On comparative views of the colonial history of the Americas and the role of borders and borderlands, see Jeremy Adelman and Stephen Aron, "From Borderlands to Borders: Empires, Nation-States, and the Peoples in Between in North American History," *American Historical Review* 104 (1999), 814–41. The War of Independence brought about an invasion, led by Benedict Arnold and Richard Montgomery, that failed partly because of inadequate food, clothing, and supplies; see Alan C. Aimone and Barbara A. Aimone, " 'Brave Bostonians': New Yorkers' Roles in the Winter Invasion of Canada," *Military Collector & Historian* 36 (1984), 134–50. The Continental Congress considered two plans to invade Canada, but it seemed unable to include French Canada in its vision of a new country, and perhaps a number of French Canadians were skeptical of the ability of the newly declared country to guarantee and respect their linguistic, religious, and cultural differences; see John M. Coleman, "How 'Continental' Was the Continental Congress?" *History Today* 18 (1968), 540–50. On the importance of the French settlers in Canada and their defeat of invading American forces in 1775 and 1813, see Robert de Roquebrune," Les Canadiens Français Vanqueurs des Américains," *Miroir de l'Histoire* 103 (1958), 77–82. The American invasion of Canada during the War of Independence and the War of 1812 (as well as the later Fenian raids) left a mark on Canada and was a factor in forging

a common nation from the different colonies of British North America. For a discussion of the aid of French settlers in the Beauce in the Chaudière valley of Québec during the American Revolution, see Barry Hadfield Rodrigue, "The Album in the Attic: The Forgotten Frontier of the Quebec-Maine Borderlands during the Revolutionary War," *Journal of the Historical Society* 3 (2003), 45–73. In 1812, French Canadians fought the Americans in a highly effective way and with strong military organization; see Martin F. Auger, "French-Canadian Participation in the War of 1812: A Social Study of the *Voltigeurs Canadiens*," *Canadian Military History* 10 (2001), 23–41. For limited British Resources in the West (Lake Erie region), the limitations of the Canadian militia, and the indifference of the Indians to fight the Americans, see Paul John Woehrmann, "The American Invasion of Western Upper Canada in 1813," *Northwest Ohio Quarterly* 39 (2) (1968), 61–73, 39 (4) (1968), 39–48 and 40 (1) (1968), 27–44. Lillian F. Gates publishes in full a letter from December 1837, in which Louis Joseph Papineau, leader of the rebellion in Lower Canada, wrote Bancroft, a democratic politician, for support and a large loan, only to receive a sympathetic response but one that advocated peaceful means of protest, which did not help to effect the invasion of Canada that Papineau may have desired; see "A Canadian Rebel's Appeal to George Bancroft," *New England Quarterly* 41 (1968), 96–104. The secret police, which began in Canada in 1864 and was built on the rural police force that was established in Lower Canada in 1837 in the aftermath of the rebellion, was often seen as necessary to protect the border from American invasion and, at the end of the American Civil War, became a force against Fenians from the United States. In 1873, the Northwest Mounted Police was formed. Canadians seem to have been more accepting of secret police powers than were Victorian Englishmen in the mother country. See Gregory S. Kealey, "The Empire Strikes Back: The Nineteenth-Century Origins of the Canadian Secret Service," *Journal of the Canadian Historical Association* 10 (1999), 3–18. About the Fenian raids, see Bill Goble, "On to Canada Again? A History of the Fenian Invasion of 1872," *Military Images* 16 (1995), 22–25. Goble also discusses the Fenians, many of whom were veterans of the American Civil War, to invade Canada in 1866 and 1870, as a means of ending British oppression in Ireland. On the role of the Fenian raids and their contribution to national unity in British North America, see W.S. Neidhardt, " 'We've Nothing Else to Do': The Fenian Invasions of Canada, 1866," *Canada: An Historical Magazine* 1 (1973), 1–20. In an article the year before, Neidhardt looks at the ambivalence of the U.S. government and the Republican party with regard to the Fenians; see "The American Government and the Fenian Brotherhood: A Study in Mutual Political Opportunism," *Ontario History* 64 (1972), 27–44. See also a discussion of a group that organized an invasion of Canada in 1866, Dennis Clark, "Militants of the 1860's: The Philadelphia Fenians," *Pennsylvania Magazine of History and Biography* 95 (1971), 98–108. Peter Berresford Ellis and Joseph A. King record the defeat of the Fenians, or the Irish Republican Army (or the Irish Army of Liberation) at the Battle of Ridgeway on June 2, 1866, at the hands of British regulars and the Canadian militia and discuss the losses; see "Fenian Casualties and Prisoners: Fenian Invasion of British North America, June 1866," *Irish Sword* 18 (1992), 271–85. These raids and the role of the Irish and Irish Americans in battling the injustices of the British Empire were keys to the ideas of Louis Riel, who led the Northwest rebellions on the Canadian Prairies in 1869 and 1885. For a more detailed account of the Fenian invasions, see Hereward Senior, *The Last Invasion of Canada: The Fenian Raids, 1866–1870* (Toronto: Dundurn Press, 1991). The government of Canada (Ontario and Quebec) fitted a squadron to fight the Fenians and the new dominion government, after Confederation in 1867, revived a navy in the second Fenian crisis in 1869–70 (while the Northwest Rebellion was going on); see Richard J. Wright, "Green Flags and Red-Coated Gunboats. Naval Activities on the great Lakes During the Fenian Scares, 1866–70," *Inland Seas* 22 (1966), 91–110. G.F.G. Stanley argues that Riel denounced such a Fenian invasion of the Northwest as a farce; see "L'Invasion Fenienne au Manitoba," *Revue d'Histoire de l'Amérique Française* 17 (1963), 258–68. On the insecurities and security of Canada from colonial times, but especially in terms of the twentieth century, which Prime Minister Wilfrid Laurier proclaimed as belonging to

Canada, see Desmond Morton, "Providing and Consuming Security in Canada's Century," *Canadian Historical Review* 81 (2000), 2–28. Even still, Canada and the United States, long-time allies, devised plans to invade each other after the First World War; see Richard A. Preston, "Buster Brown Was Not Alone: American Plans for the Invasion of Canada, 1919–1939," *Canadian Defence Quarterly* 20 (1990), 29–37. Concerning a plan by a congressman from New York to annex Upper Canada and leave Lower Canada as a vassal state that could not interfere with the development of Upstate New York, see J.C.A. Stagg, "Between Black Rock and a Hard Place: Peter B. Porter's Plan for an American Invasion of Canada in 1812," *Journal of the Early Republic* 19 (1999), 385–422. On the marginalization of Natives in Mexico, the United States, and Canada, see Anthony DePalma, *Here: A Biography of the New American Continent* (2001) and Reginald C. Stuart, "First and Further Drafts: Reappraisals of North American Identities," *Canadian Journal of History* 37 (2002), 95–101. For a discussion of the defeat of the American forces in the Niagara region of Upper Canada (now Ontario), led by Stephen van Rensselaer, see Carol Whitfield, "The Battle of Queenston Heights," *Canadian Historic Sites* 11 (1974), 9–59; Derek Smith, "Disaster at Queenston Heights," *American History* 36 (2001), 38–44. See also David G. Fitz-Enz, *The Final Invasion: Plattsburgh, the War of 1812's Most Decisive Battle* (New York: Cooper Square, 2001). A good review article on the work of F. Murray Greenwood, Françoise Noël, and Allan Greer that explores the tensions internal to Lower Canada and in relation to the American and French Revolutions, culminating in the Rebellion of 1837 (but also with implications for the Union of the two Canadas, responsible government, and Reciprocity with the United States) can be found in Peter Burroughs, " 'The Garrison Mentality' Versus 'La Survivance': English-French Relations in Lower Canada, 1791," *Journal of Imperial and Commonwealth History* 24 (1996), 296–308. As the notes to this chapter illustrate, those events have various dimensions, Canadian, British, American, inter-American, imperial, colonial, national, regional. American views on Canada, whether by John Adams or his son John Quincy or by Benjamin Franklin, and the American invasion of Canada illustrate that the idea of Canada was important not simply to those living in the southern colonies but also those in the north and in the two countries that were born at different times; see Arnold Whitridge, "Canada: The Struggle for the 14th State," *History Today* 17 (1967), 13–21. Various journals and books in different languages present distinct points of view on the same events.

50. Martin J. Griffin, "The Late Sir John Macdonald," *The Atlantic Monthly* 68 (408) (October 1891), 52. Canadian independence and identity developed politically and economically. See, for instance, R.A. Shields, "Imperial Policy and the Role of Foreign Consuls in Canada 1870–1911," *Dalhousie Review* 59 (1979–80), 717–47. Macdonald, during the campaign of 1891, appealed to loyalty of empire in the face of a a movement for commercial union with the United States; see K.A. MacKirdy, "The Loyalty Issue in the 1891 Federal Election Campaign, and an Ironic Footnote," *Ontario History* 55 (1963) 143–54. Riel's desire for the status of a province only and Macdonald's skill in diplomacy averted war with the United States, which contained annexationists in favor of annexing the Northwest Territory in Canada; see Alvin C. Gluek, Jr., "The Riel Rebellion and Canadian-American Relations," *Canadian Historical Review* 36 (1955), 199–221. On Macdonald's change of heart about Confederation in the face of American designs on the Northwest, see Donald G. Creighton, "Old Tomorrow," *Beaver* (Winter 1956), 6–10. On Macdonald's willingness to have Canadian troops participate in imperial expeditions, see C.P. Stacey, "John A. Macdonald on Raising Troops for Imperial Service, 1885," *Canadian Historical Review* 38 (1957), 37–41. For another view—this one dealing with the *Royal Commission on the Defence of British Possessions and Commerce Abroad* (July 29, 1880), see Alice R. Stewart, "Sir John A. Macdonald and the Imperial Defence Commission of 1979," *Canadian Historical Review* 35 (1954), 119–39. On the case of Nils Guzaf von Schoultz, a Swede who invaded Upper Canada as part of an American invasion force on November 12, 1838, and who was hanged less than a month later in Kingston, had an impact on John A. Macdonald's thinking about the need for a British North America united into a state; see

Lennard Sillanpaa, "Death of a Liberator, 1838," *Beaver* 70 (1990), 27–31. Macdonald had had his own struggles at unity. During the American Civil War, Abraham Lincoln had to try to flush out the actual intentions of Jefferson Davis, who had sent emissaries to Canada, by sending emissaries of his own to the South, where Davis, rather than negotiating peace, insisted on independence. Canada, then, and the British Empire, were part of the platform of American conflict, identity, and unity just as the threat of American expansion was connected to Macdonald's national dream of a united British North America (Canada), which occurred in 1867, at least in its first stages (Manitoba joined in 1870, British Columbia in 1871, and Prince Edward Island in 1873). See John R. Brumgardt, "Presidential Duel at Midsummer: The 'Peace' Missions to Canada and Richmond, 1864," *Lincoln Herald* 77 (1975), 96–102. David also sent Beverley Tucker, later the U.S. Consul in Liverpool under President James Buchanan, on a trade mission to Canada in 1864, the same year as the Charlottetown Conference on Confederation, to arrange for the exchange of Southern cotton for meat; see Ludwell Harrison Johnson, III, "Beverley Tucker's Canadian Mission, 1864–1865," *Journal of Southern History* 29 (1963), 88–89. Another account of Jefferson Davis in 1867 and 1868, as he awaited trial, generally can be found in George E. Carter, "A Note on Jefferson Davis in Canada—His Stay in Lennoxville, Quebec," *Journal of Mississippi History* 33 (1971), 133–39. The American invasion of Canada, even in a hypothetical form, has also had a long life in the literary imagination in Canada. See Valerie Broege, "War with the United States in Canadian Literature and Visual Arts," *Journal of American Culture* 9 (1986), 31–36. A work of popular history on one of these invasions is Pierre Berton, *The Invasion of Canada, Vol. 1, 1812–13* (Boston: Little Brown, 1980).

51. William Lyon Mackenzie, *Province of Upper Canada, Assembly, Committee on Grievances, Seventh Report*, April 10, 1835, quoted in *The Colonial Century: English-Canadian Writing before Confederation*, ed. A.J.M. Smith (1973; Toronto: Tecumseh Press Limited, 1986), 1:152. A recent detailed view of this key figure in Canadian and North American history occurs in John Sewell, *A Political Biography of William Lyon Mackenzie* (Toronto: Lorimer, 2002). About Mackenzie's family, see F.K. Donnelly, "The British Background of William Lyon Mackenzie," *British Journal of Canadian Studies* 2 (1987), 61–73. On Mackenzie's exile in New York State and related topics, see Lillian F. Gates, *After the Rebellion: The Later Years of William Lyon Mackenzie* (Toronto: Dundurn, 1988). A more specific work concerning Mackenzie's role as a newspaper editor occurs in Chris Raible, *A "Colonial Advocate" The Launching of His Newspaper and the Queenston Career of William Lyon Mackenzie* (Creemore, ON: Curiosity House, 1999). For an analysis of the Rebellion of 1837 in Upper Canada based on class tensions, see Andrew Bonthius, "The Patriot War of 1837–1838: Locofocoism with a Gun?" *Labour* 52 (2003), 9–43. For two divergent views of Mackenzie as mayor of Toronto, see Frederick H. Armstrong, "William Lyon Mackenzie, First Mayor of Toronto: A Study of a Critic in Power,"*Canadian Historical Review* 48 (1967), 309–31; and Paul Romney, "William Lyon Mackenzie as Mayor of Toronto," *Canadian Historical Review* 56 (1975), 416–36. Whereas Armstrong sees Mackenzie as an incompetent administrator who was fiscally irresponsible, Romney sees Mackenzie as honest and hardworking. On Mackenzie as pro-management, see Frederick H. Armstrong, "Reformer as Capitalist: William Lyon Mackenzie and the Printers' Striker of 1836," *Ontario History* 59 (1967), 187–96, and his assessment of Mackenzie's popularity and political career, "William Lyon Mackenzie: The Persistent Hero," *Journal of Canadian Studies* 6 (1971), 21–36. For a view of Mackenzie as having the agrarian values of Jacksonian Democracy and for seeing Jackson in ideal terms, see J.E. Rea, "William Lyon Mackenzie—Jacksonian," *Mid-America* 50 (1968), 223–35. Mackenzie has an important American dimension. In the *Gazette* he supported Martin van Buren in 1838 and 1840 despite van Buren's lack of sympathy to the Canadian rebels/patriots; see Lillian F. Gates, "Mackenzie's *Gazette:* An Aspect of W.L. Mackenzie's American Years," *Canadian Historical Review* 46 (1965), 323–45; for a discussion of of Mackenzie's grasp of policy, see Gates's "The Decided Policy of William Lyon Mackenzie," *Canadian Historical Review* 40 (1959), 185–208. Four hundred Americans, under H.C. Steward, crossed the ice on Lake Erie in February 1838 to invade

Pelee Island. In the battle both sides had heavy casualties; see J.P. Martyn, "The Patriot Invasion of Pelee Island, 1838," *Ontario History* 56 (1964), 153–65. See also Lillian F. Gates, "W.L. Mackenzie's Volunteer and the First Parliament of United Canada," *Ontario History* 59 (1967), 163–83 and William Dawson LeSueur, *William Lyon Mackenzie: A Reinterpretation* (Toronto: Macmillan, 1979). A classic account of Mackenzie occurs in William Kilbourn's masterful *The Firebrand: William Lyon Mackenzie and the Rebellion in Upper Canada* (Toronto: Clark, Irwin and Company Limited, 1956).

52. Mackenzie (chairman) et al., quoted in Smith, *The Colonial Century*, 155.

53. Haliburton in Smith, *The Colonial Century*, 185. For a different reading of Haliburton's views of slavery (that the satire in this quotation implies) but a view that also includes Haliburton's warning against slavery, see George Elliott Clarke, "White Niggers, Black Slaves: Slavery, Race and Class in T.C. Haliburton's *The Clockmaker*," *Nova Scotia Historical Review* 14 (1994), 13–40. For a wider discussion of slaves, see my *Contesting Empires*. Haliburton's reply—a compilation of seven letters—to Lord Durham's report of 1839 is germane especially appropriate to this chapter: Haliburton was of Loyalist stock and defended the Tory way of life against Durham's reforms; see Rhonda Bradley, "A Blazing Rage: T.C. Haliburton's *Reply to the Report of the Earl of Durham*," *Nova Scotia Historical Review* 12 (1992), 76–95. Although there are a few useful articles on Haliburton's family, the most germane one is that which speaks about his paternal grandparents, New England Planters, and the Planters' sympathy for displaced Acadians and guilt over occupying Acadian lands; see Gordon MacKay Haliburton, "The Planter Roots of Thomas Chandler Haliburton," *Dalhousie Review* 71 (1991), 292–309. Haliburton (1796–1865) was the creator of the satirical Yankee Sam Slick; a judge in Nova Scotia; and later a Member of Parliament in England from 1859 to 1865; see V.L.O. Chittick, "Haliburton as Member of Parliament," *University of Toronto Quarterly* 33 (1963), 78–88. On the paradox that Haliburton's apparently anti-Yankee satires were popular in the United States after they appeared there in 1837 because they showed a kind of Nativist regional American humor, see Matthew R. Laird, "Nativist American Humour: Sam Slick and the Defence of the New England Whig Culture," *Canadian Review of American Studies* 23 (1993), 71–88. Richard A. Davies bases his discussion of Haliburton's three decades in Britain—until his death—on accounts in contemporary British newspapers; see " 'Not at All the Man That We Have Imagined': Mr. Justice Haliburton in England (1835–65)' " *Dalhousie Review* 59 (1979–80), 683–95. On Haliburton writing of the history of Nova Scotia—he wrote two such accounts in the 1820s—see M. Brook Taylor, "Thomas Chandler Haliburton as a Historian," *Acadiensis* 13 (1984), 50–68. About Haliburton who argues for harmony among tradition, technology, and nature, see R.D. MacDonald, "Thomas Chandler Haliburton's 'Machine in the Garden': Applying Leo Marx's Criticism of America to Haliburton's *Clockmaker*," *Canadian Review of American Studies* 19 (1988), 165–81; Tension between New England and the Maritimes sometimes occurred and was two-way. According to D.G. Lochhead, at one point, New Englanders associated Halifax, which Haliburton helped to put on the literary map, with the reviled Loyalists/Tories; see "Halifax in Canadian Literature," *Transactions of the Royal Society of Canada* 19 (1981), 93–104. See also Vernon Rolfe Lindquist, "The Soil and the Seed, the Birth of the Canadian Short Story in English: Haliburton, Moodie and Others, 1830–1867," Ph.D. dissertation, University of New Brunswick, 1979; Darlene Nelita Fortier, "The European Connection: A Study of Thomas Haliburton, Gilbert Parker, and Sara Jeannette Duncan," Ph.D. dissertation, University of Toronto, 1981; Ruth Panofsky, "Thomas Chandler Haliburton's *The Clockmaker*, First, Second, and Third Series," Ph.D. dissertation, York University (Toronto), 1991.

54. Howe in Smith, *The Colonial Century*, 211. Howe's sympathetic response to Lord Durham was different from Haliburton's or Beamish Murdock's. See Philip Girard, " 'I Will Not Pin My Faith to His Sleeve': Beamish Murdoch, Joseph Howe, and Responsible Government Revisited," *Journal of the Royal Nova Scotia Historical Society* 4 (2001), 48–69. As Girard points out, Murdoch and Howe were selected to speak at the 1849 centenary of the founding of Halifax, so Nova Scotians were split. One of the principles that Howe held dear was consultation with the

people, which he thought had not been done in the Confederation debate, according to J. Murray Beck, who considered George Johnson's manuscript biography in the Public Archives of Canada the best evaluation of Howe and Confederation; see Beck, "Joseph Howe and Confederation: Myth and Fact," *Transactions of the Royal Society of Canada* 2 (1964), 137–50. See also Beck's, "Joseph Howe: Mild Tory to Reforming Assemblyman," *Dalhousie Review* 44 (1964), 44–56. Beck marks the period, 1828 to 1843 as the turning point in making Howe a leader in the reform movement. C.B. Fergusson looks at Howe's opinions on federation with the Canadian colonies from 1832 to 1869; see "Howe and the Confederation," *Nova Scotia Historical Quarterly* 4 (1974), 223–44. J.M. Beck discusses how Howe turned reluctantly from the idea of imperial union when he saw that Nova Scotia would be part of the Confederation; see "Howe and the Enactment of the B.N.A. Act: The Final Disillusionment of a Statesman of Empire," *Nova Scotia Historical Society Collections* 40 (1980), 7–30; See also J. Murray Beck, *Joseph Howe, Vol. 1: Conservative Reformer, 1804–1848* (Montreal: McGill-Queen's University Press, 1982) and his *Joseph Howe, Vol. 2: The Briton Becomes Canadian, 1848–1873* (Montreal: McGill-Queen's University Press, 1983). Joseph Howe was finely tuned to associations among the parts of British America, the connection with Britain and its empire, and the relations with the United States. U.S.–Canada relations continue to fascinate, which can be seen when an American professor taught U.S. History one year at University of Lethbridge in Alberta, Canada. See James Tag, " 'And, We Burned Down the White House, Too': American History, Canadian Undergraduates, and Nationalism," *History Teacher* 37 (2004), 309–34.

55. John L. Allen considers the first age of discovery, which includes the period that includes Cabot and Cartier, to have made great contributions to European cartography and knowledge of the New World; see his "From Cabot to Cartier: The Early Exploration of Eastern North America, 1497–1543," *Annals of the Association of American Geographers* 82 (1992), 500–21, esp. 517–19. The "discovery" has been categorized over time; see W.H. Goetzmann, *New Lands, New Men: America and the Second Great Age of Discovery* (New York: Viking, 1986). See, for example, Alan Williams, "A Newfoune Lande," *American History* 32 (1997), 16–20, 65–66. Williams discusses a number of matters, including John Day's letter to Columbus (published in 1956), Sebastian Cabot's lack of preservation of his father's memory (even a rivalry of son with father) as opposed to Las Casas's care in preserving Columbus's legacy, the rivalry in 1897 between Newfoundland and the Maritime provinces of Canada in claiming Cabot's landfall, the various accounts of John Cabot's death, the continued controversy over Cabot/Caboto. See Luca Codignola's informative review of Peter E. Pope's *The Many Landfalls of John Cabot* (Toronto: University of Toronto Press, 1997) in *The William and Mary Quarterly* 57 (2000), 660–62 that points out that Cabot became, among other things in the nineteenth century, a counterpoint of Canadian identity against the use of Columbus in the United States. See also Lucien Campeau, "Les Cabots et L'Amérique," *Revue d'Histoire de l'Amérique Française* 14 (1960), 317–52; Patrick McGrath, "Bristol and America, 1480–1631," *The Western Enterprise: English Activities in Ireland, the Atlantic, and America 1480–1650*, ed. K.R. Andrews et al. (Detroit: Wayne State University Press, 1979), 81–102; Peter Bosa, "Perche E Importante Conoscere La Nostra Storia: Giovanni Caboto," ["Why It Is Important To Know Our History: John Cabot"] *Veltro* 29 (1985), 47–51; John H. Gilcrist, "Cabotian Conjectures: Did a Cabot Reach Maine in 1498?" *American Neptune* 45 (1985), 249–52; K.E. Rowlands, "America Was Born in Bristol," *British Heritage* 10 (1989), 61–65; *Venezia e i Caboto*, ed. Rosella Mamoli-Zorzi and Ugo Tucci (Venice: Università degli studi di Venezia, 1992); Jiri Smrz, "Cabot 400: The 1897 St. John's Celebrations," *Newfoundland Studies* 12 (1996), 16–31; Brian Cuthbertson, "John Cabot and His Historians: Five Hundred Years of Controversy," *Journal of the Royal Nova Scotia Historical Society* (1998), 16–35; D.A. Muise, "Who Owns History Anyway? Reinventing Atlantic Canada for Pleasure and Profit," *Acadiensis* 27 (1998), 124–34; Glen Norcliffe, "John Cabot's Legacy in Newfoundland: Resource Depletion and the Resource Cycle," *Geography* 84 (1999), 97–109; On Portuguese voyages, see, for instance, Lucien Campeau, "Découvertes

Portugaises en Amérique du Nord," *Revue d'Histoire de l'Amérique Française* 20 (1966), 171–227 and for the connections in the North Atlantic (for example, the role of Columbus), see Marianne Mahn-Lot, "Colomb, Bristol, et l'Atlantique Nord," *Annales: Economies, Sociétés, Civilisations* 19 (1964), 522–30.

3   Recognizing Canadian Women and Women in Canada

1. Northrop Frye, "Haunted by Lack of Ghosts: Some Patterns in the Imagery of Canadian Poetry," *The Canadian Imagination: Dimensions of a Literary Culture*, ed. David Staines (Cambridge, MA: Harvard University Press, 1977), 27. For my own earlier discussion of works that made Canadian literature diverse and multicultural, see "Canadian Literature: in the Mouth of the Canon," *Journal of Canadian Studies* 23 (1988–89), 145–58. In these notes, I try to give some background, leads, and alternative routes to the brief discussions in the main text. An earlier and briefer version of this chapter appeared in "Seeing Double: Crossing Boundaries Here and There in Some Canadian Women Poets," *A World of Local Voices* (Germany: Königshausen & Neumann, 2003), 29–42.

2. Frye in Staines, *Canadian Imagination*, 37–38.

3. George Grant, *Technology and Empire* (Toronto: Anansi, 1969) and *The George Grant Reader*, ed. William Christian and Sheila Grant (Toronto: University of Toronto Press, 1998), 400.

4. Douglas LePan in *The New Oxford Book of Canadian Verse in English*, ed. Margaret Atwood (Toronto: Oxford University Press, 1982), 167–68. In his prose, LePan also had perspective views on the typology of European and Canadian mythology; see his "Some Observations on Myth and Legend: Irish and Canadian," *Proceedings & Transactions Royal Society of Canada* 17 (1979), 85–97. For more on LePan, see S.C. Hamilton, "European Emblem and Canadian Image: A Study of Douglas LePan's Poetry," *Mosaic: A Journal for the Interdisciplinary Study of Literature* 3 (1970), 62–73; J.M. Kertzer, "The Wounded Eye: The Poetry of Douglas LePan," *Studies in Canadian Literature/Etudes en Littérature Canadienne* 6 (1981), 5–23; Peter Stoicheff, "Douglas LePan," *Profiles in Canadian Literature, VI*, ed. Jeffrey M. Heath (Toronto: Dundurn, 1986), 9–16. Douglas LePan, Roberson Davies, and Timothy Findley were particularly supportive of my poetry written in youth, for which I was and am grateful as I remember them.

5. Robert, Kroetsch, "Introduction," Jonathan Hart, *Breath and Dust* (Melbourne: Mattoid/Grange; dist. Edmonton: University of Alberta Press, 2000), xi–xii. I am indebted to Robert Kroetsch, whose literary and critical work has been so suggestive in Canada and beyond. Much has been written about and by Kroetsch. As this chapter discusses home and exile, place and space, I concentrate on this aspect. Kroetsch edited a special issue in which he declares in the Introduction: "The United States is a space culture come to the edge of its space, noisily confronting time. Canada is as timeless as winter, a nightmarish dream of what might and cannot ever be. It is so much of a space culture it cannot afford a history; silence is the language of space" (1). The Canadian poet, for Kroetsch, turns in imagination to complicity, to failure, an uninvention of the world where failure and success are failure (1). See Robert Kroetsch, "A Canadian Issue," *Boundary* 2 (3) (Fall 1974), 1–3. As Mackenzie King intimated, Canada has too much geography and too little history. See Robert Kroetsch, "Occupying Landscape We Occupy Story We Occupy Landscape," *Refractions of Germany in Canadian Literature and Culture*, ed. Antor Heintz et al. (Berlin: de Gruyter, 2003), 23–29. See also Kroetsch's "The Fear of Women in Prairie Fiction: An Erotics of Space," in *Crossing Frontiers: Papers in American and Canadian Western Literature*, ed. Dick Harrison et al. (Edmonton: University of Alberta Press, 1979), 73–83; his "On Being an Alberta Writer: Or, I Wanted to Tell Our Story," *The New*

Provinces: Alberta and Saskatchewan, ed. Howard Palmer and Donald Smith (Vancouver: Tantalus Research, 1980), 217–27; and his Preface to *Gaining Ground: European Critics on Canadian Literature*, ed. Robert Kroetsch et al. (Edmonton: NeWest, 1985)—this collection contains an array of useful essays. For special issues on Kroetsch, see *Great Plains Quarterly* 14 (Summer 1994) and *New Quarterly: New Directions in Canadian Writing* 18 (Spring 1998). See Peter Thomas, "Keeping Mum: Kroetsch's 'Alberta,' " *Journal of Canadian Fiction* 2 (2) (1973), 54–56; John Moss, "Canadian Frontiers: Sexuality and Violence from Richardson to Kroetsch," *Journal of Canadian Fiction* 2 (3) (1973), 36–41; Rosemary Sullivan, "The Fascinating Place Between: The Fiction of Robert Kroetsch," *Mosaic* 11 (1978), 165–76; Peter Thomas, *Robert Kroetsch* (Vancouver: Douglas & McIntyre, 1980); Arnold E. Davidson, "History, Myth, and Time in Robert Kroetsch's *Badlands*," *Studies in Canadian Literature* 5 (1980), 127–37; Robert R. Wilson, "The Metamorphoses of Space: Magic Realism," *Magic Realism and Canadian Literature: Essays and Stories*, ed. Peter Hinchcliffe and Ed Jewinski (Waterloo, ON: University of Waterloo Press, 1986), 61–74; Georgiana M.M. Colvile, "On Coyote or Canadian Otherness in Robert Kroetsch's *Badlands* and George Bowering's *Caprice*," *Renaissance and Modern Studies* 35 (1992), 128–38; Dianne Tiefensee, *"The Old Dualities": Deconstructing Robert Kroetsch and His Critics* (Montreal: McGill-Queen's University Press, 1994); Richard Henry, "Identity Crises/Cries for Identity: Claiming the Canadian Prairie in the Novels of Robert Kroetsch," *World Literature Today* 73 (1999), 289–94; Justin D. Edwards, "Going Native in Robert Kroetsch's *Gone Indian*," *Studies in Canadian Literature* 26 (2001), 84–97; Simona Bertacco, *Out of Place: The Writings of Robert Kroetsch* (Bern: Peter Lang, 2002); Some related theses have been written on Kroetsch. The ones most relevant to our discussion are Robert Thomas Archambeau, "Wordsworth after Empire," Ph.D. dissertation, University of Notre Dame, 1995, which discusses the postimperial adaptation of Wordsworth in the framework of Robert Kroetsch, Derek Walcott, and Seamus Heaney. See Brian Ralph Swail, "Absolutely Fabulous: Fabulation in the Works of David Arnason, Robert Kroetsch, Tomson Highway and Thomas King," Ph.D. dissertation, University of Manitoba, 2003. Swail places Kroetsch in a context of European and Native Canadian writing, concentrating on Kroetsch's *What the Crow Said* in terms of postmodernism, magical realism, and mythologies in Canada.

6. Frederick J. Turner, *The Frontier in American History* (New York: Henry Holt, 1920), 2–3. See Northrop Frye's *The Bush Garden: Essays on the Canadian Imagination* (Toronto: Anansi, 1971) for an influential book on the tensions in the imagining and experience of the Canadian frontier.

7. Marshall McLuhan, "Canada: The Borderline Case," in Staines, *Canadian Imagination*, 247. McLuhan's borderlands provide a suggestive perspective that complements that of Turner and Frye.

8. For instance, see Jonathan Hart, *Theater and World: The Problematics of Shakespeare's History* (Boston: Northeastern University Press, 1992).

9. Jan Zwicky, *Lyric Philosophy* (Toronto: University of Toronto Press, 1992), 8. On Zwicky, see John Harris, "Scaffoldings of Weary Words: Jan Zwicky's *Wittgenstein Elegies*," *Essays on Canadian Writing* 37 (1989), 65–68.

10. See Gaston Bachelard, *The Poetics of Space*, trans. Maria Jolas (Boston: Beacon Press, 1969).

11. Margaret Atwood, *Survival* (Toronto: Anansi, 1972), 32.

12. Tuu'luq in *An Anthology of Native Canadian Literature in English*, second ed., ed. Daniel David Moses and Terry Goldie (Toronto: Oxford University Press, 1998), 75.

13. Hayman in *The New Oxford Book of Canadian Verse in English*, ed. Margaret Atwood (Toronto: Oxford University Press, 1982), 1.

14. Robert Giroux, Introduction in Elizabeth Bishop, *The Collected Prose*, ed. Robert Giroux (London: Chatto & Windus, The Hogarth Press, 1984), ix.

15. Giroux, *The Collected Prose*, x.

16. "Wading at Wellfleet" and "Cape Breton," in Elizabeth Bishop, *The Collected Poems 1927–1979* (London: Hogarth Press, 1984), 7 and 67 respectively.

17. Bishop, *Poems*, 203. For a discussion of Bishop's sexuality, which also includes some discussion of her early years in Nova Scotia after being removed from the United States at the age of one,

NOTES TO PAGES 94–96

see David R. Jarraway, " 'O Canada!': The Spectral Lesbian Poetics of Elizabeth Bishop," *PMLA* 113 (1998), 243–57. See also Howard Moss's article on Bishop—"The Canada–Brazil Connection," *World Literature Today* 51 (1977), 29–33.

18. Bishop, *Poems*, 125–26.

19. Bishop, *Poems* 69. On Bishop and Nova Scotia (most recent first), Steven Gould Axelrod, "Elizabeth Bishop: Nova Scotia in Brazil," *Papers on Language and Literature* 37 (2001), 279–95; Brian Robinson, "Bridging a Divided Place," *Divisions of the Heart: Elizabeth Bishop and the Art of Memory and Place*, ed. Sandra Barry, Gwendolyn Davies, and Peter Sanger (Wolfville, NS: Gaspereau, 2001), 77–90; Peter Sanger, "Elizabeth Bishop's Village," *The Antigonish Review* 91 (1992), 63–80; Alfred Corn, "In Great Village," *Grand Street* 8 (1989), 126–36; Martha Carlson-Bradley, "Lowell's 'My Last Afternoon with Uncle Devereux Winslow': The Model for Bishop's 'First Death in Nova Scotia,' " *Concerning Poetry* 19 (1986), 117–31; Peter Sanger, "Elizabeth Bishop and Nova Scotia," *The Antigonish Review* 60 (1985), 15–27; Alberta Turner, " 'First Death in Nova Scotia,' " *Field: Contemporary Poetry and Poetics* 31 (1984), 42–43.

20. Bishop, *Prose*, 250.

21. Bandeira, in *An Anthology of Twentieth-Century Brazilian Poetry*, ed. Elizabeth Bishop and Emanuel Brasil (Middletown, CT: Wesleyan University Press, 1972), 3.

22. Line 35, Cottnam in *Canadian Poetry: From the Beginnings through the First World War*, ed. Carole Gerson and Gwendolyn Davies (Toronto: McClelland & Stewart, 1994), 33. For more on Cottnam, see Gwendolyn Davies, "Researching Eighteenth-Century Maritime Writers: Deborah How Cottnam—A Case Study," *Working in Women's Archives: Researching Women's Private Literature and Archival Documents*, ed. Helen M. Buss and Marlene Kadar (Waterloo, ON: Wilfrid Laurier University Press, 2001), 35–50. See Janice Dickin's review of this collection in *Biography* 25 (2002), 513–18. Dickin mentions Davies's archival work looking through the silence to find material on Cottnam (516).The Government of Canada has excavated the How Property on Grassy Island, Nova Scotia, which belonged to Deborah's father, Edward How, and her mother, Deborah Cawley How (see collections.ic.gc.ca).

23. Bishop, *Prose*, 8.

24. Rita Joe, in Moses and Goldie, *Anthology*, 113. See Rita Joe, "The Gentle War," *Canadian Woman Studies* 10 (1989), 27–29.

25. Crawford, in Atwood, *Canadian Verse*, 20.

26. Johnson, in Atwood, *Canadian Verse*, 58–59.

27. Pickthall, in Atwood, *Canadian Verse*, 82. For more on Marjorie Pickthall, see Henry Kriesel, " 'Has Anyone Here Heard of Marjorie Pickthall?' Discovering the Canadian Literary Landscape," *Canadian Literature* 100 (1984), 173–80; Janice Williamson, "Framed by History: Marjorie Pickthall's Devices and Desire," *A Mazing Space: Writing Canadian Women Writing*, ed. Shirley Neuman and Smaro Kamboureli (Edmonton: Longspoon, 1986), 167–78; Alex Kizuk, "The Case of the Forgotten Electra: Pickthall's Apostrophes and Feminine Poetics," *Studies in Canadian Literature/Etudes en Litterature Canadienne* 12 (1987), 15–34; Diana Relke's "Demeter's Daughter: Marjorie Pickthall & the Quest for Poetic Identity," *Canadian Literature* 115 (1987), 28–43 and her Ph.D. dissertation (1988) (see note about Livesay); Sandra Campbell, " 'A Girl in a Book': Writing Marjorie Pickthall and Lorne Pierce," *Canadian Poetry* 39 (1996), 80–95; Anne Compton, "A 'Little World' in Decadence: Marjorie Pickthall's Poems on Nature and on Religion," *Canadian Poetry* 43 (1998), 10–43; Patricia L. Badir, " 'So Entirely Unexpected': The Modernist Dramaturgy of Marjorie Pickthall's The Wood Carver's Wife," *Modern Drama* 43 (2000), 216–45; Misao Dean, "Making Canada's 'Literary Land Claim': Marjorie Pickthall's 'The Third Generation'," *Journal of Canadian Studies/Revue d'Etudes Canadiennes* 36 (2001), 24–34.

28. Jean de Léry, *History of a Voyage to the Land of Brazil*, trans. Janet Whatley (Berkeley: University of California Press, 1990), 132, see 246n14.

29. On Native women's literature in Canada, see, for example, Barbara Godard, *Talking about Ourselves: The Literary Productions of the Native Women of Canada* (Ottawa: Canadian Research

Institute for Advancement of Women/Institute Canadien de Recherches sur la Femme, 1985); *Writing the Circle: Native Women of Western Canada*, ed. Jeanne Perreault (Norman: University of Oklahoma Press, 1993); Sylvia Bowerbank, "Literature and Criticism by Native and Métis Women in Canada," *Feminist Studies* 20 (1994), 565–81; Helen Hoy, *How Should I Read These? Native Women Writers in Canada* (Toronto: University of Toronto Press, 2001); On Native language, literature, arts, and culture, see Eung-Do Cook, *Linguistic Studies of Native Canada* (Vancouver: University of British Columbia Press, 1978); Penny Petrone, *Native Literature in Canada: From the Oral Tradition to the Present* (Toronto: Oxford University Press, 1990); M. Dale Kinkade, "The Decline of Native Languages in Canada," *Endangered Languages*, ed. Robert H. Robins and Eugenius M. Uhlenbeck (Oxford: Berg, 1991), 157–76; Ann Marie Plane, "Childbirth Practices among Native American Women of New England and Canada, 1600–1800," *Medicine and Healing*, ed. Peter Benes (Boston: Boston University Press, 1992), 13–24; E.F. Koerner, "Panel Discussion on 'The History of the Study of the Native Languages of Canada,' " *Actes du XVe Congrès International des Linguistes, Québec, Université Laval, 9–14 août 1992: Les Langues menacées/Endangered Languages: Proceedings of the XVth International Congress of Linguists, Québec, Université Laval, 9–14 August 1992*, ed. André Crochetière et al. (Sainte-Foy: Presses Univérsités de Laval, 1993), I:213–18; Guy Lavallée, ed., "Indian/Native Studies in Canada 1980–1992: A Bibliographical Essay," *Third National Conference on the State of Canadian Bibliography: Achievements, Challenges and Opportunities/Troisième Conférence nationale sur la bibliographie canadienne: Réalisations, défis, perspectives*, ed. Erik L. Swanick (Toronto: Bibliographical Society of Canada, 1994), 329–72; Hartmut Lutz, "Contemporary Native Literature in Canada and 'The Voice of the Mother,' " *O Canada: Essays on Canadian Literature and Culture*, ed. Jørn Carlesen and Tim Caudery (Aarhus, Denmark: Aarhus University Press, 1995), 79–96; Albert-Reiner Glaap, "Margo Kane, Daniel David Moses, Yvette Nolan, Drew Hayden Taylor: Four Native Playwrights from Canada," *Anglistik: Mitteilungen des Verbandes deutscher Anglisten* 7 (1996), 5–25; Michael Patterson, "Native Music in Canada—The Age of the Seventh Fire," *Australian–Canadian Studies: A Journal for the Humanities & Social Sciences* 14 (1996), 41–54; Coomi S. Vevaina, "Articulating a Different Way of Being: The Resurgence of the Native Voice in Canada," *Intersexions: Issues of Race and Gender in Canadian Women's Writing*, ed. Coomi S. Vevaina and Barbara Godard (New Delhi: Creative, 1996), 55–73; *Native and Christian: Indigenous Voices on Religious Identity in the United States and Canada*, ed. James Treat (New York: Routledge, 1996); Robert M. Nelson, "A Guide to Native American Studies Programs in the United States and Canada," *Studies in American Indian Literatures* 9 (1997), 49–105; Drew Hayden Taylor, "Storytelling to Stage: The Growth of Native Theatre in Canada," *TDR: The Drama Review* 41 (1997), 140–52; Shirley E. Crawford, "The Educational Value of Understanding a Culture: Selected Stories from the Native People of Western Canada," Ph.D. dissertation, Brigham Young University, 1998; Shona Taner, "The Evolution of Native Studies in Canada: Descending from the Ivory Tower," *Canadian Journal of Native Studies* 19 (1999), 289–319; Stephanie May McKenzie, "Canada's Day of Atonement: The Contemporary Native Literary Renaissance, the Native Cultural Renaissance and Post-Centenary Mythology," Ph.D. dissertation, University of Toronto, 2001; Michael J. Witgen, "An Infinity of Nations: How Indians, Empires, and Western Migration Shaped National United in North America," Ph.D. Dissertation, University of Washington, 2004. Crawford begins her study by drawing on the poetry of Dan George and Rita Joe and sets out to examine Native stories for their children past and present as a means to better education (3–5). One of the problems Crawford, who is writing in the wake of The Royal Commission on Aboriginal People (1991), sees is that non-Natives, including those who teach Natives, in Western Canada have been unaware of the Native story tradition and notes that the Alberta Teachers' Association will add her work to their resource library (8, 10). A complication is that Native language groups in Western Canada straddle borders from Alaska to Mexico, so the notion of Canadian, she implies, is national and serves as a delimitation but not something that contains language and culture (10). McKenzie focuses on myth as a means of looking at Native culture and how difficult it is to separate myth and history in any culture. She sets out to examine how some key Canadian writers of European descent, such as Leonard Cohen, Robert Kroetsch, and Margaret Atwood, searched "for a sacred historical writing" and traces the search for a national mythology, including Northrop Frye's work in the 1950s; she maintains that it was Natives who gave Canadian literature the moment Canada needed about its centennial that Archibald Lampman and others were seeking generations before (7–16). Witgen discusses claims of Canada and the United States to the West in the context of "This fact, this fiction of European and Euro-American possession" and speaks of the western interior of North America even in 1803 as "an indigenous space" (3). He argues for an understanding of the changes in the West according to indigenous points of view as "un-bordered" (3). As with Bishop, who lived in Nova Scotia and was partly of Canadian ancestry, the boundaries of being Canadian and in Canada also apply to Native writers, men and women.

30. Johnson, in Moses and Goldie, *Anthology*, 30. For more on and by Pauline Johnson, see Lucie K. Hartley, *Pauline Johnson* (Minneapolis: Dillon, 1978); George W. Lyon, "Pauline Johnson: A Reconsideration," *Studies in Canadian Literature/Etudes en Littérature Canadienne* 15 (1990), 136–59; A. LaVonne Brown Ruoff, "Justice for Indians and Women: The Protest Fiction of Alice Callahan and Pauline Johnson," *World Literature Today* 66 (1992), 249–55; Roseanne Hoefel, "Writing, Performance, Activism: Zitkala-Sa and Pauline Johnson," *Native American Women in Literature and Culture*, ed. Susan Castillo and Victor M.P. Da Rosa (Porto: Fernando Pessoa University Press, 1997), 107–18; Carole Gerson, " 'The Most Canadian of All Canadian Poets': Pauline Johnson and the Construction of a National Literature," *Canadian Literature* 158 (1998), 90–107; Mary Elizabeth Leighton, "Performing Pauline Johnson: Representations of 'the Indian Poetess' in the Periodical Press, 1892–95," *Essays on Canadian Writing* 65 (1998), 141–64; A. LaVonne Brown Ruoff, "Early Native American Women Authors: Jane Johnston Schoolcraft, Sarah Winnemucca, S. Alice Callahan, E. Pauline Johnson, and Zitkala-Sa," *Nineteenth-Century American Women Writers: A Critical Reader*, ed. Karen L. Kilcup (Malden, MA: Blackwell, 1998), 81–111; Veronica Strong-Boag, *Paddling Her Own Canoe: The Times and Texts of E. Pauline Johnson (Tekahionwake)* (Toronto, ON: University of Toronto Press, 2000); Anne Collett, "E. Pauline Johnson Tekahionwake: Mistress of Her Craft (1861–1913)," *Kunapipi: Journal of Post-Colonial Writing* 23 (2001), 130–33 and her "Red and White: Miss E. Pauline Johnson Tekahionwake and the Other Woman," *Women's Writing* 8 (2001), 359–73; Deena Rymhs, "But the Shadow of Her Story: Narrative Unsettlement, Self-Inscription, and Translation in Pauline Johnson's Legends of Vancouver," *Studies in American Indian Literatures: The Journal of the Association for the Study of American Indian Literatures* 13 (2001), 51–78; E. Pauline Johnson, *Tekahionwake: Collected Poems and Selected Prose*, ed. Carole Gerson (Toronto: University of Toronto Press, 2002); Lorraine York, " 'Your Star': Pauline Johnson and the Tensions of Celebrity Discourse," *Canadian Poetry* 51 (2002), 8–17; Carole Gerson, "Recuperating from Modernism: Pauline Johnson's Challenge to Literary History," *Women and Literary History: 'For There She Was,'* ed. Katherine Binhammer et al. (Newark: University of Delaware Press, 2003), 167–86; Sabine Milz, " 'Publica(c)tion': E. Pauline Johnson's Publishing Venues and Their Contemporary Significance," *Studies in Canadian Literature/Etudes en Littérature Canadienne* 29 (2004), 127–45. The M.A. and Ph.D. theses on Johnson show how transnational and how border-crossing Native Studies is; see Marilyn Beker, "Pauline Johnson: a Biographical, Thematic and Stylistic Study," M.A. thesis, Concordia University (Montreal), 1974; Mary Ann Stout, "Early Native American Women Writers: Pauline Johnson, Zitkala-Sa, Mourning Dove," M.A. thesis, The University of Arizona, 1992; Elizabeth Ann Grant, "Hearing the Page: Teaching the Sound of Oral Traditions in Native American Written Texts," M.A. dissertation, St. John's University (New York), 1996; Christine Lowella Marshall, "The Re-Presented Indian: Pauline Johnson's 'Strong Race Opinion' and Other Forgotten Discourses," Ph.D. dissertation, University of Arizona, 1997; Rachel Annie Kirschke Cole, "Assimilation Process as Seen through Native American Literature," M.A. thesis, University of Houston-Clear Lake, 1998; Erika E. Aigner-Varoz, "Suiting

Herself: E. Pauline Johnson's Constructions of Indian Identity and Self," Ph.D. dissertation, University of New Mexico, 2001; Cari Michelle Carpenter, "Seeing Red: Anger, Femininity, and the American Indian of Nineteenth-Century Sentimental Literature," Ph.D. dissertation, University of Michigan, 2002; Mishuana R. Goeman, "Unconquered Nations, Unconquered Women: Native Women (Re)mapping Race, Gender, and Nation," Ph.D. dissertation, Stanford University, 2003; Florence Ida Enns, "Photographing Pauline Johnson: Publicity Portraits of a Canadian 'Half Blood' Identity," M.A. thesis, University of Alberta, 2004; John Power, "First Impressions: Reconstructing Language and Identity in Pauline Johnson's 'The Cattle Thief,' Jeannette Armstrong's 'Indian Woman,' and Beth Cuthand's 'Post-Oka Kinda Woman,' " M.A. thesis, Lakehead University, 2004. Stout discusses Johnson and two other key Native women writers at the turn of the twentieth century as presaging later writing by Native women. Grant sees Johnson as part of a small canon of Native literature before what Kenneth Lincoln called, in 1983, a "Native American Renaissance." Marshall observes that Johnson, the daughter of a Mohawk chief, George Johnson (a friend of Alexander Graham Bell), and an English emigrant (Emily Howells and a cousin of the American author William Dean Howells), was exposed to Shakespeare and English literature as well as Mohawk stories, argues that she is a serious writer who disrupted colonial discourses while she was being co-opted, and lends the reminder that she was the only Native writer to earn a living from writing alone. These studies emphasize aspects of Johnson in terms of her gender, Native heritage, and political context. Moreover, Marshall says that Johnson does not receive notice, even finds erasure, in contemporary studies of Native American and Native Canadian literature, not to mention in more general studies such as Clara Thomas's, *All My Sisters: Essays on the Work of Canadian Women Writers*. Whereas Atwood does not mention Johnson's achievement, Paula Gunn Allen diminishes her (Marshall, "Pauline Johnson," 11–12). Johnson was successful as a writer who did not need any ethnographer to interpret her, although she found herself contending with stereotypes of Natives (15–16). Marshall also shows how in matrilineal Iroquois society Johnson was not considered Mohawk, but how the regulations of Canadian government did designate her Mohawk (20). She and her siblings know Mohawk (22). For more on Johnson's life, see Marcus Van Steen's *Pauline Johnson: Her Life and Work Through Native literature* (works including those of Johnson), Cole traces assimilation of Natives (see Cole, "Assimilation," 3). See also Gretchen Bataille and Kathleen Mullen Sands, *American Indian Women: Telling Their Lives*. Cole cites as an example a story from Johnson's *The Moccasin Maker* (1913), which Gunn selected in *Spider Woman's Granddaughters* (20–21). Aigner-Varoz discusses how, as a writer and an entertainer, Johnson constructed her constructions of identity in her mixed background and in the face of stereotypes and observes: "Johnson's voice was most divided in her non-fiction due to conflicting rhetorical tensions: her need to secure an income, hence a friendly audience for her articles, as well as to communicate the 'truth' about who Indians were and how they lived on Indian Reserves" (1). According to Aigner-Varoz, slave narratives and Native writing of the nineteenth century had to incorporate Eurocentric views in order to be heard (3). See also Gerald Vizenor's *Manifest Manners*, 152. In a letter to Charles Mair, Johnson denied that she got her literary gifts from her mother's side and expressed pride in her Native heritage (6). Religion, language, class, and mixed ancestry all affected the tension between self and literary identity for Johnson. Carpenter examines Johnson and S. Alice Callahan and Sarah Winnemucca in relation to Anglo-American writers such as Lydia Maria Child, Maria Susanna Cummins, and Ann Stephens in terms of how does a Native woman, given racial and gender stereotypes in the nineteenth century, express protest and anger. She also relates this obstacle— expressing protest in sentimental literature in terms of Anglo-American and African American contexts (Carpenter, "Seeing Red," 9–15). Goeman grounds her discussion of gender, nation, and Native women in terms of E. Pauline Johnson's (1861–1913) idea of space and intersection. In chapter 2, Goeman discusses Johnson in tems of race, gender, and nation because of her roles as activist, performer, and writer and because she has been neglected owing to an oversimplified view of assimilation (see also 13). Enns argues that Johnson used a dual image in her publicity photographs, both aspects of her mixed background, to transgress racist stereotypes and boundaries (see Enns, "Publicity Portraits," 1–4). Power maintains that language is a means for Native women to reclaim and construct their identities. In chapter two, he discusses Johnson as a controversial figure in this process. See also Betty Keller, *Pauline Johnson: First Aboriginal Voice of Canada* and Charlotte Gray's *The Life and Times of E. Pauline Johnson, Tekahionwake* (see Power, "First Impressions," 2–3, 14–15).

31. Sainte-Marie, in Moses and Goldie, *Anthology*, 517. Buffy Sainte-Marie, born in Saskatchewan, adopted and brought up in Maine and Massachusetts, now living in Hawaii, is a well-known figure who is readily found on the web. She is involved in educational projects in Canada and the United States and is a great supporter of Native causes. See, for instance, Bruce Weir, "Achievement Honored," *Saskatchewan Sage: Saskatchewan's Aboriginal News Publication* (April 1998), 7. It can also be found at www.sicc.sk.ca/faces/wsainbu.htm.

32. Sainte-Marie, in Moses and Goldie, *Anthology*, 175.

33. Sainte-Marie, in Moses and Goldie, *Anthology*, 176, see 175.

34. Sainte-Marie, in Moses and Goldie, *Anthology*, 177–78.

35. Armstrong, in Moses and Goldie, *Anthology*, 227, see 226. On Armstrong, see Stephen Morton, "First Nations Women's Writing and Anti-Racist Work in Institutional Locations: A Feminist Reading of Lee Maracle and Jeanette Armstrong," *Thamyris: Mythmaking from Past to Present* 6 (1999), 3–33; Manina Jones, "Slash Marks the Spot: 'Critical Embarrassment' and Activist Aesthetics in Jeanette Armstrong's *Slash*," *West Coast Line* 33 (2000), 48–62.

36. Armstrong, in Moses and Goldie, *Anthology*, 229.

37. Armstrong, in Moses and Goldie, *Anthology*, 230, see 229.

38. Armstrong, in Moses and Goldie, *Anthology*, 230. On early Native-European encounters, see Jonathan Hart, *Columbus, Shakespeare, and the Interpretation of the New World* (New York and London: Palgrave Macmillan, 2003).

39. Best, in *Fire on the Water: An Anthology of Black Nova Scotian Writing. Volume 1. Early and Modern Writers 1785–1935*, ed. George Elliott Clarke (Lawrencetown Beach, Nova Scotia: Pottersfield Press, 1991), 118. On Best, see Constance Backhouse, "'I Was Unable to Identify with Topsy': Carrie M. Best's Struggle against Racial Segregation in Nova Scotia, 1942," *Atlantis: A Women's Studies Journal/Revue d'Etudes sur la Femme* 22 (1998), 16–26. For a recent special issue, see *Black Writing in Canada, Canadian Literature* 182 (2004). And the editorial by Laura Moss. On the racism and sexism Black women suffered, see Suzanne Morton, "Separate Spheres in a Separate World: African Nova-Scotian Women in the Late-19th-Century Halifax County," *Acadiensis* 22 (1993), 61–83. Bernice Moreau discusses discrimination and hardship in the first half of the twentieth century in "Black Nova Scotian Women's Experience of Educational Violence in the early 1900s: A Case of Colour Contusion," *Dalhousie Review* 77 (1997), 179–206; see also her "Black Nova Scotian Women's Educational Experience, 1900–1945: A Study in Race, Gender and Class relations," Ph.D. dissertation, University of Toronto, 1996. The case of Québec is also informative; see, for instance, Vivien Dûchaine, "Les Femmes Haïtiennes au Québec," *Resources for Feminist Research* 15 (1986–87), 10–12, which includes the argument that Western feminism also excludes these women from Haiti and not simply racism and sexism. For other relevant work on African Canadian writing (from the most recent), see Robin Breron, "Black Theatre Canada: A Short History," *Canadian Theatre Review* 118 (2004), 25–28; Diana Brydon, "Detour Canada: Rerouting the Black Atlantic, Reconfiguring the Postcolonial," *Reconfigurations: Canadian Literatures and Postcolonial Identities/Littératures canadiennes et identités postcoloniales*, ed. Marc Maufort and Franca Bellarsi (Brussels: Peter Lang, 2002), 109–22 and her "Black Canadas: Rethinking Canadian and Diasporic Cultural Studies," *Revista Canaria de Estudios Ingleses* 43 (2001), 101–17; George H. Junne, Jr., *Blacks in the American West and Beyond-America, Canada, and Mexico* (Westport, CT: Greenwood; 2000); Gamal Abdel-Shehid, "'Who Got Next?': Raptor Morality and Black Public Masculinity in Canada," *Pop Can: Popular Culture in Canada*, ed. Priscilla L. Walton, and Lynne Van Luven (Scarborough, ON: Prentice Hall Allyn and Bacon Canada, 1999), 128–39;

Stephen Johnson, "Uncle Tom and the Minstrels: Seeing Black and White on Stage in Canada West Prior to the American Civil War," *Post-Colonial Stages: Critical and Creative Views on Drama, Theatre and Performance*, ed. Helen Gilbert (London: Dangaroo, 1999), 55–63; Rinaldo Walcott, " 'A Tough Geography': Towards a Poetics of Black Space(s) in Canada," *West Coast Line* 22 (1997), 38–51; Shirley J. Yee, "Finding a Place: Mary Ann Shadd Cary and the Dilemmas of Black Migration to Canada, 1850–1870," *Frontiers: A Journal of Women Studies* 18 (1997), 1–16; George Elliott Clarke, "Must All Blackness Be American?: Locating Canada in Borden's 'Tightrope Time,' or Nationalizing Gilroy's The Black Atlantic," *Canadian Ethnic Studies/Etudes Ethniques au Canada* 28 (1996), 56–71; Barbara Godard, "Writing Resistance: Black Women's Writing in Canada," *Intersexions: Issues of Race and Gender in Canadian Women's Writing*, ed. Coomi S. Vevaina and Barbara Godard (New Delhi: Creative, 1996), 106–15; Angela Lee, "Black Theatre in Canada/African Canadian Theatre," *Canadian Theatre Review* 18 (1995), 1–51; Lorris Elliott, "Black Writing in Canada: The Problems of Anthologizing and Documenting," *Canadian Review of Comparative Literature/Revue Canadienne de Littérature Comparée* 16 (1989), 721–27; Robin Breon, "The Growth and Development of Black Theatre in Canada: A Starting Point," *Theatre History in Canada/Histoire du Théâtre au Canada* 9 (1988), 216–28. For a historiographical survey, see Afua Cooper, "Constructing Black Women's Historical Knowledge," *Atlantis* 25 (2000), 39–50. Some M.A. and Ph.D. theses in the past twenty-five years have discussed Black women writers in Canada. For a discussion of the oppression of Black women in Canada and the United States owing to class, race, and gender, see Jacinth Samuels, "The Sound of Silence: Racism in Contemporary Feminist Theory," M.A. thesis, University of Windsor, 1991. For an analysis of Black women journalists, including an examination of Henry Bibb (*Voice of the Fugitive in Canada*) and Mary Ann Shadd Cary, who was married to Bibb and who published her own newspaper in Canada, *The Provincial Freeman*, see Bernell Elizabeth Tripp, "Black Women Journalists, 1825–1860," Ph.D. dissertation, University of Alabama, 1993. Tripp says, "To avoid the constant struggle for equal rights and the poor treatment at the hands of a seemingly unheeding society, many blacks left the country [U.S.] to start or join colonies in such places as Canada, Africa, and Haiti" (2). Another dissertation that includes a discussion of Mary Ann Shadd Cary (1823–93) is Nora Darlene Hall, "On Being and African-American Woman: Gender and Race in the Writings of Six Black Women Journalists, 1849–1936," Ph.D. dissertation, University of Minnesota, 1998. Hall examines the writings of these journalists in 91 periodicals in Canada, England, and the United States. Ann Marie Mann Simpkins also analyzes the work of Shadd (Cary), but does so in terms of rhetoric—in comparison with Mary E. Miles (Bibb); see her "The Professional Writing Practices and Dialogic Rhetoric of Two Black Women Publishers: Discourse as Social Action in the Nineteenth Century," Ph.D. dissertation, Purdue University, 1999. See also Adriane Eartha Lenora Dorrington, "Nova Scotia Black Female Educators: Lessons from the Past," Ph.D. dissertation, University of Toronto, 1995. For an extended and further discussion of Shadd (Shadd Cary), teacher, abolitionist, and the first female Black newspaper editor in North America, see Avonie Brown, "Links and Lineage: The Life and Work of Mary Ann Shadd in Media, a Black Feminist Analysis," M.A. thesis, University of Windsor, 1996. For a historical context for François Malepart de Beaucourt's "Portrait of a Negro Slave" (1786), also known as "*La Negresse*," one of Canada's best-known historical paintings, see Terry M.T. Provost, "The Shadow of a Nation: Remembering the Black Woman in the Nomadic Picture," M.A. thesis, Concordia University (Montreal), 1998.

40. Dionne Brand, *No Language Is Neutral* (Toronto: Coach House Press, 1990), 15. For a wide discussion that includes, in chapter four, an examination of Brand's *No Language Is Neutral* (1990), see Gabrielle Civil, "From Body to Nation, Black Women's Poetry in the United States, Haiti, and Canada," Ph.D. dissertation, New York University, 2000. Drawing on Antonio Gramsci's idea of the organic intellectual, Brendan John Wild discusses Brand in the context of the social, economic, and political constraints on Black Women in Canada; see his "Overhearing Dionne Brand: Genre and the Organic Intellectual Project," Ph.D. dissertation, University of Alberta,

2003. For more on Brand in context, for example, see Lynette Hunter, "After Modernism: Alternative Voices in the Writings of Dionne Brand, Claire Harris, and Marlene Philip," *University of Toronto Quarterly* 62 (1992–93), 256–81.

41. Brand, *No Language*, 28.

42. Dionne Brand, *In Another Place, Not Here* (1996; London: The Women's Press Ltd, 1997), 180.

43. Brand, *Another Place*, 189.

44. Brand, *Another Place*, 230. For some of the work on Brand in the past five years or so (most recent first), see Joanne Saul, "In the Middle of Becoming': Dionne Brand's Historical Vision," *Canadian Woman Studies/Les Cahiers de la Femme* 23 (2004), 59–63; Marlene Goldman, "Mapping the Door of No Return: Deterritorialization and the Work of Dionne Brand," *Canadian Literature* 182 (2004), 13–28; Erica L. Johnson, "Unforgetting Trauma: Dionne Brand's Haunted Histories," *Anthurium: A Caribbean Studies Journal* 2 (2004); Marie Carrière, "L'Errance identitaire dans les textes migrants du Québec et du Canada anglais," *Etudes Canadiennes/Canadian Studies: Revue Interdisciplinaire des Etudes Canadiennes en France* 54 (2003), 93–103; Johanna X.K. Garvey, " 'The Place She Miss': Exile, Memory, and Resistance in Dionne Brand's Fiction," *Callaloo: A Journal of African-American and African Arts and Letters* 26 (2003), 486–503; Joanna Luft, "Elizete and Verlia Go to Toronto: Caribbean Immigrant Sensibilities at 'Home' and Overseas in Dionne Brand's In *Another Place, Not Here*," *Essays on Canadian Writing* 77 (2002), 26–49; Maria Caridad Casas, "Orality and the Body in the Poetry of Lillian Allen and Dionne Brand: Towards an Embodied Social Semiotics," *ARIEL* 33 (2002), 7–32; Christian Olbey, "Dionne Brand in Conversation," *ARIEL* 33 (2002), 87–102; Sophia Forster, " 'Inventory Is Useless Now but Just to Say': The Politics of Ambivalence in Dionne Brand's *Land to Light On*," *Studies in Canadian Literature/Etudes en Littérature Canadienne* 27 (2002), 160–82; George Elliott Clarke, " Harris, Philip, Brand: Three Authors in Search of Literate Criticism," *Journal of Canadian Studies/Revue d'Etudes Canadiennes* 35 (2000), 161–89; Dina Georgis, "Mother Nations and the Persistence of 'Not Here,' " *Canadian Woman Studies/Les Cahiers de la Femme* 20 (2000), 27–34; Margaret Ellen Quigley, "Desiring Intersubjects: Lesbian Poststructuralism in Writing by Nicole Brossard, Daphne Marlatt, and Dionne Brand," Ph.D. dissertation, University of Alberta, 2000; Rinaldo Walcott, "At the Full and Change of CanLit: An Interview with Dionne Brand," *Canadian Woman Studies/Les Cahiers de la Femme* 20 (2000), 22–26; Jason Wiens, " 'Language Seemed to Split in Two': National Ambivalence(s) and Dionne Brand's 'No Language Is Neutral,' " *Essays on Canadian Writing* 70 (2000), 81–102; Pamela McCallum, "Written in the Scars: History, Genre, and Materiality in Dionne Brand's *In Another Place, Not Here*," *Essays on Canadian Writing* 68 (1999), 159–82.

45. *Archive for Our Times: Previously Uncollected and Unpublished Poems of Dorothy Livesay*, ed. Dean J. Irvine (Vancouver: Arsenal Pulp Press, 1998). Dorothy Livesay (1909–96) has been the subject of much work, including M.A. and Ph.D. theses, some of which I mention here. During the 1970s, Susan Jane Wood wrote a general study—"The Poetry of Dorothy Livesay, (1928–1975)," M.A. thesis, Concordia University (Montreal), 1978. Exploring Livesay's public and private worlds, from imagism to feminism, Sandra Lynn Hutchinson produced "Form and Vision in the Poetry of Dorothy Livesay, 1919–1984," Ph.D. dissertation, University of Toronto, 1986. Hutchinson calls attention to how Livesay reinvents herself and how she espouses a poetics that expands beyond lyricism, is a poetry of life, and an explorer of forms that follow feeling (1–6) and evokes land and city scapes (7–8). Diana Mary Amelia Relke traces the changes in the self-concept of female poets, including Livesay, and the attempted reconciliation of the relation between the woman and the poet; see Relke's "Canadian Women Poets and Poetic Identity: A Study of Marjorie Pickthall, Constance Lindsay Skinner, and the Early Work of Dorothy Livesay," Ph.D. dissertation, Simon Fraser University, 1986. For a related article, see Diana M.A. Relke, "The Task of Poetic Mediation: Dorothy Livesay's Early Poetry," *ARIEL* 17 (1986), 17–36. For a discussion of Livesay's expression of love, see Nadine McInnis, "Dorothy Livesay's Poetics of Desire," M.A. thesis, University of Ottawa, 1992. In a wider

context of the United States and Canada, Caren Ellen Irr discusses Livesay's combining of lyric and documentary; see Irr, "The Suburb of Dissent: Cultural Politics in the United States and Canada during the 1930s," Ph.D. dissertation, Duke University, 1994. Another study, by Duane William McDougall, takes up Livesay's essay of 1969 on the documentary poem as a Canadian genre; see his "Reconstruction and Revisionism: A Genre Study of Documentary Long Poems in Canadian Literature in English, 1789–1974," University of New Brunswick, 1995. On the relation of female subjectivity to modernist poetry, see Laura Jane McLauchlan, "Transforming Poetics: Refiguring the Female Subject in the Early Poetry and Life Writing of Dorothy Livesay and Miriam Waddington," Ph.D. dissertation, York University (Toronto), 1997. She discusses interesting parallels between Livesay and Waddington (both born in Winnipeg, studied literature and social work at University of Toronto) and mentions Livesay's mother, Florence, who was also a poet (8, see 1–7). Making use of Pierre Bourdieu's cultural theories (as well as the work of theorists such as Stuart Hall and Jennifer Slack), Peggy L. Kelly discusses how Madge Macbeth and Livesay came to terms with the masculine assumptions of literary politics in their time. Kelly also notes that nature is one of the themes of Livesay's corpus, her living in various regions of Canada and in different countries, and her talent in languages; see Kelly, "A Materialist Feminist Analysis of Dorothy Livesay, Madge Macbeth, and the Canadian Literary Field, 1920–1950," Ph.D. dissertation, University of Alberta, 1999, 1–2, 10–11. For connected work, see Peggy Kelly, "Politics, Gender, and New Provinces: Dorothy Livesay and F.R. Scott," *Canadian Poetry* 53 (2003), 54–70. On Livesay, others, and the context of literary production and poets as editors, see Dean Jay Irvine, "Little Histories: Modernist and Leftist Women Poets and Magazine Editors in Canada," Ph.D. dissertation, McGill University, 2001, esp. 3, 34–120. For related work, see Irvine's "Among Masses: Dorothy Livesay and English Canadian Leftist Magazine Culture of the Early 1930s," *Essays on Canadian Writing* 68 (1999), 183–212. An important collection is *A Public and Private Voice: Essays on the Life and Work of Dorothy Livesay*, ed. Lindsay Dorney et al. (Waterloo: University of Waterloo Press, 1986). For some works on Livesay and her context, see Jean Gibbs, "Dorothy Livesay and the Transcendentalist Tradition," *Humanities Association Review/La Revue de l'Association des Humanites* 21 (1970), 24–39, 43; Doris Leland, "Dorothy Livesay: Poet of Nature," *Dalhousie Review* 51 (1971), 404–12; Peter Stevens, "Out of the Silence and across the Distance: The Poetry of Dorothy Livesay," *Queen's Quarterly* 78 (1971), 579–91; Lee Briscoe Thompson, "A Coat of Many Cultures: The Poetry of Dorothy Livesay," *Journal of Popular Culture* 15 (1981), 53–61; Laurie Ricou, "The Naive Eye in the Poetry of Dorothy Livesay, P.K. Page, and Miriam Waddington," *Voices from Distant Lands: Poetry in the Commonwealth*, ed. Konrad Gross and Wolfgang Klooss (Würzburg: Königshausen & Neumann, 1983), 108–14; Lorraine York, " 'A Thankful Music': Dorothy Livesay's Experiments with Feeling and Poetic Form," *Canadian Poetry* 12 (1983), 13–23. Peter Stevens, *Dorothy Livesay: Patterns in a Poetic Life* (Toronto: ECW, 1992); Marvin Gilman, "Lines of Intersection: The Two Dorothys and Marxism," *New Literatures Review* 28–29 (Winter 1994–Summer 1995), 23–32; Di Brandt, "Revisiting Dorothy Livesay's *The Husband,*" *Capilano Review* 2 (32) (2000), 75–89; Esther Pardo, "Canonization or Exclusion?: Dorothy Livesay's Wayward Modernism from the 1940s," *Atlantis: Revista de la Asociación Española de Estudios Anglo-Norteamericanos* 22 (2000), 167–86; Susan Gingell, "Claiming Positive Semantic Space for Women: The Poetry of Dorothy Livesay," *Essays on Canadian Writing* 74 (2001), 1–25. On Livesay and Africa, see Fiona Sparrow, "The Self-Completing Tree: Livesay's African Poetry," *Canadian Poetry* 20 (1987), 17–30; Sandra Hutchison, "Frontiers of Imagination: The African Writings of Dorothy Livesay and Karen Blixen," *Canada and the Nordic Countries*, ed. Jørn Carlsen and Bengt Streijffert (Lund: Lund University Press; Chartwell-Bratt, 1988), 139–48.

46. For a study that brings out one related context in this period, see Dean Jay Irvine, "Little Histories: Modernist and Leftist Women Poets and Magazine Editors in Canada, 1926–1956," Ph.D. dissertation, McGill University, 2001.

47. Livesay, *Archives*, 18.

48. Livesay, *Archives*, 25.
49. Livesay, *Archives*, 28.
50. Livesay, *Archives*, 52.
51. Livesay, *Archives*, 56.
52. Livesay, *Archives*, 66.
53. Livesay, *Archives*, 72.
54. Livesay, *Archives*, 90.
55. Livesay, *Archives*, 104.
56. Livesay, *Archives*, 109.
57. Livesay, *Archives*, 114.
58. Livesay, *Archives*, 160.
59. Livesay, *Archives*, 161.
60. Livesay, *Archives*, 161.
61. Livesay, *Archives*, 201.
62. Livesay, *Archives*, 225.
63. Livesay, *Archives*, 241.
64. Livesay, *Archives*, 245.
65. Margaret Atwood, *Poems 1976–1986* (1987; London: Virago, 1992), 13. Catherine Sheldrick Ross discusses place in an Atwood novel; see her " 'Banished to This Other Place': Atwood's *Lady Oracle*," *English Studies in Canada* 6 (1980), 460–74. Fiona Sparrow places Atwood in a context of earlier works about nineteenth- and twentieth-century Canada; see her " 'This Place Is Some Kind of Garden': Clearings in the Bush in the Works of Susanna Moodie, Catharine Parr Traill, Margaret Atwood and Margaret Laurence," *The Journal of Commonwealth Literatures* 25 (1990), 24–41. For a pertinent collection about Atwood, see *Margaret Atwood: Writing and subjectivity*, ed. Colin Nicholson (New York: St. Martin's Press, 1994); on landscape, see in this volume Judith McCombs, "From 'Places, Migrations' to *The Circle Game*," 51–67. On Place in two poems by Bliss Carmen and Atwood, see S. Ramaswamy, "Time, Space and Place in Two Canadian Poems: An Indian View," *International Journal of Canadian Studies* 15 (1997), 121–33. For a discussion of space and place in one of Atwood's earliest novels, see Danielle Schaub, " 'I Am a Place': Internalised Landscape and Female Subjectivity in Margaret Atwood's *Surfacing*," *Mapping Canadian Cultural Space: Essays on Canadian Literature*, ed. Danielle Schaub (Jerusalem: Magnes, 1998), 83–103. An earlier discussion of this moment in *Surfacing* may be found in Manfred Mackenzie, " 'I Am a Place': Surfacing and the Spirit of Place," *A Sense of Place in the New Literatures in English*, ed. Peggy Nightingale (St. Lucia: University of Queensland Press, 1986), 32–36.
66. Margaret Atwood, *Second Words: Selected Critical Prose* (Toronto: Anansi, 1982), 403–04.
67. Anne Carson, *Glass, Irony and God* (New York: New Directions, 1995), 75. For more on Anne Carson, see the special issue of *Canadian Literature* devoted to her work: 176 (Spring 2003). Other works include: Adam Philips, "Fickle Contracts: The Poetry of Anne Carson," *Raritan* 16 (1996), 112–19; John D'Agata, "A Talk with Anne Carson," *Brick* 57 (1997), 14–22; Mark Halliday, "Carson: Mind and Heart," *Chicago Review* 45 (1999), 121–27; Sharon Wahl, "Erotic Sufferings: *Autobiography of Red* and Other Anthropologies," *Iowa Review* 29 (1999), 180–88. Halliday discusses this work in terms of ambition and erudition. A good overview of Carson and her work occurs in Stephen Burt, who visited Carson in the Berkeley hills near the university there; see his "Poetry without Borders," *Publishers Weekly* 247 (14) (April 3, 2000), 56–57. See also Ian Rae, " 'Dazzling Hybrids': The Poetry of Anne Carson," *Canadian Literature* 166 (2000), 17–41 and Harriet Zinnes, "What Is Time Made Of? The Poetry of Anne Carson," *Hollins Critic* 38 (2001), 1–10. David C. Ward discusses the reaction of John Kinsella, William Logan, Harold Bloom and others to Carson's poetry; see his "Anne Carson: Addressing the Wound," *PN Review* 27 (5) (May–June 2001), 13–16, esp. 13. Chris Jennings discusses *Eros of the Bittersweet* and explores desire and poetics according to Carson as well as her use of genre, fragments and ancient Greek; see Jennings, "The Erotic Poetics of Anne Carson,"

University of Toronto Quarterly 70 (2001), 923–36. Mark Scroggins examines Carson's poetics, including *charis* and her juxtaposition of culturally disparate elements, and her experiment with genre and use of *melopœia*, or the music of language, which is so memorable; see his " 'Truth, Beauty, and the Remote Control," *Parnassus: Poetry in Review* 26 (2) (2002), 127–45. Two recent works discuss Carson's *Autobiography in Red*. See Monique Tschofen, 'First I Must Tell about Seeing': (De)Monstrations of Visuality and the Dynamics of Metaphor in Anne Carson's *Autobiography of Red*," *Canadian Literature* 180 (Spring 2004), 31–50. Drawing on Jacques Lacan's reading, which includes practice, concept, and metaphor, Robert William Gray discusses melancholia in three "poetic novels," by Audrey Thomas, Kristjana Gunnars, and Anne Carson (*Autobiography in Red*). Gray's Introduction discusses the melancholia in detail, including its importance in Freud; see Gray, "Melancholic Poetics: The Vagaries and Vicissitudes of Identity in Three Canadian Poetics Novels and various Pyschoanalytical Works," Ph.D. dissertation, University of Alberta, 2003.

68. Anne Carson, *Plainwater: Essays and Poetry* (New York: Alfred A. Knopf, 1995), 39.
69. MacEwen, in *The New Oxford Book of Canadian Verse in English*, ed. Margaret Atwood (Toronto: Oxford University Press, 1982), 388, see 386, 390–91. Gwendolyn MacEwen is one of Canada's most powerful poets of her generation. Some M.A. and Ph.D. theses include or focus on a discussion of her work in terms mainly of myth, biography, and spirituality, although one study begins a study of literature of a place—Toronto—with MacEwen. See, for instance, Jan Bartley, "The Marriage of Parts: Gwendolyn MacEwen's Sources and their Applications," M.A. thesis, York University (Toronto), 1975. Drawing on Northrop Frye's theories of mythopoeia and Claude Levi-Strauss's work on South America, Ruth Frances Gillian Harding-Russell examines the poetry of MacEwen, Michael Ondaatje, and George Bowering; see her "Open Forms in Mythopoeia in Three Post-Modern Canadian Poets," Ph.D. dissertation, University of Saskatchewan, 1986. For a related vein, see Angela Catherine Dinaut, "Gwendolyn MacEwen: A Mythopoeic Writer Creates a Kanadian Identity," M.A. thesis, Dalhousie University, 1989. For more on mythology in Anglo-Canadian culture, but in conjunction with the works of Sheila Watson, see Ruth De Fehr, "The Residue of Myth: A Study of Sheila Watson's 'Five Stories' and Gwendolyn MacEwen's 'Noman,' " M.A. thesis, University of Victoria, 1991. For a discussion of spirituality in the context of other writers, see Elizabeth Ann Potvin, "Aspects of the Spiritual in Three Canadian Poets: Anne Wilkinson, Gwendolyn MacEwen, and Phyllis Webb," Ph.D. dissertation, McMaster University, 1991. This thesis dovetails with the others as it explores feminist mythopoesis and contemporary theology, especially in relation to the spiritual journeys of women, which involve Daphne's spiritual retreat from the green world as a distinction of the quest by male heroes. Potvin argues that MacEwen connects the birth of the poet with the rebirth of nature and, like her fellow female poets, uses metaphors of immanence, inwardness, and domesticity. MacEwen finds the spiritual in the personal. Sophie Rachel Levy attempts to ask with Frye and Atwood, "Where is here?" as it relates to Toronto, using MacEwen and other Toronto writers to explore this question. MacEwen's *Earthlight* (1982) and *Noman's Land* and *Afterworlds*, her last books, are central texts for Levy in her "Torontology," M.A. thesis, University of Toronto, 2001, esp. 1–3, 16–18. Levy also discusses Caribbean Toronto and writers such as Brand and Austin Clarke and Marlene Nourbese-Philip. Dorothy Shostak examines MacEwen's poetry in terms of the power of the fetish and disavowal. See Shostak, "Open Secrets: Fetishicity in the Poetry of Gwendolyn MacEwen," Ph.D. dissertation, Dalhousie University, 2001. In the Introduction, Shostak has set out a framework of anthropological, psychoanalytic, and economic fetish (see esp. 16). MacEwen herself saw her work as liminal—on the threshold between world and dream. Richard Almonte explores why Canadian literature—quite different from what might be expected from Harold Bloom's anxiety of influence—involves women as precursors, why people rewrite the lives of these predecessors to enhance their reputations against the odds of enduring literary fame for writers in Canada and uses an array of writers, including the foreshortened careers of Susanna Moodie, Gwendolyn MacEwen, and Pat Lowther. Whereas Chapter Three discusses Atwood

and Carole Shields, Chapter Four examines Moodie, Chapter Five, MacEwen, and Chapter Six, Lowther. See Almonte, "Posthumous Praise: Biographical Influence in Canadian Literature," Ph.D. dissertation, McMaster University, 2003. Almonte asserts that Moodie, MacEwen, and Lowther especially influenced later playwrights, novelists, poets, and biographers (see 12). MacEwen has been the focus of attention in fictional, dramatic, and cinematographic representations (15). The most recent thesis on MacEwen returns to the concern of myth and metaphor and to the spiritual turn of the poet. In particular, Brent Donald Wood explores performance is the bond between MacEwen and her reader; see his "Approaching Spirit: Myth, Metaphor and Technique in the Poetry of Avison, Nichol and MacEwen," Ph.D. dissertation, University of Toronto, 2003. In terms of theory and context, Wood asks whether MacEwan is a mystic, feminist, or alchemist. Wood draws on Northrop Frye, reading MacEwan's poems in relation to myth (dreams and modes), metaphor, and technique. According to Wood, MacEwen, Avison, and Nichol are, among their contemporaries, most dedicated to spiritual concerns in their poetry (10). He also calls attention to their sense of place—the Annex and downtown Toronto and the University of Toronto (12) and provides a brief biography of MacEwen (1941–87) (see 14–15). For a book-length study of MacEwen, see Jan Bartley's *Invocations: The Poetry and Prose of Gwendolyn MacEwen* (Vancouver: University of British Columbia Press, 1983), which does not include discussions of *The T.E. Lawrence Poems* and *Afterworlds*. For other significant work on MacEwen, see Clément Moisan, "Ecriture et errance dans les poesies de Gwendolyn MacEwen et Nicole Brossard," *Canadian Review of Comparative Literature/Revue Canadienne de Littérature Comparée* 2 (1975), 72–92; Ellen D. Warwick, "To Seek a Single Symmetry," *Canadian Literature* 71 (1976), 21–34; Drew O'Hagan, "Canadian Monsters: Some Aspects of the Supernatural in Canadian Fiction," *The Canadian Imagination: Dimensions of a Literary Culture*, ed. David Staines (Cambridge: Harvard University Press, 1977), 97–122; Frank Davey, *Surviving the Paraphrase: Eleven Essays on Canadian Literature* (Winnipeg: Turnstone, 1983); R.F. Gillian Harding, "Iconic Mythopoeia in MacEwen's The T.E. Lawrence Poems," *Studies in Canadian Literature/Etudes en Littérature Canadienne* 9 (1984), 95–107; Jan Bartley, "Gwendolyn MacEwen," *Canadian Writers and Their Works*, ed. Robert Lecker et al. (Toronto: ECW Press, 1985), 231–71; Rosalind Conway, " Gwendolyn MacEwen," *Profiles in Canadian Literature, VI*, ed. Jeffrey M. Heath (Toronto: Dundurn, 1986), 57–64; Shelagh Wilkinson, "Gwendolyn MacEwen's Trojan Women: Old Myth into New Life," *Canadian Woman Studies/Les Cahiers de la Femme* 8 (1987), 81–82; Penn Kemp, "A Musing I Would Have Liked to Have Shared with Gwendolyn MacEwen," *Tessera* 5 (September 1988), 49–57. R.F. Gillian Harding-Russell, "Gwendolyn MacEwen's 'The Nine Arcana of the Kings' as Creative Myth and Paradigm," *English Studies in Canada* 14 (1988), 204–17; Thomas M.F. Gerry, " 'Green Yet Free of Seasons': Gwendolyn MacEwen and the Mystical Tradition of Canadian Poetry," *Studies in Canadian Literature/Etudes en Littérature Canadienne* 16 (1991), 147–61; Liza Potvin, "Gwendolyn MacEwen and Female Spiritual Desire," *Canadian Poetry* 28 (1991), 18–39; Jan Bartley, "Gwendolyn MacEwen (1941–87)," *ECW's Biographical Guide to Canadian Poets*, ed. Robert Lecker et al. (Toronto: ECW, 1993), 264–66; Rosemary Sullivan, "Biography: An Elegiac Art," *Meanjin* 54 (1995), 329–37 [this is a brief biography that are notes toward Sullivan's biography]; María Luz González, "El Camino arquetípico del héroe: El mago y el sumo sacerdote en las novelas de Gwendolyn Macewen," *Revista Canaria de Estudios Ingleses* 39 (November 1999), 307–21; Brent Wood, "From *The Rising Fire* to *Afterworlds*: The Visionary Circle in the Poetry of Gwendolyn MacEwen," *Canadian Poetry* 47 (2000), 40–69; María Luz González Rodríguez, "Cuestiones de estructura en la colección Noman de Gwendolyn Macewen: Un puzzle de símbolos," *Polifonías textuales: Ensayos in honorem María del Carmen Fernández Leal*, ed. Manuel Brito and Juan Ignacio Oliva (La Laguna, Spain: Revista Canaria de Estudios Ingleses (RCEI), 2001), 177–85; María Luz González, "Caronte y la luna: Arquetipos míticos en *The Armies of the Moon* de Gwendolyn MacEwen," *Revista Canaria de Estudios Ingleses* 48 (2004), 179–92. For a biography, see Rosemary Sullivan, *Shadow Maker: The Life of*

Gwendolyn MacEwen (Toronto: HarperCollins, 1995). In 1998, a documentary film appeared, *Shadow Maker*, directed by Brenda Longfellow for Gerda Film Productions.

4 Writing and History: T.E. Lawrence and Bernard and Charlotte Shaw

1. T.E. Lawrence, *Correspondence with Bernard and Charlotte Shaw 1922–1926*, ed. Jeremy and Nicole Wilson (Fordingbridge: Castle Hill Press, 2000), 12–13; the edition used hereafter unless otherwise indicated. For a study germane to my chapter on TEL and the Shaws, see Stanley Weintraub, *Private Shaw and Public Shaw: A Dual Portrait of Lawrence of Arabia and G.B.S.* (New York: Braziller, 1963). On TEL and GBS, see W.R. Martin, "GBS, DHL, and TEL: Mainly Lady Chatterley and Too True," *Shaw: The Annual of Bernard Shaw Studies* 4 (1984), 107–12. A shorter version of this essay occurred in *The Waking Dream of T.E. Lawrence: Essays on His Life, Literature, and Legacy*, ed. Charles M. Stang (New York: Palgrave, 2002), 131–60. My thanks to Charles Stang for inviting my essay on Lawrence. For two earlier collections on T.E. Lawrence, see *The T.E. Lawrence Puzzle*, ed. Stephen E. Tabachnick (Athens: University of Georgia Press, 1984) and *T. E. Lawrence: Soldier, Writer, Legend: New Essays*, ed. Jeffrey Meyers (New York: St. Martin's, 1989).

2. Lawrence, *Correspondence*, 36. For work on TEL as a writer and on his biography, see Gordon Mills, "T.E. Lawrence as a Writer," *Texas Quarterly* 5 (1962), 35–45; Robert Graves, *T.E. Lawrence to His Biographers* (Garden City, NY: Doubleday, 1963); Victoria Ocampo, *T.E. (Lawrence of Arabia)* (New York: E.P. Dutton; 1963); James A. Notopoulos, "The Tragic and the Epic in T. E. Lawrence," *Yale Review* 54 (1965), 331–45; Denis Boak, "Malraux and T.E. Lawrence," *Modern Language Review* 61 (1966), 218–24; Suleiman Mousa, *T.E. Lawrence: An Arab View* (London: Oxford University Press, 1966); *Evolution of a Revolution: Early Postwar Writings of T.E. Lawrence*, ed. Stanley Weintraub (University Park: Pennsylvania State University Press, 1968); Phillip Knightley, "T.E. Lawrence," *The Craft of Literary Biography*, ed. Jeffrey Meyers (New York: Schocken, 1983), 154–72; Philip O'Brien, *T.E. Lawrence: A Bibliography* (Boston: Hall, 1988); William M. Chace, "T.E. Lawrence: The Uses of Heroism," *T.E. Lawrence: Soldier, Writer, Legend*, 128–60; C. Ernest Dawn, "The Influence of T.E. Lawrence on the Middle East," *T. E. Lawrence: Soldier, Writer, Legend*, 58–86; David Fromkin, "The Importance of T.E. Lawrence," *The New Criterion* 10 (1991), 86–98; John M. Mackenzie, "T.E. Lawrence: The Myth and the Message," *Literature and Imperialism*, ed. Robert Giddings (New York: St. Martin's, 1991), 150–81; June Turner, "T.E. Lawrence," *American Image: Studies in Psychoanalysis and Culture* 48 (1991), 395–416; James Buchan, "Romancers: John Buchan and T.E. Lawrence," *T.E. Notes: A T. E. Lawrence Newsletter* 4 (1) (1993), 1–5; Harold Orlans, "The Many Lives of T.E. Lawrence: A Symposium," *Biography: An Interdisciplinary Quarterly* 16 (1993), 224–48; Ton Hoenselaars, "Joseph Conrad and T.E. Lawrence," *Conradiana: A Journal of Joseph Conrad Studies* 27 (1995), 3–20; Albert Hourani, "The Myth of T.E. Lawrence," *Adventures with Britannia: Personalities, Politics, and Culture in Britain*, ed. William Roger Louis (Austin: University of Texas Press, 1995), 9–24; P.T. Whelan, "T.E. Lawrence's Crusade," *Studies in Medievalism* 6 (1996), 261–71; Stephen Ely Tabachnik, *T.E. Lawrence* (New York: Twayne, 1997); Michel Stanesco, "Du chevalier au cénobite: Le Médiévisme de T.E. Lawrence et le code du renoncement à soi," *Une Amitié européenne: Nouveaux horizons de la littérature comparée*, ed. Pascal Dethurens (Paris: Champion, 2002), 193–212; Maurice J-M. Larès, "Three English-Language Versions of André Malraux's Article on T.E. Lawrence: 'N'était-ce donce que cela,' " *T.E. Notes: A T.E. Lawrence Newsletter* 13 (3) (2003), 1–55; Victoria Carchidi, "Creation out of the Void: The Life and Legends of

T.E. Lawrence," *Mapping the Self: Space, Identity, Discourse in British Auto/Biography*, ed. Frédéric Regard (Saint-Etienne: Université de Saint-Etienne, 2003), 269–84. On space, an important aspect in TEL, see Gaston Bachelard (1884–1962), *La poétique de l'espace* (Paris: Presses universitaires de France, 1957). Bachelard was born about four years earlier than TEL (1888–1935) and died about twenty-seven years after TEL did.

3. For discussions of this work (more in following notes), see Rota Bertram, "Lawrence of Arabia and *Seven Pillars of Wisdom*," *Texas Quarterly* 5 (3) (1962), 46–53; Meyers, *T.E. Lawrence: Soldier, Writer, Legend*, Eugene Goodheart, "A Contest of Motives: T.E. Lawrence in *Seven Pillars of Wisdom*," *T.E. Lawrence in His Letters*, 110–27; see Meyer's essay in the same volume, 8–27; A.J. Flavell, "T.E. Lawrence, *Seven Pillars of Wisdom* and the Bodleian," *Bodleian Library Record* 13 (1990), 300–13; Susan Smith Nash, "Geology and the Hero's Body in T.E. Lawrence's *Seven Pillars of Widsom*," *T.E. Notes* 3 (1992), 6–7; Donald Mengay, "Arabian Rites: T.E. Lawrence's *Seven Pillars of Wisdom* and the Erotics of Empire," *Genre* 27 (1994), 395–416; Carola Kaplan, "Conquest as Literature, Literature as Conquest: T.E. Lawrence's Artistic Campaign in *Seven Pillars of Wisdom*," *Texas Studies in Literature and Language* 37 (1995), 72–97; David Boal, "T.E. Lawrence as Prophet: *Seven Pillars of Wisdom* and the End of Empire," *Anglophonia: French Journal of English Studies* 3 (1998), 125–33; William David Halloran, "Titan, Tome and Triumph: T.E. Lawrence's 'Seven Pillars of Wisdom' as a Modernist Spectacle," Ph.D. dissertation, University of California, Los Angeles, 2001. According to Halloran, postcolonial and modernist angles help us to understand but themselves cannot embrace the complexity of this text. TEL is part of British and international modernism but does not embrace it entirely. Halloran questions Edward Said's view of TEL as typical Orientalist [see *Orientalism* (New York: Verso, 1978), esp. 228, 239] and points to Ali Behdad's *Belated Travelers: Orientalism in the Age of Colonialism* (Durham: Duke University Press, 1994) and Leela Gandhi's *Post-Colonial Theory: A Critical Introduction* (New York: Columbia University Press, 1998) as correctives to Said's generalizations, reductions, and absolutes (3–5). Halloran applies this critique to colonizers, figures such as TEL and Edward William Lane, linguist and Sanskrit expert, who deserve better. For Halloran (8–9), an analysis that takes into account the limits of Orientalism as critique is the work of Dennis Porter (see, for instance, his *Haunted Journeys: Desire and Transgression in European Travel Writing* [Princeton: Princeton University Press, 1992]). Halloran says that TEL was aware that "his life was an assembly of contradictions" (11). He also places TEL in the context of Sir Richard Burton and Charles M. Doughty, whose legacy of representations of the Arab world TEL sought to transform (13).

4. Lawrence, *Correspondence*, 4.

5. Lawrence, *Correspondence*, 4. For some theses on TEL, see Alastair G. Bain, "T.E. Lawrence: Politics and Imagery," M.A. thesis, University of Chicago, 1964; James G. Coates, "The Influence of T.E. Lawrence on British Foreign Policy in the Middle East, 1918–1922," M.A. thesis, McGill University, 1967; Thomas James O'Donnell, "The Dichotomy of Self in T.E. Lawrence's 'Seven Pillars of Wisdom,' " Ph.D. dissertation, University of Illinois at Urbana-Champaign, 1970; Stephen Ely Tabachnick, "T.E. Lawrence's 'Seven Pillars of Wisdom' As a Work of Art," Ph.D. dissertation, University of Connecticut, 1972; John Saul Friedman, "The Challenge of Destiny: A Comparison of T.E. Lawrence's and André Malraux's Adventure Tales," Ph.D. dissertation, New York University, 1974; Robert Hall Warde, "T.E. Lawrence: A Critical Study," Ph.D. dissertation, Harvard University, 1978; Malcolm Dennis Allen, "The Medievalism of T.E. Lawrence," Ph.D. dissertation, Pennsylvania State University, 1983, which discusses TEL's study of medieval history and the lives of the saints. Victoria Carchidi, "Creation Out of the Void: The Making of a Hero, an Epic, a World, T.E. Lawrence," Ph.D. dissertation, University of Pennsylvania, 1987. Carchidi sees in *Seven Pillars* TEL's great elegy, an epic work of loss and mourning, the ironic gap between void and monument. In chapters 3 and 4, Muhammed Nasser Shoukany examines how Arab writers subvert the Orientalism of Joseph Conrad and TEL; see his "Orientalism and the Arab Literary Responses: Studies in Ahmad Faris al-Shidyaq, Charles M. Doughty, Joseph Conrad, Jabra I. Jabra and Tawfiq Yusuf

Awwad," Ph.D. dissertation, The University of Texas at Austin, 1990. James Timothy Barclay describes how the British used Lawrence to organize and train the Arab nationalists in guerilla warfare; see his "T.E. Lawrence and the Arab Revolt: Innovation and Irregular Warfare," M.A. thesis, Central Missouri University, 1991. After setting up the framework of nationalism, imperialism, Orientalism, and racism, Robert Davies discusses Richard Burton, Wilfrid Scawen Blunt, and TEL in personal and cultural terms; see his "Warriors and Gentlemen: The Occidental Context of Arabian Travel Narratives of Burton, Blunt and Lawrence," Ph.D. dissertation, University of Technology, Loughborough, 1991. See also Mohammed Nour Naimi, "T.E. Lawrence and the Orientalist Tradition," Ph.D. dissertation, University of Essex, 1991. Naimi explores Lawrence's Orientalist contexts, such as those of Rudyard Kipling and John Buchan. Joel Clark Hodson discusses the role of American journalism, film, and scholarship in the making of an Anglo-American legend; see "Transatlantic Legends: T.E. Lawrence and American Culture," Ph.D. dissertation, George Washington University, 1992. David Arthur Boxwell explores esprit de corps and anxieties over same-sex bonding and includes TEL in the authors he discusses; see his " 'Between Idealism and Brutality:' Desire, Conflict, and the British Experience of the Great War," Ph.D. dissertation, Rutgers University, 1995. Maren Ormseth Cohn examines TEL as a translator of Homer and as an Odyssean figure, shifting identities in search of self; see "T.E. Lawrence and Odysseus: A Study of Translation, Identity and Heroic Action," Ph.D. dissertation, University of Chicago, 1995. Judith Mary Alexis Schwartz maintains that heroes do not follow a developmental pattern but are often missing something or have a wound that must be healed: TEL and Churchill are among her examples and extends Auerbach's Odysseus's scar; see her "The Wounds that Heal: Heroic Endeavors and Human Development," Ph.D. dissertation, The Union Institute, 1995, see 9–10. Here, then, Schwartz confirms the connection I have made implicitly, in the structure of this book, between TEL and Odysseus, in terms of "heroism" (the protagonist and recognition) (see17–18). She also has an interesting discussion of myth in the context of developmental psychology (see 19–21). Faysal Mohammed discusses the liaison TEL chose for the British in the Arab Revolt (begun June 10, 1916); see his "Faysal ibn Al-Husayn and Britain: The Uneasy Alliance," Ph.D. dissertation, University of Toronto, 1996. Mohammed calls TEL's portrait of Faysal in *Seven Pillars* insightful (ix). Ethan Joe David Hildreth sees TEL's *Revolt in the Desert* (an abridged form of *Seven Pillars*) as a popular success, which was influential in shaping imperialist attitudes that resembled those in the late nineteenth century; see his "Writing an Imperial Narrative: Treatment of the Arab Image in Nineteenth-Century British Literature," Ph.D. dissertation, Georgia State University, 1997, esp. ch. 6. Hildreth moves from Benjamin Disraeli (especially his novel *Tancred* [1847]), artist, and prime minister, to TEL, soldier and writer, whose work, in Hildreth's view, uses romance and also undermines the Arab in representation (12–13). Sanjeev Kumar Uprety discusses ethnicity and gender when examining cross-cultural mimicry in imperial subjects such as Lawrence and Native subjects such as Gandhi; see "Mimicry, Masculinity and Modernity: Representations of Effeminacy and Hypermasculinity in Imperial and Native Narratives," Ph.D. dissertation, Brown University, 2003 (see 1). In regard to gender boundaries, which the life of TEL raises, Uprety calls attention to works such as Kaja Silverman's *Male Subjectivity at the Margins* (New York: Routledge, 1992) and Judith Halberstam's *Female Masculinity* (Durham: Duke University, 1998) and also calls on texts such as Homi Bhabha's *The Location of Culture* (London: Routledge, 1992) and Rey Chow's *The Protestatnt Ethnic and the Spirit of Capitalism* (New York: Columbia University Press, 2002) to provide a context for cross-cultural mimicry. In *Seven Pillars*, TEL, according to Uprety, represents Arab identities in a stereotypical Orientalist way but in doing so allowed himself scope to forge a masculinity at once medieval and modern (7, see 18). TEL has many sides. Brian R. Johnson discusses *Seven Pillars* in terms of representations of nomads; see his "Nomad and Nomadologies: Transformations of the Primitive in Twentieth-Century Theory and Culture," Ph.D. dissertation, Dalhousie University, 2003, esp. ch. 2. Johnson discusses Stuart Hall and James Clifford on nomadology (5) and notes TEL's enthusiasm for nomads (17).

6. Lawrence, *Correspondence*, 4.

7. Lawrence, *Correspondence*, 4.

8. Lawrence, *Correspondence*, 4.

9. Lawrence, *Correspondence*, 4.

10. Lawrence, *Correspondence*, 4.

11. Lawrence, *Correspondence*, 5.

12. Lawrence, *Correspondence*, 5; insertion on "ambiguous" is TEL's own postscript.

13. Lawrence, *Correspondence*, 5.

14. Lawrence, *Correspondence*, 6.

15. Lawrence, *Correspondence*, 7.

16. Lawrence, *Correspondence*, 7.

17. Lawrence, *Correspondence*, 8.

18. Lawrence, *Correspondence*, 10.

19. Lawrence, *Correspondence*, 10, see 8. See Jeremy Wilson, *Lawrence of Arabia: The Authorised Biography of T.E. Lawrence* (London: Heinemann, 1989), 637–38. See also Fred D. Crawford, "Richard Aldington's Biography of Lawrence of Arabia," *Richard Aldington: Reappraisals*, ed. Charles Doyle (Victoria, BC: University of Victoria Press, 1990), 60–80. For more on TEL, see Stanley Weintraub, "The Two Sides of 'Lawrence of Arabia': Aubrey and Meek," *Shaw: The Annual of Bernard Shaw Studies* 7 (1964), 54–57; Phillip Knightley, *The Secret Lives of Lawrence of Arabia* (New York: McGraw, 1970); Jeffrey Meyers, "The Secret Lives of Lawrence of Arabia," *Commonweal* 93 (1970), 100–04; Wolfgang J. Helbich, "Lawrence of Arabia," *Englische Dichter der Moderne:Ihr Leben und Werk*, ed. Rudolf Suhnel and Dieter Riesner (Berlin: Schmidt, 1971), 373–84; Stanley Weintraub, *Lawrence of Arabia: The Literary Impulse* (Baton Rouge: Louisiana State University Press, 1975); Richard Perceval Graves, *Lawrence of Arabia and His World* (New York: Scribner's, 1976); Baber Bader, "Lawrence of Arabia and H.H. Richardson," *Australian Literary Studies* 11 (1983), 99–101; Stanley Weintraub, "Lawrence of Arabia: The Portraits from Imagination, 1922–1979," *The T.E. Lawrence Puzzle*, 269–92.

20. Lawrence, *Correspondence*, 10.

21. Lawrence, *Correspondence*, 11. On Hardy, see M.H.C. Warner, "Lawrence, of Arabia, Thomas Hardy and the Four Black Tea Sets," *Thomas Hardy Yearbook* 5 (1975), 35–38.

22. Lawrence, *Correspondence*, 11.

23. Lawrence, *Correspondence*, 11.

24. Lawrence, *Correspondence*, 12.

25. Lawrence, *Correspondence*, 12.

26. Lawrence, *Correspondence*, 12.

27. Lawrence, *Correspondence*, 15.

28. Lawrence, *Correspondence*, 16.

29. Lawrence, *Correspondence*, 17.

30. Lawrence, *Correspondence*, 17.

31. Lawrence, *Correspondence*, 17.

32. Lawrence, *Correspondence*, 18–19.

33. Lawrence, *Correspondence*, 20, see 17.

34. Lawrence, *Correspondence*, 20.

35. Lawrence, *Correspondence*, 20.

36. Lawrence, *Correspondence*, 20–21.

37. Lawrence, *Correspondence*, 21.

38. Lawrence, *Correspondence*, 21.

39. Lawrence, *Correspondence*, 21.

40. Lawrence, *Correspondence*, 21.

41. Lawrence, *Correspondence*, 23n5.

42. Lawrence, *Correspondence*, 21–22.

43. Lawrence, *Correspondence*, 22.

44. Lawrence, *Correspondence*, 22.
45. Lawrence, *Correspondence*, 10.
46. Lawrence, *Correspondence*, 22.
47. Lawrence, *Correspondence*, 23.
48. Lawrence, *Correspondence*, 23.
49. Lawrence, *Correspondence*, 25.
50. Lawrence, *Correspondence*, 24.
51. Lawrence, *Correspondence*, 25–26.
52. Lawrence, *Correspondence*, 26.
53. Lawrence, *Correspondence*, 26–27.
54. Lawrence, *Correspondence*, 28.
55. Lawrence, *Correspondence*, 29.
56. Lawrence, *Correspondence*, 30.
57. Lawrence, *Correspondence*, 30–31.
58. Lawrence, *Correspondence*, 31.
59. Lawrence, *Correspondence*, 33.
60. Lawrence, *Correspondence*, 31.
61. Lawrence, *Correspondence*, 32.
62. Lawrence, *Correspondence*, 32.
63. Lawrence, *Correspondence*, 33–34.
64. Lawrence, *Correspondence*, 34.
65. Lawrence, *Correspondence*, 34.
66. Lawrence, *Correspondence*, 34.
67. Lawrence, *Correspondence*, 35–36.
68. Lawrence, *Correspondence*, 37.
69. Lawrence, *Correspondence*, 37.
70. Lawrence, *Correspondence*, 38.
71. Lawrence, *Correspondence*, 38.
72. Lawrence, *Correspondence*, 39–40.
73. Lawrence, *Correspondence*, 41.
74. Lawrence, *Correspondence*, 41.
75. Lawrence, *Correspondence*, 42.
76. Lawrence, *Correspondence*, 43.
77. Lawrence, *Correspondence*, 43.
78. Lawrence, *Correspondence*, 44.
79. Lawrence, *Correspondence*, 44.
80. Lawrence, *Correspondence*, 44.
81. Lawrence, *Correspondence*, 45–46.
82. Lawrence, *Correspondence*, 46.
83. Lawrence, *Correspondence*, 46.
84. Lawrence, *Correspondence*, 48.
85. Lawrence, *Correspondence*, 49–50.
86. Lawrence, *Correspondence*, 51.
87. Lawrence, *Correspondence*, 52–53.
88. Lawrence, *Correspondence*, 52.
89. Lawrence, *Correspondence*, 64, 67n4.
90. Lawrence, *Correspondence*, 65, see 67n6.
91. Lawrence, *Correspondence*, 70.
92. Lawrence, *Correspondence*, 70.
93. Lawrence, *Correspondence*, 70–71.
94. Lawrence, *Correspondence*, 78, see 83n3.

95. Lawrence, *Correspondence*, 150–51.

96. Lawrence, *Correspondence*, 183.

97. British Library, Add. MS 45914 and 45915; see T.E. Lawrence, *Correspondence*, Wilson and Wilson, eds., 184n2. See also R.D. Barnett, "T.E. Lawrence and the British Museum," *Times Literary Supplement*, October 16, 1969: 1210–11.

98. Lawrence, *Correspondence*, 187–88.

99. Lawrence, *Correspondence*, 189.

100. Lawrence, *Correspondence*, 68n1, 203.

101. Lawrence, *Correspondence*, 203.

102. Lawrence, *Correspondence*, 207–08.

103. Lawrence, *Correspondence*, 209–11.

104. Lawrence, *Correspondence*, 198–99.

105. Frank N. and Nelson Doubleday Collection, Box 7, Manuscripts Division, Department of Rare Books and Special Collections, Princeton University Library. On this collection, Howard C. Rice, Jr., "Additions to the Doubleday Collection (at Princeton): Kipling, T.E. Lawrence, Conrad," *Princeton University Library Chronicle* 24 (1963), 191–96.

106. TEL to F.N. Doubleday [FND], September 17, 1923, 2 recto–verso.

107. TEL to FND, November 15, 1923, 1 verso–2 recto.

108. TEL to FND on June 16, 1927, 2 recto, in Doubleday Collection, Box 7, Princeton University Library.

109. TEL to FND on June 16, 1927, 2 verso.

110. TEL to FND, August 25, 1927, 2 verso.

111. TEL to FND, August 25, 1927, 1 verso.

112. TEL to FND, June 28, 1929, 1 verso.

113. TEL to FND, December 18, 1930, 3 recto.

114. TEL to FND, January 27, 1931, 1 recto. For other library collections of TEL, see Ann Bowden, "The T. E. Lawrence Collection at the University of Texas," *Texas Quarterly* 5 (1962), 54–63; Philip O'Brien, "Collecting T.E. Lawrence Materials," *The T.E. Lawrence Puzzle*, 293–311; David H. Patrick, "The T. E. Lawrence Collection: Its Historical Uses for the Biographer," *Library Chronicle of the University of Texas* 20 (1990), 16–47.

115. TEL to Sir John Maxwell, January 4, 926, Doubleday Collection. One of the poets I discussed in the chapter on Canadian women writers was Gwendolyn MacEwen; she wrote poems on TEL; see R.F. Gillian Harding, "Iconic Mythopoeia in MacEwen's *The T.E. Lawrence Poems*," *Studies in Canadian Literature/Etudes en Littérature Canadienne* 9 (1984), 95–107.

116. John R. Woolfenden, *Columbia Pictures Presents the Sam Spiegel and David Lean Production of Lawrence of Arabia* (New York: Richard Davis, 1962). On the film (and related topics in theatre and arts), see Stanley Weintraub, "How History Gets Rewritten: *Lawrence of Arabia* in the Theatre," *Drama Survey* 2 (1963), 269–75; Gary Crowdus, "*Lawrence of Arabia*: The Cinematic (Re)Writing of History," *Cineaste* 17 (2) (1989), 14–21; Michael A. Anderegg, "Lawrence of Arabia: The Man, the Myth, the Movie," *T.E. Notes* 4 (7) (September 1993), 1–7 and, in the same issue, L. Robert Morris, "Is *Lawrence of Arabia* Really a Great Film?," 8–9; Joel Hudson, "Who Wrote *Lawrence of Arabia*? Sam Spiegel and David Lean's Denial of Credit to a Blacklisted Screenwriter," *Cineaste* 20 (4), 12–18; Michael Wilson, "*Lawrence of Arabia*: Elements and Facets of the Theme," *Cineaste* 21 (4), (1995), 30–32; Fred D. Crawford, *Richard Aldington and Lawrence of Arabia: A Cautionary Tale* (Carbondale: Southern Illinois University Press, 1998); Steven Caton, *Lawrence of Arabia: A Film's Anthropology* (Berkeley: University of California Press, 1999); Stephen Teo, "The Legacy of T.E. Lawrence: The Forward Policy of Western Film Critics in the Far East," *Film and Nationalism*, ed. Alan Williams (New Brunswick, NJ: Rutgers University Press, 2002), 181–94.

117. *Sam Spiegel and David Lean Production*, A1 recto–A2 recto.

118. *Sam Spiegel and David Lean Production*, A2 recto.

5 Poiēma, Theoria, and Tekhnē

1. An earlier version appeared in "Poetry in the Age of Theory and Technology," *Literature in the Age of Technology*, ed. Dorothy Figuiera (Provost: ICLA at Brigham Young University, 2004), 175–88. My thanks to Dorothy Figuiera, our host, and to the International Comparative Literature Association on whose executive committee I serve.

2. There are many intricacies to the relation between the key terms in this chapter. One interesting aspect occurs in reading Haney's discussion in which he discusses the ethical implications of the aesthetic, especially of literary production, in terms of phronēsis or ethical knowledge and techne or productive knowledge In Aristotle's *Nichomachean Ethics* he distinguishes three kinds of knowledge: epistēmē (theoretical), productive (technē), and phronēsis (practical). Although, for Artistotle, the literary craft is a matter of technē, even if the content is ethical, means and ends are separated and a tension exists between the ethical (phronēsis) and the aesthetic, unlike epistēmē, which is of necessary truths. Haney sees in Romanticism a realization of the tension between the prophetic and Vatic aspect of the poet with the production of poetry in an age of mechanical reproduction, a kind of recognition of the passing of the poet as prophet even under protest. Haney appeals to Levinas's idea of ethical otherness and Gadamer's interest in the interpreter of a work of art as a way of seeing a balance between the ethical and aesthetic, phronēsis and technē not being reducible one to the other. See David P. Haney "Aesthetics and Ethics in Gadamer, Levinas, and Romanticism: Problems of Phronesis and Techne," *PMLA* 114 (1999), 32–45, especially, 32–33, 43–44. For related work, see Emmanuel Levinas, *Otherwise Than Being: or, Beyond Essence*, trans. Alphonso Lingis (The Hague: Nijhoff, 1981); Hans-Georg Gadamer, "On the Contribution of Poetry to the Search for Truth"; "Poetry and Mimesis," *"The Relevance of the Beautiful" and Other Essays*, ed. Robert Bernasconi and trans. Nicholas Walker (Cambridge: Cambridge University Press, 1986), 105–15, 116–22. See also Walter Benjamin, "The Work of Art in the Age of Mechanical Reproduction," *Illuminations*, trans. Harry Zohn (New York: Schocken, 1969), 217–51 and Martin Heidegger, *Poetry, Language, Thought*, trans. Albert Hofstadter (New York: Harper, 1971); Martha C. Nussbaum, *Love's Knowledge: Essays on Literature and Philosophy* (New York: Oxford University Press, 1990); Paul Ricoeur, *Oneself as Another*, trans. Kathleen Blamey (Chicago: University of Chicago, 1992). Some interesting work on poetry, literature, and techné (tekhnē) occurs in Al Husar, " Tekhnê et poïesis," *Analele Stiintifice ale Universitatii 'Al. I. Cuza' din Iasi (Serie noua), e. Lingvist* 26 (1980), 43–47; Stephen C. Byrum, "The Greek Concept of 'techne,' " *Politics, Society, and the Humanities*, ed. Reed Sanderlin and Craig Barrow (Chattanooga, TN: Southern Humanities, 1984), 160–68; Pierre Laurette, "Apaté, mimésis, techné," *Roman, réalités, réalismes*, ed. Jean Bessière (Paris: Presses Universaires de France, 1989), 57–64; Véronique M. Fóti, *Heidegger and the Poets: Poiesis, Sophia, Techne* (Atlantic Highlands, NJ: Humanities, 1992); Pierre Laurette, *Lettres et techné: Informatique, instrumentations, méthodes et théories dans le domaine littéraire* (Candiac, PQ: Balzac, 1993); Franc Schuerewegen, "Tekhnè telepathikè (sur Marguerite Duras)," *(En)jeux de la communication Romanesque*, ed. Suzan van Dijk and Christa Stevens (Amsterdam: Rodopi, 1994), 61–70; Paolo Quintili, "La Couleur, la téchne, la vie: L'Esthétique épistémologique des Salons (1759–1781)," *Recherches sur Diderot et sur l'Encyclopédie* 25 (1998), 21–39; Cynthia Haynes, "Virtual Diffusion: Ethics, Techné and Feminism at the End of the Cold Millennium," *Passions, Pedagogies, and 21st Century Technologies*, ed. Gail E. Hawisher and Cynthia Selfe (Logan: Utah State University Press, 1999), 337–46; R.L. Rutsky, *High Techne: Art and Technology from the Machine Aesthetic to the Posthuman* (Minneapolis, MN: University of Minnesota Press, 1999); Joanna Hodge, "Freedom, Phusis, Techne: Thinking the Inhuman," *Inhuman Reflections: Thinking the Limits of the Human*, ed. Scott Brewster et al. (Manchester: Manchester University Press, 2000), 38–56; Nicoletta Pireddu, "Towards a Poet(h)ics of Techne: Primo Levi and Daniele Del Giudice," *Annali d'Italianistica* 19 (2001), 189–214. The study of rhetoric and communication is also concerned with technē: for instance, see Terry

Papillion, "Isocrates' Techne and Rhetorical Pedagogy," *Rhetoric Society Quarterly* 25 (1995), 149–63; the special issue on technē—ed. Tracy Bridgeford—of *Technical Communication Quarterly* 11 (2) (Spring 2002), 125–240; Ekaterina V. Haskins, "Paideia versus Techne: Isocrates's Performative Conception of Rhetorical Education," *Professing Rhetoric: Selected Papers from the 2000 Rhetoric Society of America Conference*, ed. Frederick Antczak, Cinda Coggins, and Geoffrey D. Klinger (Mahwah, NJ: Erlbaum, 2002), 199–206.

3. On theoria (theory), see Malcolm Mackenzie Ross, "Ruskin, Hooker and 'the Christian Theoria,' " *Essays in English Literature from the Renaissance to the Victorian Age Presented to A.S.P. Woodhouse, 1964*, ed. Millar MacLure and F.W. Watt (Toronto: University of Toronto Press, 1964), 283–303; Gregory Ulmer, "Op Writing: Derrida's Solicitation of Theoria," *Displacement: Derrida and After*, ed. Mark Krupnick (Bloomington: Indiana University Press, 1983), 29–58. Miklós Szabolcsi, György M. Vajda, and Eva Kushner, "Theoria litterarum et litterae comparatae," *Neohelicon* 13 (1986); Éric Méchoulan, "Theoria, Aisthesis, Mimesis and Doxa," *Diogenes* 151 (1990), 131–48; Michael J.C. Echeruo, "Derrida, Language Games, and Theory," *Theoria: A Journal of Social and Political Theory* 86 (1995), 99–115; Ian Rutherford, "Theoria and Darsan: Pilgrimage and Vision in Greece and India," *Classical Quarterly* 50 (2000), 133–46; Claire Colebrook, "Happiness, Theoria, and Everyday Life," *Symploke* 11 (2003), 132–51. For a suggestive discussion of the intersections of theory and poetics, see Earl Miner, *Comparative Poetics: An Intercultural Essay on Theories of Literature* (Princeton: Princeton University Press, 1990).

4. See Harold Innis, *The Strategy of Culture* (Toronto: University of Toronto Press, 1952) and his *Empire & Communications*, ed. David Godfrey, illustrated ed. (Victoria, BC: Press Porcépic, 1986); Marshall McLuhan, *The Mechanical Bride: Folklore of Industrial Man* (New York: Vanguard Press, 1951) and his *The Gutenburg Galaxy: The Making of Typographic Man* (Toronto: University of Toronto Press, 1962); Walter J. Ong, *Orality and Literacy: The Technologizing of the Word* (London; New York: Methuen, 1982). See also Marshall McLuhan, "The Later Innis," *Queen's Quarterly* 60 (1953), 385–94; Donald F. Theall, "Exploration in Communications since Innis," *Culture Communication, and Dependency: The Tradition of H.A. Innis*, ed. William H. Melody, Lioira Salter, and Paul Heyer (Norwood: Ablex, 1981), 225–34; Northrop Frye, "Criticism and Environment," *Adjoining Cultures as Reflected in Literature and Language*, ed. John Evans and Peter Horwath (Tempe: Arizona State University, 1983), 9–21; and Carolyn Marvin, " Innis, McLuhan and Marx," *Visible Language* 20 (1986), 355–59.

5. On poetics generally, see, for instance, *Encyclopedia of Poetry and Poetics*, ed. Alex Preminger (Princeton: Princeton University Press, 1965); Don Geiger, *The Dramatic Impulse in Modern Poetics* (Baton Rouge: Louisiana State University Press, 1968); George Calinescu, *Studies in Poetics* (Bucharest: Univers, 1972); Jonathan Culler, *Structuralist Poetics: Structuralism, Linguistics and the Study of Literature* (Ithaca: Cornell University Press, 1975); Wilbur Samuel Howell, *Poetics, Rhetoric, and Logic: Studies in the Basic Disciplines of Criticism* (Ithaca: Cornell University Press, 1975); Tzvetan Todorov, *The Poetics of Prose* (Ithaca: Cornell University Press, 1977); K. Viswanatham, *Essays in Criticism and Comparative Poetics* (Waltair: Andhra University Press, 1977); Stuart Friebert, *A Field Guide to Contemporary Poetry and Poetics* (London and New York: Longman, 1980); Tzvetan Todorov, *Introduction to Poetics* (Minneapolis: University of Minnesota Press, 1981); Peter Stallybrass, *The Politics and Poetics of Transgression* (Ithaca: Cornell University Press, 1989); Lubomír Doležel, *Occidental Poetics: Tradition and Progress* (Lincoln: University of Nebraska, Press 1990); Christopher Collins, *The Poetics of the Mind's Eye: Literature and the Psychology of Imagination* (Philadelphia: University of Pennsylvania Press, 1991); Wai-lim Yip, *Diffusion of Distances: Dialogues between Chinese and Western Poetics* (Berkeley: University of California Press, 1993); James Elkins, *The Poetics of Perspective* (Ithaca: Cornell University Press, 1994); Jacques Rancière, *The Names of History: On the Poetics of Knowledge* (Minneapolis: University of Minnesota Press, 1994); Richard Kearney, *Poetics of Modernity: Toward a Hermeneutic Imagination* (Atlantic Highlands, NJ: Humanities, 1995); Masaki Mori, *Epic Grandeur: Toward a Comparative Poetics of the Epic* (Albany: State University of New York Press,

1997); Catherine Brown, *Contrary Things: Exegesis, Dialectic, and the Poetics of Didacticism* (Stanford, CA: Stanford University Press, 1998); Marc Froment-Meurice, *That Is to Say: Heidegger's Poetics* (Stanford, CA: Stanford University Press, 1998); Richard Kearney, *Poetics of Imagining: Modern to Post-Modern* (New York: Fordham University Press, 1998); Giorgio Agamben, *The End of the Poem: Studies in Poetics* (Stanford, CA: Stanford University Press, 1999); Eleazar M. Meletinky, *The Poetics of Myth* (New York: Routledge, 2000).

6. George Orwell, " Politics and the English Language," *Horizon* (April 1946).

7. Johann Wolfgang von Goethe, *The Sorrows of Young Werther,* trans. Michael Hulse (London and New York: Penguin, 1989). Wilde has Vivian support her proposal to write an article called "The Decay of Lying" when she proclaims, with the usual Wildean comic reversal or inversion that so characterizes his wit in the plays: "The ancient historians gave us delightful fiction in the form of fact, the modern novelist presents us with dull facts under the guise of fiction" (37) and Vivian ends the dialogue with some main points, for instance, "Life imitates Art far more than Art imitates Life" (55) and "Lying, the telling of beautiful untrue things, is the proper aim of Art" (55–56). See Oscar Wilde, "The Decay of Lying: A Dialogue," *The Nineteenth Century: A Monthly Review,* ed. James Knowles (January–July 1889), 35–56. On the editing of this and other Wilde's texts, see David Holdeman's review of the Bobby Fong and Karl Beckson first volume of *The Complete Works of Oscar Wilde* (Oxford: Oxford University Press, 2000) and of Nicolas Frankel's *Oscar Wilde's Decorated Books* (Ann Arbor: University of Michigan Press, 2000) at www.textual.org/text/reviews/holdeman.htm. Wilde's essay also appears in his *Intentions;* the edition I consulted was (New York: Brentano's, 1905). Fyodor Dostoevsky, *Notes from the Underground,* trans. Constance Garnett (1918; New York: Dover, 1992). The narrator meditates on his spite, which includes the sentence: "Why, the whole point, the real sting of it lay in the fact that continually, even in the moment of the acutest spleen, I was inwardly conscious with shame that I was not only not a spiteful but not even an embittered man, that I was simply scaring sparrows at random and amusing myself by it" (2). In a few sentences, he says: "I was lying when I said just now that I was a spiteful official. I was lying from spite." The twists of introspection, meditation, roles, and other shifts in psychology play out in the narrator's thoughts on spite and related topics. For secondary sources, see *Dostoevski and the Human Condition,* ed. Alexaj Ugrinsky et al. (New York: Greenwood, 1986)—see in particular in this volume, Rado Pribic, *"Notes from the Underground*: One Hundred Years after the Author's Death," 71–77 and Phyllis Berdt Kenevan, "Rebirth and the Cognitive Dream: From Dostoevski to Herman Hesse and C.G. Jung," 181–90. Another interesting connection between literature and psychology is apparent in David Fred Burgess, "Narrative Fits: Freud's Essay on Dostoevsky," Ph.D. dissertation, University of Washington, 2000. The philosophical dimension is discussed in Alec D. Hope, "Dostoevski and Nietzsche," *Melbourne Slavonic Papers* 4 (1970), 38–45 and Martin P. Rice, "Dostoevski's *Notes from the Underground* and Hegel's Master and Slave," *Canadian-American Slavic Studies* 8 (1974), 359–69.

8. Jerome Bruner, *Actual Minds, Possible Worlds* (Cambridge, MA: Harvard University Press, 1986); Thomas G. Pavel, *Fictional Worlds* (Cambridge, MA: Harvard University Press, 1986); Jonathan Hart, "A Comparative Pluralism: The Heterogeneity of Methods and the Case of Possible Worlds," *CRCL/RCLC* 15 (1988), 320–45.

9. Plato, *The Republic of Plato,* trans. Francis Macdonald Cornford (New York: Oxford University Press, 1947); Aristotle (see also Longinus), [Greek and English] *The Poetics / Aristotle On the sublime / "Longinus". On style / Demetrius* (Cambridge: Harvard University Press, 1927); Longinus (see entry for Aristotle); Thomas Aquinas, *Aristotle: On interpretation. Commentary by St. Thomas and Cajetan (Peri hermenias),* trans. from the Latin with an intro. by Jean T. Oesterle (Milwaukee: Marquette University Press, 1962).

10. Northrop Frye, *Anatomy of Criticism: Four Essays* (Princeton: Princeton University Press, 1957, rpt. 1973); Jacques Derrida, *Of Grammatology,* trans. Gayatri Chakravorty Spivak (Baltimore: Johns Hopkins University Press, 1976) and his *Acts of Literature,* ed. Derek Attridge

(New York: Routledge, 1992); Jonathan Hart, *Northrop Frye: The Theoretical Imagination* (London and New York: Routledge, 1994).

11. Charles-Augustin Sainte-Beuve, "Des soirées littéraires, ou Les poètes entre eux," *Paris, ou Le livre des Cent-et-Un*, tome second (Paris: Ladvocat, 1831), 121–39; I.A. Richards, *Practical Criticism; A Study of Literary Judgment* (London: K. Paul, Trench, Trubner, 1929).

12. *Oxford English Dictionary (OED)* online: http://80-dictionary.oed.com.

13. Richard Hooker, *Of the lawes of ecclesiastical politie: eight bookes* (Lond [London]: Will: Stansby . . ., [1611?]) For a suggestive discussion of how Hooker's views of church and state affected Samuel Johnson's, see Jack Lynch, "Johnson and Hooker on Ecclesiastical and Civil Polity," *Review of English Studies* 55 (2004), esp. 58–59, see 45–57. Hooker's theory has a number of dimensions, one of them being law. See Paul E. Forte, "Richard Hooker's Theory of Law," *Journal of Medieval and Renaissance Studies* 12 (1982), 133–57. John Florio prefers the forms in Italian that contain "h": for instance, his dictionary contains two relevant definitions— "Theoría, *contemplation, speculation, deep study, insight or beholding*" and "Theórico, *a speculator or contemplative man. Also belonging to contemplation and view.*" These definitions occur in John Florio, *Qveen Anna's New World Of Words, Or Dictionarie og the "Italian" and "English" "tongues* (London, 1611), 562; Florio's smaller and earlier edition of 1598 is also instructive. For discussions of Florio's Italian–English dictionary and translations, see James L. Rosier, "Lexical Strata in Florio's *New World of Words*," *English Studies: A Journal of English Language and Literature* 44 (1963), 415–23; D.J. O'Connor, "John Florio's Contribution to Italian-English Lexicography," *Italica* 49 (1972), 49–67. David O. Frantz, "Florio's Use of Contemporary Italian Literature in *A Worlde of Wordes*," *Dictionaries: Journal of the Dictionary Society of North America* 1 (1979), 47–56; William Edward Engel, "Knowledge that Counted: Italian Phrase-Books and Dictionaries in Elizabethan England," *Annali d'Italianistica* 14 (1996), 507–22; David O. Frantz, "Negotiating Florio's *A Worlde of Wordes*," *Dictionaries: Journal of the Dictionary Society of North America* 18 (1997), 1–32 and Michael William Wyatt, "John Florio and The Cultural Politics of Translation," Ph.D. dissertation, Stanford University, 2000. See also Frances Yates, *John Florio: The Life of an Italian in Shakespeare's England* (Cambridge: Cambridge University Press, 1934).

14. Jonathan Swift, *[Gulliver's travels] Travels into several remote nations of the world: In four parts / By Lemuel Gulliver, first a surgeon, and then a captain of several ships*, third ed. (London: Printed for Benj. Motte, 1726); Thomas Sprat, *The History of the Royal-Society of London for the Improving of Natural Knowledge* (London: Printed by T.R. for J. Martyn . . ., and J. Allestry . . ., 1667).

15. See Galifridus Anglicus, *Promptorium Parvulorum sive Clericorum, Lexicon Anglo-Latinum Princeps* (1499; reprinted by AMS Press, New York).

16. See Geoffrey Chaucer, *The boke of Chaucer named Caunterbury tales* (Emprynted at Westmestre: By Wynkyn de Word the, yere of our lord. M.CCCC.lxxxxviii [1498]).

17. *Ars Poetica*, in *Horace, Satire, Epistles, Ars Poetica*, trans. H.R. Fairclough, Loeb Classical Library (Cambridge, MA: Harvard University Press, 1936), see 333–65. Perhaps the key line is "Omne tulit punctum qui miscuit utile dulci, / lectorem delectando pariterque monendo" (343–44). This can be loosely translated as: "He wins every vote who can mix the useful and the sweet, at once delighting and teaching the reader" (my translation).

18. Philip Sidney, *[Defence of poetry]. An apologie for poetrie. Written by the right noble, vertuous, and learned, Sir Phillip Sidney, Knight* (At London: Printed [by James Roberts] for Henry Olney, and are to be sold at his shop in Paules Church-yard, at the signe of the George, neere to Cheapgate, Anno. 1595); William Shakespeare, *Mr. William Shakespeares comedies, histories & tragedies: published according to the true originall copies* (London: Isaac Iaggard and Ed. Blount, 1623); for Keats, I have in mind the culminating lines of "Ode on a Grecian Urn,"—" 'Beauty is truth, truth beauty,'—that is all / Ye know on earth, and all ye need to know" (lines 49–50) [I have left out the quotation marks in these lines in keeping with the first printing of the poem in *Annals of Fine Arts* (James Elmes, editor), January 1820; on this debate over the quotation, see Dennis R. Dean, "Some Quotations in Keats's Poetry," *Philological Quarterly* 76 (1997), 69–85;

William Butler Yeats, *The Collected Poems of W.B. Yeats*, Definitive ed. with the Author's Final Revisions (New York: Macmillan, 1956, rpt. 1960).

19. Plutarch, *The lives of the noble Grecians and Romaines / compared together by that graue learned philosopher and historiographer, Plutarke of Chaeronea; translated out of Greeke into French by Iames Amiot . . .; with the liues of Hannibal and of Scipio African, translated out of Latine into French by Charles de l'Escluse, and out of French into English, by Sir Thomas North Knight; hereunto are also added the liues of Epaminondas, of Philip of Macedon, of Dionysius the Elder, tyrant of Sicilia, of Augustus Caesar, of Plutarke, and of Seneca, with the liues of nine other excellent chiefetaines of warre, collected out of Aemylius Probus, by S.G.S. and Englished by the aforesaid translator* (Imprinted at London: By Richard Field for George Bishop, 1603); Michel de Montaigne, *Essays vvritten in French by Michael Lord of Montaigne, Knight of the Order of S. Michael, gentleman of the French Kings chamber: done into English, according to the last French edition, by Iohn Florio reader of the Italian tongue vnto the Soueraigne Maiestie of Anna, Queene of England, Scotland, France and Ireland, &c. And one of the gentlemen of hir royall priuie chamber* (London: Printed by Melch. Bradvvood for Edvvard Blount and William Barret, 1613). For poetic novels and prose, which recalls the possibility of poetic prose in the face of prosaic verse, see especially, James Joyce, *Ulysses* (Paris: Shakespeare and Company, 1922); Virginia Woolf, *To the Lighthouse* (London: L. & V. Woolf at the Hogarth Press, 1927). There is also a conflation of epic and novel, which are already closely related, in these works. Narrative poetry also complicates the relation between the storytelling in the novel and that in history, historical poetry and poetry, generally. On Joyce and style, see William S. Fleming, "Formulaic Rhythms in Finnegans Wake," *Style* 6 (1972), 19–37; E.A. Levenston, "Narrative Technique in Ulysses: A Stylistic Comparison of 'Telemachus' and 'Eumaeus,' " *Language and Style* 5 (1972), 260–75; William B. Warner, "The Play of Fictions and Succession of Styles in Ulysses," *James Joyce Quarterly* 15 (1977), 18–35; Seamus Deane, "Heroic Styles: The Tradition of an Idea," *Ireland's Field Day* (Notre Dame: University of Notre Dame Press, 1986), 45–58; Massimo Bacigalupo, "Pound/Joyce: Style, Politics, and Language," *Joyce Studies in Italy, II*, ed. Carla de Petris (Rome: Bulzoni, 1988), 161–72; Hugh Kenner, "Mutations of Homer," *Classic Joyce*, ed. Franca Ruggeri (Rome: Bulzoni, 1999), 25–92. On stream-of-consciousness, which Joyce and Woolf developed, see Weiping Li, "The Rhetorical Forms in Stream-of-Consciousness Style," *Waiguoyu/Journal of Foreign Languages* 3 (1995), 49–54, 80, and on Joyce and Woolf, see John Andrews Whittier-Ferguson, "Framing Pieces: Designs of the Modernist Glosin in Joyce, Woolf, and Pound," Ph.D. dissertation, Princeton University, 1990. On Woolf's style, see N. Elizabeth Monroe, "The Inception of Mrs. Woolf's Art," *College English* 2 (1940), 217–30; Muriel R. Schulz, "A Style of One's Own," *Women's Language and Style*, ed. Douglas Butturff and Edmund L. Epstein (Akron: L & S Books; 1978), 75–83; Julia Penelope Stanley, "Consciousness as Style; Style as Aesthetic," *Language, Gender, and Society*, ed. Barrie Thorne, Cheris Kramarae, and Nancy Henley (Rowley, MA: Newbury House, 1983), 125–39; Gerald Levin, "The Musical Style of 'The Wave' " *Journal of Narrative Technique* 13 (1983), 164–71; André Dommergues, "Virginia Woolf et le dire fragmenté," *Bulletin de la Societé de Stylistique Anglaise* 7 (1985), 175–88; Teresa L. Ebert, "Metaphor, Metonymy, and Ideology: Language and Perception in Mrs. Dalloway," *Language and Style* 18 (1985), 152–64; Pamela J. Transue, *Virginia Woolf and the Politics of Style* (Albany: State University of New York Press, 1986); Garrett Stewart, "Catching the Stylistic D/rift: Sound Effects in 'The Waves,' " *ELH* 54 (1987), 421–61; Diane Lee Richards, "Crossing Boundaries: Genre, Voice and Marginality in the Monologues of Robert Browning, William Faulkner and Virginia Woolf," Ph.D. dissertation, University of California, Berkeley, 1997; John Parras, "The Dangerous Gift of Poetry: Woolf's Critique of the Lyric," *Virginia Woolf Miscellany* 51 (1998), 5–6; Harvena Richter, "The Hidden Poetry of Virginia Woolf," *Virginia Woolf Miscellany* 57 (2001), 3–4; Emily Blair, "Virginia Woolf and the Nineteenth-Century Domestic Aesthetic: Poetry the Wrong Side Out," Ph.D. dissertation, University of California, Davis, 2002; Cornelia D.J. Pearsall, "Whither, Whether, Woolf: Victorian Poetry and A Room of One's Own," *Victorian Poetry* 41 (2003), 596–603. The Authorized Version or

King James Bible blurs the line between poetry and prose, something that, given the mixture of poetics, dialectics, and rhetoric in language, is no surprise, but something that rarely takes on the beauty and power as it does in English in this sacred book.

20. Friedrich Wilhelm Nietzsche, *The Birth of Tragedy [Geburt der Tragödie. English]*, trans. Douglas Smith (Oxford: Oxford University Press, 2000); Roland Barthes, *Mythologies* (Paris: Éditions du Seuil, 1957) and his *Le plaisir du texte* (Paris: Éditions du Seuil, 1973); Marshall McLuhan, *The Mechanical Bride: Folklore of Industrial Man* (New York: Vanguard Press, [1951]). For Nietzsche and/on style, see Allan L. Carter, "Nietzsche on the Art of Writing," *Modern Language Notes* 39 (1924), 98–102; Paul Cantor, "Friedrich Nietzsche: The Use and Abuse of Metaphor," *Metaphor: Problems and Perspectives*, ed. David S. Miall (Brighton: Harvester, 1982), 71–88; Geoffrey Waite, "Nietzsche and Deconstruction: The Politics of 'The Question of Style,'" *BMMLA* 16 (1983), 70–86; Eugen Biser, "Nietzsche: Critic in the Grand Style," *Studies in Nietzsche and the Judaeo-Christian Tradition*, ed. James C. O'Flaherty et al. (Chapel Hill: University of North Carolina Press, 1985), 16–28; Geoffrey Waite, "The Politics of 'The Question of Style': Nietzsche/Höderlin," *Identity of the Literary Text*, ed. Mario J. Valdés and Owen Miller (Toronto: University of Toronto Press, 1985), 246–73; Jeffrey Schnapp, "Nietzsche's Italian Style: Gabriele D'Annunzio," *Stanford Italian Review* 6 (1986) and in *Nietzsche in Italy*, ed. Thomas Harrison (Saratoga, CA: ANMA Libri, 1988), 247–63; Babette E. Babich, "On Nietzsche's Concinnity: An Analysis of Style," *Nietzsche Studien: Internationales Jahrbuch für die Nietzsche-Forschung* 19 (1990), 59–80, her "Towards a Post-Modern Hermeneutic Ontology of Art: Nietzschean Style and Heideggerian Truth," *Analecta Husserliana*, ed. M. Kronegger (Dordrecht: Kluwer Academic, 1990), 195–209, and her "Self-Deconstruction: Nietzsche's Philosophy as Style," *Soundings* 73 (1990) 105–16; Claudia Crawford, "Nietzsche's Great Style: Educator of the Ears and of the Heart," *Nietzsche Studien: Internationales Jahrbuch für die Nietzsche-Forschung* 20 (1991), 210–37; Geneviève Finke-Lecaudey, "Le Langage poétique de Nietzsche à la lumière de 'Also sprach Zarathustra': Analyse du chapitre 'Von der grossen Sehnsucht' ('Du grand désir')," *Le Langage poétique: Métrique, rythmique, phonostylistique* (Aix-en-Provence: Centre des Sciences du Langage, Université de Provence, 1991), 111–33; John Carson Pettey, *Nietzsche's Philosophical and Narrative Styles* (New York: Peter Lang, 1992); Douglas A. Gilmour, "On Language, Writing, and the Restoration of Sight: Nietzsche's Philosophical Palinode," *Philosophy and Rhetoric* 27 (1994), 245–69; Thomas Leddy, "Nietzsche on Unity of Style," *Historical Reflections/Réflexions Historiques* 21 (1995), 553–67; Vincent Fornerod, "Jeux et enjeux de la métaphore chez Nietzsche," *Etudes de Lettres* 1–2 (1996), 13–25; Bernd Magnus, "Philosophy as a Kind of Writing: *Der Fall Nietzsche,*" *REAL: The Yearbook of Research in English and American Literature* 13 (1997), 125–47; Jacques Derrida, "The Question of Style," *Feminist Interpretations of Friedrich Nietzsche*, ed. Kelly Oliver and Marilyn Pearsall (University Park: Pennsylvania State University Press, 1998), 50–65; Lohren David Green, "Interpreting Nietzsche: The Role of Style in the History of Philosophy," Ph.D. dissertation, University of California, Berkeley, 1998; Dorothea B. Heitsch, "Nietzsche and Montaigne: Concepts of Style," *Rhetorica* 17 (1999), 411–31; Kathleen Merrow, " 'The Meaning of Every Style': Nietzsche, Demosthenes, Rhetoric," *Rhetorica* 21 (2003), 285–307. For Barthes on style, see Roland Barthes, "Style and Its Image," *Literary Style: A Symposium*, ed. Seymour Chatman (New York: Oxford University Press, 1971), 3–10; Josue V. Harari, "The Maximum Narrative: An Introduction to Barthes' Recent Criticism," *Style* 8 (1974), 56–77; Jean A. Moreau, "Plaisir du texte, plaisir du style," *L'Arc* 56 (1974), 78–82; Roland A. Champagne, "The Dialectics of Style: Insights from the Semiology of Roland Barthes," *Style* 13 (1979), 279–91; Louis-Jean Calvet, "Les Barthes: Morceaux choisis," *Le Francais dans le Monde* 254 (1993), 56–57; Louis-Jean Calvet, "Un Barthes des Barthes," *Le Francais dans le Monde* 254 (January 1993), 55–60; Robert K. Martin, "Roland Barthes: Toward an 'écriture gaie,' " *Camp Grounds: Style and Homosexuality*, ed. David Bergman (Amherst: University of Massachusetts Press, 1993), 282–98; Kathleen Woodward, "Late Theory, Late Style: Loss and Renewal in Freud and Barthes," *Aging and Gender in Literature: Studies in Creativity*, ed. Anne Wyatt-Brown and Janice Rossen (Charlottesville: University Press of Virginia, 1993), 82–101; Nicholas Harrison,

"Camus, écriture blanche and the Reader, between Said and Barthes," *Nottingham French Studies* 38 (1999), 55–66; D.A. Miller, "Foutre! Bougre! Ecriture!," *Yale Journal of Criticism: Interpretation in the Humanities,* 14 (2001), 503–11. For McLuhan on/and style, media, and related topics, see Marshall McLuhan, "The Relation of Environment to Anti-Environment," *University of Windsor Review* 2 (1966), 1–10; his "Erasmus: The Man and the Masks," *Erasmus in English* 3 (1971), 7–10; his "Alphabet, Mother of Invention," *ETC. A Review of General Semantics* 34 (1977), 373–83; his "Figures and Grounds in Linguistic Criticism," *ETC.: A Review of General Semantics* 36 (1979), 289–94; and his "Lewis's Prose Style," *Wyndham Lewis: A Revaluation: New Essays,* ed. Jeffrey Meyers (Montreal: McGill-Queen's University Press, 1980), 64–67. For work on McLuhan, see Lloyd Reynolds, "Comment: Marshall McLuhan and Italic Handwriting," *Journal of Typographic Research* 3 (1969), 293–97; James J. Murphy, "The Metarhetorics of Plato, Augustine, and McLuhan: A Pointing Essay," *Philosophy and Rhetoric* 4 (1971), 201–14; Lloyd W. Brown, "Misunderstanding Media: McLuhan on Language, Culture and Race," *Conch: A Sociological Journal of African Cultures and Literatures* 4 (1972), 1–10; Bruce E. Gronbeck, "McLuhan as Rhetorical Theorist," *Journal of Communication* 31 (1981), 117–28; David R. Olson, "McLuhan: Preface to Literacy," *Journal of Communication* 31 (1981), 136–43; Thomas W. Cooper, "Marshall McLuhan: Style as Substance," *American Review of Canadian Studies* 12 (1982), 120–32; Hwa Jung, "Misreading the Ideogram: From Fenollosa to Derrida and McLuhan," *Paideuma* 13 (1984), 211–27; Jeffrey Kittay, "Recent Research on McLuhan's Theory of Content," *Studies in Communication: Communication and Culture: Language Performance, Technology, and Media,* ed. Sari Thomas (Norwood, NJ: Ablex, 1990), 208–14; Jay Rosen, "The Messages of 'The Medium Is the Message,' " *ETC.: A Review of General Semantics* 47 (1990), 45–51; Robert J. Scholes, "Linguists, Literacy, and the Intensionality of Marshall McLuhan's Western Man," *Literacy and Orality,* ed. David R. Olson and Nancy Torrance (Cambridge: Cambridge University Press, 1991), 215–35; Robert Owen Fiander, "Marshall McLuhan, the Printed Word, and Nineteenth-Century Outcasts of Literacy," Ph.D. dissertation, University of New Brunswick, 2000.

21. William Blake, "Jerusalem," *Milton* (London, 1804).

22. Francis Bacon, *The two bookes of Sr. Francis Bacon: Of the proficience and advancement of learning, divine and hvmane* (London: W. Washington, 1629).

23. Dwight Eisenhower, *Military-Industrial Complex Speech, 1961,* The Avalon Project at Yale Law School, Public Papers of the Presidents, Dwight D. Eisenhower, 1960, 1035–40.

24. George Grant, *Technology and Empire: Perspectives on North America* (Toronto: House of Anansi, 1969); see Jacques Ellul, *L'empire du non-sens: l'art et la société technicienne* (Paris: Presses Universitaires de France, 1980); *Technology & the West: A Historical Anthology from Technology and Culture,* ed. Terry S. Reynolds and Stephen H. Cutcliffe (Chicago: University of Chicago Press, 1997). See volumes 1 and 2 especially of the Loeb Classics bilingual edition, *Sophocles,* ed. Hugh Lloyd-Jones (Cambridge, MA: Harvard University Press, 1994); Louise Labé, *Oeuvres . . .* (Lyon: [s.n.], 1555); and Margaret Atwood, *The Edible Woman* (Toronto: McClelland & Stewart, 1969).

25. C.P. Snow, *The Two Cultures and the Scientific Revolution* (Cambridge: Cambridge University Press, 1959).

26. Umberto Eco, *Interpretation and Overinterpretation/Umberto Eco with Richard Rorty, Jonathan Culler, Christine Brooke-Rose,* ed. Stefan Collini (Cambridge: Cambridge University Press, 1992); Louise Erdrich, *Baptism of Desire* (New York: Harper & Row, 1990); Frantz Fanon, *Peau noire, masques blancs* (Paris: Éditions du Seuil, 1952); Gabriel García Márquez, *Of Love and Other Demons,* trans. Edith Grossman (New York: Alfred A. Knopf, 1995) [*Del amor y otros demonios*]; Allen Ginsberg, *Contexts of Poetry / Robert Creeley, with Allen Ginsberg, at the Vancouver Conference, July 1963* (Buffalo, NY: Audit, 1968); Günter Grass, *My Century,* trans. Michael Henry Heim (New York: Harcourt, 1999); Nancy Huston, *The Goldberg Variations* [translated by the author] (Montréal, Québec: Nuage Editions, 1996); Joy Kogawa, *Obasan* (1981; Boston: D.R. Godine, 1982); Toni Morrison, *Playing in the Dark: Whiteness and the Literary Imagination* (Cambridge, MA: Harvard University Press, 1992); V.S. Naipaul, *Reading &*

Writing: A Personal Account (New York: New York Review of Books, 2000); *All My Relations: An Anthology of Contemporary Canadian Native Fiction*, ed. Thomas King (Toronto: McClelland & Stewart, 1990); Derek Walcott, *The Antilles: Fragments of Epic Memory* (New York: Farrar, Straus and Giroux, 1993).

27. Plato, *The Republic of Plato*, trans. Francis M. Cornford (New York: Oxford University Press, 1941, rpt. 1968).

28. *Apocalypse Now* (1979), producer/director Francis Ford Coppola, released: November 9, 1999, Paramount Home Entertainment, runtime: 2 hours, 33 minutes.

29. Matthew Arnold, *Essays in Criticism* (London: Macmillan, 1865).

30. William Carlos Williams, "The Red Wheelbarrow," *The Collected Poems of William Carlos Williams*, ed. A. Walton Litz and Christopher MacGowan (New York: New Directions, 1988).

31. Terry Eagleton, *Literary Theory: An Introduction* (Minneapolis: University of Minnesota Press, 1983); see *Structuralism and Since: from Lévi Strauss to Derrida*, ed. John Sturrock (Oxford: Oxford University Press, 1979).

32. See Jonas Barish, *The Antitheatrical Prejudice* (Berkeley: University of California Press, 1981).

33. See Frye, *Anatomy*.

34. Paul De Man, *Blindness & Insight: Essays in the Rhetoric of Contemporary Criticism* (New York: Oxford University Press, 1971).

35. Percy Bysshe Shelley, *A Defence of Poetry*, ed. Mrs. Shelley, reprinted from the edition of MDCCCXLV (Indianapolis: The Bobbs-Merrill Company, 1904); *Defence of Poetry. Part First.* Also at www.library.utoronto.ca/utel/rp/criticism/shell_il.html; see Shelley Sig. 10r–12r on Dante. See Dante, *Vita Nuova. Italian and English. The canzoniere of Dante Alighieri; including the poems of the Vita nuova and Convito, Italian and English*, trans. Charles Lyell (London: J. Murray, 1835); see Alfred Lord Tennyson, especially "The Poet" and his sonnet "Alexander" (1872) as well as "The Lotus-Eaters" in *Poetical Works* (London, 1886); T.S. Eliot, *The Waste Land* (New York: Boni and Liveright, 1922); Hilda Doolittle (H.D.), *Heliodora, and Other Poems* (Boston: Houghton Mifflin & Company, 1924).

36. See Louis Althusser, *Essays on Ideology* (London: Verso, 1984).

6 Poetry and Mythology: Coda

1. This section is a later version of a talk delivered at "A World of Local Voices," a conference organized by Klaus Martens and his group at Universität des Saarlandes in October 1998, which, along with a poetry reading, constituted my contribution there. My thanks to him and to my other hosts. A revised version of that talk appeared as "Poetry and Mythology," *Wascana Review* 37 (2) (Fall 2002), 182–86; this appeared in the same issue with another poem "The Story of Our Making," 187; my thanks to the editor Michael Trussler.

2. Four works in the past decade will serve as examples of this widening concern with the relation between music and ideology both in classical and the popular expressions in various parts of the world. Gregory B. Lee's *Troubadours, Trumpeters, Troubled Makers: Lyricism, Nationalism, and Hybridity in China and Its Others* (Durham: Duke University Press, 1996) devotes a chapter— chapter 6—to Chinese trumpeters and French troubadours and examines Nationalist ideology and the cultural dimension of popular music. More generally, Lee explores the ways the lyrics of poets and songwriters answered cultural imperialism and nationalistic ideology. Lee analyzes the manner in which lyrics transgress ideological boundaries in China and the Chinese diaspora. Leslie David Blasius, *Schenker's Argument and the Claims of Music Theory* (Cambridge and New York: Cambridge University Press, 1996), leads up to a discussion of the function of ideology. *Music/Ideology: Resisting the Aesthetic: Essays,* ed. Adam Krims (Amsterdam: G + B Arts International, 1998) shows an array of points of view. In this volume, Adam Krims provides an introduction in which he discusses the relation of postmodern musical poetics to close reading,

and, in a commentary, Henry Klumpenhouwer explores poststructuralism and issues of music theory. Among the interesting essays are one by Jean-François Lyotard and another, on feminist theory and music theory, by Suzanne G. Cusick. Mark Carroll, in *Music and Ideology in Cold War Europe* (Cambridge and New York: Cambridge University Press, 2003), brings together issues and perspectives (esp. 1–7). His discussion of freedom of Nabokov is interesting with regard to means and ends and of the nature of the freedom of expression in the act of creation (see 9–21, esp. 21).

For other works during the 1980s, 1990s, and beyond, see also Lucy Green, *Music on Deaf Ears: Musical Meaning, Ideology, Education* (Manchester: Manchester University Press, 1988); Richard D. Leppert, *Music and Image: Domesticity, Ideology, and Sociocultural Formation in Eighteenth-Century England* (Cambridge: Cambridge University Press, 1988); Rose Rosengard Subotnik, *Developing Variations: Style and Ideology in Western Music* (Minneapolis: University of Minnesota Press, 1991); John Beverley, *Against Literature* (Minneapolis: University of Minnesota Press, 1993), which includes a discussion of the ideology of postmodern music and Left politics; John Daverio, *Nineteenth-Century Music and the German Romantic Ideology* (New York: Maxwell Macmillan International, 1993); John Potter, *Vocal Authority: Singing Style and Ideology* (New York: Cambridge University Press, 1998), which discusses classical ideology; *The Pleasure of Modernist Music: Listening, Meaning, Intention, Ideology*, ed. Arved Mark Ashby (Rochester, NY: University of Rochester Press, 2004).

3. Aristotle, *The Poetics / Aristotle. On the sublime / "Longinus." On style / Demetrius* (Cambridge, MA: Harvard University Press, 1927); Greek and English texts.

4. Here I have in mind Orwell's essay, "The Politics of the English Language" (1946): see George Orwell, *The Collected Essays, Journalism, and Letters of George Orwell*, ed. Sonia Orwell and Ian Angus (London: Secker & Warburg, 1968), esp. vol. 1, 1920–40. See Raymond Williams, *Orwell* (London: Flamingo, 1971). For a discussion of Orwell and the relation between ideology and form, see Carl Howard Freedman, *George Orwell: A Study in Ideology and Literary Form* (New York: Garland, 1988) and for the connection between Orwell and the politics of ideology, see Stephen Ingle, *George Orwell:A Political Life* (Manchester: Manchester University Press, 1993), ch. 5; Roland Barthes's *Mythologies* (Paris: Seuil, 1957), which has almost twice as many articles or essays than the Annette Lavers's translation into English, is a key discussion of the relation between nature and culture and the estrangement of the everyday into an ideological awareness. Barthes, who wrote on Bertolt Brecht's theory of theatre, shares this alienation effect with Brecht. Reality, which is socially and politically constructed, is often presented as natural in a society. Barthes sees the entanglement of ideology and power in language. On Barthes, for instance, see Jonathan Culler, *Roland Barthes* (London: Fontana, 1983); M. Moriarty, *Roland Barthes* (Cambridge: Polity, 1991); Andrew Leak, *Roland Barthes: Mythologies* (London: Grant & Cutler, 1994); *Barthes, au lieu de roman*, ed. Marcielle Macé and Alexandre Gefen (Paris: Desjonquères, 2002) and *R/B, Roland Barthes*, ed. Marianne Alphant and Natalie Léger (Paris: Seuil, 2002). Many American writers engage the French on ideology in the nineteenth century. For instance, John Adams expressed his skepticism about the ability of the fledgling United States to establish a free republican government as Thomas Jefferson had envisioned. In a letter to Jefferson on July 13, 1813, Adams expresses this doubt and notes: "Napoleon has lately invented a Word, which perfectly expresses my Opinion at that time and ever since. He calls the Project Ideology"; see *The Founders' Constitution*, ed. Philip B. Kurland and Ralph Lerner (Chicago: University of Chicago Press, 1987, 2000), chapter 15 (Equality), document 59. Apparently, Bonaparte considered the welter of ideas in the French Revolution to about 1792 to be ideology. Thomas Jefferson himself had outlined, in an undated document [Elements (Of) Ideology], his own view of the word, which he took to mean "our means of obtaining knowledge" in an outline for what would appear to be a projected study or book [*The Thomas Jefferson Papers* Series 1, Library of Congress, ms. 1 p.]. As Destutt de Tracy in the 1790s conceived of ideology, it was a science or system of ideas, but the world could also mean abstract speculation, idealism, and the way ideas are expressed. The *Oxford English Dictionary* (second ed. 1989) sets this out clearly. The word "ideology" changed then and is still contested.

5. See especially *Northrop Frye, Anatomy of Criticism: Four Essays* (Princeton: Princeton University Press, 1957, rpt. 1973), which is based on the mythological and natural cycles of the seasons.

6. Narrative and argumentation were often seen as being opposed. Plato opposes philosophy to poetry, whereas Plato's philosophy involved a good deal of narrative, especially in the form of allegory, so that the actual foundation of philosophy was narrative as well as dialectical and dialogical. The usefulness of knowledge is one of the reasons Plato places philosophy above poetry. Universality is something that is applied through practicality. Philip Sidney saw poetry as a means of moving people to virtue. This *telos* is the same for Plato and Sidney—virtue—but they construct related arguments and narratives with a different preference about whether philosophy or poetry best serves that end. The ethnological turn, as exemplified by Michel de Montaigne, Jean de Léry, and others so vitally in the sixteenth century, as well as the anthropological or ethnological aspect of history and literary theory and criticism, as exemplified by Natalie Zemon Davis, Jean-François Lyotard, and Stephen Greenblatt, as well as the importance of the work of Clifford Geertz in anthropology, blur the distinction between story and argument into what I have called story-argument. For my earliest use of the idea of story-argument, see "Stephen Greenblatt's Shakespearean Negotiations," *Textual Practice* 5 (1991), 429–48. Oscar Wilde, who used his wit to create plays and stories, wrote: "Arguments are to be avoided; they are always vulgar and often convincing."

7. As I have said elsewhere, in *Mythologies*, Barthes attacked mythology in 1957, the same year Frye was defending it in *Anatomy*. In some ways Barthes idea of mythology is similar to Frye's notion of ideology. This relation between mythology and ideology is a central concern of my *Northrop Frye: The Theoretical Imagination* (London and New York: Routledge, 1994), esp. ch. 7 (see 194–95 for the discussion of Barthes and Frye). Terminology can change and blur and cause misapprehension in the connection between mythology and ideology. "Myth" can be a misguided view or belief or can be, in its more technical sense, the root of story and perhaps even of imagination, or much else between. One of the tensions in ideology has been the notion of it as a matter of ideas or ideas as matter (that is, as part of the human material social process). See Raymond Williams, *Marxism and Literature* (Oxford: Oxford University Press, 1977), 55–60. On the history of ideology, beginning with Destutt de Tracy, see J. Plamenatz, *Ideology* (London: Macmillan, 1985). A recent brief study is Michael Freeden's *Ideology: A Very Short Introduction* (Oxford: Oxford University Press, 2003); chapter 3 discusses theory and ideology. Some of the many recent discussions of ideology and its theoretical, social, and historical effects are Richard Brian Miller, *Casuistry and Modern Ethics: A Poetics of Practical Reasoning* (Chicago: University of Chicago Press, 1996); *Ideology and the Politics of (In)exclusion*, ed. Linda Ware (New York: Counterpoints, 2004); *Feminist Communication Theory: Selections in Context*, ed. Lana F. Rakow and Laura A. Wackwitz (Thousand Oaks, CA: Sage, 2004); Leon P. Baradat, *Political Ideologies: Their Origins and Impact*, eighth ed. (Upper Saddle River, NJ: Prentice Hall, 2003); Richard Kearney, *On Paul Ricoeur: The Owl of Minerva* (Aldershot: Ashgate, 2004); *Critical Theories, Radical Pedagogies, and Global Conflicts*, ed. Gustavo Fischman et al. (Lanham, MD: Rowan & Littlefield, 2005); Robert Conquest, *The Dragons of Expectation: Reality and Delusion in the Course of History* (New York: Norton, 2005).

Richard Miller's discussion of poetics in the context of rhetoric and casuistry occurs in chapter 9. In the collection on feminist communication, Teresa de Lauretis discusses the role of images and ideology in relation to women of color. Linda Ware's collection examines the relation of ideology to exclusion in education, especially as that pertains to special education, and social and cross-cultural elements—something that, as I note in this book, affects our reading of texts including literature. Baradat's textbook provides students with a definition, history, and recent context for ideology and the spectrum of ideologies from radical to reactionary. Kerney discusses, in study four, the relation between ideology and utopia; in Dialogue 1, he also explores the view that myth enables possible worlds; Fischman's collection examines in various ways by different authors a number of ideas, such as ideology and social justice, in a time in which neoliberalism is not seen as radical enough and utopian thinking gets beyond history and the global and dystopian realities facing students, teachers, and others. For instance, in this collection, there is a contribution that seems to unmask the ideology of standardized testing. Conquest sees the original nurturing of dragons, with their delusions and idealizations in democratic, Left, and liberal discourse as being the French Enlightenment, which, oddly enough I might add, has been the target of a fair number of theorists upholding the very ideals that Conquest criticizes.

The relation among poetics, philosophy and mythology is another crucial topic, although not as much a problem of these times as its connection to ideology. A good introduction to representation, poiesis, and the boundaries between philosophy and literature is *Beyond Representation: Philosophy and Poetic Imagination*, ed. Richard Eldridge (Cambridge: Cambridge University Press, 1996); see J.M. Bernstein's discussion of the ideology of the aesthetic in this volume. Another earlier book on this topic is Terry Eagleton's *The Ideology of the Aesthetic* (Oxford: Blackwell, 1990); a collection on the topic is *Aesthetics and Ideology*, ed. George Levine (New Brunswick, NJ: Rutgers University Press, 1994). Cornell University Press has a series on myth and poetics. Some of the books most pertinent to our discussion are Claude Calame, *Récit en Grèce ancienne: enunciations et representations de poètes* (Paris: Méridiens Klincksieck, 1986); Gregory Nagy, *Greek Mythology and Poetics* (Ithaca: Cornell University Press, 1990); *The Craft of Poetic Speech in Ancient Greece*, trans. Janice Orion [Ithaca: Cornell University Press, 1995]); *Poetry and Prophecy: The Beginnings of a Literary Tradition*, ed. James L. Kugel (Ithaca: Cornell University Press, 1990); Nicole Loraux, *Né de la Terre. Mythe et politique à Athènes* (Paris: Le Seuil, 1996) [see *Born of the Earth: Myth and Politics in Athens*, trans. Selina Stewart (Ithaca: Cornell University Press, 2000)]; Egbert J Bakker, *Poetry in Speech: Orality and Homeric Discourse* (Ithaca: Cornell University Press, 1997).

8. Plato, *The Republic of Plato*, trans. Francis Macdonald Cornford (New York: Oxford University Press, 1947), bk. 10.

9. Buffon's most celebrated discussion of style may be found in Georges Louis Leclerc, comte de Buffon, *Discours sur le Style; texte français avec version latine de J. A. Nairn* (Paris: Société d'édition 'Les belles letters,' 1926). The original text is 1753. For Buffon, style was integral to the person. In "An Essay in Criticism," Alexander Pope wrote: "For diff'rent Styles with diff'rent Subjects sort," defining decorum. Pope begins this poem with the musing of whether a poet or critic suffers most on his craft: " 'Tis hard to say, if greater Want of Skill / Appear in Writing or in Judging ill"? Matthew Arnold's use of the phrase "grand style" is in keeping with his notion of the high aims of poetry and poetry as something that would take the place of religion and philosophy, a kind of knowledge that would supplant dogma. For Arnold, poetry might have had a higher use, but it had a use. See his essay from 1864, "The Function of Criticism at the Present Time." An interesting analysis of Arnold is Irving Babitt's review of Stuart P. Sherman's *Matthew Arnold: How to Know Him*, in *The Nation* (August 2, 1917).

10. "What is a cynic? A man who knows the price of everything and the value of nothing." See Oscar Wilde, *Lady Windermere's Fan* (1892), act 3.

11. Expatriation is a common theme among Conrad, Grove/Greve and Huston. The peripatetic Conrad was born in the Ukraine and became a British subject; Grove/Greve had a German and then a Canadian career writing in English (both careers were recently connected); Nancy Huston was born an Anglophone in Calgary, Alberta, but has become a major French writer living in Paris. On Conrad, see, for instance, Jeffrey Meyers, *Joseph Conrad: A Biography* (London: Murray, 1991); John Batchelor, *The Life of Joseph Conrad: A Critical Biography* (Oxford: Blackwell, 1994); Michael Greaney, *Conrad, Language, and Narrative* (Cambridge: Cambridge University Press, 2002); *Conrad in the Twenty-First Century: Contemporary Approaches and Perspectives*, ed. Carola Kaplan et al. (New York: Routledge, 2005). On Grove (Greve), see, for example, Klaus Martens, *F.P. Grove in Europe and Canada: Translated Lives*, trans. Paul Morris (Edmonton: University of Alberta Press, 2001); *The Politics of Cultural Mediation: Baroness Elsa von Freytag-Loringhoven and Felix Paul Greve*, ed. Paul Hjartarson and Tracy Kulba (Edmonton: The University of Alberta Press, 2003). See Nancy Huston, *Nord perdu; suivi de, Douze France* (Arles: Actes sud, 1999) and the English version *Losing North: Musings on Land, Tongue and Self* (Toronto: McArthur, 2002).

12. On Plato and myth, see Stanley Rosen, *The Quarrel between Philosophy and Poetry: Studies in Ancient Thought* (New York: Routledge, 1988, rpt. 1993), particularly on the quarrel between philosophy and poetry and on Plato's myth of the reversed cosmos; Christopher Janaway, *Images of Excellence: Plato's Critique of the Arts* (Oxford: Clarendon Press, 1995), especially his discussion of mimesis and anti-mimesis and of the connection among myth, madness, and pleasure (chs. 5–7); *Essays on Plato's "Republic,"* ed. Erik Nis Ostenfeld (Aarhus: Aarhus University Press, 1998), especially Lars Albinus's discussion of the katabasis of Er and Plato's use of myth; Kathryn A. Morgan, *Myth and Philosophy from the Presocratics to Plato* (Cambridge: Cambridge University Press, 2000). See Toynbee's "Not the age of atoms but of welfare for all," *Technology and Social Change*, ed. Wilbert Ellis Moore (Chicago: Quadrangle Books [1972]); *Toynbee: Reappraisals*, ed. C.T. McIntire (Toronto: University of Toronto, 1989); William Hardy McNeill, *Arnold J. Toynbee: A Life* (New York: Oxford University Press, 1989); Christopher Brewin, "Arnold Toynbee, Chatham House, and Research in a Global Context," *Thinkers of the Twenty Years' Crisis: Inter-War Idealism Reassessed*, ed. David Longe and Peter Wilson (Oxford: Clarendon Press, 1995), ch. 11.

13. See Philip Sidney, [*Defence of Poetry*] *An apologie for poetrie. VVritten by the right noble, vertuous, and learned, Sir Phillip Sidney, Knight* (At London: Printed [by James Roberts] for Henry Olney, and are to be sold at his shop in Paules Church-yard, at the signe of the George, neere to Cheap-gate, Anno. 1595) and Percy Bysshe Shelley, *A Defence of Poetry*, ed. Mrs. Shelley, reprinted from the edition of MDCCCXLV (Indianapolis: The Bobbs-Merrill Company, 1904), Part First.

7 Creating the Word: Northrop Frye and Writing

1. Although I have been asked to write about Frye for many years and have published widely on him, the most ready place to find my views on his theory, criticism, and writing are in *Northrop Frye: The Theoretical Imagination* (London and New York: Routledge, 1994). A previous version of this chapter was published as "The Quest for the Creative Word," *Rereading Frye: The Published and Unpublished Works*, ed. David Boyd and Imre Salusinszky (Toronto: University of Toronto Press, 1999), 55–71.

2. Hart, "The Road Not Taken: The Fictions of Northrop Frye," *The British Journal of Canadian Studies* 9 (1994), 216–37. I wish to thank Robert Denham for his kind help over the years, especially in providing me copies of his transcriptions of Frye's unpublished fiction and his comments on fiction in the diaries-notebooks. In a letter to me (February 23, 1996), Denham clarifies that the novel in Frye's notebooks that we had been calling the Kennedy-Megill fragment or novel is the *Locust-Eaters*. See also my "Northrop Frye and the End/s of Ideology," *Comparative Literature* 47 (1995), 160–74 and "Northrop Frye and the 1960s: The Crisis in Canadian Education," *Canadian Literature* 152/153 (1997), 93–106; special issue, "Remembering the Sixties."

3. This is a phrase I use in my book on Frye and as its subtitle. In chapter 7, I discuss the relation between ideology and mythology. For other discussions of ideology in Frye, see David Cayley, *Northrop Frye in Conversation* (Toronto: Anansi, 1992), and Imre Salusinszky, "Frye and Ideology," Lee and Denham, eds., *The Legacy of Northrop Frye* (Toronto: University of Toronto Press, 1994), 76–83.

4. John Ayre, *Northrop Frye: A Biography* (Toronto: Random House, 1989), 100.

5. Ayre, *Northrop Frye*, 96, 99–100.

6. I avoid a discussion of this novel, the problems of which I have discussed elsewhere. See Hart, *Northrop Frye: The Theoretical Imagination* (London and New York: Routledge, 1994), 267–68, 287 and Hart, "Road Not Taken," 221. More generally, I have avoided repeating what I have said about Frye's fiction elsewhere.

7. The Correspondence of Northrop Frye and Helen Kemp, 1932–1939, ed. Robert D. Denham (Toronto: University of Toronto Press, 1996), Vol 1, 463–4.

8. Notebook 4, Notes on Fiction. From 1939 onwards. Transcription from Robert D. Denham. From the typescript he supplied me. E.J. Pratt Library, Victoria University, Toronto, 23 pp. 3.

9. Notebook 4, 14.

10. Notebook 4, 15, see 21, 55, 62, 86.

11. Northrop Frye, "Affable Angel," *Acta Victoriana* 64 (January 1940), 4.

12. Notebook 4, 95.

13. Notebook 20, A draft of "Reflections in a Mirror." No date. Transcription from Robert D. Denham. From the unedited typescript he supplied me. E.J. Pratt Library, Victoria University, Toronto, 8 pp. [p. 1]. There is no notation for the file number in Denim's transcription, so I have substituted the page number.

14. On Frye's visionary criticism, see A.C. Hamilton, "Northrop Frye: The Visionary Critic." *CEA Critic* 42 (1979), 2–6, Hart, "The Mystical-Visionary Criticism of Northrop Frye," *Christianity and Literature* 41 (1992), 277–98, and Hart, *Northrop Frye*, ch. 8. In these works I call Frye a Paradoxical Visionary.

15. Notebook 4, 22.

16. Notebook 4, 34, 45, 58, 76.

17. Northrop Frye, "1949 Diary," paras. 1–3, in *Northrop Frye Newsletter* 7 (Fall 1996), 1. The following citations from the "1942 Diary" are from the same source.

18. "1942 Diary," in *NFN* 7 (Fall 1996), 16.

19. Notebook 16, 69.

20. "1949 Diary," p.1.

21. 1949 Diary," 16–17.

22. For discussions on Frye and Canada, see Margaret Atwood, *Survival* (Toronto: Anansi, 1972); "A Tribute to Northrop Frye," *Vic Report* 1991; Ian Balfour, *Northrop Frye* (Boston: Twayne, 1988), ix–x, 78–88, and the pieces in "II. Imagined Community: Frye and Canada," in Lee and Denham, *The Legacy*, by Linda Hutcheon, James Reaney, Sandra Djwa, Milton Wilson, David Staines, Clara Thomas, and Margaret Atwood (105–73). Rather than repeat myself, I refer the reader to my review article on the Lee and Denham volume (Hart, "Poetics and Culture: Unity, Difference, and the Case of Northrop Frye," *Christianity and Literature* 46 (1996), 61–79). For my views on Frye in Canada, see Hart, "Northrop Frye and the 1960s," *Canadian Literature* (special issue, 1997), an essay completed in 1992.

23. "1942 Diary 8," (Notebook 8, p. 27).

24. I have added p. and pp. for pages, which is contrary to the most recent MLA format for parenthetical citations, to avoid confusion when there are also entry numbers."1942 Diary 22, pp. 6–7.

25. "1942 Diary" 40, p. 11.

26. "1942 Diary" 32–3, pp. 9–10.

27. Notebook 20, p. 10, file 20, p. 8. I have decided to use notes here because Denham's notation here is long and is different here from his usual practice of giving the paragraph numbers for the notebooks.

28. Notebook 4, 31, p. 11.

29. Notebook 20, p. 9, file 20, p. 8.

30. Notebook 20, p. 10, file 20, p. 8.

31. Notebook 20, p. 11, file 20, p. 9.

32. Notebook 20. See Hart, *Northrop Frye*, 269–74.

33. Notebook 20

34. Notebook 20, p. 13, file 20, p. 10. As I have said elsewhere, including my writing on Frye, religion in literary and cultural studies is often occluded and suppressed but represents a return of the repressed. For recent discussions on Frye, religion, and culture, see the essays by

A.C. Hamilton, Thomas Willard, Hayden White, Craig Stewart Walker, Margaret Burgess, Imre Salusinszky, Deanne Bogdan, and Michael Dolzani in "I. The Double Vision: Culture, Religion, and Society," in Lee and Denham, *The Legacy*, 3–102.

35. See Frye, *Anatomy of Criticism: Four Essays* (Princeton: Princeton University Press, 1957), 127.
36. Qtd. in Frye, *The Double Vision: Language and Meaning in Religion* (Toronto: University of Toronto Press, 1991), 22.
37. Notebook 20, p. 13, file 20, p. 10.
38. Notebook 20, p. 14, file 20, p. 11.
39. Notebook 20, p. 15, file 20, p. 10.
40. Notebook 20, p. 15, file 20, p. 11.
41. Notebook 20, p. 16, file 20, p. 12.
42. Notebook 2, 16.
43. Notebook 2, 17.
44. Notebook 2, 18.
45. Notebook 2, 19.
46. Notebook 1, Notes on *The Locust Eaters*. Written 1940s. Transcription from Robert D. Denham. From the typescript he supplied me. NFF, 1991, box 34, file 2. E.J. Pratt Library, Victoria University, Toronto. 21pp, [p. 16]. Denham's transcriptions here lack the numbered paragraphs I have been using elsewhere in my references to the notebooks. I have, therefore, used the page numbers in brackets after the notebook number.
47. Notebook 1, 60, [p. 17]
48. Notebook 1, 60, [p. 17]
49. Notebook 1, 60, [p. 17]
50. Notebook 1, [p. 17]
51. Notebook 1, [p. 17]
52. Notebook 1, 63, [p. 17]
53. Notebook 20, p. 17, file 20, p. 13.

8   Seeing Inside Willy Loman's Head: The Tragedy of the Commoner on Film

1. In this production, Hoffman's *Salesman*, only because that is the most ready way to identify it and that is the way it will probably be remembered, when I talk about the director, Volker Schlondorff, as if he controlled the artistic decisions of the production, it may be a fiction, for theatre and television drama are collaborative arts and in television drama, producers may have much say in the final product as I know Sam Levene did when producing *The Tempest* with director John Hirsch, at Stratford, Ontario, for the production of the Canadian Broadcasting Corporation. Having made this assumption, I have picked the director as the representative most commonly responsible for artistic decisions. Lee J. Cobb played Willy in the first film. A draft of this essay was first presented at the Fifth International Conference on Television Drama at Michigan State University. This earlier version became "The Promised End: The Conclusion of Hoffman's *Death of a Salesman*, "*Literature/Film Quarterly* 19 (1991), 60–65. My thanks to the editors of that journal, especially James M. Welsh, for their original interest and for their permission to reprint and to my host at MSU, Philip McGuire. Besides reframing this argument in a larger context in relation to other parts of my study on recognition and interpreting culture generally, I have tried to update the notes whenever more recent works are germane. For Miller generally, see *The Cambridge Companion to Arthur Miller*, ed. and intro. Christopher Bigsby (Cambridge, England: Cambridge University Press, 1997). For Miller and film, see R. Barton Palmer, "Arthur Miller and the Cinema," *The Cambridge Companion to Arthur Miller*,

ed. and intro. Christopher Bigsby (Cambridge, England: Cambridge University Press, 1997), 184–210. For overviews of criticism on Miller, see Tetsumaro Hayashi, *Arthur Miller Criticism (1930–1967)* (Metuchen, NJ: Scarecrow, 1969); Stephen Barker, "Critic, Criticism, Critics," in Bigsby, *The Cambridge Companion*, 230–44.

2. John V. Hagopian, "Arthur Miller: The Salesman Two Cases," *Modern Drama* 6 (1963), 117. Brian Parker, "Point of View in Arthur Miller's *Death of a Salesman,*" in *Arthur Miller, A Collection of Critical Essays,* ed. Robert W. Corrigan (Englewood Cliffs, NJ: 1969), 95; rpt. from *University of Toronto Quarterly* 35 (1966), 144–57.

3. Arthur Miller, "Tragedy and the Common Man" in *The New York Times*, February 27, 1949, 11, 1–3, rpt. in Arthur Miller, *Death of a Salesman* (Text and Criticism: The Viking Critical Library), ed. Gerald Weales (New York: Viking 1967, rpt. 1977), 147. For more on tragedy and tragic elements, see Vernon Elso Johnson, *Dramatic Influences in the Development of Arthur Miller's Concept of Social Tragedy, Dissertation Abstracts* 23 (1962), 2135–36; Esther Merle Jackson, "Death of a Salesman: Tragic Myth in the Modern Theatre," *College Language Association Journal* 7 (1963), 63–76; Chinmoy Banerjee, "Arthur Miller: The Prospect of Tragedy," *An English Miscellany* 3 (1965), 66–76; William R. Brashear, "The Empty Bench: Morality, Tragedy, and Arthur Miller," *Michigan Quarterly Review* 5 (1966), 270–78; Clinton W. Trowbridge, "Arthur Miller: Between Pathos and Tragedy," *Modern Drama* 10 (1967), 221–32; Robert A. Martin, "Arthur Miller and the Meaning of Tragedy," *Modern Drama,* 13 (1970): 34–39; B.S. Field, Jr., "Hamartia in Death of a Salesman," *Twentieth Century Literature: A Scholarly and Critical Journal* 18 (1972), 19–24; William P. Fleming, Jr., *Tragedy in American Drama: The Tragic Views of Eugene O'Neill, Tennessee Williams, Arthur Miller, and Edward Albee, Dissertation Abstracts International* 33 (1972), 308A (Toledo); R.K. Gupta, "Death of a Salesman and Miller's Concept of Tragedy," *Kyushu American Literature,* 15 (1974), 10–19; Alfred R. Ferguson, "The Tragedy of the American Dream in Death of a Salesman," *Thought: A Review of Culture and Idea* 53 (1978), 83–98; Ana Lucia Almeida Gazolla de Garcia, "Tragedy and Value: A Study of Dias Gomes' O Pagador de Promessas and O Santo Inquerito and Arthur Miller's Death of a Salesman," *Dissertation Abstracts International* 39 (1979): 6749A; Philemon V. Gomwalk, "The Tragic Element in Arthur Miller's Death of a Salesman," *Kuka: Journal of Creative and Critical Writing* (1980–81), 34–40; William Aarnes, "Tragic Form and the Possibility of Meaning in Death of a Salesman," *Furman Studies* 29 (1983), 57–80; Rita Di Giuseppe, "The Shadows of the Gods: Tragedy and Commitment in 'Death of a Salesman'," *Quaderni di Lingue e Letterature* 14 (1989), 109–28; Robert A. Martin, "The Nature of Tragedy in Arthur Miller's *Death of a Salesman,*" *South Atlantic Review,* 61 (4) (1996), 97–106; Harksoon Yim, "Arthur Miller's Theory of Tragedy and Its Practice in *All My Sons, Death of a Salesman,* and *The Crucible,*" *Publications of the Mississippi Philological Association* (1996), 57–63.

4. Miller, "The 'Salesman' Has a Birthday," in *The New York Times*, February 5, 1950, I1, 1, 3, rpt. in Viking ed., 149–50. For more on *Salesman*, see Stephen A. Lawrence, "The Right Dream in Miller's *Death of a Salesman,*" *College English* 25 (7) (1964), 547–49; Barclay W. Bates, "The Lost Past in *Death of a Salesman,*" *Modern Drama* 11 (1968), 164–72; Guerin Bliquez, "Linda's Role in *Death of a Salesman,*" *Modern Drama* 10 (1968), 383–86; Chester E. Eisinger, "Focus on Arthur Miller's Death of a Salesman: The Wrong Dreams," in *American Dreams, American Nightmares,* ed. David Madden and Harry T. Moore (Carbondale and Edwardsville: Southern Illinois University Press, 1970), 165–74; Christopher Innes, "The Salesman on the Stage: A Study in the Social Influence of Drama," *English Studies in Canada* 3 (1977), 336–50; Diane Long Hoeveler, "*Death of a Salesman* as Psychomachia," *Journal of American Culture* 1 (1978), 632–37; Ina Rae Hark, "A Frontier Closes in Brooklyn: *Death of a Salesman* and the Turner," *Postscript* 3 (1986), 1–6; Harold Bloom, ed., *Arthur Miller's Death of a Salesman* (New York: Chelsea, 1988); Peter J. Burgard, "Two Parts Ibsen, One Part American Dream: On Derivation and Originality in Arthur Miller's *Death of a Salesman,*" *Orbis Litterarum: International Review of Literary Studies*" 43 (4) (1988), 336–53.; Leah Hadome, "Fantasy and Reality: Dramatic Rhythm in *Death of a Salesman,*" *Modern Drama* 31 (2) (1988), 157–74; Robert A. Martin, "Arthur Miller: Public Issues, Private Tensions," *Studies in the Literary Imagination* 21 (2) (1988), 97–106; Kay Stanton, "Women and

the American Dream of *Death of a Salesman*," *Feminist Rereadings of Modern American Drama*, ed. June Schlueter (Rutherford: Fairleigh Dickinson University Press, 1989); Harry Harder, "*Death of a Salesman*: An American Classic," in ed. Nicholas J. Karolides, Lee Burress, and John M. Kean *Censored Books: Critical Viewpoints* (Metuchen, NJ: Scarecrow, 1993), 209–19; John S. Schockley, "*Death of a Salesman* and American Leadership: Life Imitates Art," *Journal of American Culture* 17 (2) (1994), 49–56; Matthew Roudané, ed., *Approaches to Teaching Miller's Death of a Salesman* (New York: Mod. Lang. Assn. of America, 1995), for instance, 3–18; Bigsby, *The Cambridge Companion*; Matthew Roudané, "*Death of a Salesman* and the Poetics of Arthur Miller," in Bigsby, *The Cambridge Companion*, 60–85; Jonathan Witt, "Song of the Unsung Antihero: How Arthur Miller's Death of a Salesman Flatters us," *Literature & Theology: An International Journal of Theory, Criticism and Culture* 12 (2) (1998), 205–16; Brenada Murphy, " 'Personality Wins the Day': *Death of a Salesman* and Popular Sales Advice Literature," *South Atlantic Review* 64 (1) (1999), 1–10; Terry Otten, "*Death of a Salesman* at Fifty-Still 'Coming Home to Roost,' " *Texas Studies in Literature and Language* 41 (3) (1999), 280–310; a collection, *Readings on Death of a Salesman*, ed. Thomas Siebold (San Diego, CA: Greenhaven, 1999); a special issue (of writers and scholars on *Salesman*) of *Michigan Quarterly Review* 37 (4) (1998 Fall), for instance, Colby H. Kullman, "*Death of a Salesman* at Fifty: An Interview with Arthur Miller," *Michigan Quarterly Review* 37 (4) (1998), 624–34; "*Salesman Has a Birthday*": *Essays Celebrating the Fiftieth Anniversary of Arthur Miller's Death of a Salesman* (Lanham, MD: University Press of America, 2000); Fred Ribkoff, "Shame, Guilt, Empathy, and the Search for Identity in Arthur Miller's *Death of a Salesman*," *Modern Drama* 43 (1) (2000), 48–55; Ramón Espejo Romero, "*Death of a Salesman*, de Arthur Miller, en España durante los años 50," *Atlantis: Revista de la Asociación Española de Estudios Anglo-Norteamericanos* 24 (1) (2002), 85–107; James E. Walton, "*Death of a Salesman's* Willy Loman and *Fences's* Troy Maxson: Pursuers of the Elusive American Dream," *CLA Journal* 47 (1) (2003), 55–65.

5. Parker, "Point of View," 95.

6. Arthur Miller, "Introduction," *The Collected Plays* (New York, 1957), rpt. in Viking ed., 155. On Arthur Miller and his work generally, see Joseph A. Hynes, "Arthur Miller and the Impasse of Naturalism," *South Atlantic Quarterly* 62 (1963), 327–34; Robert Hogan, *Arthur Miller* (Minneapolis: University of Minnesota Press, 1964); Leonard Moss, *Arthur Miller* (New York: Twayne, 1967, rpt. 1980); Edward Murray, *Arthur Miller: Dramatist* (New York: Frederick Ungar, 1967); Robert W. Corrigan, "The Achievement of Arthur Miller," *Comparative Drama* 2 (1968), 141–60; Richard I. Evans, *Psychology and Arthur Miller* (New York: Dutton, 1969); Benjamin Nelson, *Arthur Miller: Portrait of a Playwright* (New York: McKay, 1970); Sidney H. White, *Guide to Arthur Miller* (Columbus, Ohio: Charles E. Merrill, 1970); Harriet Ungar, "The Writings of and about Arthur Miller: A Check List 1936–1967," *Bulletin of the New York Public Library* 74 (1970), 107–34; John H. Ferres, *Arthur Miller: A Reference Guide* (Boston: Hall, 1979); V. Rajakrishnan, "After Commitment: An Interview with Arthur Miller," *Theatre Journal* 32 (1980), 196–204; *Essays on Modern American Drama: Williams, Miller, Albee, and Shepard*, ed. Dorothy Parker (Toronto: University of Toronto Press, 1987); Robert A. Martin, "Arthur Miller: Public Issues, Private Tensions," *Studies in the Literary Imagination* 21 (2) (1988), 97–106; Lothaar Bredella, "Literary Texts and Intercultural Understanding: Arthur Miller's Play *Death of a Salesman*," *Understanding the USA: A Cross-Cultural Perspective,* ed. Peter Funke (Tübingen: Narr, 1989), 200–19; Jan Balakian, "An Interview with Arthur Miller," *Studies in American Drama, 1945-Present* 6 (1) (1991), 29–47; Ron Rifkin, "Arthur Miller," *BOMB* 49 (1994), 52–56; Chris Banfield, "Arthur Miller," *American Drama*, ed. Clive Bloom (New York: St. Martin's, 1995), 82–96; Jan Balakian, "Arthur Miller," *Speaking on Stage: Interviews with Contemporary American Playwrights,* ed. Philip C. Kolin and Colby H. Kullman (Tuscaloosa: University of Alabama Press, 1996), 40–57; Alice Griffin, *Understanding Arthur Miller* (Columbia: University of South Carolina Press, 1996); a special issue on Miller by Norma Jenckes, ed., "Arthur Miller," *American Drama* 6 (1) (1996), including, for instance, Roudané, "Arthur Miller and His Influence on Contemporary American Drama," *American Drama* 6 (1) (1996), 1–13; Martin Gottfried, *Arthur Miller: His Life and Work* (Cambridge, MA: Da Capo,

2003); Paul Roazen, "Arthur Miller's Words and Deeds," *Queen's Quarterly* 111 (2004), 405–15; Steven R. Centola, "Arthur Miller and the Art of the Possible," *American Drama* 14 (2005), 63–86.

7. Miller, Introduction, 156. See Parker, "Point of View," 101.

8. Jo Mielziner, "Designing a Play: *Death of a Salesman*," from his *Designing for the Theatre* (New York, 1965), rpt. in Viking ed., 193.

9. Miller, *Death of a Salesman* (Viking Critical Edition), 125. All references to and quotations from the text are from this edition.

10. *Salesman*, 16, 61.

11. *Salesman*, 128–29 ff. On awareness, mind, and perception, which are related to my own discussion of recognition and interpretation, see P.P. Sharma, "Search for Self-Identity in *Death of a Salesman*," *Literary Criterion* 11 (2) (1974), 74–79; C.J. Gianakaris, "Theatre of the Mind in Miller, Osborne and Shaffer," *Renascence: Essays on Value in Literature* 30 (1977), 33–42; Charles Eugene McKay, "The Themes of Awareness, Self-Knowledge, and Love in Arthur Miller's Major Dramatic Works," Ph.D. dissertation, University of Mississippi, 1976.

12. *Salesman*, 133.

13. *Salesman*, 137.

14. See Parker, "Point of View," 101; for a view that argues for Willy's centrality but also for a multiplicity of points of view, see Miller, Introduction, 163. On the tragedy and common man, see Helen M. McMahon, "Arthur Miller's Common Man: The Problem of the Realistic and the Mythic," *Drama and Theatre* 10 (1972), 128–33, and her "Arthur Miller's Common Man: The Problem of the Realistic and the Mythic," *Dissertation Abstracts International* 32 (1973): 326A-27A (Purdue). For more on Willy Loman, see Paul N. Siegel, "Willy Loman and King Lear," *College English* 17 (6) (1956), 341–45; Richard T. Brucher, "Willy Loman and the Soul of a New Machine: Technology and the Common Man," *Journal of American Studies* 17 (3) (1983), 325–36; Harold Bloom, ed., *Willy Loman* (New York: Chelsea House, 1990); Thomas E. Connolly, "Oedipus, Lear, and Willy Loman," *Hypotheses: Neo-Aristotelian Analysis*, 31/32 (1999–2000) 9–12; Granger Babcock, " 'What's the Secret?': Willy Loman as Desiring Machine," *American Drama* 2 (1) (1992), 59–83; Dana Heller, "Salesman in Moscow," *The Futures of American Studies* ed. and introd. Donald E. Pease, and Robyn Wiegman, (Durham, NC: Duke University Press, 2002) 183–210; James E. Walton, "*Death of a Salesman*'s Willy Loman and *Fences*'s Troy Maxson," 55–65.

15. *Salesman*, 98, *125–27*. By repeating the word "remarkable," Miller has Willy's discovery of Biff's love echo his discovery of Charley's friendship (98, 133).

16. *Salesman*, 139.

17. Parker, "Point of View," 108–09. The director also substitutes sentimental music for the sound of the symbolic flute and does not show Linda taking Charley's arm and moving through the wall-line of the kitchen to the grave.

18. Miller, Introduction, 168–69.

19. Orm Overland, "The Action and Its Significance: Arthur Miller's Struggle with Dramatic Form," *Modern Drama* 18 (1975), 6.

20. For an early discussion of the controlling point of view as Willy's mind, see Edward Groff, "Point of View in Modern Drama," *Modern Drama* 2 (1959): 268–82, esp. 275, 282. For other views of tragedy as well as on expressionism and realism in *Salesman*, see John Gassner, *Form and Idea in the Modern Theater* (New York: Dryden Press, 1956), 13, 135–36; Miller et al., "A Matter of Hopelessness in *Death of a Salesman*, a Symposium . . ." *Tulane Drama Review* 2 (1958): 63–69, rpt. in *Two Modern American Tragedies*, ed. John D. Hurrell (New York, 1961), 76–81; Richard J. Foster, "Confusion and Tragedy: The Failure of Miller's *Salesman*," in Hurrell, *American Tragedies*, 82–88; Leonard Moss, *Arthur Miller* (rev. ed.) (Boston: Twayne, 1980), 24–36; Nell Carson, *Arthur Miller* (London: Methuen, 1982), 1–2, 12–13, 44–59; Dennis Welland, *Miller the Playwright* (1983), passim.

21. Miller, Introduction, 159.

22. Miller, Introduction, 159–60. Many dissertations have discussed Miller as part or the central focus of their research. There is space to mention only a few of the multitude that examine *Salesman*. Denis C. Phillips explores, from the perspective of education, the problem of obsolescence in relation to ideologies of success, which comprise part of the American dream and does so based on a close reading of *Salesman*; see his "Obsoleting Culture: An Educational Reading of Arthur Miller's 'Death of a Salesman' " Ph.D. dissertation, Stanford University, 2004. Phillips sees Miller's play as making problematic this construction of success in the American dream (2) and examines this in chapter 1. In discussing the idea that every man and woman is a hero, Leslie Goss Erickson discusses four key African American works and what she calls Anglo-American culture, including *Salesman*; see her "The Search for Self: Everyday heroes and the Integral Re-Visioning of the Heroic Journey in Postmodern Literature and Popular Culture," Ph.D. dissertation, University of Nebraska-Lincoln, 2004. Erickson draws on Joseph Campbell's analysis of myth, whose egalitarian nature she finds attractive (1–2) and other critics and theorists of myth, and, in chapter 3, she concentrates on Biff's journey to autonomy although examining other characters' quests (8–9). Kathryn Mercedes O'Rourke looks at the relation between initiation and identity in works that include *Salesman*; see her "Rites of Passage: Studies in Literature, Film and Culture from 1950 to the Present," Ph.D. dissertation, University of California, Riverside, 2003, esp. ch. 4 (52–83). Salesman involves postadolescent males in this initiation—including Biff's rebellion against his father, Willy (1, 7). For a discussion of the relation among technology, individual, and social life, including an analysis of *Salesman*, see Dennis George Jerz, "Soul and Society in a Technological Age: American Drama, 1920–1950, Ph.D. dissertation, University of Toronto, 2001. Jerz discusses Mielziner's set design for *Salesman* (1949) in terms of expressionism (3) and this play in connection with Tennessee Williams's *A Streetcar Named Desire* (1947) (see 201–57). In discussing *Salesman* in the theatre (scenic conventions, acting, lights and music, intrinsic elements, film realism and stage symbolism, aesthetic experience, and intellectual content), Darin Lee Grebel explores how it could be made into a film in the setting of a high school class; see his " 'Death of a Salesman': From Play to Film, "M.A. thesis, California State University, Dominguez Hills, 2000. For a study that includes a discussion of *Salesman* as a memory play in which Miller articulates a social vision, see Janet Nafena Balakian, "The Evolution of Arthur Miller's Dramaturgy," Ph.D. dissertation, Cornell University, 1991. A comparative study includes an examination of *Salesman*: see Maureen Ryan Waldron, "Hubris and Hamartia in Greek and American Tragedy" M.S. thesis, Southern Connecticut State University, 1987. On the tensions between the individual and the social in *Salesman* and other Miller plays, see Emmanuel Njegani Ngwang, "Survival and Personal Identity in Arthur Miller's Major Plays," Ph.D. dissertation, Oklahoma State University, 1986. This study covers topics such as democratic humanism, survival, and identity in family, legal system, and religion. Ngwang mentions Biff's realization that life is about family and not being number one in a career and how he awakens Willy to this view (3). For a suggestive comparison, see Niki S. Hare, "Tragedy, Classical and Modern: A Comparative Study of *Ajax* and *Death of a Salesman*, M.A. thesis, Dalhousie University, 1972.

9   Placing Ireland: Some Lyric Poets

1. Line 1, p. 7. All quotations from the poetry of Yeats are, unless otherwise indicated, from W.B. Yeats, *The Poems: A New Edition* (New York: Macmillan, 1983). My thanks to the editors of *New Delta Review*, especially Nat Hardy, for inviting earlier versions of this and a piece on Paul Muldoon and for granting permission to reprint this collocation, revision, and supplemented version here. See Jonathan Hart, "Some Thoughts on Irish Lyric Poetry," *New Delta Review* 19 (1) (Fall/Winter 2001), 92–107 and, in the same issue, my review of *"Poems*

1968–1998 by Paul Muldoon," 113–16. Wherever possible I have tried to discuss relevant criticism since I first wrote this discussion of Irish poetry and to fill out the notes otherwise as my essays first appeared in a literary journal.

2. Yeats, lines 9–10, p. 7. Some earlier work on Yeats and landscape is suggestive. See John Unterecker, "The Yeats Landscape, *Yeats, Joyce, and Beckett: New Light on Three Modern Irish Writers*, ed. Kathleen McGrory and John Unterecker (Lewisburg: Bucknell University Press); Sister M. Bernetta Quinn, "Symbolic Landscape in Yeats: County Sligo," *Shenandoah* 16 (1965), 37–62 and her "Symbolic Landscape in Yeats: County Galway," *The Hidden Harmony: Essays in Honor of Philip Wheelwright*, ed. Oliver Johnson et al. (New York: Odyssey, 1966), 145–71; Deborah Fleming, "Landscape and the Self in W.B. Yeats and Robinson Jeffers," *Ecopoetry: A Critical Introduction*, ed. J. Scott Bryson (Salt Lake City, UT: University of Utah Press, 2002), 39–57. My own emphasis is different owing to the context—especially poetics and description—and relation to other specific writers. Whereas I have talked about land, landscape, and place in some of Yeats's poems, Natalie Crohn Schmitt has discussed similar terrain in *At the Hawk's Well* (1916), *The Dreaming of the Bones* (1919), and *The Cat and the Moon* (1924); see her " 'Haunted by Places': Landscape in Three Plays by W.B. Yeats," *Comparative Drama* 31 (1997), 337–66 (reprinted in *Land/Scape/Theater*, ed. Elinor Fuchs and Una Chaudhuri [Ann Arbor: University of Michigan Press, 2002], 53–83). On Yeats and the natural world, see Jacqueline Genet, "La Dialectique de la nature et de l'esprit dans la poésie de W.B. Yeats," *Autour de l'idée de Nature: Histoire des idées et civilization: Pédagogie et divers* (Paris: Didier, 1977), 137–57; Patrick Rafroidi, "Yeats, Nature and the Self," *Yeats, Sligo and Ireland: Essays to mark the 2st Yeats International Summer School*, ed. Alexander Norman Jeffares (Totowa, NJ: Barnes & Noble, 1980), 189–96; Ronald G. Hoover, "W.B. Yeats and Nature: Change, Permanence or Both," *The Image of Nature in Literature, the Media, and Society*, ed. Will Wright and Steven Kaplan (Pueblo, CO: Society for the Interdisciplinary Study of Social Imagery, University of Southern Colorado, 1993), 48–52.

3. Yeats, line 34, p. 8. On empowerment of the colonized Irish by making English sing, see Richard Bizot, "Mastering the Colonizer's Tongue: Yeats, Joyce, and Their Successors in the Irish Schoolroom," *Studies in the Literary Imagination* 30 (1997), 63–76. See also Alasdair Macrae, *W.B. Yeats: A Literary Life* (New York: St. Martin's, 1995); Spurgeon Thompson, "The Romance of Simulation: W.B. Yeats and the Theme-Parking of Ireland," *Eire-Ireland* 30 (1995), 17–34; Deidre Toomey, "Moran's Collar: Yeats and Irish Ireland," *Yeats Annual* 12 (1996), 45–83; *Yeats and Women*, ed. Deirdre Toomey (London: Macmillan, 1997). Some recent works on Yeats are germane. As Oliver Hennessey suggests, Yeats, like Leo Africanus, Edmund Spenser, and others, had an identity caught between the imperial center and location of birth or settlement, but this leads to some differences in discussing place from mine (including a reading of "No Second Troy"); see his " 'Talking with the Dead: Leo Africanus, Esoteric Yeats, and Early Modern Imperialism," see 293–301. Another view of Yeats and empire can be found in Joseph Lennon, "Writing across Empire: W.B. Yeats and Rabindranath Tagore," *Rabindranath Tagore: Universality and Tradition*, ed. Patrick Colm and Lalita Pandit (Madison, NJ: Fairleigh Dickinson University Press, 2003), 213–29. For an interesting discussion of the importance of Yeats in the art of poetry and his influence on the younger generation of poets, such as Seamus Heaney, see Ronald Schuchard, "The Legacy of Yeats in Contemporary Irish Poetry," *Irish University Review* 34 (2004), 291–313. Schuchard discusses how Heaney negotiated Yeats and some of the influence of Yeats writing about Ireland and its politics; see Heaney, *The Government of the Tongue* (New York: Farrar, Straus, and Giroux, 1989). Another context for Yeats and his use of imagery is Helen Vendler's *Poets Thinking: Pope, Whitman, Dickinson, Yeats* (Cambridge, MA: Harvard University Press, 2004). On Yeats and his wife, George Hyde-Lees Yeats, see Ann Saddlemyer, *Becoming George: The Life of Mrs. W.B. Yeats* (Oxford: Oxford University Press, 2002). On Maud Gonne and others in Yeats, see Dennis Haskell, "W.B. Yeats," *Kenyon Review* 23 (2001), 168–75. For useful review articles on Yeats (and books about him) from a textual point of view, including his habit of constant revision, as well as iden-

tity, context, and belief, see Daniel T. O'Hara's back-to-back articles, "The Division of Yeats Studies," *Journal of Modern Literature* 24 (3–4) (2001), 511–18 and, in the same issue, "Recent Yeats Studies," 518–24. On the influence of Yeats, see Steven Matthews, *Yeats as Precursor: Rereadings in Irish, British and American Poetry* (Basingstoke: Macmillan, 2000). For a discussion of Yeats in terms of decolonization (which Edward Said also discussed), including the view that Yeats's use of his own culture and of the international literary resources and his "cosmopolitan nativism" gives him affinities with later postcolonial writers, see Johan Ramazani, "Is Yeats a Postcolonial Poet?" *Raritan* 17 (1998), 64–89. See also R.F. Foster, *W.B. Yeats: A Life.I: The Apprentice Mage*, 1865–1914 (Oxford: Oxford University Press, 1997).

4. Yeats, p. 13.

5. Yeats, pp. 21–22. The *Oxford English Dictionary* (Second Edition 1989) on-line defines "sleeven" (of which sleiveen is said to be a variant) as "An untrustworthy or cunning person" (used in Ireland and Newfoundland) and "shoneen" as "to indicate a person's inclination towards English rather than Irish standards and attitudes in cultural life, sport, etc." (Anglo-Irish).

6. Yeats, lines 1–2, p. 33.

7. Yeats, lines 7, 12, p. 39.

8. Yeats, lines 1–4, p. 39.

9. Yeats, p. 41.

10. Yeats, lines 7–8, p. 41.

11. Yeats, lines 31–32, p. 50.

12. Yeats, lines 1–4, pp. 56–57.

13. Yeats, lines 1–4, pp. 58–59.

14. Yeats, lines 1–5, pp. 77–78.

15. Yeats, lines 7–9, pp. 80–81.

16. Yeats, lines 4–5, p. 82.

17. Yeats, lines 8–10, p. 91.

18. Yeats, "The Fascination," lines 11, 1, p. 93.

19. Yeats, lines 5–8, p. 93.

20. Yeats, line 12, p. 93.

21. Yeats, lines 7–8, 15–16, 23–24, and variation 31–32; ll. 17–18, pp. 108–09.

22. Yeats, lines 1–4, p. 131.

23. Yeats, lines 14–16, 38–40, 77–80, pp. 180–82.

24. Yeats, lines 1–4, p. 180.

25. Yeats, lines 56–59, p. 181.

26. Yeats, lines 3–6, p. 187.

27. Yeats, line 21, p. 187.

28. Yeats, line 57, p. 189.

29. Yeats, line 80, p. 190; see line 1, p. 188 and line 33, p. 189.

30. Yeats, lines 1–3, p. 188.

31. Yeats, lines 4–6, p. 193.

32. Yeats, lines 3, 6–8, p. 193.

33. Yeats, lines 17–18, p. 193.

34. Yeats, line 25, p. 193.

35. Yeats, lines 9–11, p. 193.

36. Yeats, lines 21–23, p. 193.

37. Yeats, line 24, p. 193.

38. Yeats, lines 26, 32, p. 194.

39. Yeats, lines 2, 8–9, p. 237.

40. Yeats, lines 16–18, p. 237.

41. Yeats, lines 31, 34, p. 238.

42. Yeats, lines 45–48, pp. 238–39.

43. Yeats, lines 52–54, p. 239.
44. Yeats, lines 4–8, p. 294.
45. Yeats, lines 43–46, p. 295.
46. Yeats, lines 68–69, p. 327.
47. Yeats, lines 85–86, p. 327.
48. Yeats, lines 92–94, p. 328.
49. See Yeats, lines 5–16, p. 325.
50. Yeats, lines 38–40, pp. 347–48.
51. Yeats, lines 1–38, pp. 346–47.
52. Yeats, p. 348.
53. Yeats, lines 9–12, p. 348.
54. Seamus Heaney, *New Selected Poems 1966–1987* (London: Faber and Faber, 1990), p. 1.
55. Heaney, *New Selected Poems*, 1. Some critics explore the relation between Heaney and Yeats. See, for instance, Jon Stallworthy, "The Poet as Archeologist: W.B. Yeats and Seamus Heaney," *Review of English Studies* 33 (1982), 158–74; Robert F. Garratt, *Modern Irish Poetry: Tradition and Continuity from Yeats to Heaney* (Berkeley: University of California Press, 1986; 1989 ed. includes a new epilogue); Charles Lee O'Neill, "Circumventing Yeats: Austin Clarke, Thomas Kinsella, Seamus Heaney," Ph.D. dissertation, New York University, 1987; Joseph Zwier, "Stephen Spender Remembers Three Irish Poets: MacNiece, Yeats, Heaney," *Irish Literary Supplement* 8 (1) (1989), 22–23; Jonathan Allison, "Community and Individualism in the Poetry of W.B. Yeats and Seamus Heaney," Ph.D. dissertation, University of Michigan, 1988; Elizabeth Butler Cullingford, " 'Thinking of Her . . . as . . . Ireland': Yeats, Pearse, and Heaney," *Textual Practice* 4 (1990), 1–21; Susan Shaw Sailer, "Time against Time: Myth in the Poetry of Yeats and Heaney," *Canadian Journal of Irish Studies* 17 (1991), 54–63; Sidney Burris, "Pastoral Nostalgia and the Poetry of W.B. Yeats and Seamus Heaney," *Learning the Trade: Essays on W. B. Yeats and Contemporary Poetry*, ed. Deborah Fleming (West Cornwall, CT: Locust Hill, 1993), 195–201; Fergal Columba O'Doherty, "The Garden, the Pasture and the Bog: William Butler Yeats, John Hewitt and Seamus Heaney on Colonialism and National Identity," Ph.D. dissertation, City University of New York, 1995; Jonathan Allison, "Seamus Heaney's Yeats," *Yeats* 14 (1996), 19–47; Michael Cavanagh, "Tower and Boat: Yeats and Seamus Heaney," *New Hibernia Review/Iris Éireannauch Nua* 4 (2000), 17–38; Eugene O'Brien, "The Question of Ireland: Yeats, Heaney, and the Postcolonial Paradigm," and Raphael Ingelbien, "Decolonizing Ireland/England? Yeats. Seamus Heaney and Ted Hughes," *W.B. Yeats and Postcolonialism*, ed. Deborah Fleming (West Cornwall, CT: Locust Hill, 2001), 51–70 and 71–100 respectively.
56. Heaney, *New Selected Poems*, 2.
57. Heaney, *New Selected Poems*, 2. An interesting view of return, in which the place for poetry is something Heaney expresses through a natural image in his memoir "Mossbawn," see Michael Cavanagh, "Seamus Heaney Returning," *Journal of Modern Literature* 22 (1998), 117–30. On Heaney and nature in a particular context, see Terry Gifford, "Saccharine or Echo Soundings? Notions of Nature in Seamus Heaney's *Station Island*," *The New Welsh Review* 3 (1990), 12–17. On place and landscape in Heaney, see Anthony Bradley, "Landscape as Culture: The Poetry of Seamus Heaney," *Contemporary Irish Writing*, ed. James D. Brophy and Raymond J. Porter (Boston: Twayne for Iona College Press, 1983), 1–14; Douglas Norman Houston, "Myths of Place: The Importance of Landscape in the Poetries of W.H. Auden and Seamus Heaney," Ph.D. dissertation, University of Hull, 1986; Thomas Docherty, "Ana-: or Postmodernism, Landscape, Seamus Heaney," *Contemporary Poetry Meets Modern Theory*, ed. Antony Easthope (Toronto: University of Toronto Press, 1991), 68–80, rpt. in *Seamus Heaney*, ed. Michael Allen (New York: St. Martin's, 1997), 206–22; Brian Robinson, "Negotiations: Religion, Landscape, and the Postcolonial Moment in the Poetry of Seamus Heaney," *Mapping the Sacred: Religion, Geography and Postcolonial Literatures*, ed. Jamie S. Scott and Paul Simpson-Housley (Amsterdam: Rodopi, 2001), 5–36.

58. Seamus Heaney, *Eleven Poems* (Belfast: Festival Publications, n.d.), n.p. [p. 3].

59. Heaney, *New Poems* [1990], lines 4–5, p. 10.

60. Heaney, *New Poems* [1990], line 16, p. 10.

61. Seamus Heaney, *Hailstones* (Dublin: Gallery Books, 1984), ll. 6–7, p. 21.

62. Seamus Heaney, *Station Island* (London: Faber and Faber, 1984), ll. 8–11, p. 53.

63. Seamus Heaney, *Seeing Things* (London: Faber and Faber, 1991), ll. 1–4, p. 22.

64. Seamus Heaney, *Sweeney's Flight: Based on the Revised Text of "Sweeney Astray."* Photographs by Rachel Giese (London: Faber and Faber, 1992), ll. 1–4, p. 70.

65. Seamus Heaney, *Opened Ground: Poems 1966–1996* (London: Faber and Faber, 1998), ll. 1–5, p. 151.

66. Seamus Heaney, *Wintering Out* (London: Faber and Faber, 1972), 14–15, 47–48. "The Tollund Man" also appears in Seamus Heaney and Derek Mahon, *in their element* (Belfast: Arts Council of Northern Ireland, 1977).

67. Heaney, "Bogland," *Door into the Dark* (1969), p. 47.

68. Heaney, "Bogland," *Door into the Dark,* lines 17–18, see 6, p. 47.

69. Heaney, "Bogland," *Door into the Dark,* lines 41–44, p. 48.

70. Heaney, "Westering," *Wintering Out,* lines 26, 31, 33–36, p. 80. Heaney also includes "Westering" in Seamus Heaney and Noel Connor, *Gravities: A Collection of Poems and Drawings* (Newcastle upon Tyne: Charlotte Press Publications, 1979), p. 16.

71. Seamus Heaney, *An Open Letter* (Derry: Field Day Theatre Company, 1983), stanza 33, p. 13.

72. Seamus Heaney, *Sweeney Astray* (1983; London: Faber and Faber, 1984). Heaney has also produced a version of Sophocles's *Philoctetes,* a drama.

73. Heaney, "Clearances," *The Haw Lantern,* Poem I, ll. 1–4, p. 225.

74. Heaney has also explored the relation of public and private in his version of Sophocles's *Philoctetes*; see his *The Cure at Troy* (London: Faber and Faber, 1990).

75. Muldoon, "The Boundary Commission," *Mules* (1977). All quotations from the poetry of Muldoon are from Paul Muldoon, *Poems 1968–1998* (New York: Farrar, Strauss and Giroux, 2001). This citation comes from p. 80.

76. Muldoon, "The Boundary Commission," *Poems 1968–1998*, p. 80. On Muldoon and the land, see Tim Hancock, " 'Mad Images and a Very Fixed Landscape': Paul Muldoon and the New Narrative," *Critical Review* 37 (1997), 133–40. On the relation to Yeats, see William A. Watson, "Yeats, Muldoon, and Heroic History," Fleming, *Learning the Trade*, 21–38; Christian Llywelyn Lloyd, "Dialogising the Lyric: Politics and Prosaics in the Poetry of W.B. Yeats, Ciaran Carson and Paul Muldoon, Ph.D. dissertation, Queen's University, 1999. Other work germane to this chapter is Richard Brown, "Bog Poems and Book Poems: Doubleness, Self-Translation, and Pun in Seamus Heaney and Paul Muldoon," *The Chosen Ground: Essays on the Contemporary Poetry of Northern Ireland,* ed. Neil Corcoran (Bridgend: Seren, 1992), 171–88; Kevin Brady, "Northern Exposures: Politics, Pressure and Tradition in the Poetry of Montague, Heaney, and Muldoon," Ph.D. dissertation, Drew University, 1996; Clair Wills, *Reading Paul Muldoon* (Newcastle: Bloodaxe Books, 1998); Shane Murphy, " 'The Eye that Scanned It': The Picture Poems of Heaney, Muldoon, and McGuckian," *New Hibernia Review* 4 (4) (2000), 85–114; Ingo Berensmeyer, "Identity or Hybridization? Mapping Irish Culture in Seamus Heaney and Paul Muldoon," *Etudes Irlandaises* 28 (2003): 65–83, Lars-Håkan Svensson, "Heaney and Muldoon in Conversation," *Nordic Irish Studies* 3 (2004), 17–33. Christopher T. Malone examines the "Mythos of place" with regard to Irish poets, such as Heaney and Muldoon, who are trying to negotiate the legacy of Yeats and the question of modern Irish identity and postcolonial and postmodern community for Irish poets, especially those from the north; see his "Writing Home: Spatial Allegories in the Poetry of Seamus Heaney and Paul Muldoon," *ELH* 67 (4) (2000), 1083, see 1084–109. Steven Matthews discusses poetry about inanimate objects, which allows male poets from the north of Ireland, such as Heaney and Muldoon, to understand art, politics, and the relation of the poet to "the history of division"; see his "The Object Lessons of Heaney, Carson, Muldoon and Boland," *Critical Survey* 15 (2003), 18, see 19–33.

77. Muldoon, "Meeting the British," *Poems 1968–1998*, p. 161.
78. Muldoon, "Hay," *Poems 1968–1998*, p. 418.
79. Mary O'Malley, "The Otter Woman," in *A Special Issue: Contemporary Irish Poetry and Criticism of The Southern Review* 31 (3) (July 1995), 689. On O'Malley, see Bernard McKenna, " 'Such Delvings and Exhumations': The Quest for Self-Actualization in Mary O'Malley's Poetry," *Contemporary Irish Women Poets: Some Male Perspectives* (Westport, CT: Greenwood, 1999), 151–72.
80. Brendan Kennelly's "The Hag of Beare" in *Irish Women Poets*, 401. On Kennelly, see, for example, "On Language and Invention: Interview with Brendan Kennelly," *Literary Review* 22 (1979), 197–204, which includes a discussion of Yeats and his influence. See also Åke Persson, *Betraying the Age: Social and Artistic Protest in Brendan Kennelly's Work* (Göteborg: Acta Universitatis Gothoburgensis, 2000); John McDonagh, " 'Blitzophrenia': Brendan Kennelly's Post-Colonial Vision," *University Review* 33 (2003), 322–36.
81. Kennelly, "The Hag of Beare," lines 1–6, p. 401.
82. Medbh McGuckian's translation of Nuala Ní Dhomhnaill's "An Mhurúch san Ospidéal" ("The Mermaid in the Labour Ward") in parallel texts, special issue of *The Southern Review* (1995), lines 1–6, p. 439, see p. 438. On Dhomhnaill, see, for instance, Loretta Qwarnström, "Travelling through Liminal Spaces: An Interview with Nuala Ní Dhomhnaill," *Nordic Irish Studies* 3 (2004), 65–73; See Nuala Ní Dhomhnaill, "Why I Chose to Write in Irish, the Corpse that Sits Up and Talks Back," *Representing Ireland: Gender, Class, Nationality*, ed. Susan Shaw Sailer (Gainesville: University Press of Florida, 1997), 45–56.
83. W.B. Yeats, *Uncollected Prose by W.B. Yeats*, collected and edited by John P. Frayne and Colton Johnson, vol. 2 (New York: Columbia University Press, 1976), 195.
84. Seamus Heaney, *Among Schoolchildren: A Lecture Dedicated to the Memory of John Malone* (Belfast: John Malone Memorial Committee, 1983), 11.
85. Seamus Heaney, *Opened Ground: Poems 1966–1996* (London: Faber and Faber, 1998), 447.

10 Being Novel, Almost and Not

1. Jonathan Hart, "A Comparative Pluralism: the Heterogeneity of Methods and the Case of Possible Worlds," *CRCL/RCLC* 15 (1988), 320–45. In 1710, Leibniz published *Théodicée* a philosophical work on good, evil, and possible worlds. In 1714, Leibniz wrote *Monadologia*, which built on *Théodicée*. My thanks to Jüri Talvet for inviting an earlier version of this chapter and for permission to reprint it; see "Novels, Almost Novels and Not Novels: Fiction, History, European Colonial Expansion and After," *Interlitteraria* 9 (2004), 9–27.
2. For the motto, see the Bond film, "On Her Majesty's Secret Service," 1969. This phrase is used in other contexts, see Torben S. Hansen: "Non sufficit orbis—Castile and the Spanish Empire 1492–1659," *Denjske Historiker*, Forside—Nyeste Numre—Nummer 91/92, Årgang 2000/2001 [Torben S. Hansen, Non sufficit orbis—Kastillien og det spanske imperium 1492–1659], which is about the overreach or overextension of the Spanish Empire. In a review of Geoffrey Parker's *The Grand Strategy of Philip II* (London and New Haven: Yale University Press, 1998), Robin G. Macpherson notes of Philip: "In spite of the seemingly insurmountable difficulties, Philip can truly be said to have ruled the first empire on which the sun never set and, long before James Bond, used the motto *Non Sufficit Orbis*—the World is not Enough!" see Reviews on the Home Page of the Institute of Historical Research, University of London.
3. Juvenal, "The Satires of Juvenal," *Juvenal and Persius*, trans. G.G. Ramsey (London: William Heinemann, 1930), 10: 168–70; Latin, p. 206 and English on p. 207.
4. See *The Republic of Plato*, trans. B. Jowett, second ed., rev. and corrected (Oxford: Clarendon, 1881), book 10.

5. See Marshall McLuhan, *The Gutenberg Galaxy: The Making of Typographic Man* (Toronto: University of Toronto Press, 1962) and his *Understanding the Media: The Extensions of Man* (New York: New American Library, 1964).

6. Plato shows some skepticism about the power of poets and imagination rather than the reason of philosophers. The importance of the imagination has been long discussed in relation to Samuel Taylor Coleridge and other Romantics in Britain and the Continent. The Wordsworth Trust lists on its website, under themes, the section "Wordsworth and Imagination," which is as follows: "Wordsworth saw imagination as a powerful, active force that works alongside our senses, interpreting the way we view the world and influencing how we react to events. He believed that a strong imaginative life is essential for our well-being. Often in Wordsworth's poetry, his intense imaginative effort translates into the great visionary moments of his poetry." See http://www.wordsworth.org.uk/poetry/ww.htm. Much has been written on Romanticism, which often includes discussions of fancy and imagination. Two sources that are especially suggestive are Northrop Frye, "The Drunken Boat: The Revolutionary Element in Romanticism," in Northrop Frye, ed., *Romanticism Reconsidered: Selected Papers from the English Institute* (New York and London: Columbia University Press, 1963), 1–25 and Isaiah Berlin, *The Roots of Romanticism*, ed. Henry Hardy (1965; Princeton: Princeton University Press, 2001).

7. *Aristotle's Poetics*, trans. George Whalley, ed. John Baxter and Patrick Atherton (Montreal and Kingston: McGill-Queen's University Press, 1997), 73.

8. On Russian culture, expansion, and empire, see, for instance, Geoffrey Hosking, *Russia: People and Empire, 1552–1917* (London: HarperCollins, 1997) and Orlando Figes, *Natasha's Dance: A Cultural History of Russia* (2002; London: Penguin, 2003).

9. Jonathan Swift, *Gulliver's Travels*, ed. Philip Pinkus (Toronto: Macmillan, 1968), 141–42.

10. The authoritative study of this topic is Terence Cave, *Recognitions: A Study in Poetics* (1988; Oxford: Clarendon Press, 1990).

11. *The Four Voyages of Columbus*, ed. Cecil Jane (1929 and 1932; New York: Dover, 1988), 1: 10. The original reads:

> Y luego que legué á las Indias, en la primera isla que hallé tomé por fuerça algunos d'ellos, para que deprendiesen y me diesen noticia de lo que avía en aquellas partes, é así fué que luego entendieron, y nos á ellos, quando por lengua ó señas; y estos han aprovechado mucho. (11)

12. Jane, *Columbus*, 12.

13. G.R. Crone, "Introduction," *The Voyages of Cadamosto and Other Documents on Western Africa in the Second Half of the Fifteenth Century*, xxx–xlv. It is possible that Cadamosto wrote some parts before 1460. The apparently late-fourteenth-century manuscript is in a cursive semi-Gothic hand, probably that of a copyist and not in Cadamosto's autograph. See *Paesi novamente retrovati* (Vicenza, 1507).

14. Crone, *Voyages*, xliii–iv. Crone's translation is based on the *Paesi*.

15. Amerigo Vespucci, *Van de nieuwer werelt oft landtscap nieuwelicx gheounden* (Antwerp, 1508).

16. Benedetto Bordone, *Isolario di Benedetto Bordone nel qual si ragiona di tutte l'isole del mondo* (Venice, 1534). For an early account of the settlement of Madeira, the Canaries, the Azores, and Cape Verde, see Edgar Prestage, *The Portuguese Pioneers* (London: Adam & Charles Black, 1933, rpt. 1966), 35–75

17. Hans Staden, *Warhaftige Historia und Beschreibung einer Landtschaft der wilden nacketen grimmigen Menschenfresser Leuthen in der Newenwelt America gelegen* (Marburg, 1557); Jean de Léry, *Histoire d'vn voyage fait en la terre du Bresil, autrement dite Amerique* (La Rochelle, 1578).

18. Michel de Montaigne, *Les essais: reproduction typographique de l'exemplaire annoté par l'auteur et conservé à la bibliothèque de Bordeaux* (Paris, 1906–31); for the earliest English translation, see Michel de Montaigne, 1533–92, *The essayes or morall, politike and millitarie discourses of Lo: Michaell de Montaigne, Knight of the noble Order of St. Michaell, and one of the gentlemen in ordinary*

of the French king, Henry the third his chamber. The first booke. First written by him in French. And now done into English by him that hath inviolably vowed his labors to the aeternitie of their honors, whose names he hath severally inscribed on these his consecrated altares. . . . *Iohn Florio* (London: Val. Sims for Edward Blount, 1603).

19. *Essays vvritten in French by Michael Lord of Montaigne* . . . (London: Melch. Bradvvood for Edvvard Blount and William Barret, 1613), 106, see 107. Cambridge University Library copy.

20. *Oroonoko: Or, The Royal Slave. A True Story. By Mrs A. Behn* (London: Will. Canning, 1688), 10.

21. Marco Polo, *The most noble and famous trauels of Marcus Paulus, one of the nobilitie of the state of Venice, into the east partes of the world, as Armenia, Persia, Arabia, Tartary, with many other kingdoms and prouinces. No lesse pleasant, than profitable, as appeareth by the table, or contents of this booke. Most necessary for all sortes of persons, and especially tor trauellers. Translated into English* (London: Ralph Nevvbery, 1579). The entry on Marco Polo in *The Catholic Encyclopedia* gives a good account of the early textual circumstances: "The 'Book of Marco Polo' dictated to Rusticiano was compiled in French. A more correct version, revised by Marco Polo, was sent by him in 1307 to Thibaud of Cepoy, the agent of Charles of Valois at Venice, to be presented to that prince, who was a candidate for the Crown of Constantinople and the promoter of a crusading movement. The Latin, Venetian, and Tuscan versions are merely translations which are often faulty, or abridgments of the first two texts." See the classic edition of 1914 at www.newadvent. org/cathen.

22. Salman Rushdie, *Imaginary Homelands: Essays and Criticism, 1981–1991* (London: Granta Books, 1991).

23. See Bartolomé de las Casas, *A Short Account of the Destruction of the Indies*, trans. Nigel Griffin (London: Penguin, 1992). See also Lewis Hanke, *Aristotle and the American Indians* (Bloomington: University of Indiana Press, 1959) and Anthony Pagden, *The Fall of Natural Man: The American Indian and the Origins of Comparative Ethnology* (1982; Cambridge: Cambridge University Press, rev., 1986).

24. On this topic, see Jonathan Hart, *Representing the New World: English and French Uses of the Example of Spain* (New York and London: Palgrave Macmillan, 2001). See also various versions of Las Casas's *Short Account of the Destruction of the Indies*, such M.M.S., *The Spanish Colonie* (London, 1583) and *Le Miroir De La Tyannie Espagnole Perpetree aux Indes Occidentales* (Amsterdam, 1620). See William S. Maltby, *The Black Legend in England* (Durham, NC: Duke University Press, 1971).

25. Thomas Mann, *The Magic Mountain*, trans. H.T. Lowe-Porter (1927; New York: Vintage Books, 1969), 716.

26. Mann, *Magic*, 727.

27. Mann, *Magic*, 727.

INDEX

mimesis (see also imitation,
representation), 4–5, 9–14, 16, 35, 45,
53, 214–19, 226, 238, 303n12
mind, 1, 5–7, 11, 15, 25, 29, 36, 40, 44,
46–7, 57, 59–62, 64, 67, 69–70, 72,
90, 115, 118–19, 121, 125–7, 135–6,
139, 143–4, 152, 157, 173, 181, 185,
187–9, 195, 198–9, 209, 213, 226–7,
230, 242n55, 245n23, 295n18, 300n4,
307n11, 308n20; high-mindedness,
114; mindless, 91
misrecognition, 5, 8, 13, 17, 88, 106,
195, 215, 222, 227, 229, 231–2, 235,
238, 240n15
modern, 9–10, 45, 47, 52, 106, 124, 143,
199, 201–2, 207, 214, 232, 235–7,
260n2, 263n36; modernism/modernist,
69, 159, 282n45, 287n3, 288n5,
294n7, 313n76; modernity, 21, 104,
108, 143, 194, 222, 236
Montaigne, Michel de, 54, 57, 145, 147,
173, 218, 228, 237, 253n112,
254n125; "On Cannibals," 57–8
moral/morality, 43, 46, 58, 62, 66, 126,
129, 132, 154, 174, 193, 212, 220,
246n51, 251n102; morality play, 193,
220; *Everyman*, 220; *Mankind*, 220
Morrison, Samuel Eliot, 80
Morrison, Toni, 151, 221, 298n26
Mozart, Wolfgang Amadeus, 152
Muldoon, Paul, 17, 206–9, 235–6,
309n1; *Hay,* 207; *Meeting with the
British*, 207; *Mules*, 207;
multiplicity, 6, 89–91, 104, 161, 213,
227, 232, 307n14
Murray, Gilbert, 10, 22, 244n10
music, 4, 26, 69, 90, 92, 102, 136, 150,
158–9, 161, 163, 171, 175, 195, 197,
201, 212, 284n67, 299–300n2,
308n17, 309n22; music of
mathematics, 158
muthos, 25, 28, 32–3, 152, 158, 169–70,
173, 179, 224–5, 238; mythos, 156,
158–60, 313n76; myth/mythology, 9,
12, 15–16, 23–35, 40, 47, 52–4, 56, 58,

65, 67–72, 87, 91, 102–3, 113, 121,
124, 143, 150, 152–3, 156–63,
169–70, 180, 193, 195, 197–8, 200–3,
206–8, 213, 219, 224–5, 229–30, 235,
238, 245n24, 256n150, 273n4, 274n5,
276–78n29, 284–5n69, 288n5, 301n5,
302n7, 303n12, 303n3, 308n22,
313n76

Naipaul, V. S., 151, 221, 298–9n26
Napoleon, 82, 84, 116, 300n4
narrative, 10, 12, 15, 17, 28, 35–8, 41–2,
53–4, 77, 10p8, 117, 132, 148, 153,
155–6, 158–9, 173, 181, 192, 195,
197, 212, 214, 216–19, 221–2, 225–6,
228–9, 236–8, 278n30, 296n19,
301n6; travel narratives, 214, 221–2,
237, 261n11
Native(s), 2, 4, 13, 16, 26, 76, 83, 85,
89–90, 92, 96–8, 104, 152, 156, 173,
207, 209, 211, 213–14, 216, 218–21,
231, 253n112, 264n43, 273n1, 274n5,
276–7n29, 277–9n30, 279n31
natural philosopher/philosophy
(see philosophy, science), 10,
145–6, 149
nature/natural, 1–6, 9–10, 14–16, 23,
25–6, 29, 35–6, 45, 48, 51, 54, 58–9,
66–7, 71, 78, 80, 84, 89, 93, 96, 100,
102–4, 109, 123, 136, 138, 144–6,
148–9, 152–3, 158, 162, 168, 170,
172–3, 177–7, 180, 186–7, 193–209,
217, 220, 226, 234, 236, 238, 239n1,
242n51, 245n19, 249n89, 259n169,
271n53, 282n45, 284n69, 300n2, 4,
301n5, 308n22, 309n2, 312n57;
naturalism, 9, 26, 193
Nerval, Gérard de, 175–6
Netherlands, 84–5, 117; Holland, 220
New Criticism/New Critics, 155,
197, 214
New England, 82, 92–4, 103, 264n43,
271n53; Boston, 94, 188–9, 260n2;
Cape Cod, 94; Maine, 96, 232,
268n49, 279n31; Massachussetts, 93–6,